Practicality of Grace in Protestant Theology

Practicality of Grace in Protestant Theology

Foreword by Dr. Peter Lillback
President, Westminster Theological Seminary

Introduction by Dr. Michael G. Maness
Managing Editor, *Testamentum Imperium*

Kevaughn Mattis
Founder, *Testamentum Imperium*

www.PreciousHeart.net/ti

WIPF & STOCK · Eugene, Oregon

THE PRACTICALITY OF GRACE IN PROTESTANT THEOLOGY

Copyright © 2021 Wipf and Stock Publishers. All rights reserved. Except for brief quotations in critical publications or reviews, no part of this book may be reproduced in any manner without prior written permission from the publisher. Write: Permissions, Wipf and Stock Publishers, 199 W. 8th Ave., Suite 3, Eugene, OR 97401.

Wipf & Stock
An Imprint of Wipf and Stock Publishers
199 W. 8th Ave., Suite 3
Eugene, OR 97401

www.wipfandstock.com

PAPERBACK ISBN: 978-1-7252-8418-0
HARDCOVER ISBN: 978-1-7252-8419-7
EBOOK ISBN: 978-1-7252-8420-3

May the grace of God inspire all
to search out the riches of our great
inheritance in eternal security in Christ.

2 Corinthians 1:3–4

[3] Praise be to the God and Father of our Lord Jesus Christ,
the Father of compassion and the God of all comfort,
[4] who comforts us in all our troubles, so that
we can comfort those in any trouble with
the comfort we ourselves receive from God.

Contents

most have detailed outlines at the beginning of each chapter

Foreword by **Dr. Peter Lillback** ix

Introduction by **Dr. Michael G. Maness** xiii

1. God's Condescension in Action: Nature of Divine Redemptive Love
   by **Dr. Glenn R. Kreider** 1

2. Is Yahweh's Faithfulness Contingent Upon Human Obedience?—
   "For I Am God and No Mortal"
   by **Dr. Terry Ann Smith** 29

3. Suicide the Unpardonable Sin and the Multi-Dimensional
   History of a Theological Error
   by **Dr. Timothy J. Demy** 43

4. Luther's Theology of the Cross as Foundation for Sanctification in
   Latin American Liberation Theology
   by **Dr. Patricia Cuyatti Chavez** 67

5. How God Wrestles with the Shortcomings of His People
   on the Ontological Level
   by **Dr. Leon Harris** 83

6. Irrevocable Nature of Salvation as a Basis for Trusting God with
   the Daily Affairs of Life
   by **Rev. Christopher D. Surber** 111

7. Pastoral Care Treasures in Prison and the Golden Hour
   by **Dr. Michael G. Maness** 127

8. Pastoral Care in Public Settings: A Theoretical & Theological Premise
   with Effective Outcomes of Chaplaincy
   by **Dr. Keith A. Evans** 141

9. Use of the Concept of New Identity in Christ in Counseling
   Sexual Addiction in Young Men
   by **Dr. Alan M. Martin** 157

10. New Identity in Christ—Counseling Women Who Have Been
    Sexually Abused or Raped
    by **Dr. LaVerne Bell-Tolliver** 171

11. Justification through Union with Christ with His Faith Becoming
    Our Own into New Creation
    by **Dr. John DelHousaye** 185

12. A Non-legalistic Doctrine of Sanctification: Christian Failure and
    Christian Growth
    by **Rev. Dr. Enrique Ramos** 199
13. How Does the Doctrine of Justification by Faith
    Impact Christian Counseling?
    by **Sabrina N. Gilchrist** 223
14. Christian Spirituality of Eschatological Hoping (*Promissiology*):
    Towards a Theological Hermeneutics of Human Anticipation
    and the Quest for Meaning in Suffering
    by **Professor D. J. Louw** 233
15. Divine Forgiveness and Freedom from the Shame of Past Mistakes:
    A Communitarian Perspective
    by **Kevaughn Mattis** 265

Bibliography 275
Indices 295
    Persons 295
    Scripture & Semi-sacred References 298
    Books and Publications 301
    General 304

Foreword
by Dr. Peter Lillback
President, Westminster Theological Seminary[1]

It is my honor to introduce *The Practicality of Grace in Protestant Theology*. Here you have a selection of fifteen essays from the online journal *Testamentum Imperium*, edited by Dr. Michael G. Maness. The title of this collection reminds me of a maxim of Theodore Roosevelt: "Be practical as well as generous in your ideals. Keep your eyes on the stars, but remember to keep your feet on the ground." This book achieves this balance by lifting our eyes to the glories of the gospel of the risen Christ, and by leading us into the spiritual struggles and physical traumas that confront believers in a world that groans for the adoption of sons (cf. Romans 8:19–22).

This anthology is remarkable in my estimation for four reasons: (1) the diversity of the contributors, (2) the range of theological issues engaged, (3) the relevance of that theology to the deep issues facing people in a broken world, and (4) the practical application of those theological insights to the needs of the church. Let me briefly illustrate each of these points.

First, consider the diversity of the contributors. They represent Dallas Theological Seminary, Talbot Seminary, New Brunswick Theological Seminary, the US Naval Chaplaincy, the Lutheran School of Theology in Chicago, Temple Baptist Seminary, Banner Thunderbird Medical Center in Glendale, Arizona, Oklahoma Christian University, the University of Arkansas, Phoenix Seminary, a counseling ministry in Puerto Rico, North-West University, South Africa, Wake Forest University, Stellenbosch University in South Africa, and BPP Law School in Manchester UK. Clearly the global

---

[1] Lillback is president of Westminster Theological Seminary, at which he earned his Ph.D., and serves there as professor of historical theology and church history. He also serves as the president of The Providence Forum (www.ProvidenceForum.org) and senior editor of the new *Unio cum Christo: An International Journal of Reformed Theology and Life* (www.uniocc.com). He has written several books and articles, including his magisterial *George Washington's Sacred Fire* (Bryn Mawr, PA: Providence Forum Press, 2006; 1,208p.), *George Washington & Israel* (Bryn Mawr, PA: Providence Forum Press, 2012); with David Hall, *A Theological Guide to Calvin's Institutes: Essays and Analysis (Calvin 500)* (P&R Publishing, 2018; 616p.), and with Charles Colson, Wayne Grudem, and Philip Ryken, *Biblical Perspectives on Business Ethics* (Basking Ridge, NJ: Center for Christian Business Ethics Today, 2012). See bibliography for more of Lillback's work.

range of the online theological conversation of *Testamentum Imperium* is remarkable.

Second, reflect on the broad range of issues engaged herein under the themes of salvation in Christ and the process of sanctification. These two salvific blessings, justification and sanctification, were denominated the *duplex gratiae,* or double graces of the covenant of grace, by Protestant Reformer, John Calvin. These great theological truths are addressed from varying standpoints to be sure. But in the process, the richness of the theological heritage of the Christian faith shines with coruscating succinctness.

Thus you will encounter the classic Christian creeds, Trinity, Christology, and Ontology. But these weighty concerns lead to the Lordship of Christ, relationships, and reconciliation. Philosophers and knotty questions like election, predestination, and eschatology appear, yet they are brought into dialogue with covenant, fidelity, obedience, and forgiveness. The Bible's stories of Hagar, the woman at the well and the theology of Hosea are mined for spiritual nurture. Church historians will find insightful reflections on ancient, medieval, reformation and modern theologians.

You will find helpful and careful discussions of the nature of divine redemptive love, the shortcomings of the people of God, the relationship of the Lord's faithfulness to human obedience, suicide and the unpardonable sin, the significance of Luther's theology of the cross for sanctification, the certainty of salvation and daily trust in God, the impact of identity in Christ for men facing sexual addiction, the value of understanding identity in Christ for women who have been sexually harmed, Christ's faith as the believer's faith through union with Christ, a critique of various understandings of the relationship of justification with sanctification, the impact of justification by faith on Christian counseling, the impact of the Christian's ultimate hope on suffering and meaning, and God's forgiveness that leads to freedom from shame. There is something useful here for every reader whether theologian or counselor. These themes will deepen your spiritual wisdom.

Third, this set of articles manifests the relevance of theology for addressing the weighty issues of the human predicament facing believers in this imperfect and fallen world. Here you will wrestle with redemption, sin, the unpardonable sin, the people of God, the community of faith. salvation's certainty, divine faithfulness, the cross, identity in Christ, the faith of Christ, Latin American liberation theology, feminist theology, hermeneutical contextualization of the cross, justification by faith, union with Christ, sanctification, ultimate hope, and forgiveness. You will be enriched personally by contemplating these carefully considered themes.

Fourth, *The Practicality of Grace in Protestant Theology* lives up to its title. Here, the practical application of great Protestant theological insights clearly connects with the critical concerns of many in the church. Reading this anthology will enable you to immerse yourself in real and often thorny issues of life in Christ, such as: love, shortcomings, human obedience, suicide and salvation, certainty and trust, addiction, sexual abuse and rape, personal faith, law and grace, failure and growth, Christian counseling, suffering and meaning, and freedom from shame.

These relevant emphases are not only due to the insights of the practically minded contributors, but also because of the theological leadership of the editor of the collection and the founder of the online journal. The real-world focus of the articles emanates in part due to the labors of the editor and the founder of the journal. The first, Michael Maness, has served as a prison chaplain and the second, Kevaughn Mattis, is a trained attorney. Their life experiences have given them an eye and a heart to select the best of their journal's writings to bless the contemporary church's troubling concerns.

Undoubtedly, there will be disagreements with viewpoints and positions taken by various writers. There may be those who take issue with the contextualization of Luther's theology for Liberation theology and Feminist hermeneutics. Some will disagree with the critical assessment of Federal Vision theology and Lordship Salvation. Some will find too much Calvinism in some of the articles. Some may question why certain politically and theologically charged issues of our day are not addressed herein. Some may find internal tensions between one author and another who have contributed to the volume. Such responses are expected and inevitable given the range of writers as they address vexing issues from differing communities and theological perspectives. The diversity will sharpen your thinking and deepen your understanding of views maintained by Protestants today.

This, however, is evident. The authors are not flummoxed by the difficult themes they address. Each reflects the historic Protestant spirit that recognizes that authentic Christians consider themselves not as fulfilling the dreadful mandates of a strict task-master, but as joyfully meeting the debt of sincere gratitude. They consciously address their themes from the vantage point of divine grace. They recognize their greatest contribution to the reader is to engage them with the unmerited favor of God in Christ. For this alone offers living hope to the daily lives of those struggling with the burdens of sin in a world lapsed far from its pristine glory.

Indeed, these essays echo the message of William Wilberforce who once described real Christianity:

> It makes no sense to take the name of Christian and not cling to Christ. Jesus is not some magic charm to wear like a piece of jewelry we think will give us good luck. He is the Lord. His name is to be written on our hearts in such a powerful way that it creates within us a profound experience of His peace and a heart that is filled with His praise.

Wilberforce added, "What a difference it would be if our system of morality were based on the Bible instead of the standards devised by cultural Christians."

This is the kind of Christianity our authors wish to impart as they enable us to consider the amazing grace of God that meets us in every need when we turn afresh to Christ. For it is our God's grace alone in Christ alone that enables us to sing from the heart, "I once was lost, but now am found, was blind, but know I see." I commend this book to you as you seek to grow in grace and in the knowledge of our Lord and Savior Jesus Christ (2 Peter 3:18).

Dr. Peter A. Lillback, President
Westminster Theological Seminary, Philadelphia
February 8, 2019

Introduction
by Dr. Michael G. Maness
Managing Editor, *Testamentum Imperium*[2]

What an honor it has been to work with so many fine scholars.

Kevaughn Mattis began *Testamentum Imperium—An International Theological Journal* in 2005 with a vision to gather scholarly dialogue from a multitude of disciplines on the security of the Christian believer, our "Great Testament," which in Latin is *Testamentum Imperium*.

Our first publication in 2009 was *Perspectives on Eternal Security* with 13 articles from the 60 published in the 2007 journal.[3]

This volume brings together 13 carefully chosen articles from the 163 articles published in the 2011 journal, plus one by Dr. Keith Evans and another by me. All 163 relate a facet of the practicality of grace. We felt these 15 represented not only the diversity but also met needs in unique venues in fresh, relevant, and intriguing ways.

Plus, each seemed to touch a news headline today.

While several bestsellers from scientific atheists deride all things religious and slander Christ's divinity in the ugliest ways (cf. Richard Dawkins and Sam Harris), Glenn Kreider resolutely anchors the gospel in the stupendous incarnation where the Creator in Christ exemplifies humility to humanity in practical tenderness.

Timothy Demy's masterly and historically-linked exposition on suicide corrects the depressive "unpardonable sin" in that horrendous

---

[2] Maness earned a D.Min. at NOBTS and a M.Div. at SWBTS, and is a retired senior clinical chaplain from the Texas Department of Criminal Justice (20 years). He is the author of nine books and over 100 articles, including, *How We Saved Texas Prison Chaplaincy 2011—Immeasurable Value of Volunteers and Their Chaplains* (AuthorHouse, 2015; 414p.; www.PreciousHeart.net/Saved), which chronicled the networking that saved the Texas prison chaplaincy from cancellation in 2011; *Ocean Devotions—from the Hold of Charles H. Spurgeon* (2008); *Would You Lie To Save a Life?—A Theology on the Ethics of Love, Love Will Find a Way Home* (2007); *Heaven—Treasures of Our Everlasting Rest* (2004); and *Heart of the Living God—Love, Free Will, Foreknowledge, Heaven—A Theology of the Treasure of Love* (2004; 728p.); *Queen of Prison Ministry—the Story of Gertha Rogers, First Woman to Minister on Texas Death Row* (2008); and *Precious Heart, Broken Heart—Love and the Search for Finality in Divorce* (2003). He is web master of www.PreciousHeart.net with links to over 10k sites to resources all over the world and hosts perhaps the largest collection of papers and data on prison chaplaincy in the world, and the most for Texas. He has been managing editor and publisher of *Testamentum Imperium* for most of its publication history, www.PreciousHeart.net/ti.

[3] See www.PrciousHeart.net/ti/2007.

tragedy to a more biblical view of forgiveness for all parties. His veteran military chaplaincy experience, so apropos today, touches all affected by suicide, especially veterans and law officers.

Evans reveals the skill set of the hospital chaplain and the inherent contributions of caring for the soul to the entire mission of medical and healthcare.

Alan Martin's carefully resolute pastoral care of male sexual addiction seems to head off those afflicted—we hope—before more embarrassment ensues for the church, indeed, before more headlines expose clergy abuse in both Protestant and Catholic churches.

LaVerne Bell-Tolliver beseeches the church in a powerfully prescient treatise to *finally* deal with rape—perfect timing here—and hits our hearts hard today as the #MeToo movement has *finally* empowered more brave women to speak up. Her experience as a victim and a top clinician resonate with a determined heart to help all in Christ survive such trauma and overcome.

In a world that conspires to gut God out of any meaning of life, D. J. Louw pushes us in heavy existential theologizing to view the cross of Christ and the resurrection as the quintessential necessity for every authentic sense of certain hope. Without the resurrection, there is no hope in this life, and Louw takes us to the root of our being in Christ.

Every article seems to hit a U.S. headline in a uniquely exquisite revelation, melding the academic with the deeply practical. How can we say this? In many ways, if grace cannot be made

Practical

or in some way reach and *aid* the hurting, then grace seems to lose some of its most elemental and living treasure.

Grace—the unmerited favor from God through his son Jesus Christ allows us access to the Throne of God, all of us, everywhere, where we all stand on level ground. All need grace, and the Christian is guaranteed grace when they come to God with a humble heart.

Grace—with the above definition—many faith traditions have refined their understanding for centuries. However, when the church meets the lost person, the poor person, and the victim of crime and exploitation, it seems to us at *Testamentum Imperium* that we lose many of our differences and coalesce around "loving our neighbor."

In such, we become the witness of God's grace to the hurting, to those wounded, and to those scarred by the evils of the world. Each of us in our faith traditions becomes a unique vehicle for God to use. May God help us—the church—bring healing, give comfort, and strengthen a soul in their unique trial of affliction.

These 15 articles touch a broad scope of affliction, real areas of struggle, from physical suffering to moral and theological dilemmas. And part of the choice was *not* to find from the 163 those who see eye-to-eye theologically or philosophically. We desired to share the unique expertise of 15 in 15 unique oceans, as it were, who feel with a *pastoral heart* and have set sail in their rugged crafts upon 15 separate tumultuous oceans of pain. Each of the 15 chart a course through a unique deep seas of pain. Each weathered captain ferry in the hold of their vessels a precious cargo of healing balm from God to help bring a soul to a port of healing and peaceful victory—in Christ.

We hope these articles bless you, challenge you, and encourage you in the

Practical Grace

that God energizes and facilitates in you, as Christian readers, and expands the horizons of your own service on the open wild seas in your lives throughout the precious Kingdom of our loving God.

Rev. Dr. Michael G. Maness
Managing Editor, *Testamentum Imperium*
Retired Senior Clinical Chaplain
Texas Department of Criminal Justice
www.PreciousHeart.net

1.
God's Condescension in Action:
Nature of Divine Redemptive Love
by Dr. Glenn R. Kreider
Professor of Theological Studies
Dallas Theological Seminary[4]

Preface on Creeds 1
Introduction 2
A. The Humility of God in the Incarnation 4
B. The Son's Works Emulate the Father's Works 8
C. Jesus Meets the Samaritan Woman at the Well of Sychar (John 4) 12
D. Yahweh Meets Hagar at the Spring on the Road to Shur (Gen 16) 15
E. Some Similarities in the Two Stories 22
Conclusion 26

Preface on Creeds

Nicene-Constantinopolitan Creed[5]

We believe in one Lord, Jesus Christ, the only Son of God, eternally begotten of the Father, God from God, Light from Light, true God from true God, begotten, not made, of one Being with the Father. Through him all things were made. For us and for our salvation he came down from heaven: by the power of the Holy Spirit he became incarnate from the Virgin Mary, and was made man.

Definition of Chalcedon[6]

Our Lord Jesus Christ . . . is perfect both in deity and in humanness; . . . actually God and actually man, with a rational soul and a body. He is of the same reality as God as far as his deity is concerned and of the same reality as we ourselves as far as his humanness is concerned; thus like us in all respects, sin only excepted. Before time began he was begotten of the Father, in respect of his deity, and

---

[4] Kreider wrote *God with Us: Exploring God's Personal Interactions with His People Throughout the Bible* (P&R Publishing, 2014) and *Jonathan Edwards' Interpretation of Revelation 4:1–8:1* (University Press of America, 2004); he co-edited others, including *Eschatology: Biblical, Historical, and Practical Approaches* (Kregel Academic, 2016) and *Exploring Christian Theology: The Church, Spiritual Growth, and the End Times* (Bethany House Publishers, 2014), and wrote many articles for *Bibliotheca Sacra* and the *Criswell Theological Review*, many on Jonathan Edwards.

[5] Nicene-Constantinopolitan Creed (381), accessed 11-6-10, www.iclnet.org/pub/resources/text/history/nicene381.html.

[6] Definition of Chalcedon (451), accessed 11-6-10, www.iclnet.org/pub/resources/text/history/creeds.chalcedon.txt.

now in these last days, for us and behalf of our salvation, this selfsame one was born of Mary the virgin, who is God-bearer in respect of his humanness. We also teach that we apprehend this one and only Christ-Son, Lord, only-begotten in two natures; and we do this without confusing the two natures, without transmuting one nature into the other, without dividing them into two separate categories, without contrasting them according to area or function. The distinctiveness of each nature is not nullified by the union. Instead, the properties of each nature are conserved and both natures concur in one person and in one reality. They are not divided or cut into two persons, but are together the one and only and only-begotten Word of God, the Lord Jesus Christ.

Cornelius Plantinga[7]

When we say Jesus is Lord, we are talking about God's greatest reversal, and we are saying that we trust not only in Jesus, but also his *program of dying and rising*. We trust his redemptive program in which self-expenditure leads to life, and not just to burnout. We trust that in his death Jesus absorbed the world's evil into himself, and cut the loop of vengeance, that in his resurrection Jesus led out all the captives of the world.

Introduction

In the incarnation, the eternal Son of the eternal Father, the Lord of all creation, humbled Himself and became a creature. He submitted Himself to His own creation, for the sake of the world and its inhabitants that He had made.[8] This act of condescension did not include the forfeiture of His divinity; rather, to His full deity was added full humanity so that the incarnate Son is "perfect both in deity and in humanness . . . of the same reality as God as far as His deity is concerned and of the same reality as we ourselves as far as His humanness is concerned; thus like us in all respects, sin only excepted."[9]

That the sovereign of the universe, the one who spoke creation into existence, the one who still holds it all together by His powerful word, would (or even could) condescend to become a creature is the

---

[7] Alvin Plantinga, "A Sermon for Advent: I Believe in Jesus Christ, God's Only Son, Our Lord," in *Exploring and Proclaiming the Apostles' Creed*, ed. Roger E. Van Harn (Grand Rapids: Eerdmans, 2004), 76.

[8] "He was in the world, and though the world was made through him, the world did not recognize him. He came to what which was his own, but his own did not receive him" (John 1:10–11).

[9] Plantinga, "A Sermon for Advent," 76.

ultimate mystery.[10] A greater act of submission could never be conceived. Although it does require a degree of humility to submit to one who is greater or to one's equal, to submit to one's inferior requires a great deal more. To submit to one who is infinitely inferior is the ultimate demonstration of humility.

Only the second person of the Trinity condescended to become human. Neither the Father nor the Spirit became a creature, but is divine humility limited to the incarnation? In a sermon on the incarnation, Cornelius Plantinga proposes that condescension is a family tradition for the Trinity. He asserts, "The Son of God just does what he sees his father doing. He empties himself and takes the form of a servant because that's the way they do it in his family. And God exalts Jesus Christ and gives him the name above every name because that too is the Godly way—to exalt the humble, to get very enthusiastic about those who spend themselves for others."[11] According to Plantinga, the incarnation is a manifestation in history of the divine family's longstanding tradition of condescension for the sake of the creation.

The goal of this paper is to provide some biblical support for Plantinga's thesis, beginning with a brief examination of the text for his sermon.[12] Then, two biblical stories will be read in defense of his claim, one from the life of Jesus and the other from the Pentateuch. The similarities between these two stories seem too great to be merely coincidental. It would seem that the Gospel writer intended his audience to read these stories together, or at least to hear the echoes of the Old Testament story in the New. Further, it is possible that John wants his readers to consider that Jesus behaved as He did on this day

---

[10] J. I. Packer puts it this way: "The real difficulty, the supreme mystery with which the gospel confronts us, does not lie ... in the Good Friday message of atonement, nor in the Easter message of resurrection, but in the Christmas message of Incarnation. The really staggering Christian claim is that Jesus of Nazareth was God made man—that the second person of the Godhead became the 'second man' (1 Cor 15:47), determining human destiny, the second representative head of the race, and that he took humanity without the loss of deity, so that Jesus of Nazareth was as truly and fully divine as he was human." J. I. Packer, *Knowing God*, 20th Anniversary Edition (Downers Grove: IVP, 1993), 53.

[11] Alvin Plantinga, "A Sermon for Advent," 77.

[12] The goal is not to prove this thesis but to provide evidence for it and then to illustrate its significance in the reading of two biblical stories. To say it another way, rather than providing sufficient evidence demanded to establish proof, this paper argues for the plausibility of Plantinga's thesis and then presents some of its implications.

because He was following the example of His Father. Since Jesus understood the Scriptures to be about Him, it would seem that one means by which He grew in wisdom and knowledge (Luke 2:40, 52) was by studying the Scriptures. So, on this day, when He found himself beside a well in Samaria and He met a woman who came to draw water, He knew how to treat her because of His familiarity with a similar story in the Pentateuch.

But, first, it might be helpful to provide some New Testament exegetical support for reading these two texts in this way. We turn first to the biblical text for Plantinga's sermon, the Christological hymn in Philippians 2, and then to Jesus' instructions on the Christological reading of the Scriptures in John 5.

A. The Humility of God in the Incarnation

In his epistle to the Philippians, the apostle Paul encourages Christians to pursue unity in the church and to love one another. Specifically, he asks them to "do nothing out of selfish ambition or vain conceit, but in humility consider others better than yourselves (Phil. 2:3)."[13] This lifestyle of humility evidences itself in self-sacrifice, in submission. The admonition to consider others better clearly does not necessarily mean that the others are better. In fact, the illustration of Christ would make little sense in that case.

Paul also does not encourage Christians to ignore or discount their own interests, their own needs. Instead, "Each of you should look not only to your own interests, but also to the interests of others," he says (Phil. 2:4). Paul is describing a lifestyle which does not demand one's rights and privileges or disregard taking care of one's needs; rather, it is a lifestyle marked by an appropriate and proper care of one's own interests "but also" looks out for the interests of others.

To drive this point home to his audience, Paul uses an illustration. Paul's use of Christ here is an example; he seems to be reminding this church of something they already know. To make the point, Paul does not compose his own doctrinal statement. Rather, he uses a Christological confession that was almost certainly already familiar to these believers. Gerald Hawthorne concludes,

---

[13] Unless indicated otherwise, all biblical citations are from the New International Version (Colorado Springs, CO: International Bible Society, 1984).

Here is at least one thing that calls forth almost universal agreement. It is that vv. 6–11 constitute a beautiful example of a very early hymn of the Christian church.[14]

This hymn was likely part of the liturgy of the church, perhaps even part of the service on the day this letter was read publicly for the first time.[15] Thus, in this passage, Paul does not set out to write a high Christology, to defend the doctrine of Christ apologetically, or to engage in academic theologizing. Rather, His focus is ethical, practical, and liturgical.[16] The audience is already grounded in the faith. They already know who Christ is.[17] In order to drive home his instruction about humility, love, unity, and similar Christian virtues, Paul uses Christ as an example: "Your attitude should be the same as that of Christ Jesus" (Phil. 2:5).

In what way should Christians be like Christ? Paul's answer here is simple, yet profoundly not simplistic. Christians should emulate His humility. Christ is the perfect example of one who did nothing out of selfish ambition or vain conceit. He demonstrated His humility by considering others better than Himself.[18] His actions demonstrated His attitudes. He was and is God, "in very nature" (Phil. 2:6). He who is fully God "did not consider equality with God something to be grasped but made himself nothing" (Phil. 2:7).[19] Jesus humbled

---

[14] Gerald F. Hawthorne, *Word Biblical Commentary: Philippians* (Dallas: Word, 1998), 76, Logos Library System, electronic.

[15] Of course, this claim is speculative. No records of the order of worship survive. But if this is an early confession of faith, it is likely that the church would have used it as a common confession in a corporate worship setting.

[16] All good theology is intensely practical. Perhaps that is one of the major methodological implications of this text. Paul here provides a model for practical theology, for liturgical theology that includes both confession and ethical implications.

[17] One implication of this early confession of faith is that it provides evidence of a Nicene Christology during the New Testament era. Thus, the Council of Nicaea confirmed Christian orthodoxy, it did not choose between a smorgasbord of "Christianities." See D. Jeffrey Bingham, "Development and Diversity in Early Christianity," *Journal of the Evangelical Theological Society* 49 (2006): 45–66.

[18] At first glance this seems a bit strong, perhaps even blasphemous. Does Paul really say that Christ considered others better than Himself? Of course, no one is greater than Christ, and no one knows that better than Christ. So then, how could He have considered others better than Himself? Note that He considered others greater does not mean that they are greater than He. But to treat those who are inferior to Him as greater, to submit Himself to them for their sakes is the height of, and perhaps even the definition of, humility. I am indebted to my friend and colleague Dorian Coover Cox for this insight.

[19] Clearly, Paul is not affirming that Jesus ceased to be, or that he ceased to be God in the incarnation. Rather, he "emptied himself" (NASB) or "made himself nothing" (NIV) or "made himself of

[Footnote continued on next page]

Himself, He sacrificed Himself, He gave Himself, He poured Himself out, He submitted His own desires and interests for others, and He condescended to become something He was not. To His divine nature He added a human nature. God himself became human; He who was "in very nature God" took "the very nature of a servant, being made in human likeness." The Creator of the universe became a creature, without ceasing to be the Creator. This is the wonder and mystery of the incarnation; not simply that the second person of the triune God became fully human, but in doing so He remained fully God.[20]

So, Paul's encouragement to the Philippians, and to all Christians, is to be like Christ. Consider others better than yourselves, humble yourselves (cf. James 4:10), and serve others, he says. Christians should follow the example of the one whose name they claim.[21]

This is one of the major ethical implications of the incarnation found throughout the New Testament. Jesus Christ shows His followers how to live, how to treat others. Paul put it this way in his letter to the Romans, "God demonstrated his love for us in this: while we were still sinners, Christ died for us" (Rom. 5:8). The apostle John explains that sacrifice is the essence of love, "This is how we know what love is: Jesus Christ laid down his life for us" (1 John 3:16a; cf. 4:9). "God is love" (1 John 4:8, 16) and "we love because he has first

---

no reputation" (KJV and NKJV). Hawthorne explains, "Hence, the hymn states that Christ, who shared the nature of God, who was equal with God, ἑαυτὸν ἐκένωσεν ('emptied himself')! The emphatic position of ἑαυτόν ('himself') and the form of the verb strongly suggest that this act of 'emptying' was voluntary on the part of the preexistent Christ" (Hawthorne, *Philippians*, 85). In the incarnation, Jesus remained fully and completely divine; he gave up nothing of his deity. Instead, he gave himself. For a helpful survey of the interpretations of this text see Hawthorne (ibid.). He concludes: "The Philippian text does not say that Christ gave up anything. Rather it says that he added to himself that which he did not have before—'the form of a servant,' 'the likeness of a man.' Thus the implication is that at the incarnation Christ became more than God, if this is conceivable, not less than God."

[20] "Here are two mysteries for the price of one—the plurality of persons within the unity of God, and the union of Godhead and manhood in the person of Jesus. It is here, in the thing that happened at the first Christmas, that the profoundest and most unfathomable depths of the Christian revelation lie. 'The Word became flesh' (John 1:14): God became man; the divine Son became a Jew; the Almighty appeared on earth as a helpless human baby, unable to do more than lie and stare and wriggle and make noises; needing to be fed and changed and taught to talk like any other child. And there was no illusion or deception in this: the babyhood of the Son of God was a reality. The more you think about it, the more staggering it gets. Nothing in fiction is so fantastic as this truth of the Incarnation." Packer, *Knowing God*, 53.

[21] This use of Christ as an example is not to propose an example model of the atonement. Rather, in His atoning work, Christ died as a substitute for sinners, the righteous for the unrighteous (2 Cor. 5:21). But the substitutionary atonement of Christ is an example of humility, self-sacrifice, condescension for the sake of the hopeless and helpless.

loved us" (1 John 4:19). John, too, emphasizes the ethical impact of this truth, "and we ought to lay down our lives for our brothers" (1 John 3:16b). The New Testament writers interpret the incarnation as establishing or grounding their instructions about proper behavior of the members of the body of Christ.[22]

Paul, in Philippians 2:6, goes one step further. Not only does he use Jesus as the example of humility for humans, he links Jesus' condescension in the incarnation to the character of God. Gerald Hawthorne writes:

> Hence, in this connection the participial phrase that begins v.6—ὅς ἐν μορφῇ θεοῦ ὑπάρχων ("who *being* in the form of God"), often wrongly translated as a concessive participle—who *though* he was in the form of God (RSV, NASB, Beck, Confraternity, Goodspeed, Williams), is more correctly translated as a causative: "precisely *because* he was in the form of God he reckoned equality with God not as a matter of getting but of giving" (Moule, "Manhood," 97). This then makes clear that contrary to whatever anyone may think about God, his true nature is characterized not by selfish grabbing, but by an open-handed giving.[23]

Plantinga draws a similar conclusion:

> The Greek text doesn't say that *although* he was in the form of God he emptied himself. What it says is, "*Being* in the form of God he emptied himself." You might almost read, *because* he was in the form of God he emptied himself. Because he was in the form of God he took the form of a servant, washing the feet of disciples who would never dream of doing the same thing for each other.[24]

Let me be clear: it is not my claim that this is the only way to read Philippians 2:6. Many interpreters argue for a concessive force of the participial phrase.[25] But it is legitimate to read it with a causative force. Such is a plausible and defensible reading. Nor is it my claim that the humility of God is defended from the exegesis of this one

---

[22] Similarly, James rebukes showing favoritism (James 2:1–4) and insists that faith without works is dead, worthless, and useless (James 2:14–26). Many other biblical examples could be cited.

[23] Hawthorne, *Philippians*, 85.

[24] Plantinga, "A Sermon for Advent," 76. For a comparison of this hymn and Jesus' washing his disciples' feet, see Greg Perry, "To Know and Be Known: How Christ's Love Moves Us into Intimacy, Humility, and Risk. A Sermon on John 13:1–17," in *All for Jesus—A Celebration of the 50th Anniversary of Covenant Theological Seminary*, ed. Robert A. Peterson and Sean Michael Lucas (Ross-shire, Great Britain: Mentor, 2006), 371–76.

[25] See, for example, Daniel B. Wallace, *Greek Grammar Beyond the Basics: An Exegetical Syntax of the New Testament* (Grand Rapids: Zondervan Publishing House, 1996), 634–35.

text. Whether or not the participle has a concessive or a causative force is a decision made on theological grounds.[26] On what basis should one conclude that the active humility of Jesus is because He is God? Such a decision must be informed by the teaching of the Scriptures, since no text should be interpreted as something disconnected from the rest of the canon.

We turn now to the Gospel of John, to a text in which Jesus defends himself to His critics and gives them instructions on how to read the Bible. He rebukes their hermeneutical approach, pointing out their failure to read the Bible with the correct theological perspective.

B. The Son's Works Emulate the Father's Works

In the fifth chapter of his gospel, John records a healing miracle of Jesus. Like many of His miracles, this healing occurred on the Sabbath; and as regularly happened when Jesus healed on the Sabbath, there were objections and opposition from the Jewish leaders.[27] "Because Jesus was doing these kinds of things on the Sabbath," John says, "the Jews persecuted Him" (John 5:16).[28] In this case, Jesus' response to His critics was direct and clear: "My Father is always at his work to this very day, and I, too, am working" (John 5:17). In this statement, Jesus affirms several things. He claims that the Father's work is constant. Thus, it would seem, the Father is working even on the Sabbath. Jesus also affirms a consistency between His work and the work of the Father. In short, Jesus seems to link His work, even on the Sabbath, with the work of the Father.

His answer infuriated His hearers: "For this reason the Jews tried all the harder to kill him; not only was he breaking the Sabbath, but he was even calling God his own Father, making himself equal to God" (John 5:18). They clearly recognized the implications of what He said. If Jesus was claiming here to be the Father and that He (the

---

[26] All exegetical decisions are informed by theology. It could hardly be otherwise.

[27] John refers to the opposition as "the Jews" (John 5:10, 15, 16, 18). It would seem that the opposition was particularly coming from the Jewish leaders. It would be inappropriate to see here evidence of inappropriate anti-Jewish rhetoric in Jesus or John. Rather, the leaders of the Jews opposed him, and it is they who receive Jesus' rebuke.

[28] It might seem to go without saying that it was not just what Jesus did that was seen as the problem, it was the time when He was doing these acts. It appears that Jesus was intentionally calling attention to Himself by His violation of the traditional Sabbath regulations.

Father) was working, there likely would not have been as strong a reaction.[29] But His critics knew that Jesus was making the claim as a human, and that was the heart of the problem for them, for humans were not allowed to work on the Sabbath.[30] They also understood that Jesus was asserting his deity in making himself equal to God. Jesus was, implicitly, claiming to be both human and divine, to be God incarnate.

Jesus' answer to this objection is an extended teaching on how to read the Bible. The Scriptures, Jesus said, testify about Him (John 5:39). So, if they are read properly, the readers will see Him there and come to Him for life (John 5:40). He reminds them of the testimony of John the Baptist, who proclaimed Christ (John 5:31–36). He reminds them of Moses, who wrote about Christ (John 5:45–47). "If you believed Moses," Jesus said, "you would believe me, for he wrote about me. But since you do not believe what he wrote, how are you going to believe what I say?" (John 5:46–47). To those who respected Moses and thought themselves to be the authoritative interpreters of Moses, these were harsh words of rebuke. But it is not just John and Moses who testify about Christ, Jesus says, all the Scriptures point to Him.

Jesus claims that His critics are blind and deaf, that they have rebelled against God and the prophets He had sent, and that they had even rebelled against God's Son. They have been unable to hear God and to see Him, even though He has been speaking plainly and has been present in their midst. Jesus said, "You have neither heard his voice nor seen his form, nor does his word dwell in you, for you do not believe the one he sent. You diligently study the Scriptures because you think that by them you possess eternal life. These are the Scriptures that testify about me, yet you refuse to come to me to have life" (John 5:37–40).

This is a firm and strong rebuke of the way these Jewish scholars were reading the Scriptures. They considered themselves to be experts

---

[29] This text, then, would seem to provide evidence of a trinitarian view of God. It would be hard to conceive the reason for the opposition on a unitarian or modalistic reading of this text.

[30] Whether Jesus was breaking the Mosaic Sabbath laws or only the traditions of the rabbis is not the issue here. The critics recognized that He was claiming a unique relationship with the Father and that this was the basis of His Sabbath work.

in the law, but Jesus points out to them that their approach was wrong and, thus, their readings of the Scriptures were in error.[31] Their misunderstanding was that studying the Scriptures was the way to have eternal life, that the study of the Scriptures was the end in itself. The flaw in their approach is that the Scriptures are not the means of life—Jesus is! The Scriptures testify to Him. Those who read the Scriptures correctly recognize that and come to Him for life. To study the Scriptures without recognizing their proper aim is to misread the Scriptures.[32]

Jesus' point is that the study of the Scriptures is not enough, for they must be studied correctly. It is not enough to read the Word of God; it must be read properly. Every reading is an interpretation; the Scriptures do not simply speak for themselves. Since the Scriptures testify about Jesus, any reading that fails to hear Jesus, any interpretation that fails to elevate Jesus, any study that fails to focus on Jesus is incorrect and is worthy of judgment. These Jewish leaders were failing to read the Scriptures correctly.

Thus, Jesus said that Moses himself will be called to accuse these rebels before the Father (John 5:45). They had elevated Moses and his law, thinking that in doing so they were honoring God. Instead, they were missing the whole point of the Scriptures, since Moses wrote about Jesus (John 5:46).[33] When God Himself, in the incarnation, came to them and spoke to them they failed to hear His voice. When God Himself came and appeared before them in Jesus of Nazareth, they failed to see Him. When God himself came and did His work in their midst they failed to perceive Him.

In John 5:19, Jesus claims that "the Son can do nothing by himself, he can do only what he sees his Father doing, because whatever the Father does the Son also does." Jesus seems to be affirming that His actions are not only consistent with the works of His Father but that He learned what to do by watching His Father work. Of course, the

---

[31] Thus, the Scriptures must be read with the theological conviction that they are about Christ. This presupposition must ground every reading of the text.

[32] Cf. 1 Tim 3:15 where Paul wrote to Timothy reminding him of what he had learned from infancy, that the Scriptures "are able to make you wise for salvation through faith in Christ Jesus."

[33] It is unlikely that Moses understood that he was speaking of Christ. But Moses, rightly interpreted, wrote of the Son.

eternal Son had been watching the Father work prior to the incarnation. In fact, the Father and Son had been working together in perfect harmony. But when the Son humbled Himself and took on humanity, He had a new perspective on His Father. As He grew in wisdom (Luke 2:40, 52), as He studied the Scriptures, He watched His Father work.[34] As Jesus read the Scriptures, He learned to recognize and to tell the story of God's work of creation and redemption.[35] As He read the Old Testament stories, He recognized the hope of the culmination of redemption. Jesus read the Scriptures as God's testimony about Him and, it would seem, He patterned His life after the example of His Father.[36] In short, Jesus read the Scriptures as the story of God's work in the created order and He emulated His Father in what He did.[37]

The Son is not the Father, but in His works He reveals the Father because He is the Son of His Father. His critics got it right. They understood Jesus to be claiming to be in a unique relationship with the Father (John 5:18). He was. They should have believed Him, not simply because He said it, but because the Scriptures the Jews were reading testify about Him. Their attention to the Scriptures was a good thing, but because they were not reading them properly, their study of the Scriptures brought them condemnation not life. Their

---

[34] Of course, "watching" the Father work in the Scriptures is a metaphor for interpreting the Scriptures accurately as relating the work of God.

[35] One of the many mysteries of the incarnation is the relationship between the divine and human attributes. Although omniscience is an attribute of deity, humans come to learn and develop in their understanding. That Jesus grew and learned is clearly taught in Scripture (Luke 2:40, 52; Heb. 5:8). On the temptations of Jesus, Wayne Grudem concludes, "As difficult as it may be for us to understand, Scripture affirms that in these temptations Jesus gained an ability to understand and to help us in our temptations. '*Because he himself has suffered and been tempted*, he is able to help those who are tempted' (Heb. 2:18)." Gruden, *Systematic Theology—An Introduction to Biblical Doctrine* (Grand Rapids: Zondervan, 1994), 537. It would seem that Jesus learned how to read and how to read the Bible the same way that all others humans learn.

[36] Article 1 of the Dallas Theological Seminary Doctrinal Statement says, "We believe that all the Scriptures center about the Lord Jesus Christ in His person and work in His first and second coming, and hence that no portion, even of the Old Testament, is properly read, or understood, until it leads to Him." John 5:39 is included in the list of biblical support. See the *Dallas Theological Seminary Catalog 2011–2012*, 187.

[37] His approach to making decisions was to ask, "What would Yahweh do?" It is, however, unlikely that Jesus wrote a "WWYD" bracelet. It is also unlikely that any of His disciples wore "WWJD" bracelets.

Bible study did not contribute to faith and godliness, because they were studying incorrectly.[38]

C. Jesus Meets the Samaritan Woman at the Well of Sychar (John 4)

The healing miracle that precipitated this lesson on hermeneutics took place at the pool near the Sheep Gate in Jerusalem (John 5:2). It follows, in John's narrative, another incident some time earlier at another body of water, a well near Sychar in Samaria (John 4:5). This story of the healing of an invalid at a pool evidences Jesus' mercy and compassion toward an outsider, one who was marginalized from the faith community because of his thirty-eight-year disability. In the story recorded in John 4, Jesus met a woman at a well in Samaria. She too was an outsider because she was a woman, a Samaritan, and she was living with a man who was not her husband.[39] It would seem that the narrator's arrangement of these stories was not coincidental. In short, the reader of John 5 has the incident in John 4 in the background when reading Jesus' teaching about the relationship between His and the Father's works and Jesus' criticism of a non–Christological hermeneutic.

In John 4, Jesus has an extended conversation with this unnamed Samaritan woman.[40] Jesus and His disciples were on their way from Judea to Galilee.[41] On their way through Samaria Jesus stopped to rest

---

[38] Christian Bible study is not simply Bible study performed by Christians, it is Bible study which approaches the text confessing that Jesus is the Christ, that He is God in the flesh, that the hope of the resurrection and the regeneration of all things is found in Him. In short, Christian Bible study is not unbiased and objective, it is intentionally and confessionally convinced of the truth of Christian orthodoxy. Exegesis cannot be disconnected from theology, at least not Christian exegesis.

[39] It would seem that this woman was not only marginalized from the Jewish community but from the Samaritan religious community as well.

[40] Frank Anthony Spina, *The Faith of the Outsider—Exclusion and Inclusion in the Biblical Story* (Grand Rapids: Eerdmans Publishing Co., 2005), 142, writes, "In the story of the woman at the well, John's Gospel arguably contains the longest and most elaborate narrative in the entire New Testament on the outsider theme."

[41] John says that Jesus "had to go through Samaria." The necessity seems connected to the "divine appointment" with this woman, not that the only or even usual way to get from Judea to Galilee was to go through Samaria. In John's gospel, the theme of divine intention and the accomplishing of God's plan commonly occur. Spina's conclusion seems accurate: "Granted, it's difficult to see anything transparently providential right away; yet, by the end of the story, that dimension must surely be considered. Supporting this claim, this same Greek word [*dei*] elsewhere in John's Gospel underscores a number of 'necessities' that are anything but ordinary (see John 3:7, 14, 30; 4:20, 24; 9:4; 10:16; 12:34; 20:9)" in *Faith of the Outsider*, 145.

at a well. John, who likely was with Jesus on this trip and thus was an eyewitness to some of these events, says that Jesus was tired (John 4:6), so He rested by the well by Himself while His disciples went into the town to buy food (John 4:9). While Jesus waited, a woman from Samaria came to draw water. Jesus engaged her in conversation, which was surprising to the woman, since "Jews do not associate with Samaritans" (John 4:9).[42] Further, this is not simply a Samaritan, but a Samaritan woman. Jesus' private conversation with a Samaritan woman violated a number of social mores. Even in our day, in our much more enlightened culture, a private conversation between a Christian leader and a woman not his wife would lead some to question the leader's wisdom and discretion, and perhaps even his theology. In the culture of his time, Jesus' behavior would have been deemed inappropriate by almost everyone. So this is not a minor point in the story, and this is magnified by the disciples' reaction when they return. John says that they "were surprised to find him talking with a woman" (John 4:27). The disciples seem more surprised that He was talking to a woman than that she was a Samaritan.

The conversation begins with the subject of water, which is not surprising, because of the setting. Jesus asks this woman to serve Him, to give Him a drink of water. The woman apparently understood some of the implications of Jesus' request. She expresses surprise that He would be unaware of the cultural expectations. She reminds him that there is conflict between Jews and Samaritans. When Jesus explains that if she really understood who He was she would have asked Him for living water, the woman is even more confused. She does, however, seem to understand that Jesus was claiming to be able to provide something she desperately needed. She finally asks for the water Jesus is offering her. His intention seems clear, to use water as a means of focusing her attention on Him. The water is not the end; it is a means to a much more important end. If all divine revelation points

---

[42] Whether or not the NIV reading is adopted or the alternative, "Jews do not use dishes Samaritans have used," the point remains the same. There was significant conflict between Jews and Samaritans; there was blame on both sides.

to Christ, then things like food and water would be opportunities to recognize the giver of every good gift and the gift itself.[43]

Rather than providing what she requests, and what He had implicitly encouraged her to desire, Jesus then told her to call her husband (John 4:16). She admits that she is not married and is stunned when Jesus is able to relate her marital history of five husbands and a current live-in relationship with a man not her husband. She is convinced that He is a prophet, one who is able to see what humans cannot normally see. Eventually she confesses her belief that when the Messiah comes, He will explain everything. In clear and unambiguous terms, Jesus declares to her that He is the Messiah (John 4:26).[44]

At that time the disciples returned and were surprised to see Jesus talking with a woman, but none of them said anything to Him about it (John 4:27). The woman left to return to her village, leaving her water jar at the well. Her testimony to the people of the village is, "Come, see a man who told me everything I ever did. Could this be the Christ?" (John 4:29). The question seems rhetorical, since there are several indications in the narrative that she does believe in Him. Many from the village accompany her back to the well where Jesus and the disciples wait.

Meanwhile, the disciples are trying to get Jesus to eat. He refuses, and instead calls their attention to the fields ripe for harvest (John 4:34–38). There is little reason to think that the disciples understand what he was saying. The woman's confusion about "living water" seems matched by their confusion about "ripe fields."

Many of the Samaritans believed in Jesus, because of the woman's testimony: "He told me everything I ever did" (John 4:39). They urged Jesus to stay with them, so He spent two days in their village.

---

[43] "I am the bread of life," Jesus said (John 6:35). As the Creator He is the source of bread but He is also the bread itself. Of course, the "bread of life" has several levels of meaning. Jesus is the source of the actual food we eat to sustain life and He is life itself. He is also the source of living water, the water of life, the Holy Spirit.

[44] Such clarity of confession of His Messiahship is rare in the Gospels. Seldom does Jesus speak so explicitly and directly. Later, He will speak similarly to Pilate (cf. John 18:37), another outsider to the people of faith and the promises of God.

He spent two days in the Samaritan village.[45] The disciples also, apparently, spent two days in the Samaritan village. The story ends with the testimony of the Samaritan believers: "We no longer believe just because of what you said; now we have heard for ourselves, and we know that this man really is the Savior of the world" (John 4:42).

As this story begins, Jesus is resting by a body of water. The readers know something that most of the characters in the story do not know, that He was here by necessity, as part of the divine plan (John 4:4).[46] This is not an accidental encounter between Jesus and a woman. Could it be that John intends his readers to connect this story to the revealed plan of God, to another story of God's redemptive encounter with a woman? Could it be that Jesus was not only aware of that story but He intentionally re-enacted it on this day? God having a conversation with a woman at a body of water, bringing salvation to her, condescending to relate to her when no one else would, providing for her needs, and even using her to bring others to faith—did such a thing ever happen in redemptive history prior to the time of Jesus?

D. Yahweh Meets Hagar at the Spring on the Road to Shur (Gen 16)

In Genesis 16, Moses records a story from the life of the patriarch Abram. After a decade in the land of Canaan, during which Abram has been waiting patiently for God to begin to build a nation through him, Sarai is still childless. Abram and Sarai became more and more concerned about the ticking of Sarai's biological clock. She concluded, correctly, that "the LORD has kept me from having

---

[45] The repetition is for emphasis. This is a stunning reversal of expected social behavior. Not only are social mores being shattered, so our deeply-held stereotypes. These Samaritans practiced hospitality, inviting Jesus to stay with them. Jesus' experiences with the Jews were frequently less pleasant (cf. John 5:18; 7:1). But perhaps more surprising is that Jesus and his disciples accepted the hospitality of the Samaritans. It is unlikely that in two days in the town that they could have avoided using dishes used by the Samaritans (cf. John 4:9), not to mention having contact with the Samaritans in the town. In fact, the point seems to be that Jesus had a great deal of interaction and contact with these Samaritans and that such contact was good and worthy of emulation by His followers.

[46] It could be that even Jesus is unaware of His divine appointment with this woman. J. I. Packer writes, "The Word had become flesh: a real human baby. He had not ceased to be God; he was no less God then than before; but he had begun to be a man. He was not now God *minus* some elements of his deity, but God *plus* all that he had made his own by taking manhood to himself. He who made man was now learning what it felt like to be man." *Knowing God*, 57.

children" (Gen. 16:2). She then conceived a plan; she will offer her maid to Abram as a surrogate and build a family through her.

Sarai's evaluation of the cause of the situation is accurate. The LORD is the cause of her childlessness. The flaw is in her plan to give her maidservant to her husband and to attempt to build a family through her. Surprisingly, or perhaps not, Abram agreed with her plan and took Hagar the Egyptian maidservant as his wife (Gen. 16:3).[47] He slept with her and she conceived a child.[48] The echoes of Genesis 3 in this story seem deliberate. As in the fall narrative, the man "listened to his wife," and his wife "took and gave to her husband."[49]

---

[47] On the other hand, Abram's behavior here might not be surprising at all. He has demonstrated himself to be a man who cared more about himself than others, one who looks for the easy way out of conflict without consideration for the effects of his decisions on others. Attempts to absolve Abram of guilt in this incident abound. Some have proposed that since the law which prohibits adultery had not get been given, adultery is not yet a sin, or at least Abram could not be aware that it is wrong. But this story is written not from the perspective of Abram's day, but in the context of the exodus. The audience in that context did know that adultery is wrong and that Abram's behavior here is not an act of faith. Furthermore, the narrator indicates that Hagar became Abram's wife, so there was no adultery. Abram is a polygamist. Polygamy was widely practiced and not forbidden to the people of God. But, it must be noted, the problem here is not polygamy or adultery but Abram's mistreatment of his wife and unborn child.

In over a decade of teaching this material, I have never had a female student defend Abram's behavior. The attempts to defend Abram have always come from men. I do not know if this gender divide is significant or representative, but I believe that my female students have it right.

For a representative defense of Abram, see Augustine, *City of God* 16.25: "Abraham is in no way to be branded as guilty concerning this concubine. For he dealt with her for the begetting of progeny, not for the gratification of lust, and not to insult her but to obey his wife, who supposed it would be solace of her barrenness if she could make use of the fruitful womb of her handmaid to supply the defect of her own nature. By that law of which the apostle says, 'Likewise also the husband has not power of his own body, but the wife' [1 Cor. 7:4]. Sarah could, as a wife, do benefit to him through childbearing by another, when she could not do so in her own person. Here there is no wanton lust, no crude lewdness. The handmaid is delivered to the husband by the wife for the sake of progeny and is received by the husband for the sake of progeny, each seeking not guilty excess but natural fruit. Thus the pregnant bondwoman despised her barren mistress, and Sarah, with womanly jealousy, rather laid the blamed of this on her husband. Yet even then Abraham showed that he was not a slavish lover but a free begetter of children and that in using Hagar he had guarded the chastity of Sarah his wife and had gratified her will and not his own. He had received her without seeking her, gone in to her without being attached, impregnated without loving her. For he says, 'Behold, your maid is in your power; do to her as you please.' Here is a man able to treat different women as they require—his wife temperately, his handmaid compliantly, neither intemperately!" *Ancient Christian Commentary on Scripture, Genesis 12–50*, edited by Thomas Oden and Mark Sheridan (Downers Grove: IVP, 2002), 45.

[48] The implication seems to be that after ten years of trying to conceive a child with Sarai, one attempt with Hagar results in pregnancy.

[49] See Wenham, who writes, "It is clear from the outset that the narrator does not endorse Sarai's scheme. Her very first words blame her creator for her predicament, suggesting that she is in her own way going to sort out God's mistakes, hardly a model of piety. Then in the deliberate echoes of Gen 3, Abram 'obeying his wife,' Sarai 'taking and giving to her husband,' the narrator suggests we are witnessing a rerun of the fall. Though the consequences are not as calamitous as the disobedience in

[*Footnote continued on next page*]

As in the fall narrative, the result of this decision has immediate and long term tragic consequences.

Immediately, things are different in Abram's family. When Hagar discovers she is pregnant, she begins to despise Sarai. Sarai rebukes Abram, blaming him for this conflict. She tells him, "You are responsible for the wrong I am suffering.... May the LORD judge between you and me" (Gen. 16:5). She is correct. It was Abram's actions which resulted in Hagar's pregnancy. But, as is usually the case when humans play the "blame game," she ignores her own culpability in the plan.

How will Abram respond to Sarai's implicit request to do something about the conflict between the two wives? His reply is chilling: "'Your servant is in your hands,' Abram said. 'Do with her whatever you think best'" (Gen. 16:6a). It is very difficult to read this description of Abram's behavior charitably, since the narrator goes on to tell us that Sarai mistreated Hagar (Gen. 16:6b). Surely Abram knew, or should have known, that this would have been the result. If he could not have known that Sarai would treat Hagar cruelly, he surely knew it when it happened.[50] There is no hint in the narrative that Abram did anything to protect Hagar. Remember, this is not simply Sarai's or Abram's servant. Hagar is Abram's wife, and she is pregnant with Abram's son.[51]

Hagar endured the abuse for as long as she could, but eventually she ran away to the desert. At a spring in the desert on the road to Shur, on the way back to Egypt, she was met by "the angel of the LORD" (Gen. 16:7).

Although there are several ways to interpret the identity of the "angel of the Lord," what is beyond question is that this messenger is connected to Yahweh and is here as part of the divine plan. The

---

Eden, they were sufficient to abort Sarai's enterprise had not the Lord intervened to salvage the situation." Gordon J. Wenham, *Word Biblical Commentary: Genesis 16–50* (Dallas: Word, 1998), 12, Logos Library System.

[50] There is no way to justify Abram by pointing out that it was Sarai who mistreated Hagar not Abram. Abram is the patriarch. This is his family and he is responsible for ruling justly. If someone under his care is mistreated, is he not culpable? Furthermore, Hagar is no longer simply the servant of Sarai. She is Abram's wife (Gen. 16:3) and she is bearing Abram's child. Abram is not ignorant of her pregnancy.

[51] The readers know something that no other character in the story knows, to this point. Hagar is not simply bearing Abram's child, she is carrying his son.

narrator intends the reader to recognize this as an act of Yahweh. This character could be an angel, a messenger sent by Yahweh to Hagar.[52] In that case, when the angel speaks, he is communicating the message sent by God. But it would be better to understand this "angel" as Yahweh himself, for the narrator tells us that Hagar gave a name to the LORD who appeared and spoke to her (Gen. 16:13). In short, this seems to be a theophany, an appearance of God on earth in human form. The story reveals a God who condescends to enter into the life experience of this Egyptian slave woman. Whether God sent a messenger or He himself left heaven to come to earth in the form of a being that this woman can see and hear, the Creator has humbled himself to care for a creature on earth and to bless a creature. But this is not simply any creature; this is Hagar, an Egyptian slave woman, the unwanted wife of the patriarch Abram.[53]

In the Abram stories, we have been introduced to a man chosen by God to be the mediator of blessings to all peoples on earth (Gen. 12:3). In a later chapter, Abram's name will be changed to Abraham by Yahweh, because "I have made you the father of many nations" (Gen. 17:5).[54] In the story in Genesis 16, the mother of one of those

---

[52] For a representative defense of the view that the angel of the Lord is an angel, see Didymus the Blind, *On Genesis 249*, from *Ancient Christian Commentary on Scripture, Genesis 12–50*, ed. Oden and Sheridan, 49. Didymus explains, "She names him 'Lord' and 'God.' It is not too much of a stretch to say that the angel was not in the service of his own words but of God's, as are also the prophets. For, in a certain sense, when angels exercise their ministry and when they foretell the future, they do the work of prophets. The name *angel* indicates an activity, not a substance; the same is true of the name *prophet*, [Since] the angel was speaking the words of God, Hagar called him God because of the One who lived in him. Similarly, when Isaiah prophecies, he sometimes speaks in his own person, as a man who has within himself the prophetic spirit, and he sometimes, as it were, makes God the character who speaks, without adding 'says the Lord." For example, he writes, 'I made the earth and created man upon it' [Isa. 45:12], but (it is he himself speaking) as one sent by the Lord he proclaims, 'Hear, O heavens, and give ear, O earth; for the Lord has spoken' [Isa. 1:2]. We say this to show that the words of Isaiah are not all spoken as though he were merely an intermediary but that participation in God confers also the authority of God; and because of God's dwelling in them, those who share in him are called gods. This is so true that an angel speaking to Moses was also called God. It is written in fact: And the angel of the Lord called him and said to him. 'I am the God of Abraham, the God of Isaac and the God of Jacob' [Exod. 34:6, LXX]. If one looks at the minister, these are words of angels, but if one looks at the sense, they are words of God."

[53] This is not some decontextualized or generic appearance of God. He came to earth (or sent a representative to earth) at a specific time in a specific place in a specific form to appear to a specific person.

[54] At this time in the story, Abraham is not yet the father of many nations. He is only the father of Ishmael. But, the promises of God are sure, so this one can be stated as if it is already accomplished. Also not to be missed is that this promise of Abraham's fruitfulness (Gen. 17:6) comes when he is 99 years old. Abraham's fruitful years of producing children are delayed until he is well into his second

[*Footnote continued on next page*]

nations is blessed by God. This blessed person is not a descendent of Abram, she is an Egyptian. She is a woman, a servant of the patriarch's wife who, because of the patriarch's actions, will be elevated to the status of favored wife in his household.[55] She is, after all, the only one of Abram's wives to this point to provide him a son, and it will be nearly fourteen years before Sarah bears Isaac (Gen. 16:16; cf. 17:1 and 21:5).

Why is Hagar a recipient of God's intervention here? The answer seems simple: she is bearing Abram's child.[56] Abram was chosen by God to be a mediator of God's blessing to all peoples. But Abram is not even willing to preserve the life of his unborn child. God, who sees all, condescends to intervene and to protect this child and her mother from harm.

The angel found Hagar near a spring in the desert. He asked her where she has come from and where she is going (Gen. 16:8). This conversation is clearly not so that the angel can gather information from Hagar. God already knows why Hagar is here. He is, after all, the God who sees everything.[57] Further, the angel's greeting, "Hagar,

---

century (cf. Gen. 25:1–6; where the narrator names six sons and refers to the additional sons of his concubines).

[55] It is almost universally acknowledged that Hagar joined the patriarch's family during Abram's brief sojourn in Egypt (Gen. 12:10–20). Perhaps she was given to Sarai when she was taken into the Pharoah's household (Gen. 12:15–16). Thus, this was not the first time that Hagar was elevated and blessed in the context of Abram's sin. His trip to Egypt, and his lie about his marital status in order to avoid any harm to himself (Gen. 12:12–13) resulted in Hagar joining the family of God's blessing. Now, pregnant with Abram's son, she will be elevated again, not because of Abram's great faith, but because of God's great grace.

[56] Although it might be possible to justify Abram's behavior in agreeing to sleep with this woman, even though I do not think so, there is no way to justify him when he allows his wife Sarai to mistreat the mother of his unborn child and to drive her away from the family. My purpose is not the "bash" Abram for his sin. It is, rather, to recognize how much in need of grace our father Abraham was. He was not blessed by God because of his faithfulness and obedience to God. He was blessed by a gracious God for reasons known only to God.

[57] The parallels to God's question to Adam ("Where are you?") in Genesis 3 and to Cain (Where is your brother?") in Genesis 4 seem obvious. Wenham writes: "For the first time, Hagar is addressed by name and is called 'Sarai's maid.' This may have surprised Hagar. How could a stranger have known about her identity? The reader, knowing that the stranger is the angel of the Lord, is not surprised. But the question that follows, "Where have you come from?" although sounding quite natural to Hagar, strikes the reader as rhetorical. It is as unnecessary as the Lord asking Adam "where are you?" (Gen. 3:9) or Cain "where is Abel?" (4:9). This is, in fact, the first time the Lord has asked someone their whereabouts since Gen. 4, and it emphasizes the parallel between this story and those earlier ones.

"But whereas Adam and Cain prevaricated, Hagar is perfectly honest in her answer, 'I am running away from Sarai, my mistress.' She admits that she is a runaway slave, and her chosen verb 'run away' implies she has very good reason to escape (cf. v. 6)." Wenham, *Genesis 16–50*, 9.

[*Footnote continued on next page*]

servant of Sarai" (Gen. 16:8), indicates that he already knows her name and where she has come from. The angel instructs Hagar to return to the home of her mistress and to submit to her.[58] The implication seems to be that the God who sees everything will take care of her. The appearance of God and his promises to her imply that Hagar should trust Him in the future.[59]

After giving these instructions, the angel of the LORD added several words of blessing. Hagar hears the words: "I will so increase your descendants that they will be too numerous to count" (Gen 16:10). These are very similar to the words Abram had heard from Yahweh: "Look up at the heavens and count the stars—if indeed you can count them.... so shall your offspring be" (Gen. 15:5). The promise of innumerable descendants for Abram is now repeated for the son of the slave woman. Why? Because this as-yet-unborn child is a descendent of Abram, and his mother is the wife of the patriarch (cf. Gen. 17:20).

The angel continued:

> You are now with child and you will have a son. You shall name him Ishmael, for the LORD has heard of your misery. He will be a wild donkey of a man; his hand will be against everyone and everyone's hand against him, and he will live in hostility toward all his brothers (Gen. 16:11–12).[60]

This child's life will be marked by conflict and hostility. But this child bears the name of the God who hears. Allen Ross comments on the theological significance of the name Ishmael:

The contrast in response is stunning. Whereas Adam and Cain, when confronted by God had refused to answer or had blamed others, Hagar, the Egyptian slave woman, answered honestly. Her faithfulness in contrast to the faithlessness of Abram and Sarai is also clear.

[58] This text has sometimes been used to develop the principle that a woman in an abusive relationship must return to the abuser and submit to him. Such an interpretation is unconscionable. This text is not teaching abused spouses to submit to their abuser anymore than it is teaching that the children of the patriarch Abraham should practice polygamy. A commitment to life and to protection of the helpless (widows, orphans, strangers, and slaves seem to receive special protection from God and should also receive such from God's people) means that we should protect those who are being abused, even to the point of removing them from abuse and giving them a place to stay where they will be safe. Nor does this story prove that God will always protect the abused (and their children) in such conditions, as the graves of many who were killed by their abusers silently testify.

[59] That Hagar apparently obediently returns to her mistress demonstrates her faith in Yahweh, in the God who sees.

[60] Readers of the New Testament might hear here echoes of this angelic announcement in another angel's message to Mary: "You will be with child and give birth to a son, and you are to give him the name Jesus" (Luke 1:31).

God *sees* distress and affliction, and He *hears*. Sarai should have known this. Since God knew Sarai was barren, she should have cried out to the Lord. Instead she had to learn a lesson the hard way—from the experience of a despised slave-wife who, ironically, came back with a faith experience. How Abram must have been rebuked when Hagar said God told her to name her son Ishmael, 'God hears.'[61]

When the angel finished speaking, Hagar gave a "name to the LORD who spoke to her" (Gen. 16:13). It would seem that the narrator is thus identifying the one who spoke as the LORD.[62] There are several things significant about this act of naming. First, in the book of Genesis, naming has particular importance. The one who names exercises dominion over the one named.[63]

In this story, the Creator, Yahweh, is infinitely greater than the creature. Yet it is the greater who condescends to come to the aid of the lesser. It is the greater who humbles Himself, who submits His rights, and grants the privilege of naming to the inferior.[64] The greater one gives up the rights and privileges of His position to allow this subordinate to be honored. The greater abases Himself in order to elevate the inferior. Of course, the greater remains the one with all power and authority. The greater one does not cease to be greater in this act of condescension. When God humbles Himself in this way, He does not cease to be God. For if He did, then the promises He makes and the name He is given would be a cruel joke.

---

[61] Ross, "Genesis," in *The Bible Knowledge Commentary: An Exposition of the Scriptures*, edited by John F. Walvoord and Roy B. Zuck, electronic ed. (Dallas: Word, 1998), 57, Logos Library System.

[62] That the "angel of the Lord" in Gen. 16 seems to be Yahweh himself does not necessarily mean that every occurrence of this designation in the Hebrew Scriptures is thus to be understood this way. Each case should be examined in its own context.

[63] See Wayne Grudem, *Systematic Theology*, 462: "The fact that Adam gave names to all the animals Gen. 2:19–20) indicated Adam's authority over the animal kingdom, because in Old Testament thought the right to name someone implied authority over that person (this is seen both when God gives names to people such as Abraham and Sarah, and when parents give names to their children)."

[64] The writer of Hebrews makes a similar point about blessing. He argues that "the lesser person is blessed by the greater" (Heb. 7:7). He explains that when Abram met Melchizedek and was blessed by him (Gen. 14:19–20) and when Abram paid tithes to Melchizedek, this king and priest was greater than Abram. Thus, Melchizedek's priesthood is greater than Levi's and Aaron's (Heb. 7:9–19). When God called Abram and sent him to the land of promise, it was not because there was no worship of God in the land. One greater than Abram was already there. And this greater one was both a priest and king. Although Abram would function was a priest, mediating God's blessing to others, he would never be a king. He was a nomad in the land of promise. The only land to which he had title was a burial plot (cf. Gen. 23).

It is not merely Hagar's naming God that is significant. So is the name she gives Yahweh. She names Him, "The God who sees me" (Gen. 16:13). Yahweh is not just the God who sees. Hagar confesses that Yahweh is "the God who sees *me*." The Creator of the universe, she says, has noticed her and has condescended to care for her. The lasting influence of this name is such, the narrator notes, that the well between Kadesh and Bered is called "Beer Lahai Roi; it is still there" (Gen. 16:14). Apparently, Hagar's influence was so great that generations later this place retained the name she had given it.[65] In the stories of the patriarchs, the narrator often calls attention to the names given to places, particularly when the places are named after the God of the patriarchs. But God's condescension to Hagar, to allow her to name him, is unique in the biblical story.[66]

This story ends suddenly. Many questions remain unanswered. But what is clear is that Hagar returned to Abram and Sarai. By doing so she demonstrated her faith in the God who had appeared to her. As the messenger had declared, she bore a son and Abram gave him the name Ishmael. Thus, he demonstrated his faith in the God who had appeared to Hagar and probably also his trust in her.

E. Some Similarities in the Two Stories

The similarities between these two stories are stunning. The New Testament story elevates most of the details of the Old Testament

---

[65] Note that after Abraham's death, Isaac makes his home near Beer Lahai Roi (Gen. 25:11).

[66] Abraham called the place where God provided a ram as a substitute sacrifice for his son Isaac, "The LORD will provide" (Gen. 22:14). Jacob recognized the presence of God at the place where he saw the vision of the angels ascending and descending on a ladder and he called the place "Bethel," or "house of God" (Gen. 28:19). After the night of wrestling with the man, Jacob called the place "Peniel, saying, 'It is because I saw God face to face, and yet my life was spared'" (Gen. 32:30). Moses called the altar he constructed after the defeat of the Amalekites, "The LORD is my banner" (Exod. 17:15).

The LORD's zeal to protect his name is clearly stated in the third commandment, "You shall not misuse the name of the LORD your God, for the LORD will not hold anyone guiltless who misuses his name" (Exod. 20:7) and in the later statement, "Do not worship any other god, for the LORD, whose name is Jealous, is a jealous God" (Exod. 34:14). The strong connection between Yahweh and His name is also seen in the use of His name as a metonymy for Yahweh Himself, "Our help is in the name of the LORD, the Maker of heaven and earth" (Ps. 124:8). That this God, who takes the protection, preservation, and purity of his name so seriously would allow Himself to be named by this Egyptian slave woman, the estranged and pregnant wife of the patriarch Abraham indicates His condescension to her. That Yahweh changes the name of Abram (to Abraham) and Sarai (to Sarah) in Gen. 17, without any indication that He changed Hagar's name heightens the emphasis on His graciousness to Hagar. Note that the reason for the change of name for Abraham and Sarah seems to be their lack of faith in the promises of Yahweh. The obedience of Hagar to the message from the angel of the LORD and the retention of her given name seems to evidence her faith in Yahweh.

story, but in both cases, God condescends to engage in a redemptive encounter with a daughter of Eve, the mother of all the living (Gen. 3:20).[67] Both Hagar and the unnamed Samaritan woman are outcasts, outsiders to the people of faith. Both have husband problems. Hagar has been mistreated, rejected, and sent away by her husband. The narrator does not tell us why the Samaritan woman has had five husbands, and it would be speculative to assume whether desertion, divorce, or death were the cause. Both have been involved in inappropriate sexual relationships.[68] Both are at a source of water, drawing water for themselves and their families.[69]

Both are fleeing from something. Hagar is fleeing an abusive relationship. The Samaritan woman seems to be fleeing her past and

---

[67] Again, this point is not dependent upon the interpretation that the angel of the LORD is Yahweh himself. Even if God sent a messenger, an ambassador, a representative, He still is the one who acts on behalf of Hagar and He does so in an unusual and unexpected way. This is almost beyond conception; the sovereign Lord of the universe condescends to meet the needs of this pregnant, Egyptian, slave woman. All the while the patriarch Abraham, the father of all who believe, is not only not active in preserving her life and the life of his unborn child, he is passively (at least) the reason why she needs divine protection and provision.

A few examples of reading Gen. 16 and John 4 together have been found. Keith Krell, "Beware of Shortcuts," www.Bible.org/page.php?page_id=4513, accessed 27 September 2007, sees a connection between John 4 and Genesis 16 based upon his identification of the Angel of the LORD as the preincarnate Christ. He notes, "If this is Jesus, this is similar to the time in John 4 when Jesus sat with the woman at the well. Both women were not Jews and both were sexually sinful women. Yet, Jesus met them both with grace and mercy." Although I do not think it is helpful to try to identify the person of the godhead who appeared to Hagar, I do agree that the two stories are similar.

Bob Deffinbaugh, "The Woman at the Well," www.Bible.org/page.php?page_id=2357, accessed 27 September 2010, observes the similarities to Gen. 16, 24, and 29, important events which occurred at a well. Arthur W. Pink, *Gleanings in Genesis*, accessed 27 September 2010, connects the well in Gen. 16 with "the living Water" in John 4, www.BibleBelievers.com/Pink/Gleanings_Genesis/genesis_21.htm.

Particularly interesting is John T. Spike's explanation of the painting by the 17th century Italian artist Andrea Sacchi, "Hagar and Ishmael." Spike explains: "The Old Testament chronicle becomes a kind of Easter story in Sacchi's telling. Hagar's fervent prayers at the side of Ishmael, supine on a white linen with his arms outstretched, are joyfully interrupted by the angel who points with both hands towards the life-giving water only a few steps away. The darkness and desolation behind the boy gives way, on the angel's side, to warm, redolent air and soft green foliage. Faithful Hagar, blessed although she is a pagan, is thus portrayed as a Genesis antecedent of the Samaritan woman to whom Christ said at the well, 'whoever drinks of this water shall thirst again, but whoever drinks of the water that I give shall never thirst' (John 4:26)."

See www.TheItalians.com.au/theitalians/Detail.cfm?IRN=161277&ViewID=2, accessed 9-27-10.

[68] Although the narrator does not condemn Abraham or Sarai explicitly for their behavior in Gen. 16, it would seem that, at the very least, they have demonstrated a lack of faith in the promises of Yahweh.

[69] Hagar's family includes the child she is bearing. The Samaritan woman's family includes the man with whom she is living, and perhaps children.

is almost certainly fleeing the judgmental citizens of her village.[70] Both have something to hide. Both bear shame and guilt, some of it is even deserved. Both appear to have "ears to hear" the voice of God; they are sensitive to God. Both listen to the voice of God when He speaks. Both recognize that the one speaking is God, and both name Him, "The God Who Sees Me." Hagar explicitly gives Yahweh that name. The Samaritan woman recognizes that Jesus knows her secret thoughts and deeds. She said of Him, "He told me everything I ever did" (John 4:39). Both express faith in God and both act on their faith in Him. Hagar returns to Abram's household. The Samaritan woman returns to her village. Both return to their previous "home," which in neither case is really their home at all. Both are blessed by God. Both are beneficiaries of God's grace.

Both share their stories with others and others come to faith in God through them. When Hagar returns to Abram, he apparently believes her because when the child is born, Abram names him Ishmael, the name given him by the God who sees. Many Samaritans believe in Jesus because of this woman's testimony. Both are used by God to rebuke and encourage the faith of great men. It is hard to miss the contrast between Hagar and Abram in this story. Hagar hears from God and she believes. Abram is still struggling to obey God. It is also hard to miss the contrast between the Samaritan woman and the disciples. She hears from Jesus and believes. They are still struggling to understand who Jesus is.[71]

It is possible, perhaps, that these similarities between these stories are merely coincidental. On the other hand, the similarities might be the *very point* the divine author (and perhaps the human author, John) intends in the telling of the two stories. I think the latter is much more compelling.

---

[70] Even in our more "enlightened" culture, a woman who has been married five times and is now living with a man not her husband would not be viewed as a paragon of virtue and her lifestyle would likely be the subject of some discussion, especially among Christians.

[71] Even at the end of the Gospel of John the disciples are still struggling with their understanding of Jesus. (See their questions in John 14.) John records their deliberation together: "They kept asking, 'What does he mean by 'a little while?' We don't understand what he is saying'" (John 16:18). Even after His death and resurrection, they seemed to have a hard time recognizing Jesus, thinking Him to be a ghost (cf. Luke 24:36–37). The Samaritan woman seems to have understood that Jesus is the Messiah, the one of whom Moses spoke.

Ironically, it seems that there is one other point of similarity between these two women. Both are largely overlooked by readers of the biblical story. Many times, the Hagar story is read within the context of the Abraham stories as telling us something about Abraham. Such a reading is appropriate, but it would seem that the focus in the Abraham stories is not primarily Abraham at all, but Abraham's God. The patriarch, in this story, does not look very much like a man of faith worth emulating. He shows little concern for his unborn child. His concern seems to be to avoid having to face the truth that what he did in sleeping with Hagar did not turn out the way he had hoped. So, "out of sight out of mind" seems to be his way of dealing with the problem. But God, who had promised to bless all people on earth through Abraham, intervenes to preserve Abraham's child so that he can build a great nation through Ishmael.

Similarly, the story of the Samaritan woman is often used to draw principles for evangelism, and that would seem appropriate. It is also an important text for developing a theology of worship.[72] It seems legitimate to read it as an example of how Jesus treated women.[73] What is seldom appreciated by Bible readers is that this woman, an outsider in all kinds of ways, encounters the incarnate Son of God and becomes a believer.[74] She then responds evangelistically, telling everyone she can about this one she met. Perhaps most surprisingly, people believe her and go to meet Jesus themselves. They told her,

---

[72] God is seeking a specific kind of worshippers, those who worship in Spirit and truth. This seems to indicate, at the very least, that the Spirit is necessary for true worship. Perhaps the only people who can worship in Spirit and truth are those who are indwelt and empowered by the Spirit of God. Thus, the Church's function is to be a worshipping community. It is made up of those who worship the God who is in the power of the Holy Spirit. This is a distinctive function of the Church in this age. None other than those who are part of the body of Christ by means of the work of the Spirit of God can be spiritual worshippers.

[73] Although this story does illustrate how Jesus related to women, it would seem best not to use this story to develop principles for such interaction today. This conversation, although it took place in public, was a private conversation without eyewitnesses.

[74] "It is difficult to miss the implication that the Samaritan woman, the quintessential outsider in this particular episode, is on the verge of becoming an insider, while the natural insiders, none other than Jesus' own disciples, are depicted as awkward and puzzled. They are still insiders, of course, but a true understanding of the really important matters raised in the previous conversation seems to have alluded them completely. The Samaritan woman has hurried back to her town without paying the slightest attention to her (or her household's) need for water. Ordinary thirst no longer seems to matter; for her, another thirst is about to be slaked. In contrast, the disciples have been concentrating only on the rumble in their stomachs." Spina, *Faith of the Outsider*, 156.

"We no longer believe just because of what you said; now we have heard for ourselves, and we know that this man really is the Savior of the world" (John 4:42).[75]

Conclusion

When Jesus finds himself alone at a well with a woman of Samaria, how will He respond? Will He treat her according to the norms of His culture? Will He view her as His disciples did, as almost everyone in her village did? Or will He view her according to the perspective of His Father? Will He perhaps use this as an opportunity to engage the culture in a redemptive way? Will He put aside his own reputation and look out for the interests of another?

It would seem that when Jesus found Himself in such a situation, He recognized the opportunity to reenact the biblical story found in Genesis 16. At least, it would seem that the narrator of the story in John 4 intends his audience to hear the echoes of that Old Testament story. As he constructs the story, its similarity to the narrative in the Hagar story seems too striking to be coincidental.[76] It seems the author constructed the story in such a way as to make those echoes obvious. Since this is an historical incident in the life of Jesus, the reader should also recognize the intention of the God-man in His actions in this story.

How will Jesus respond in this situation? He will mimic what He learned from the actions of His own Father (cf. John 5:18). In John 5:19, Jesus said, "I tell you the truth, the Son can do nothing by himself; he can do only what he sees his Father doing, because whatever the Father does the Son also does." Later, He puts it this way, "Do not believe me unless I do what my Father does. But if I do it, even though you do not believe me, believe the miracles, that you may know and understand that the Father is in me, and I in the

---

[75] Although such language would be anachronistic (since the founding of the church is still in the future at the time the events in John 4 take place), it is tempting to observe that this woman is the first church planter in this town of Samaria, similar in many ways to the work of Lydia, the seller of purple, in Philippi (Acts 16). Such an interpretation need not establish biblical support for women as church planters or church leaders today.

[76] I will grant that these similarities might be mere coincidences. It would, however, seem to take more faith (perhaps even of the blind variety) to read it that way than to observe these similarities as indications of authorial intention.

Father" (John 10:37–38).⁷⁷ It is not simply what He said that revealed His identity but His works as well (John 10:25). To His disciples, He said, "The words I say to you are not just my own. Rather, it is the Father, living in me, who is doing his work. Believe me when I say that I am in the Father and the Father is in me; or at least believe on the evidence of the miracles themselves" (John 14:10–11). It would seem that Jesus' training in the Old Testament Scriptures gave Him the biblical ground for His behavior here.

Although He was a product of His culture, Jesus was also a student of it. He came to earth not as some de-contextualized, docetic, or Gnostic Christ. Rather, He came as a first century Jewish man, by which I mean "male" as well as "human." He understood the culture in which He was raised. He knew where the boundaries were. He understood the cultural mores of His time. He knew how important it was to immerse Himself in that culture. He did not isolate or separate Himself from the culture. He knew how dangerous it could be to break society's conventions. He regularly faced conflict; for example, when He broke the Sabbath traditions and when He associated with social outsiders like Gentiles, tax collectors, lepers, poor, prostitutes, and Samaritan women. He embraced that conflict, and at times even sought it out. He was not afraid to speak and act in a provocative way, yet He did so judiciously. He looked for ways to be redemptive in the culture. He had the wisdom to know when to submit to the cultural mores and when to rebel against them.

Jesus was a student of the Scriptures. He was so immersed in the biblical stories, and in the biblical story of redemption, that when He found himself at a well in a setting like in John 4, He re-enacted the story of Yahweh and Hagar in Genesis 16. In so doing, He provides a model of us. He provides us a model for how to read the Old Testament Christologically as well as an example of how His followers should engage the culture redemptively. Because He was in very nature God, He humbled himself and considered others better than Himself. To His followers, the Apostle Paul says, "Your attitude [and actions] should be the same as that of Christ Jesus" (Phil. 2:5).

---

⁷⁷ "Works" would seem to be more inclusive of all of His works, not just his miracles, as indicated by the NIV translation here as "miracles."

When his followers do that, they emulate the Father and the Son, empowered by the Spirit.

2.
Is Yahweh's Faithfulness Contingent Upon Human Obedience?—"For I Am God and No Mortal"

by Dr. Terry Ann Smith
Associate Dean of Assessment and Academic Initiatives
and Assistant Professor of Biblical Studies
New Brunswick Theological Seminary[78]

Covenant—as a concept common to a multiplicity of cultures across the Ancient Near East—is typically associated with the formulaic expressions of commitment, responsibility, and promise that were foundational to ancient treaty constructions occurring between imperial rulers and their vassals. Despite this commonality, one still finds variable meaning and usage of the concept as it appears in the Hebrew Bible. For instance, we witness human-to-human commitments forged between the biblical characters of Jonathan and David (1 Sam. 20) and Ruth and Naomi (Ruth 1:16–17) alongside the more prevalent Abrahamic, Mosaic, and Davidic covenants (Gen. 12–17, Ex. 19–24, 2 Sam. 7:4–16, and 1 Chron. 17:3–15) which signified the reciprocal relationships occurring between humans and the divine. Strikingly, the human-divine bond in the Hebrew Bible displays a provocative disparity in which human participation in the covenantal arrangement appears as both obligatory and non-obligatory.

Given this disparity, we could ask whether it is possible to reconcile what appears as two incompatible views of covenant with

---

[78] Smith also received the Rabbi Dr. Sheldon J. Weltman Prize for Excellence in Biblical Studies, Drew University, Madison, in 2011; the Benjamin Lanham Rogers Prize for outstanding competence in Old Testament Studies, New Brunswick Theological Seminary, in 2002; and the Reverend Edward Lodewick Prize for excellence in preaching, New Brunswick Theological Seminary, in 2002.

She is the author of several books and articles including: *Think About It, Consider It, Tell Us What to Do: Can Some of the Most Violent Texts of the Old Testament Be Redeemed?* (Canada: Essence, 2002); "Warring Words in the Book of Daniel" in *The Oxford Handbook of Biblical Narrative* (Oxford University Press, 2016): 266–275; and co-author with Deborah A. Appler of *Ezra-Nehemiah*, vol. 14, *Wisdom Commentary Series* (Liturgical Press, forthcoming).

respect to Yahweh and the Israelites.[79] David Noel Freedman's inquiry aptly captures the matter,

> Can covenant bond be broken—and at the same time persist? Can God sever a relationship as a result of covenant violations—and nevertheless maintain it in perpetuity?[80]

While the larger context of covenant and covenantal fealty may be understood primarily as overtly political, the Hebrew Bible often yields a unique and illuminating portrait of divine commitment in which the deity Yahweh appears heavily invested and therefore profoundly affected by the human-divine covenantal relationship.

Nowhere is this dedication more demonstrable than in chapter eleven of Hosea. The prophet Hosea attributes Israel's religious disintegration to the people's proclivity toward certain forms of Canaanite (Baal) worship, which he interprets as the Israelites' reckless abandonment of their covenantal obligations to Yahweh.[81] To capture the significance of this offense, the prophet juxtaposes Israel's disobedience with Yahweh's faithfulness, presented as divine speech; and according to Yahweh, His fidelity comes with a cost, not to the Israelites, but rather to the deity. With this portrayal, the concepts of covenantal obligation and divine commitment intertwine such that the reader is afforded an arresting glimpse into what may be construed as the heart and mind of God.

The most striking features found in the book of Hosea are his novel and varied application of familial and animalistic metaphors to depict the tumultuous relationship between the Israelites and Yahweh, his concerns with cultic worship, and the affinities between his covenant theology and that of Deuteronomy. Hosea 11 begins with a contrasting view of the past: "When Israel was young, I loved him and from Egypt I called my son" (1:1). Most translations render *na'ar* as child (or youth), which lends support to the familial imagery

---

[79] David Noel Freedman, "Divine Commitment and Human Obligation: The Covenant Theme," in *Divine Commitment and Human Obligations: Selected Writings of David Noel Freedman*, ed. John R. Huddlestun (Grand Rapids: Eerdmans Publishing Company, 1997), 176.

[80] Ibid., 177.

[81] The inference here is to Canaanite fertility rites.

projected throughout the book.[82] However, along with the sense of innocence denoted by child or youth, the reference to Egypt permits some flexibility to render the term "young" allowing a contrast to be made between Israelite religion in its earlier pre-exilic state (i.e., new and evolving) and its later more developed state (i.e., post-exilic and beyond).[83] The apparent connections between *ʾāhēb* (love) and the covenantal promises found in Deuteronomy, when applied here may be interpreted as an expression of the deity's profound affection for and allegiance to this particular group.[84] The biblical witness to Yahweh's commitment to Israel is not new, for the history of this people is rooted in the promises that Yahweh made to Israel's patriarchal ancestors Abraham, Isaac, and Jacob. In Deuteronomy 7:6–8, Yahweh declares,

> For you are a people holy to the LORD your God; the LORD your God has chosen you out of all the peoples on earth to be his people, his treasured possession, out of all the peoples who are in the earth. It was not because you were more numerous than any other people that the LORD set his heart on you and chose you, for you were the fewest of all peoples. But it was because the LORD loved you and kept the oath that he swore to your ancestors, that the LORD has brought you out with a mighty hand, and redeemed you from the house of slavery, from the hand of Pharaoh king of Egypt.

In the above, we find Yahweh's unilateral and unconditional commitment to the Israelites, a dedication couched in the covenantal language of choice thus highlighting the voluntary nature of Yahweh's actions. Therefore, it is not surprising that the deity's explicit claim and acknowledgement of this group expresses a kind of exclusivity and particularity that implicitly conveys the intrinsic character of Yahweh as a compassionate, caring albeit possessive deity. As such, these select passages do not simply call attention to the Hebrews' liberation from Egyptian bondage, but they also convey

---

[82] New Revised Standard Version, King James Version, and New International Version.

[83] The Hebrew נַעַר can be translated "boy," "child," "youth," or "servant." Although not age specific, the inference can denote both innocence and immaturity due to age. In contrast, J. Andrew Dearman suggests the term denotes a portrait of servitude and dependence that reinforces the relationship between Israel and Yahweh. J. Andrew Dearman, *The Book of Hosea* (Grand Rapids, Eerdmans Publishing Company, 2010), 278.

[84] Douglas Stuart, *Word Biblical Commentary, Hosea-Jonah*, vol. 32, ed. Hubbard A. David and Glenn W. Barker (Texas: Word Books, 1987), 178.

the group's privileged position as the deity's own special and beloved people. In Hosea 11:2, Yahweh's accusation that Israel "sacrificed to the Baals and burned incense to idols" alerts us to the problem at hand, whereby the syncretization of Israelite worship is viewed as a rejection of the God who "caused them to walk" (11:3). Israel has rejected Yahweh's love, which may be understood here as a rejection of the covenant. While one may detect a bit of divine condescension, the verbal constructions "I loved," "I called," "I caused," "I took," and "I drew" (1–4), affirm the deity's benevolent actions on behalf of this group.

When taken together, the opening verses of Hosea 11 function to contrast who the Israelites should have been versus what they had become. That is, they should have been adherents of the covenant rather than covenant violators. With this metaphorical construction, an ancient and modern audience is made aware of the deity's complaint voiced as the group's failure to uphold their end of the divine-human relationship. Herein lies the *first* concern, which surfaces as one of human obligation. Given Yahweh's steadfast behavior concerning the Israelites, is the group obligated to respond to the deity in kind? More importantly, will Israel's non-compliance alter the divine-human relationship such that it affects Yahweh's beneficent actions toward this group?

Closer inspection of covenantal fidelity among the patriarchs reveals models of human obedience that made the patriarchs suitable covenantal partners, while the disobedient were deemed undesirable participants (who were subsequently punished).[85] Similarly, we detect models of obedience and disobedience in the Deuteronomistic accounts of the kings of Israel and Judah. Thus, it appears that validation of the covenant was initially contingent on human faithfulness rooted in an understanding of Yahweh as one who rewards and punishes.[86]

Nonetheless, there exists other biblical accounts in which this requirement of obedience was absent and yet the human-divine bond,

---

[85] Ellen Juhl Christiansen, *The Covenant in Judaism and Paul—A Study of Ritual Boundaries as Identity Markers*, Arbeiten zur Geschichte des Antiken Judentums und Des Urchristen, vol. 27 (Leiden: Brill Academic Publishers, 1997), 112.

[86] Ibid.

though fragile, remained intact (cf., Isa. 43). If the former understanding of covenant validity was formative in the construction of the book of Hosea, we would expect Yahweh's irritation at the Israelites' rejection in Hosea 11:2 to result in the group's imminent judgment. We are not disappointed, since 11:5 informs us, "They shall return to the land of Egypt, and Assyria shall be their king, because they refuse to return to me," reaffirming both the deity's complaint as well as his unfilled expectation of human obedience. The text continues:

> a sword will whirl in his city and his gates will be destroyed and his counselors will be consumed, but my people are bent on turning from me and to a yoke he calls him, altogether he will not exalt them (Hos. 11:6–7).[87]

Yahweh had exalted the Israelites, adopted them as sons (and daughters), and liberated them from the yoke of their imperial oppressors. In an act tantamount to spiritual adultery, one of the overarching themes in Hosea, the people respond to the beneficent actions of the deity by becoming yoked to foreign gods, which according to Yahweh, would or could not respond to them in a reciprocal fashion. Clearly, the allusion to Egypt as a return to bondage, along with the reference to Assyria, which foreshadowed the destruction of Samaria, was meant to be taken as both divine indictment and judgment for their violation of the covenantal commitment to exclusively worship Yahweh (Exod. 20:1, Deut. 5:6).

Still, even with this indictment, the text insists upon Yahweh's unwillingness to cast the group aside despite the deity's annoyance at their betrayal. Rhetorically, the profundity of the moment is captured by the series of questions announced in 11:8.

> How can I give you up, Ephraim? How can I hand you over, O Israel? How can I make you like Admah? How can I treat you like Zeboiim? My heart recoils within me; my compassion grows warm and tender.

The internal parallelism between the Hebrew verbs *ntn* (give, deliver into the hand of), *miggēn* (piel: deliver up, hand over) and *śym* (put,

---

[87] This chapter is ripe with textual difficulties: Hosea 11:4–7 are extremely difficult to decipher and have the dubious honor of being possibly the most corrupt verses in the entire chapter, particularly verse 7 in which the entire verse with its emendations is clearly ambiguous.

place, set) function to intensify Yahweh's extreme anguish over the situation and offsets the accusatory tone found in 11:1–7.

Scholars, such as Hans W. Wolff and James L. Mays, offer somewhat differing translations for the *c* portion of verse, respectively, "My heart turns against me, my remorse burns intensely" and "My heart has turned itself against me; my compassion grows completely warm."[88] Others, such as J. G. Janzen, find these translations an unacceptable solution to the theological impasse posed by the tension created with the portrayal of Yahweh's internal struggle.[89]

Yet, it is precisely in verse 8 that the vulnerability of Yahweh bursts forth with an intensity that completely overshadows the previous verses that contained the deity's displeasure. Guenther Allen comments,

> God the parent is also the covenant Lord. The agony of a mother's compassion and a father's love appears in the How…. The exclamation signals deep and intense emotion, usually grief, occasionally of joy. Here one must envision Yahweh, hands extended in love, sobbing at the thought of punishing this wayward son. Pain pervades the scene. Those who have known such pain need no descriptions; for others, words cannot serve.[90]

Yahweh's self-professed love for this people has been portrayed as an emotional attachment, and therefore, the audience becomes exposed to the deity's emotional response in light of that attachment. When read as reflecting the mental state of one in the process of an emotionally heightened decision, Janzen's inquiry are certainly worth consideration regarding whether Yahweh can entertain questions of being or must all God speech in this regard be deemed rhetorical.[91] Yes, God is wrestling with God's self! Introspectively, Yahweh performs a self-assessment and evaluates *this* particular divine-human relationship, an association that the deity has coveted as special and

---

[88] Hans W. Wolff, *A Commentary on the Book of Hosea*, trans. G. Stansell, ed. P. Hanson, (Philadelphia: Fortress Press, 1974), 193. See also James L. Mays, *Hosea* (Philadelphia: Westminster Press, 1969).

[89] J. Gerald Janzen, "Metaphor and Reality in Hosea," *Semeia 24* (Chico: Society of Biblical Literature, 1982), 26.

[90] Guenther R. Allen, "Hosea, Amos," *Believers Church Bible Commentary* (Pennsylvania: Herald Press, 1998).

[91] Janzen, "Metaphor and Reality in Hosea," 36.

unique. Here, we find expressed the anguish of one deeply torn and conflicted over a relationship gone awry. This relationship had withstood a great deal since the people's dramatic and extraordinary liberation from Egyptian bondage.

Going forward, the Israelites would experience moments of prosperity with accompanying occasions of distress. Despite their complaints, Yahweh provided for this group in the wilderness. Succumbing to their request, Yahweh gave them kings, allowing them to conquer and be conquered so that the people might realize the deity's abiding presence. We can only imagine that it is with great sorrow of heart that Yahweh now looks at this beloved group and says, "How can I give you Ephraim, delivery you up Israel."

Thus, the *second* issue before us is one of divine commitment. Will Yahweh choose this people once again? Restated, will the Israelites once again experience the salvation of Yahweh?

The text intimates that the prevailing portrait of the human-divine relationship is fraught with tensions: even the faithful find themselves at odds with their creator. It is apparent that Yahweh's desire for the Israelites' steadfast participation in the covenant too often has yielded the reverse response. In this, they are not alone, since the abandonment of God also manifests in modern society, surviving if you will in human proclivities toward self-actualization, conflict and chaos.

Nevertheless, these verses suggest that God's love transcends these human tendencies toward abandonment by portraying the deity's response to Israel's rejection as *hesed,* unconditional and steadfast faithfulness. Nelson Gleuck is right to assert the interrelationship between *hesed* and *b^{e}rith* (covenant), "*hesed* is the premise and effect of *b^{e}rith*; it constitutes the very essence of a *b^{e}rith* but is not yet a *b^{e}rith,* even though there can be no *b^{e}rith* without *hesed.*" [92] Therefore, it is possible to suggest that undergirding the divine-human covenantal relationship is God's own commitment to perform *hesed* over and against the intentions and non-reciprocal actions of the humans who were created in God's very own image.

---

[92] Nelson Gleuck, *Hesed in the Bible* (Jersey City: KTAV Publishers, Inc., 1978), 68.

A similar sentiment resonates within the book of Isaiah. Throughout Isaiah, we find an ill-proportioned depiction of Yahweh's fidelity to Israel without a corresponding response by the people.[93] Referring to this lack of reciprocity on the part of Israel, Susan Ackerman writes,

> there is no mention that the people will give God their love as part of this reconciliation, and this despite the fact that it is within these oracles that we find what is perhaps the Bible's most powerful expression of Yahweh's love for the people.[94]

The anachronistic reference to "Ephraim" provides further evidence of the personal and intimate nature of Yahweh's relationship with this group.

Can we read this textual allusion to Ephraim as a term of endearment that identifies and emphasizes the place Israel holds in God's heart? The tone of the text undoubtedly lends itself to such an interpretation,

> How can I make you like Admah? How can I treat you like Zeboiim? My heart recoils within me; altogether my compassion grows warm and tender. (Hosea 11:8).

Stuart posits,

> Yahweh's change of mind ... is a product not of whim or circumstance, but of God's eternal consistent nature. God is a compassionate God whose basic desire toward God's people is to win them back to God's self.[95]

Similarly, Andersen and Freedman assert,

> These expressions of the utmost reluctance to exercise the fierce anger achieve two effects. They remove from the judgments all suggestions of vindictiveness. And, if the judgment is unleashed in spite of this effort to restrain it—if, as the Psalmist says, Yahweh's nostrils are stronger than his intestines (Ps. 77:10)—it is because Israel's sin has gone to the extreme, with no hope of renewal and no trace of contrition to give grounds for compassion.[96]

---

[93] Susan Ackerman, "The Personal Is Political: Covenantal and Affectionate Love ('āhēb, 'ahăbâ) in the Hebrew Bible," *Vetus Testamentum* 52 (2002): 446.

[94] Ibid., 446.

[95] Stuart, *Word Biblical Commentary*, 181.

[96] Francis I. Anderson and David Noel Freedman, *Hosea—A New Translation with Introduction and Commentary,* Anchor Bible 24 (Garden City: Doubleday & Company, Inc., 1980), 588.

Yet, the relationship between Yahweh and Israel has always been one infused with hope. Indeed, the prophetic critique of impending judgment is often companioned with hopeful ruminations of restoration (cf. Isa. 49–54; Jer. 31, 33:10–13; Ezek. 37).

Here, as elsewhere, Hosea 11:8 portrays Yahweh as one who is not willing to abandon a faithless and disobedient Israel. Insistently, Yahweh refuses to allow this people to share the same fate that the deity once visited upon the destroyed cities of Admah and Zeboiim. Consequently, rather than annihilation, Israel will experience divine mercy.

This dimension of divine love and forgiveness is captured elsewhere in the biblical record. For instance, in the book of Jonah, we find a wayward and contentious Jonah admitting, "For I knew that you are a gracious God and merciful, slow to anger, and abounding in steadfast love, and ready to relent from punishing" (Jonah 4:2b). Likewise, the Psalmist declares in Psalm 103:2–4,

> Praise the Lord, O my soul, and forget not all his benefits—who forgives all your sins and heals all your diseases, who redeems your life from the pit and crowns you with love and compassion.

As portraits of divine dedication, these and other biblical passages make it apparent that the desire of God to win back God's people has less to do with Israel's, and by extension, our own faithlessness and more to do with God's faithfulness toward us. As such, it is conceivable that God's steadfast loyalty with respect to covenantal fidelity is not predicated upon human obligation or obedience.

Based on this assessment, we can only surmise that the divine commitment to covenant fidelity, as well as the relationship forged from that commitment, is important to God, so much so that God is willing to expose God's self to mend and restore that which had been ruptured. Thus, the answer to whether Israel will once again experience the salvation of Yahweh becomes a resounding yes! Yahweh declares, "I will not execute my fierce anger; I will not again destroy Ephraim; for I am God and no mortal, the Holy One in your midst, and I will not come in wrath" (Hosea 11:9).

For the most part, the initial tension generated by verse 8 appears resolved by the three series of negation in verse 9, "I will not execute," "I will not again destroy," and "I will not come in wrath." Yahweh's self-examination has culminated in divine choice wherein the deity who could destroy makes a conscious decision that results in an act of grace rather than retaliation and annihilation. Triumphantly, Yahweh's compassion arises over and against Israel's rejection of the deity. The three verbal constructions in verse 9 not only complement the initial verbal constructions of 11:1–4, "I loved," "I called," "I taught," "I cared," and "I drew," but they also function to defuse the deity's brooding disposition. Elsewhere in the Hebrew Bible, we encounter situations whereby human intervention provided the initial impetus for neutralizing, delaying or mitigating the deity's anger (Gen. 18:22–33; Exod. 4:24–26). In this case, no human intercessor is needed nor consulted in Yahweh's monumental moment of decision. Having set aside the indictment, Israel's long list of offenses are not catalogued, weighed and brought to bear on the matter.

The sole determining factor and rationale for this change of heart is found in the words of Yahweh himself, "I am God and no mortal, the Holy One in your midst." With striking clarity, the contrast between God and God's creation is made abundantly clear: God is not human, and conversely, humans are not divine. With these words, we are invited to envision not only the distinction between heavenly and earthly realms, but we are also reminded that the ways of God differ from the ways of humanity. To be God, is to be wholly other, timeless and eternal, unencumbered by the vicissitudes that plague human life. To be mortal implies limitations and weaknesses. Mortality pits humans against each other in the never-ending battle for supremacy, power, prestige, and wealth. Ecclesiastes 3:1–8 summarizes the mortality of human existence.

> For everything there is a season, and a time for every matter under heaven:
> a time to be born, and a time to die; a time to plant, and a time to pluck up what is planted; a time to kill, and a time to heal; a time to break down, and a time to build up;
> a time to weep, and a time to laugh; a time to mourn, and a time to dance; a time to throw away stones, and a time to gather stones together; a time to embrace, and a time to refrain from embracing;
> a time to seek, and a time to lose; a time to keep, and a time to throw away; a time to tear, and a time to sew; a time to keep silence, and a time to speak;
> a time to love, and a time to hate; a time for war, and a time for peace.

By acknowledging the temporality of human existence, the passage underscores the fragility of our constructed lives.

Nevertheless, for the vast number of religious believers, this fragility finds itself grounded in the conviction that an omnipotent and righteous God stands at the apex of all of life, efficacious and eternal. Thus, the claim "I am God and no mortal, the Holy One in your midst" functions for both an ancient and contemporary audience to affirm the sovereignty of God. James Mays aptly captures the significance attending Yahweh's self-disclosure asserting,

> The actions and feelings of Yahweh can be translated into representations of human, and even animal, life. In the dramatic metaphor the personal reality of Yahweh's incursion into human life and history is present and comprehensible. But he transcends the metaphor, is different from that to which he is compared, and free of all its limitations."[97]

As humans, we are necessarily cognizant that individual or collective attitudes of "retribution" and "retaliation" manifest regularly within society for a variety of reasons.

By contrast, the phrase unequivocally declares the same cannot be said of God, whose very essence, if doing so, would be counter-intuitive to God's nature as holy and just. Here, as in other instances of divine initiative, the unwillingness of Yahweh to annihilate this group represents neither the deity's "concession to their sin" nor the curbing of his judgment, but rather corresponds to "a declaration that his relationship in history with Israel shall not end because of their sin and his wrath."[98] Hence, the phrase suggestively advocates that the human-divine relationship is held together and firmly anchored by the deity's rather than humanity's commitment to *hesed*.

As a continuation of the writer's unfolding witness to the steadfast faithfulness of Yahweh, the audience is invited to contemplate the myriad ways in which the holiness of God transcends the world of human reason while simultaneously exposing the depths to which God has through *choice* obligated God's self to humanity. The unconditional nature of that choice confirms the elasticity and continuity of both the divine-human covenantal relationship and the expectation of hope that the relationship can and will triumph over the shifting attitudes that accompany human weakness and defiance. For

---

[97] James Luther Mays, *Hosea: A Commentary* (Philadelphia: The Westminster Press, 1969), 158.
[98] Ibid., 158.

an ancient and contemporary audience, the claim of God's holiness in Hosea 11:9 passionately captures this facet of God's character, emitting rays of hope for the purposes of reconciliation. It is the "Holy One" in our midst who enacts justice for the weak and makes provision for those that have been cast aside and forgotten. This same "Holy One" is willing to forgive the transgressions of his people and call the unfaithful to repentance. Taken together 11:8–9 instructively articulate the struggle and compassion of a God that feels and feels deeply.

The God who has been in the midst of the Israelites all along now seeks to restore the relationship in 11:10–11:

> They will go after Yahweh, like a lion he will roar. For he will roar and their sons will tremble from the West. They will tremble like a bird from Egypt and like a dove from the land of Assyria and I will return them to their houses declares Yahweh.

On the surface, these verses appear a bit disturbing as the writer symbolically presents Yahweh as a mighty lion and Israel as a helpless bird, which could be interpreted as the powerful deity exerting power and extracting compliance from his much weaker constituents. As such, it is apparent that Yahweh has extracted a penalty for Israel's disobedience. Nonetheless, there exists the insistent reverberation of anticipated reconciliation. It is a homecoming invigorated by the knowledge that Yahweh still champions the cause of his people. That is, Yahweh still saves, redeems, and delivers!

Contrasting the human obligation attending the old covenantal promises associated with a pre-exilic Israel and those of its post-exilic progenitors, Freedman asserts,

> The basis of a new order would be the divine promise, the unconditional commitment—the single happy constant in the whole tragic picture—as guarantee of the new age. Since the oath was made to himself, God will carry it out; he will restore his people.[99]

Still, he is right to assert that the "moral element" in the human-divine relationship cannot be dismissed.[100] When applied to the present text,

---

[99] Freedman, "Divine Commitment and Human Obligation," 177.
[100] Ibid., 178.

God has acknowledged Israel's inability to honor their covenantal obligation, and yet, is still prepared to receive this wayward group back into the fold. In this case, it is clear that the textual aim is to further demonstrate Yahweh's care, concern and commitment to this group.

Metaphorically, the roar, as a beacon of guidance, harkens and welcomes the community back into its privileged position as those cherished by God. Furthermore, we find noticeably absent any indication of repentance as a condition of the group's restored state. Thus, the juxtaposition sets forth an inverted portrait of divine acquiescence as the mighty lion waits to shelter the trembling bird, rather than pursue it as prey. It is the promise of a renewed life and a renewed relationship.

As it stands, God's love and forgiveness continually interceded to redeem Israel, repeatedly enabling pathways for the group's salvation, restoration, and reconciliation. As far as the writer of Hosea is concerned, Yahweh is willing to honor Yahweh's part of the covenant, in spite of Israel's failure to do so, and thus affirming the theological assertion that even if human love fails,

God's love never fails.

3.
Suicide the Unpardonable Sin and the Multi-Dimensional History of a Theological Error

by Dr. Timothy J. Demy
Professor, College of Leadership and Ethics
U.S. Navy War College[101]

Introduction	43
A. Historical-Theological Considerations	45
1. Suicide and the Classical World	46
2. Suicide and the Early Church	46
3. Suicide and Medieval Theology	50
a. Twelfth-Century Precursors to Aquinas	51
b. Thomas Aquinas	53
4. Suicide and the Reformation	54
a. John Calvin (1509–1564)	55
b. Martin Luther (1483–1546)	56
c. English Reformation	57
B. Literary Considerations	58
C. Biblical Considerations	61
D. Cultural-Pastoral Considerations	64
Conclusion	65

Introduction

The development of doctrine is rarely pristine and lineal from revelation to articulation and application.[102] Popular religious beliefs come from many sources. Some beliefs are grounded in Scripture and in theology. Sometimes beliefs derive from tradition and history. On other occasions beliefs may be primarily grounded in cultural

---

[101] Demy earned a Ph.D. Salve Regina University and a Th.D. from Dallas Theological Seminary. Prior to appoint at the war college, Demy served as a chaplain for 27 years with the Navy, Marine Corp, and Coast Guard. He is a U.S. Advisor for International Network for the Study of War and Religion in the Modern World. He is the author and editor of articles and books on historical, ethical, and theological subjects, including co-ed. with Gary P. Stewart, *Suicide—A Christian Response* (Kregel Academic & Professional, 1998); co-ed. with Gary P. Stewart, *101 Most Puzzling Bible Verses* (Eugene, OR: Harvest House, 2006); and co-author of *War, Peace, and Christianity—Questions and Answers from the Just-War Perspective* (Crossway, 2010); co-author with Gary P. Stewart, William R. Cutrer, Dónal P. O'Mathúna, Paige C. Cunningham, John F. Kilner, and Linda K. Bevington of *Basic Questions on Suicide and Euthanasia: Are They Ever Right?* (Grand Rapids, MI: Kregel Publications, 1998).

[102] For an overview of the history of Christian doctrine, see John D. Hannah. *Our Legacy—The History of Christian Doctrine* (Colorado Springs: NavPress, 2001). See also Maurice Wiles, *The Making of Christian Doctrine—A Study in the Principles of Early Doctrinal Development* (Cambridge: Cambridge University Press, 1975).

practices and values. At other times beliefs may have their origins in literature. Finally, theological ideas may be an amalgamation of any or all of the above. The process of untangling the many strands of a doctrine and belief are compounded significantly when working with medieval history and theology. Historian Alexander Murray astutely observes that "to understand anything medieval at all you must give a lot of time to it, and specialize."[103] Such is the case with the idea of suicide as the unpardonable sin, an idea with an unclear history but heavily indebted to medieval thought.

Values have consequences. So, too, do beliefs. Personal, cultural, historical, and theological ideas converge daily in the lives of individuals as they face the trials, traumas, and tragedies of life, and life's many uncertainties. Perhaps nowhere, apart from the ravages of war and cataclysmic disasters, is the personal challenge of theodicy and the ramifications of the Adamic fall more intense than in matters of health and bioethics. This is especially true of the issue of suicide. No one who is touched by it remains unchanged.

Is there an action or sin so great and significant that either by timing or consequence it deprives the Christian of redemption and the blessings of eternal life with God? Why would it do so? If there is such an act, it would do so because the finality of it prohibits the individual from the opportunity to ask divine forgiveness. If so, is suicide such an act, and perhaps the only such act? Such a sin would be unpardonable. It seems from the vantage point of time alone that if such an action existed, it would be suicide since there is no opportunity for the individual who commits suicide to ask forgiveness after the fact. Yet, if this is true, and assuming that suicide is a sin, would not *any* sin that was not confessed prior to the individual's death cause the same result? If so, this then might lead one to categorize sins according to their severity (and this is exactly what happened in the history of the doctrine of sin—hamartiology).

The question under consideration in this essay is that of the possibility of future redemption for those whose lives are terminated through suicide. It is a theological response to a multifaceted issue. In considering the answer, it is understood that the question pertains

---

[103] Alexander Murray, *Suicide in the Middle Ages*, vol. 2, *The Curse on Self-Murder* (New York: Oxford University Press, 2000), 483.

primarily to the suicide of a Christian, and as such, it is an issue relating to the doctrines of sin and salvation (hamartiology and soteriology). While the same question may be asked regarding the non-Christian, the response in such an instance need not be linked directly to the act of suicide.

The issue of redemption for the non-Christian who commits suicide is one of soteriology and tied to beliefs of about either universalism or a post-death final opportunity for repentance regardless of the cause of the physical death. Considerations of universalism and second-chance possibilities for repentance are beyond the scope of this presentation and are not addressed, although the author considers acceptance of such views to be unbiblical.

This essay presents a negative response:

suicide does not prohibit redemption.

And we present this proposition within four facets: historical-theological, literary, biblical, and cultural-pastoral. In doing so, we argue that acceptance of the view is grounded in history and culture rather than in interpretations of the biblical text. Although some might argue for no redemption for those who commit suicide based on biblical texts, in the history of the idea of "no redemption for those who commit suicide," such arguments are secondary and tangential. The history of that idea is one that primarily is a theological misconception rooted primarily in medieval theology and the influence of Dante Alighieri's fourteenth-century epic poem *Divine Comedy* (*Commedia*, AD 1320), specifically the first part of the three-part poem, *Inferno*. In short, when one asks the question of those who commit suicide and affirms that there is no redemption, the ideological lineage of the question and answer is historical, literary, and cultural. It is not biblical, even though biblical texts may (or may not) be cited.

A. Historical-Theological Considerations

Suicide is not a new issue in Christian thought. Today, when a person asks the question about redemption and suicide, he or she is not asking so much a question of theology, but a question of history and the misconception of an idea about theology. The arguments and presuppositions are not grounded primarily in the biblical text and contemporary theology, but are mostly grounded in medieval views influenced by theology and literature of that era.

1. Suicide and the Classical World

The intellectual world in which Christianity emerged was well acquainted with the concept of suicide. In Jewish history, there were the deaths of the defenders at Masada, and in Greek history there was the famous death the philosopher Socrates (though he considered his death not a suicide, but rather, capital punishment imposed by the Athenian polis).[104] Plato, citing Socrates, believed that individuals were the possession of the gods just as a slave was the possession of the master, and therefore an individual's life was not his or her own to destroy.[105] This same idea, but based upon biblical revelation and worship of God, would be expressed later by Christians. Aristotle rejected the idea that there were any extenuating circumstances in which suicide was permitted.[106]

In Roman society, suicide was often imposed by the state as punishment, and the practice reached its apex under the rule of Nero from AD 58–64. Breaking with earlier philosophical thought, the Stoic philosophers of Roman society did not consider suicide morally unjust or evil but, instead, found it at times desirable—something Christians of the era such as Augustine (AD 354–430) rejected.[107]

2. Suicide and the Early Church

The issue of suicide was not in and of itself a major social concern in the patristic era although it was addressed, especially in opposition to the views of the Stoics. Among the writers voicing theological and biblical objections to it were Ignatius (*Romans* 4.1f; 5.2f; c. AD 100),

---

[104] On the deaths at Masada (AD 73), see Barry R. Leventhal, "The Masada Suicides: The Making and Breaking of a Cultural Icon," in *Suicide: A Christian Response*, ed. Timothy J. Demy and Gary P. Stewart (Grand Rapids: Kregel, 1998), 269–83.

[105] Plato (c. 427–347 BC), *Phaedo* 62.

[106] Aristotle (384–322 BC), *Nicomachean Ethics* V.11.

[107] Marcus Aurelius (AD 121–180), *Meditations,* VIII, 50 and X, 8. In Georgia Noon "On Suicide," *Journal of the History of Ideas* 39, no. 3 (Jul–Sept. 1978): 371–86, which is an overview of the history of the idea of suicide, Noon states that the Stoic response was eclipsed by "religious hysteria" (375). This misconstrues the nature of the Christian response. The response was decisive and dogmatic, but that is not the same thing as the uncontrolled panic and emotion of hysteria. Likewise, she later misunderstands and misconstrues the doctrine of predestination which she argues creates a spiritual atmosphere conducive to suicide (377).

Lactantius (*Div. inst* iii.18; c. AD 303), Chrysostom (*De consolatione Mortis*; c. AD 375), Jerome (*Commentary ad Matthew* 4.17; c. AD 400), and Augustine (AD 354–430) who used the sixth commandment to say it was wrong, an act of cowardice and did not give opportunity for repentance (*Civ. Dei* 1.4–26). Such views, especially those of Augustine would be formalized and reinforced in the councils of Gaudix (305), Carthage (348), and Braga (563).

While it was not one of the greatest social concerns of the Fathers, suicide was a tangential concern insomuch as it intersected with realities of the persecution and martyrdom of Christians.[108] Also addressed by the early church was the issue of the suicide of women facing sexual assault. Even so, classics scholar Professor Darrel W. Amundsen observed, "There is absolutely no evidence in the corpus of Christian literature for the first 250 years of the Christian era that any Christian under any circumstances committed suicide for any reason, unless one should argue that Judas is the one exception."[109] With respect to suicide and illness, Amundsen notes, "So foundational are the goodness and sovereignty of God in patristic theology and so consistently is patient endurance of affliction stressed as an essential Christian virtue, that it is not at all surprising that patristic texts do not refer to suicide by the ill."[110]

In recent years, as debates regarding suicide, physician-assisted suicide, and euthanasia became more prevalent in social discourse and public policy, some theologians and historians argued that martyrdom was a form of suicide that was accepted, sought, and applauded by early Christians.[111] Such views, however, distort history and confuse the motives of the martyred Christians. There is a very great difference between seeking death and being willing to die. Suicide,

---

[108] On historical and theological concerns relating to the martyrdom of early Christians, see W. H. C. Frend, *Martyrdom and Persecution in the Early Church* (Oxford: Blackwell, 1965). Regarding suicide and early Christianity, see Darrel W. Amundsen, *Medicine, Society, and Faith in the Ancient and Medieval Worlds* (Baltimore: The Johns Hopkins University Press, 1996), 70–126. See also his essay "Did Early Christians 'Lust After Death'?" in *Suicide—A Christian Response*, ed. Timothy J. Demy and Gary P. Stewart (Grand Rapids: Kregel, 1998), 284–95.

[109] Darrel W. Amundsen, *Medicine, Society, and Faith in the Ancient and Medieval Worlds* (Baltimore: The Johns Hopkins University Press, 1996), 71.

[110] Amundsen, "Did Early Christians 'Lust After Death'?" 292–93.

[111] See for example, Arthur J. Droge and James D. Tabor, *A Noble Death—Suicide and Martyrdom among Christians and Jews in Antiquity* (San Francisco: HarperCollins, 1992).

assisted or otherwise, is an act in which someone *intends* to die and actively pursues that end. Martyrdom is an act in which someone who is *willing* to die for his or her beliefs and is then killed by the hand or order of another. There is no intent to die in martyrdom. Whereas martyrdom is the ultimate act of suffering and sacrifice for one's faith, suicide is often the ultimate and final act of escape from suffering. Amundsen said, "Suicide in the face of illness can be seen as analogous to martyrdom only if God is viewed as either significantly less than sovereign or as an oppressive tyrant."[112]

The apostles of the early church understood very well that their commitment to Jesus Christ might cost them their lives. Jesus had warned them of the world's hatred of Him and of them because of their discipleship (John 15:18–25). Some Christians will pay the ultimate price for their faith and proclamation of the gospel. However, to compare such sacrifices with suicide is to confuse an act of selfless love with self-centered destruction.

No individual in the early church had greater influence on theology and Christianity in the West than Augustine (AD 354–430). His views on many subjects shaped western thought for centuries to come. Augustine's views on suicide heavily influenced subsequent Roman Catholic and Protestant theologians and perspectives. While some have argued that he first articulated and developed the Christian attitude toward suicide, such is not the case. Augustine affirmed earlier understandings and, said Amundsen, "by removing certain ambiguities, he clarified and provided a theologically cogent explanation of and justification for the position typically held by earlier and contemporary Christian sources."[113] Several earlier and Augustinian-era Christian writers and sources rejecting suicide include Clement, Cyprian, Justin Martyr, *Epistle of Diognetus,* the Clementine *Homilies,* Tertullian, Lactantius, Ambrose, Jerome, and Chrysostom.[114] Arguing against suicide as something honorable as viewed by the Stoics, Augustine believed suicide to be self-murder and sin. He writes:

---

[112] Amundsen, "Did Early Christians 'Lust After Death'?" 292–93.
[113] Amundsen, *Medicine, Society, and Faith in the Ancient and Medieval Worlds,* 73.
[114] Ibid., 89–101.

> It is not without significance, that in no passage of the holy canonical books there can be found either divine precept or permission to take away our own life, whether for the sake of entering on the enjoyment of immortality, or of shunning, or ridding ourselves of anything whatever. Nay, the law, rightly interpreted, even prohibits suicide, where it says, *"You shall not kill."* [115]

Augustine covers suicide in depth in Book 1 chapters 16–28 of *City of God* (*De civitate Dei,* c. AD 413–426) as well as in various letters.[116] In chapter 26, Augustine alludes to the inability to repent stating:

> No man ought to inflict on himself voluntary death, for this is to escape the ills of time by plunging into those of eternity; that no man ought to do so on account of another man's sins, for this were to escape a guilt which could not pollute him, by incurring great guilt of his own; that no man ought to do so on account of his own past sins, for he has all the more need of this life that these sins may be healed by repentance; that no man should put an end to this life to obtain that better life we look for after death, for those who die by their own hand have no better life after death.[117]

Augustine and the early Christians were firmly opposed to suicide and acknowledged that suicide was a sin of enormous consequence. What he does not expound upon further is the meaning of the last phrase "for those who die by their own hand have no better life after death." However, his strong views regarding predestination would seem to rule out any idea of loss of eternal life due to suicide.

Furthermore, Augustine wrestled with the possibility that Christian women might be tempted to commit suicide rather than allowing themselves to be raped by barbarians. Some had done so earlier and had been declared saints by Christian leaders. Women had been raped in the sack of Rome in AD 410, and Augustine was writing the chapters on suicide in the *City of God* probably around 413. On this matter, Augustine was opposed in principle to suicide, but in Book I chapter 26 stated that he would avoid rash judgments. Though opposed to suicide, he argued that in such cases, suicide might be permitted if divinely commanded in special instances such as those of Samson. And such cases were primarily ones that had already

---

[115] Augustine, *De civitate Dei,* 1.20.
[116] Amundsen, *Medicine, Society, and Faith in the Ancient and Medieval Worlds,* 111–17.
[117] Augustine, *De civitate Dei,* 1.26.

occurred and not those that might occur in the future. They were exceptional rather than normative.[118]

3. Suicide and Medieval Theology

The Middle Ages was an era rich in theological development and history. It was during this era that theology as the formal discipline of the systematization of biblical teaching came into existence. The breadth and depth of theological inquiry was enormous; and suicide as biblical, theological, legal, and pastoral issue received attention, sparingly at first, and then in greater detail by the eleventh and twelfth centuries. Historian Alexander Murray notes:

> When confronted by suicide, medieval theologians of all periods accepted that suicide was not only bad but very bad indeed *gravissumum* ["gravest"—a term widely used], and indeed, in the opinion of many, the worst sin it was possible to commit. That *nec plus ultra* ["highest" or "ultimate"] judgment is found as far apart in spirit and time as Lactantius, in fourth-century Constantinople, and late medieval urban law in Europe, and at innumerable places in between." [119]

The tragedy of suicide from an intellectual perspective was two-fold—theological and legal. Murray adds, "It gathers force from the semantic elision, general for much of the Middle Ages and traceable throughout appropriate dictionaries, of our words for sin (*peccatum*) and for crime (*crimen*), since suicide could be said to be both the worst sin *and* the worst crime."[120]

It is during this era that the theological gravity of suicide is linked exegetically with the words of Jesus in Matthew 12:31–32 regarding blasphemy of the Holy Spirit:

> Therefore I say to you, any sin and blasphemy shall be forgiven people, but blasphemy against the Spirit shall not be forgiven. Whoever speaks a word against the Son of Man, it shall be forgiven him; but whoever speaks against the Holy Spirit, it shall not be forgiven him, either in this age or in the age to come. (NASB)

---

[118] Alexander Murray, *Suicide in the Middle Ages. Vol. II, The Curse on Self-Murder* (Oxford: Oxford University Press, 2000), 110–21. Murray's work is the most extensive history available and provide an enormous amount of information and documentation.

[119] Ibid., 189–90. Murray's work is the most extensive history available and provide an enormous amount of information and documentation. See also his first volume *Suicide in the Middle Ages: Volume I: The Violent against Themselves* (Oxford: Oxford University Press, 1999).

[120] Ibid., 190.

Murray contends (with documentation) that the linkage was argued by "some divines, throughout the period," noting that Thomas of Strasbourg (ca. 1275–1357) identifies the belief as a tradition.[121]

So grave was suicide, that it was believed that the only rationale for the act was that the person did so at the instigation of the Devil (*diabolo instigante*)—a view that would continue to be part of the theology of suicide for several centuries.[122] The most frequent comments on suicide in biblical commentaries during the Middle Ages are those pertaining to the death of Judas, and usually drew from the writings of Augustine. One interesting commentary is that of Paschasius Radbertus (785–865). Murray writes:

> Paschasius seems to echo Origen, in speculating on Judas' motives. Judas had tried to repent, Paschasius points out, and he goes further. Judas may even have hanged himself in the mistaken hope of being in the next world before Jesus so he could fall at Jesus' feet and ask for pardon the moment that Jesus himself died. Paschasius here makes his own a reading he may have found in Origen, and whose presence is a legend fairly well known in the East.[123]

Apart from the novelty of the view, Paschasius' perspective is indicative of the nature of comments regarding suicide in the early Middle Ages. They were largely tied to biblical commentary rather than the articulation of theology.

a. Twelfth-Century Precursors to Aquinas

Peter Abelard (1079–1142) was one of the greatest theologians of the age. In his work *Sic et non,* chapter 155, a work looking at theological issues from views affirming and denying doctrines, he discusses whether or not suicide was permitted in the case of impending sexual attack. As noted above, this is something earlier Christians had considered in view of the barbarian invasions and persecutions. Eusebius, Jerome, and Ambrose had answered *yes* and Augustine and Macrobius had answered *no.*[124] Abelard also discussed suicide in his *Christian Theology.*

---

[121] Ibid., 190 and n. 3.
[122] Ibid., 191.
[123] Ibid., 196.
[124] Ibid., 202.

It was in the twelfth century that the term suicide, *suicidium,* was first coined by Walter of St Victor (d. c. 1180). Suicide was also discussed by John of Salisbury (c. 1115–1180) in his work *Policraticus.* [125] John of Wales (d. 1285), like Augustine, acknowledges that some women committed suicide to avoid sexual assault, but did so with divine approval or divine command (as they said, did Samson) and concludes in his work *Communiloquium,* "May the faithful therefore eschew the aforesaid error, by which a person might knowingly and voluntarily put himself to death."[126]

Peter Lombard c. 1100–1160, famous for his influential theological work *The Four Books of Sentences* (*Libri Quattuor Sententiarum,* c. 1150) did not address suicide, and this probably explains why the subject was not addressed more fully by others at the time. Murray noted, "The reticence of Peter Lombard goes a long way to account for that of other contemporary theologians."[127]

However, there was not complete silence on the subject. Bernard of Clairvaux (1090–1153) and Hildegard von Bingen (1098–1179) wrote against suicide. Hildegard, in her work *Scivias,* writes of one committing suicide as one who is

> performing the separation himself without any hope of mercy. Wherefore he falls to perdition, since he kills that by means of which he should do penance.[128]

In her dire words "without any hope of mercy," we see a glimpse of the idea of no forgiveness for those who take their lives.

By the thirteenth century and coinciding with the many classical authors being translated from Greek and Arabic, suicide was beginning to find greater discussion in theological writings. The first of those to do so was Alexander of Hales (ca. 1185–1245) in his theology text *Summa Alexandri* in which he references Augustine.[129] But it would be in the thought of Aquinas that the topic of suicide received its fullest medieval evaluation.

---

[125] Ibid., 206–11.
[126] Ibid., 213.
[127] Ibid., 216.
[128] Ibid., 217.
[129] Ibid., 219–21.

b. Thomas Aquinas

Thomas Aquinas (1225–1274), the most famous of medieval theologians, gave three arguments for why suicide is a sin. Suicide, he argued, was a sin against self, neighbor, and God. First, suicide is contrary to nature in that every living organism naturally desires to preserve its life, and suicide is an unnatural rejection of that instinct. Second, suicide is contrary to human social obligations, because the entire community is injured by self-killing. Third, suicide is contrary to human religious rights and responsibilities, because God alone should decide when a person lives or dies. Aquinas argued:

> to bring death upon oneself in order to escape the other afflictions of this life, is to adopt a greater evil in order to avoid a lesser. In like manner it is unlawful to take one's own life on account of one's having committed a sin, both because by so doing one does oneself a very great injury, by depriving oneself of the time needful for repentance, and because it is not lawful to slay an evildoer except by the sentence of the public authority.[130]

Following the thought of the era regarding the doctrine of sin, Aquinas distinguished between venial sins and mortal sins with the latter being far more serious.[131] McDonagh observes:

> The scholastics attempted a systematic exposition of this distinction between mortal (deal-dealing) and venial sins. Aquinas insisted, in line with the tradition, that venial sins were called sins analogically; mortal sins were truly sins. Since then sins have been seen as venial either because of the imperfection of the act (lack of knowledge of consent) or the triviality of the matter involved. For mortal sin there must be full knowledge (awareness), full consent, and grave matter.[132]

Theological and philosophical discussions of sin were detailed and serious. The thought of Aquinas and his *Summa* epitomized the scholastic method. Nineteenth-century American medievalist Henry Charles Lea observed:

---

[130] *Summa Theologica* II–II 64.5

[131] Ibid., I–II 71–88. However, based upon interpretations of 1 John 5:16–17, the distinction was made earlier in the history of the doctrine. Hubert Louis Motry's *The Concept of Mortal Sin in Early Christianity* (Washington, D.C.: The Catholic University of America, 1920) argues that the technical theological usage of *mortal* with reference to sin is traced to Tertullian.

[132] E. McDonagh, "Mortal Sin," *New Catholic Encyclopedia* 2nd ed., vol. 9 (Washington, D.C.: The Catholic University of America, 2003), 903.

> When we turn to the schoolmen, who endeavored through their dialectics to solve in the minutest detail every problem of the moral and spiritual world, we find the greatest of them all, Aquinas, discussing with his accustomed thoroughness how far the imputation of sin is modified by passion, or influences the character of the sin and renders it either mortal or venial. He admits freely the mitigating influence of passion in depriving a man of the use of reason and inducing temporary ignorance through absence of advertence, but to relieve an act of sin the passion must be such as to subvert the will and render the act wholly involuntary. If the will precedes the passion, the greater the passion the greater the sin; if the passion is antecedent, the greater it is the less the sin; an act suddenly performed without reflection may be venial when if committed with deliberation it would be mortal.[133]

Without ambiguity or dissent, suicide was considered a mortal sin. After the death of Aquinas, two subsequent Dominicans, Remigio de' Girolami (1235–1319), who was an early student of Aquinas, and Guido Verani (n.d.), did much to spread the ideas of Aquinas with respect to suicide. Efforts such as these, along with developments in canon law, the rise of penitential books, and the popularization of theology in writings such as those of Dante, set the idea of suicide as unforgivable into the collective Christian consciousness.

4. Suicide and the Reformation

In the sixteenth century Roman Catholic and Protestant theologians viewed suicide as sinful and abhorred it. There were some differences in how it was viewed with regard to its origins, but all viewed it as wrong and sinful. Yet, the distinction of suicide as a mortal sin was something that remained within Roman Catholic theology. There was no idea of it being an unpardonable sin in Protestant theology. "Wycliffe, and after him Martin Luther, Calvin, and others among the Reformers, rejected the distinction so far at least as it supposed a difference in the sin rather than the sinner."[134] What did remain, though, were severe civil consequences for the property of the deceased, restrictions on burial, and, often, mandatory desecration of the corpse.

---

[133] Henry Charles Lea, "Philosophical Sin" *International Journal of Ethics* 5, no.3 (April, 1895): 325–26.

[134] I. McGuiness, "Venial Sin," *New Catholic Encyclopedia* 2nd ed., vol. 13 (Washington, D.C.: Catholic University of America, 2003), 155.

a. John Calvin (1509–1564)

A lawyer as well as pastor and key Protestant theologian, John Calvin wrote very little about suicide. It is not addressed in any edition of the *Institutes*. In other writings, he addressed the subject only twice, and those instances were in sermons pertaining to suicides recorded in 1 Samuel 31 on King Saul and in 2 Samuel 17 on Samson.[135] Using the imagery of a soldier serving as a sentry at a post, Calvin argued that God has placed every person at a post "which we must not abandon until God orders us to do so."[136] Showing continuity of thought, Calvin followed the views of Augustine on the matter. Similar imagery was used in classical thought in the writings of Pythagoras and later the Roman lawyer-orator Cicero.[137] Calvin acknowledged that Christians, as all people, sometimes face difficult circumstances. However, such times did not warrant suicide. In an environment where Reformed Christians in France often faced persecution, Calvin was realistic about matters of life and death. Though non-Christians might choose suicide as a means of avoiding trials, Christians were not to do so—"unbelievers at once panic and despair and try to end their lives, which the faithful, having received from God the creator, shall give back to Him."[138] Calvin then continued and argued against "pagan philosophers" (Stoics) who supported suicide. For Calvin, suicide was a theological and civil breach of trust and stewardship. It was "the worst crime."[139] While there were social and civil consequences of a suicide, such a death, for Calvin the issue was primarily theological. Aquinas and Aristotle had found strong civil ramifications in that a suicide deprived society of one of its members. Although this was true, it was not an emphasis in Calvin's comments.[140]

While he followed Aquinas on some ideas regarding suicide, Calvin and the Reformers did not argue that suicide was a mortal sin.

---

[135] Jeffrey R. Watt, "Calvin on Suicide," *Church History* 66, no. 3 (Sept. 1997): 464.

[136] Ibid., 464.

[137] Watt, 465–66.

[138] Cited in Watt, 467.

[139] Ibid., 466.

[140] Ibid., 470.

Instead, he argued that it was diabolical in origin, because it made the individual go against the divinely given instinct for self-preservation. This perspective of Satan participating in suicide arose after Aquinas but before the Reformation era.[141] In such instances, the individual is not beyond the salvific mercy and grace of God, as Jeffrey Watt notes that we "cannot help but conclude that the devil has put such a rage in [that man]; such a man is no longer himself and no longer knows what he is doing and what he is saying."[142]

In Calvin's era, there was the denial of ecclesiastical burial for suicides, something that had been adopted in Christianity as far back 563 and the Council of Braga. There was also in some areas such as France, secular law requiring forfeiture of the property of the deceased and desecration of the corpse. All of these traditions had roots in pagan antiquity and neither Augustine nor Aquinas said anything about the body or burial of a person who committed suicide.[143] Thus, although they were not actions originating in Christian theology, such practices reinforced the cultural stigma of suicide and may have added to the theological misconception of suicide as an unpardonable sin.

The seventeenth-century Westminster Shorter Catechism, which remains authoritative for Calvinists, follows Augustine in relating one of the Ten Commandments to suicide. It declares:

> Q. 68. What is required in the sixth commandment?
> A. The sixth commandment requireth all lawful endeavors to preserve our own life, and the life of others.[144]

b. Martin Luther (1483–1546)

Reformer Martin Luther likewise does not comment much on suicide. He is adamant that suicide was not an unforgivable sin. In 1532 in one of his famous *Table Talks*, Luther commented, "I don't have the opinion that suicides are certainly to be damned. My reason is that they do not wish to kill themselves but are overcome by the

---

[141] Ibid., 469.
[142] Cited in Watt, 470.
[143] Watt, 472–73.
[144] Same prohibition against suicide is in the Larger Catechism in Questions 135 and 136.

power of the devil."[145] With such a diabolical origin, he agrees with Calvin. Luther expresses a concern not be misunderstood or misused in a way that lessens the danger and seriousness of suicide as a sin. He argues, "It is not plain that their souls are damned."[146] Rather, the person who commits suicide is "like a man who is murdered in the woods by a robber."[147] Luther is more lenient on suicide than theologians in previous centuries.

c. English Reformation

During the English Reformation there does not appear to have been any identification of suicide as the unpardonable sin, although Richard Hooker (1554–1600) in polemics against Arminianism discusses an individual who feared he had committed an unpardonable sin and committed suicide.[148] Yet, as with the remainder of Europe during the Reformation era, there was an enormous stigma against suicide and significant social and legal consequences. Michael MacDonald and Terence R. Murphy detailed:

> Suicide was a terrible crime in Tudor and early Stuart England. Self-killing was a species of murder, a felony in criminal law and a desperate sin in the eyes of the church. "For the heinousness thereof," observed Michael Dalton, "it is an offense against God, against the king, and against Nature." Suicides were tried posthumously by a coroner's jury, and if they were convicted as self-murderers, they and their heirs were savagely punished. Their moveable goods, including tools, household items, money, debts owed to them, and even leases on the land that they had worked were forfeited to the crown or to the holder of a royal patent who possessed the right to such windfalls in a particular place. Self-murderers were denied Christian burials; their bodies were interred profanely, with a macabre ceremony prescribed by popular custom. The night following the inquest, officials of the parish, the churchwardens and their helpers, carried the corpse to a crossroads and threw it naked into a pit. A wooden stake was

---

[145] Martin Luther, *Luther's Works*, American Edition, vol. 54 *Table Talk* (Philadelphia: Fortress Press, 1967), 29.

[146] Ibid.

[147] Ibid.

[148] Baird Tipson, "A Dark Side of Seventeenth-Century English Protestantism: The Sin against the Holy Spirit," *The Harvard Theological Review* 77, no. 3/4 (July–Oct. 1984): 328.

hammered through the body, pinioning it in the grave, and the hole was filled in. No prayers for the dead were repeated; the minister did not attend.[149]

By the later years of the Reformation there was in England a legal circumstance by which the judgment on suicides could be lessened. The finding of suicide need not bring on the harsh punishment that was customary if the individual who committed suicide was found by a court to be *non compos mentis* (not in their right mind). However, this was not often declared. What this shows however is the beginning of a cultural shift on ideas about suicide. With the coming of the Enlightenment and the desire by its proponents to eradicate revelation and religion as a foundation for moral judgments and social standards, there were the beginnings of the secularization of theories about suicide. There was also fuller consideration of the separate ideological strands that viewed suicide as primarily a mental illness. In the history of suicide, the act is not so much a definitive unpardonable sin, but rather a mortal sin (Roman Catholic theology) or a sin sometimes enacted because one believes he or she has committed an unpardonable sin. This latter view is found more in Protestant history and culture.

B. Literary Considerations

Literature is very powerful in conveying ideas in a culture and this is true more so in previous centuries. In the aftermath of the medieval distinction between mortal and venial sin, nonreligious literature also portrayed the seriousness of suicide. Especially noteworthy was Dante Alighieri's (1265–1321) epic poem *Divine Comedy* (*Commedia*), specifically, the first part of the poem, *Inferno* written in the wake of the life of Aquinas (1225–1274). Dante's allegorical pilgrimage of the soul heavily influenced western thought and imagination for centuries to come. In it, he assigns the souls of those who committed suicide to the seventh circle of lower hell. See Dante's description in Canto 13, line 94-105:

> When the ferocious soul departs from the body where from itself has torn itself, Minos sends it to the seventh gulf. It falls into the wood, and no part is chosen for it, but where fortune flings it there it sprouts like a grain of spelt; it rises in a

---

[149] Michael MacDonald and Terence R. Murphy, *Sleepless Souls* (Oxford: Oxford University Press, 1990), 15.

sapling and to a wild plant: the Harpies, feeding then upon its leaves, give pain, and to the pain a window. Like the others we shall go for our spoils, but not, however, that anyone may revest himself with them, for it is not just for one to have that of which he deprives himself.[150]

Georgia Noon said writes of this passage:

> The poet is filled with fear and great pity at the anguish and eternal torment of these souls and stands in horror at the awareness of their dreadful sin which has placed them beyond redemption. *It may well be that it is in the combination of this passage with medieval theological acceptance of the idea of mortal and venial sins that the popular idea of suicide as the unpardonable sin emerges.*[151]

In the nineteenth century, Dante's image was transmitted into English art in *The Wood of the Self-Murderers—The Harpies and the Suicides*, a pencil, ink, and watercolor work by the English poet, painter, and printmaker William Blake (1757–1827). In French culture, the Dante scene was portrayed by engraver and illustrator Gustave Doré (1832–1883) in his 1861 work on *The Divine Comedy*.

In English literature, in the works of John Milton (1608–1674) and William Shakespeare (1564–1616), both writing in the aftermath of the Reformation, there is also imagery of suicide. Other writers such as John Donne (1572–1631) and, earlier, Thomas More (1478–1535) also addressed the topic but from a different perspective. Shakespeare does so in the musings of Hamlet. Milton draws upon the thought of Lactantius and Augustine and writes negatively of two suicides from classical literature in *Paradise Lost*.[152]

In American literature, Herman Melville (1819–1891) and Nathaniel Hawthorne (1804–1864) both write of unpardonable sins.[153] However, only Hawthorne ties it to a suicide, and the suicide is not the unpardonable sin but the sin does end in a suicide. Hawthorne's

---

[150] Cited in Noon, 376. The harpy was a winged creature in Greek mythology known for stealing. Longfellow's translation goes, "When the exasperated soul abandons the body whence it rent itself away." *Writings of Henry Wadsworth Longfellow*, vol. 9 of 11, *Divine Comedy of Dante Alighieri, Inferno* (Cambridge, 1886), 80.

[151] Noon, 376. Italics hers.

[152] Joseph Horrell, "Milton, Limbo, and Suicide," *The Review of English Studies* 18, no. 72 (Oct. 1942): 422.

[153] See, James E. Miller, Jr. "Hawthorne and Melville: The Unpardonable Sin," *PLMA* 70:1 (March 1955): 91–114. See also, Nina Baym, "The Head, the Heart, and the Unpardonable Sin," *The New England Quarterly* 40, no. 1 (March 1967): 31–47; and Ely Stock, "The Biblical Context of 'Ethan Brand.'" *American Literature* 37:2 (May 1965): 115–34.

suicidal figure is Ethan Brand in the story "Ethan Brand—A Chapter from an Abortive Romance." The short story was originally titled "The Unpardonable Sin." In it, Ethan Brand tells a man and his son who operate a lime kiln that he once worked the same kiln until he went in search of the "unpardonable sin." Brand then claims to have found it. When asked what it is, Brand points to his heart:

> "What! Then are Ethan Brand himself?" cried the lime-burner, in amazement. "I am a newcomer here, as you say, and the call it eighteen years since you let the foot of Graylock. But, I can tell you, the good folks still talk about Ethan Brand, in the village yonder, and what a strange errand took him away from his lime-kiln. Well, and so you have found the Unpardonable Sin?"
> "Even so!" said the stranger, calmly.
> "If the question is a fair one," proceeded Bartram, "where might it be?"
> Ethan Brand laid his finger on his own heart.
> "Here!" replied he. . . .
> "What is the Unpardonable Sin?" asked the lime-burner; and then he shrank further from his companion, trembling lest his question should be answered.
> "It is a sin that grew within my own breast," replied Ethan Brand, standing erect, with a pride that distinguishes all enthusiasts of his stamp. "A sin that grew nowhere else! The sin of an intellect that triumphed over the sense of brotherhood with man and reverence for God, and sacrificed everything to its own mighty claims! The only sin that deserves a recompense of immortal agony! Freely, were it to do again, would I incur the guilt. Unshrinkingly I accept the retribution!"
> "The man's head is turned," muttered the lime-burner to himself. "He may be a sinner, like the rest of us—nothing more likely—but, I'll be sworn, he is a madman too."[154]

Then after interacting with others from the nearby village and with a wandering Jew, later in the night Brand decides his "task is done, and well done," and climbs to the top of the kiln and falls into it immolating himself. While literary portrayals of suicide such as those above do not declare suicide to be an unpardonable sin, they did much to influence readers by providing literary and cultural awareness of the linking of suicide with other acts thought to be unpardonable.

---

[154] Nathaniel Hawthorne (1804–1864), "Ethan Brand—A Chapter from an Abortive Romance, *The Snow-Image, and Other Twice-told Tales*," accessed April 1, 2011, www.ibiblio.org/eldritch/nh/eb.html. From Hawthorne's *The Snow-Image, and Other Twice-told Tales* (Boston: Ticknor, Reed, & Fields, 1851).

C. Biblical Considerations

Even though the concept and act of suicide—the deliberate killing of oneself—is present in the Bible, the word itself is not found in the Bible or classical literature, although there are many terms and phrases used that denote the idea.[155] Amundsen observes that "Ancient Greeks and Romans, whether pagans or Christians, were quite able to distinguish between various circumstances, motives, and methods of self-killing."[156] The term comes into English in the early to mid-seventeenth century from modern Latin (not classical) *suicidium* (*sui* "of oneself" and *-cidium* "a killing").

There are six suicides recorded in the Bible, five in the Old Testament (Jud. 9:50–55; 1 Sam. 31:1–6; 2 Sam. 17:23; 1 Kings 16:18) and one in the New Testament (Mt. 27:3–10; Acts 1:18–19). The death of Samson (Judges 16) is debated as whether or not it was a suicide. It could be viewed as an act in which Samson knew he probably would die, but in which death was not his intent. The intent was the defeat of his enemies. In none of the other cases is there a moral approval of the act. In none of these passages is there any mention of suicide being an unpardonable sin.

How then should we understand Matthew 12:31? What is blasphemy against the Holy Spirit, and why did Jesus say it isn't forgiven? Evangelical commentary on these verses is readily available, and for the present purposes a summary explanation is presented.[157]

These are among the most enigmatic and emphatic words Jesus speaks in the New Testament. His words in this verse (also in Mark 3:28–30 and Luke 12:10) certainly raised the eyebrows of the religious leaders, the Pharisees, to whom he was speaking. Not surprisingly, many people since then have also wondered about this unforgivable sin. In the Gospel of Mark's account of this much

---

[155] Amundsen, "Did Early Christians 'Lust After Death'?" 291.

[156] Ibid., 291–92.

[157] See for example David L. Turner's *Matthew, Baker Exegetical Commentary on the New Testament* (Grand Rapids: Baker Books, 2008) or Grant R. Osborne and Clinton E. Arnold's *Matthew, Zondervan Exegetical Commentary on the New Testament* (Grand Rapids: Zondervan Publishing, 2010). On commentary in parallel passages, see Robert H. Stein's *Mark, Baker Exegetical Commentary on the New Testament* (Grand Rapids: Baker Books, 2008) and Darrell L. Bock's *Luke 1:1–9:50 Baker Exegetical Commentary on the New Testament* (Grand Rapids: Baker Books, 1994).

debated saying (Mark 3:29), Jesus declares that not only is blasphemy against the Holy Spirit unforgivable, it is also eternal.

When Jesus spoke of this unpardonable sin, He had been confronted by the Pharisees, who condemned Him for healing a man who was blind, unable to speak, and demon possessed. The Pharisees accused Jesus of being under the power and influence of Satan and mockingly called Beelzebub after an Old Testament pagan deity (2 Kings 1:2). It was in response to these charges that Jesus spoke the words regarding blaspheming the third divine person of the Trinity, the Holy Spirit.

To blaspheme means to slander someone. In the Bible, blasphemy was an act in which the person, name, or character of God was insulted or demeaned. Rather than honoring God, a person guilty of blasphemy cursed or reviled God and His name through derogatory words and actions.

When the Pharisees proclaimed that Jesus' actions were tied to Satan, they were rejecting Jesus as Messiah and on the brink of making an irreversible decision with far-reaching consequences: They would never find national or individual salvation and forgiveness. Because they incorrectly attributed to Satan the power of the Holy Spirit exercised by Jesus in His miracles, they blasphemed the Holy Spirit. The religious establishment of Jesus' day misidentified divine actions as demonic actions and rejected the person and work of Jesus Christ as Messiah and Savior. Because Jesus was physically present when the rejection occurred, some interpreters of this verse hold that blasphemy against the Holy Spirit cannot occur today, although rejection of the Spirit's work is certainly possible.

In this passage (Mt. 12:32), Jesus states that a specific or single act of blasphemy against himself, the Son Man, can be forgiven; that is, speaking out against Jesus and his ministry is subject to forgiveness, because such words or acts of rejection come from misunderstanding the reality of His person and work. However, once the Holy Spirit works in a person's life convicting and convincing them of the truth of the gospel (John 16:8–11) or correcting misunderstandings about Jesus, a subsequent persistent and decisive rejection of the Holy Spirit's work regarding Jesus results in permanent judgment.

Persistent obstinacy leads to permanent condemnation.

Jesus tells His listeners that all blasphemies can be forgiven except this one against the Holy Spirit, because it is a blasphemy that entails in attitudes, actions, beliefs, and practices a defiant hostility toward God. It does so by rejecting God's offer of salvation expressed through the power of the Holy Spirit manifested in the words and work of Jesus. Although the Pharisees had been exposed to Jesus the Light of Truth (John 3:19), they permanently rejected Jesus, preferring spiritual darkness to light. In so doing, they blasphemed. Though apparently being convicted by the Holy Spirit that Jesus was indeed the Messiah, in rejecting Jesus the Pharisees and others refused to believe, and they rejected the only means of salvation offered by God (John 14:6). An unrepentant heart leads to an unforgivable heart. Present choices have eternal consequences. What a person believes about Jesus and His death on the cross has eternal significance. Accepting or rejecting Jesus Christ as Savior is the greatest decision we make in life.[158]

Other than the linking of Matthew 12:31–32 with suicide during the Middle Ages, one looks in vain for support for the idea of suicide as the unpardonable sin in the history of interpretation of specific verses. Apart from Roman Catholic interpretations of 1 John 5:16–17 supporting categories of mortal and venial sin, a view rejected in evangelical Protestantism, specific texts supporting forfeiture of redemption due to suicide are not present. It is likely that the contemporary *misunderstanding* of suicide and salvation should be traced back to the medieval interpretation of Matthew 12:31–32—a view that was accepted, but without extensive or unanimous presentation.

Certainly one might raise the question of verses that pertain to the doctrine of eternal security such as Hebrews 6:4–6, but discussions of the doctrine and specific texts pertaining to it are beyond the scope of this presentation. What is important for present purposes is that if one accepts eternal security (and the author does), then there is no sin that is so severe that it excludes an individual Christian from receiving eternal redemption. Conversely, if one rejects the doctrine of eternal security, then any sin has the potential of excluding the individual from eternal redemption. In either view, suicide does not in and of itself soteriologically mandate eternal separation from God.

---

[158] Adapted from the author's comments in Timothy J Demy and Gary Stewart, *101 Most Puzzling Bible Verses* (Eugene, OR: Harvest House Publishers, 2006), 95–96.

D. Cultural-Pastoral Considerations

We live in a culture of death wherein there is growing acceptance of suicide and assisted suicide as legitimate actions. It is in the realm of pastoral care that one often hears the idea that suicide is an unpardonable sin. In the author's pastoral experience of ministry inside the context of several dozen suicides, there is then often a reference or allusion to Matthew 12:31 and blasphemy of the Holy Spirit. It is an illogical and hermeneutically unsupportable leap and linkage—but one that is very common. The most reasonable explanation for this biblical and theological misappropriation and misunderstanding is that it stems from the convergence of the theological and literary ideas discussed earlier. Articulation of the idea that suicide is the unpardonable sin illustrates the complexity of ideas and the consequences they may have. Yet, for those who are contemplating suicide or who have lost friends or loved ones to suicide, the issues are very real and should never be minimized.[159]

It also raises questions regarding human forgiveness and divine forgiveness. Must sin be forgiven only after the action? Is this true for divine and human responses, or only the divine response? For example, can a person forgive an individual who is in the process of murdering or executing them?

Yet, Jesus asks the Father to forgive those who were killing him before the completion the death. This then raises the question of whether there can be forgiveness before an offense or only after it. Though it is true that the request might be that Father would forgive once the death was complete, the process of killing had already started and likely could not have been humanly reversed, even though it was not yet final.

This consideration aside, it is important to realize and communicate the truth that a post-conversion confession of sin, precluded in the case of suicide, is not the criteria for complete realization of redemption in the future.

---

[159] In addition to the author's edited volume *Suicide—A Christian Response*, referenced above, see also Gary P. Stewart, William R. Cutrer, Timothy J. Demy, Dónal P. O'Mathúna, Paige C. Cunningham, John F. Kilner, and Linda K. Bevington, *Basic Questions on Suicide and Euthanasia: Are They Ever Right* (Grand Rapids, MI: Kregel, 1998), and Timothy J. Demy, "Feel Trapped? A Biblical Perspective on Suicide," *Kindred Spirit* (Autumn 1999): 10–12.

Conclusion

Prior to the Reformation and even after it in Roman Catholic theology, the idea of suicide as unpardonable stems largely from medieval theology and distinctions between mortal and venial sin. To be sure, there has been much in more recent Catholic theology that views suicide as stemming from mental problems, but the core theological ideas remain. This perspective along with a long history of literary rejection and condemnation of suicide has informed and shaped popular cultural and religious ideas about suicide.

In post-Reformation Protestant societies, the vestiges of distinctions between mortal and venial sins along with literary and cultural ideas about suicide likely created a mindset to which was then added confusion about Matthew 12:31 and 1 John 5:16–17. The idea of suicide as an unpardonable sin is not uncommon in contemporary society, but one searches with difficulty and little success to find articulation of it in contemporary theological writings.

For Christians today, the idea of suicide as the unpardonable sin and a sin that causes forfeiture of salvation is an idea grounded in a misunderstanding of the biblical text, a misunderstanding of theology, and an idea then coupled with legal, historical, and literary concepts that yield a confusing, harmful, and erroneous conclusion. Suicide does not in itself condemn a person who has been saved.

We should help to the uttermost every person contemplating such, communicating the love of God in a fashion that rescues.

4.
Luther's Theology of the Cross as Foundation for Sanctification in Latin American Liberation Theology

by Dr. Patricia Cuyatti Chavez
Area Secretary for Latin America and the Caribbean
Focal Person for North America, Lutheran World Federation[160]

Introduction 67
A. Sanctification as Being Simultaneous Just and Sinner 67
   1. The Cross, Place of Revelation of the Hidden God 69
   2. Grace Revealed to Benefit Human Beings Integrally 71
B. Tracks on the Emphasis Made in Latin America on Sanctification 72
1. Sanctification as Active Reflection and Living in Liberation Theology 75
2. The Way of Living Sanctification among Women and the
      Feminists' Perspective 77
C. On the Contextualization of the Lutheran Heritage 80

Introduction

When I think of sanctification, concepts like connection, relationship, vocation, life in communion and in community come to me, because they inform and form part of the spiritual life. But that life is lived and exercised with and from the cross. In the Lutheran context, the cross becomes one of the major topics to develop the notion of justification and also of sanctification. This article will follow the intrinsic connection between them.

A. Sanctification as Being Simultaneous Just and Sinner

The Lutheran perspective on sanctification is based on the tension of being reconciled by the action of Jesus Christ in the cross. But reconciliation does not erase the human condition, because humans continue living in the tension between being free and sinner at the same time (*simul justus et peccator*). Sanctification happens exactly in that tension by virtue of faith granted by God's grace on the cross. Only through faith—that is, by the gracious action of God justifying all humanity—does justification takes place not because of human merits but because of God's will. The principle of justification is

---

[160] Cuyatti Chavez holds a Ph.D., Systematic Theology, Lutheran School of Theology in Chicago.

rooted in the message of the Gospels where incarnation, cross, and resurrection shape the approach to sanctification bearing witness to the constant salvific action of God in favor of the entire creation.

> Also they teach that men cannot be justified before God by their own strength, merits, or works, but are freely justified for Christ's sake, through faith, when they believe that they are received into favor, and that their sins are forgiven for Christ's sake, who, by His death, has made satisfaction for our sins. This faith God imputes for righteousness in His sight, Rom. 3 and 4.[161]

The emphasis on justification for sanctification is central and focuses on the action of God. There is a relationship built up through the entire ministry of Jesus Christ. The incarnated and resurrected God restores the image of God in the entire creation and maintains it by the action of the Holy Spirit. The work of the Holy Spirit is central to the continuing process of restoration. The broken relationship between God and God's creatures can only be done by God self. There is no need for merits that can justify or restore relations.

In this relationship, God originates faith by the power of the scriptures preached and lived out through the sacraments, the means of grace, and the active presence of the Holy Spirit. It is only by faith that access to grace takes place, and in that grace sanctification by the action of God is real. The human reality is never canceled nor divided; God acts completely in the human reality. Lutheran theology does not remain in the sphere of sanctification in the soul-body dualism; rather, God's action considers the entire humanity, and justification takes place exactly in that reality of struggle. In this human reality, sin and justification occur simultaneously. Therefore, the continuous struggles to maintain the relationship with God drives humans to depend on the gracious action of the cross, which is renewed constantly. Grace becomes relevant when living in such tension.

Sanctification according to the Lutheran perspective considers that tension. The fact that human beings are "simultaneously" free by God's grace and yet remain sinners is a reality seriously considered. The tension is encompassed by the fact that human beings, despite the grace of God and the benefit of faith alone, they continue to be

---

[161] *The Book of Concord, The Confession of the Lutheran Church*, Articles 4.1, 4.2, and 4.3.

sinners. Conscious of this human condition, the Lutheran theology of sanctification brings the tension into the concrete sphere of the reality. In this atmosphere, sanctification becomes a process that happens again and again during life. This notion also reshapes the identity of the body of Christ (*ekklesia*) because it is reformed by a relationship mediated by compassion and mercy. The church lives the benefits of the gracious God offered through salvation. Believers who form the communion of saints (communion sanctorum) are, at the same time, members of the church formed by sinners (*ekkesia peccatorum*). The balance in this tension does not come from any action by the church but by the invitation to live in reconciliation. It is the understanding that sanctification is translated in faithful actions that continue moving relationships while acknowledging the human condition and the action of God on them.

In the context of the First Testament, sanctification implied belonging to God (Exodus 13:2) and being part of God's people; they were called to obey and keep God's commands (Exodus 19:4). In the notion that the whole earth and people pertained to God the creator, the relationship became holy by actions of purification and worship that motivated a holy relationship between humans and God. The second Testament affirms the continued presence of God among God's followers, and it is emphasized by God's work on the cross. God justifies and promotes relationships. There is no need for rituals of purification that mediate that relationship. God touches the human vulnerabilities through grace.

> Faith is God's work in us ... is a living, bold trust in God's grace, so certain of God's favor that I would risk death a thousand times trusting in it. Such confidence and knowledge of God's grace makes you happy, joyful and bold in your relationship to God and all creatures. The Holy Spirit makes this happen through faith. Because of it, you ... serve everyone, suffer all kinds of things, love and praise the God who has shown you such graces.[162]

1. The Cross, Place of Revelation of the Hidden God

Redemption happens on the cross. The cross is the visible space where the revelation of God reaches its high point. The cross is the place of action and space where God is known. The crucified reveals

---

[162] Martin Luther, *Luther's German Bible of 1622*, trans. Robert E. Smith from Dr. Martin Luther's *Vermischte Deutsche Schriften*, vol. 63 (Erlangen: Heyder and Zimmer, 1854), 124.

the hidden God,[163] "the one living God who is manifest as he is concealed in the cross of Christ."[164] In the cross, God becomes visible and becomes a gift for humans. The revelation of God happening on the cross already confirms how God acts continuously. Through the cross, God preaches and reveals other attributes than that of being omnipresent, omniscient. God is the closest, most compassionate and merciful presence. The cross speaks of the incarnated Word revealing the meaningfulness of worship and communion. In that context, the sacramental offering of God regains sense.

> God confronts us first of all in his word. In his word he is 'known to us' and 'has dealing with us.' In it he has offered to us. We are directed to God's revelation in the word ... God grasps himself in his word. He becomes the 'clothed' God ...the revealed God is nothing else than the word of God.[165]

The cross reveals the unconditional will of God for salvation. In the cross, God works in order to heal people's wounds. Healing takes place because it restores relationships, it is a faithful process of healing that happens simultaneously among the communion and at the personal level. Coming back to the relationship between the hidden God and the revealed one, it is important to assert that Luther uses it to explain that it is the same God. Methodologically, the use of this distinction helps to express how God is acting through the Word, since the creation, now on the cross. The word acting in salvation is a word that speaks out of God's mystery that creates and recreates life. But the word is only accessed by faith. "The faith character of the knowledge of God is preserved by uniting revelation and concealment as two inseparable aspects in one and the same act."[166] It is in faith that the hidden God is known. Faith is the access promoted by God, access to know, "in the Word, and in the sacraments God is revealed and seen."[167] God becomes visible in a perseverant relationship

---

[163] Luther does not use the concept of hidden God in a speculative-metaphysical sense although it is open to such an interpretation ... Luther warns against this idea, while at the same time it remains a basic perspective of his theological thought. In order to safeguard the true concern of the idea, he warns against the speculative misunderstood hidden God." Walter von Loewenich, *Luther's Theology of the Cross* (Minneapolis: Augsburg Publishing House, 1976), 48.

[164] Ibid., 30.

[165] Ibid., 33.

[166] Ibid., 37.

[167] Ibid., 41.

through faithful prayer, constant reading and sharing of the good news, and faithful practice of that faith in concrete actions of love and diakonia. Faith is the element that helps to hold the tension between the hidden God and the God revealed on the cross.

The relationship built up through faith is established "under the paradoxical synthesis between the transcendence of God's salvific will and the subjective experience of the incalculable double will on the one hand, and the transcendence of the absolute double will and the subjective experience of the unconditional salvific will on the other hand."[168] It is in the reality of the work of salvation that God continues to create; the movement of life is possible without the need to speculate about the notion of the hidden God but as a source to confirm that on the cross God was revealed.

2. Grace Revealed to Benefit Human Beings Integrally

The Lutheran theology of the cross affirms that whatever is taught and preached addressing the work of God on the cross (the gospel, the sacraments, the word) is deeply connected to the action of the Holy Spirit. The Spirit of God acts in the human reality by sanctifying and consecrating. Life lived in consecration does not expect harmonious and heavenly experiences. Peace is a reality offered by God and in God. In this manner, God contributes to peace because God is the source of it. The relationship that God builds on the cross is done following the principle of peace and justice. The constant struggle of humans in life to build up peace needs to consider that peace is a principle of life. Because we humans are part of a church composed of both sinners and saints, we need to be open to the action of the Holy Spirit.

Justification is constant in the process of sanctification. It considers the totality of human beings. In that consideration, we humans embrace our nature of being simultaneously just and sinners. It is in this acknowledgment that change takes place. It is in this process of caring that the message of the gospel can challenge realities of suffering and that caring and merciful action of the Holy Spirit take place. It is also in this reality that the notion of the dualistic battle between the dimensions of the spiritual and the material are

---

[168] Ibid., 45 and 46.

overcome. The recovery of the precious and fallen humanity in us and the consideration of us as integral is a gift that allows restarting again and again the process of sanctification. Sanctification never ends; rather, it is an invitation to come to God, to the cross, to the baptism, and to the communion to restore relationships.

B. Tracks on the Emphasis Made in Latin America on Sanctification

The Indigenous populations in Latin American experienced the notion of salvation and sanctification during the arrival of Christianity in the fifteenth century through a Christology that proclaimed a celestial and monarchical Christ. The heavenly Christ confused Indigenous populations because in the proclamation Christians called for obedience to follow and relate to God, but this was a different kind of relation than the Indigenous had with their gods. Religiously, the concept of the Christian God was completely different from the concept of the divinities the Indigenous populations had.

The cross, at the core of the Christian life, was more tangible since the crucifixion was a symbol used to emphasize suffering. Many Indigenous populations identified with the crucified one because they knew that Christ was suffering with them. They were not far from understanding the message of the good news, but it was used by the church to believe in spiritual suffering. The imposition of the crucified Christ is beautifully addressed in the novel *Taita Cristo* (*Father Christ*) by Eleodoro Vargas Vicuña.[169] The small narration of Good Friday captures a suffering contradicting the meaning of the death of God. It is known that Good Friday needs to be read together with the day of resurrection. Without this perspective, it loses its message.

Tayta Cristo uses irony to express how the indigenous life is impregnated by suffering and oppression. The notion of crucifixion does not end with Good Friday, but exactly because of the conditions that the conquest forced down, the indigenous understood that their lives was a punishment or the way towards the Golgotha. The cross was used to reinforce the acceptance of suffering. Vargas brilliantly describes the way the community relates to the narration of Jesus'

---

[169] Eleodoro Vargas Vicuña, *Taita Cristo* (Lima: 1963).

death. To carry the cross has the connection to a vision of triumphalism. To carry the cross meant to overcome shameful experiences, including the fact that indigenous were not considered completely humans or that their heretical/sinner spiritual practices were given up. In the novel, one of the characters literally carries the cross. As incredible as it sounds, everyone in town sees his suffering and suffers with him. They are shocked with his death. But there is no recognition of their sufferings and struggles, because their neighbor's death has the aim to cover their sufferings.

In this irony, the author offers two perspectives of the crucified Christ. Being in the temple, Aurelia Ramos and Jacinto Navarro contemplate the figure of the crucified from two different perspectives. Jacinto praises the excellent artwork developed by the artist while Aurelia feels the suffering of the poor guy hanging on the cross. Aurelia suffers with Christ until the point to feel the pain and sadness. Capturing the irony, Vargas discloses the meaning of Good Friday and how stuck people are within it. Both attitudes of Aurelia and Jacinto invite readers to address the cross from different perspectives, but at the same time both do not raise the point. It is, of course, the great artwork that depicts the suffering that the cross expresses, but the cross also reveals the presence of God—God present among the suffering people. God is present among them, moving from suffering to active actions of faith and to concrete expressions of life that already speak of sanctification. The broader picture of the narration invites us to consider how merits are needed for consecration. But the tension remains; it is in suffering that the impossibility takes place. It is impossible to carry our personal crosses if we humans do not become followers of a gracious God. In this incapacity, the acceptance of suffering moves to a passive and obedient attitude, and in these circumstances there is the need for mediators, others than Christ, to confess in order to maintain control. In this condition God becomes literally hidden and salvation is not mediated.

Confession (as acknowledgment of failure) and sanctification are two inseparable topics. They remain central for the Christian life, and these are mediated by the crucified and risen Christ. Even today, it is possible to identify daily sufferings as part of spirituality imprinted over people in order to defeat them, to maintain social control over them or to maintain inequalities. The image of the crucified is not an invitation to support suffering, but to understand that in the midst of human suffering, God's grace takes place and that God suffers with the sufferers. This gracious character of the cross must be always used to promote transformation and consciousness.

Returning to the irony that Vargas raises, it links to another difficulty, the acceptance of Jesus Christ as celestial God. Even though the indigenous populations found it difficult to understand theological concepts contained in Christianity, as for example in the notion of the trinity, the two natures of Christ, etc., they accepted and believed in it. In some cases, Jesus Christ was welcomed as one more among the other gods, but that discussion needs more space elsewhere.

At the end of the 18th and the beginning of the 19th centuries, independent movements, in some countries in Latin America, encouraged immigration with the aim to promote religious freedom and development. Protestants who migrated from Europe focused on serving their parishioners without engaging in mission in the traditional sense. Diaconal actions where developed through schools, daycare, and health centers with the goal to respond to their call to serve the needy. The European pietism of the 18th and 19th centuries that arrived in the USA also reached the southern countries of Latin America. Harold Senkbeil noted that Pietism emphasized the awakening of spirituality in the "inner life and the subject experiences of the heart as an aid toward a living, vibrant commitment to Christ that showed itself in action."[170] The emphasis on the spiritual Christ, calling for moral changes and life regeneration, was a counter proposal to sinner practices that during the end of the 19th and early 20th centuries. This message was carried out by Pentecostal churches and movements that grew rapidly on the continent.

Sanctification, influenced by Pentecostalism, called on people to search for new life integrated with visible changes done and moved by the action of the Holy Spirit. God, through the Holy Spirit, sanctifies "hearts as assurance for salvation. Pietism in general and Methodism in particular stressed a brand of holiness that strove for

---

[170] Harold L. Senkbeil, *Sanctification. Christ in Action* (Wisconsin: Northwestern Publishing House, 2005), 27.

moral perfection ... reached by post-conversion experience."[171] Conversion, a necessary step in a consecrated life, bases its theology on the second coming of Christ to establish God's kingdom. Conversion happens personally and is a foundational experience for sanctification that encompasses a whole lifestyle, i.e., a relationship on the earth demarcated by the exigencies of the heavenly world. The emphasis on the spiritual side and the struggle with the challenges of the earth and sin searching for celestial salvation also aims to reinforce sanctification on the personal and emotional side.

1. Sanctification as Active Reflection and Living in Liberation Theology

The notion of sanctification offered in Liberation Theology is connected to a compromised Christian life with the suffering and oppression of people. The opportunity to make people's lives better is addressed by the liberating action of God. Instead of continuing to stress the hope of heaven because of the notion that the kingdom of God that will become complete when the promise of return takes place, Liberation Theology affirms that it has already arrived with Jesus the Christ. Liberation Theology interprets the historical presence and action of God in Christ using hermeneutics as a tool to affirm that salvation also happens in the reality of the poor. The poor struggle faithfully, and it is in this space or in community were "Jesus of Nazareth arrived always already interpreted by people or groups interested in him."[172] The need to return to Jesus of Nazareth was grounded in the affirmation that Christ is not other than Jesus. This first circularity confirms that justification methodologically begins when the presence of the incarnated God happens among the poor. Jesus' presence affirmed in the indwelling of God is real in the context of misery and oppression in order to de-pacify these realities and to continue inspiring people toward actions of love.[173]

---

[171] Ibid, 31.

[172] Juan Luis Segundo, *El Hombre de Hoy ante Jesús e Nazaret, II/1* (Madrid: Cristiandad, 1982), 32.

[173] Jesus trusted, thanked, and prayed the Father knowing the kindness which defined the ministry of love and service. Jon Sobrino, *Jesucristo Liberador, Lectura Histórico-Teológica de Jesús de Nazaret* (Madrid: Trotta, 1991) 186–188.

Liberation Theology in Latin America did question the way that the good news was proclaimed. Mary Solberg noted that the epistemology of liberation drives "to live knowing of such suffering and of [its] implications ... not to fix what was wrong [but to make humans aware of the personal] implications in it." [174] The "epistemological conversion" is the "transformation of a way of knowing"[175] in order to become conscious of a faith that drives to concrete liberation based on the ministry of Jesus. Salvation is not only a spiritual and future event; it is an immediate reality happening in the world of the poor who are liberated from the political, social, and economic oppression.[176] The specific context in which Jesus reveals the Christ helps to better understand God's relationship with the entire creation. The context of the poor is a theological sphere where the second circularity is expressed and where the reality of the poor illuminates the meaning of the scriptures, thereby refreshing them and making possible a contextual message. In this circularity the reading of the scriptures will always be new and will build continuity with the good news and discontinuity with what oppresses.[177]

In the context of suffering, it is possible to know Jesus through the poor. The poor is the reality where God incarnates and therefore becomes the scandalous presence of God.[178] The movement of God actualizes the promise of the kingdom of God. Jesus brings historic salvation to the poor and the poor become the place of salvation. A third circularity emphasizes the message of the kingdom of God. The connection between the message of the kingdom of God and the God of the kingdom is closely related, not only to the proclaimed event of God's presence in human history but also to the affirmation of who is God and what are these actions that deny God and promote idolatry. Here the intention is to know how humans relate to God and the gods

---

[174] Mary Solberg, *Compelling Knowledge—A Feminist Proposal for an Epistemology of the Cross* (Albany: State University of New York Press, 1997), x–xi.

[175] Ibid., xiii.

[176] The poor leads to a better understanding of the scriptures and helps to develop theology. The poor helps in the capacity to be moved to think. Jon Sobrino, *Jesús en América Latina, su significado para la fe y la cristología* (Santander: Salterrae, 1982), 52–56.

[177] Ibid., 112–113.

[178] Ibid., 44.

that intensifies the demand to choose between the incarnated God or the idols that separate humans from God.

Liberation Theology took a position against the alienating images of Christ whose emphasis on sanctification was largely used to oppress. The recovery of Jesus of Nazareth and the reinterpretation of God's presence among the oppressed break the ideology of the celestial Christ and promote relationships mediated by God who suffers with the poor and who liberates them from oppression. Liberation and salvation become one, and therefore Christians are challenged to live out a sanctified life following and promoting liberation in the transformation of society. If transformation takes place, then believers are active agents who oppose oppression and exploitation based on their relationship with God.

2. The Way of Living Sanctification among Women and the Feminists' Perspective

Sometimes out of the influence of Liberation Theology, other theologies made by women, those of African descent, and the indigenous emphasized liberation in their specific ways. The new theologies try to underline the specific needs and struggles by emphasizing what salvation means and to live it out today. It is remarkable the emphasis on daily life done by women and feminist theologians and scholars who developed reflection considering their ongoing struggles in life.

The re-reading of the scriptures[179] through women's eyes in daily life (*cotidiano*) and women's bodies were used as hermeneutical keys to make society conscious of women's condition, and oppression determined through roles socially and culturally constructed.[180] Women also considered the socio-political and economical inequalities within the social and religious structures. Feminization of poverty addressed the spirituality of embodiment, affirming that God's presence in the experiences of discrimination of women in their different context has a specific meaning for salvation, and called to promote relationships based on justice and equality.

---

[179] Ibid., 80.

[180] Elsa Tamez, "Women Re-reading the Bible," in *With Passion and Compassion—Third World Women Doing Theology*, ed. Virginia Favella and Mercy Amba Oduyoye (Oregon: Wipf & Stock Publishers, 2006), 179.

Not only women, nature too was systematically exploited and abused. Ecofeminism, stressing the relationship of God with the entire creation, is a theology for life based on the just relationship between humans and the entire creation.

Women scholars addressed many topics, like reproductive rights, ordination of women, involvement of women in decision making at many levels in the church and society. They called for a Christian life characterized by relations developed out of consideration and respect. Sanctification, in this sense, was also understood as a continuous process. The strength built upon God's presence among women in struggle, suffering, and oppression lays a foundation for opportunities to develop strong relationships and to nourish them through everyday actions. This invitation moves followers toward faithful and compassionate service already expressed by God. In addressing God's attributes, which are not only male ones, women developed a relationship based in the affirmation that God interrupts what is not meaningful and encompasses a continuity in life. God is a close friend, is part of the community, and is present in the communion. God nourishes, relates as wisdom, is present, and promotes new beginnings.

In the re-reading of the Bible, the new and fresh encounter with the divine wisdom promotes redemption and salvation to both men and women who became Jesus' followers and disciples. This active grace of God is reaffirmed daily so that the daily relationship with God means the renovation of that discipleship and resurrection, as metaphors to affirm that life continues to be possible, engaging also the *"hermanas"*[181] in ministry and service. Women become friends of God and part of the body of Christ; they also work to promote relations of solidarity strengthened by the meaning of the cross and resurrection. The dimension of God incarnated among creation and the presence of God as consoler beautifully refreshes memories and moves God's winds in order to make visible what is mystery in the familial dimension of the servant community that is strengthened in the communion. The relational and affectionate God moves people to

---

[181] Elsa Tamez, *Las Mujeres en el Movimiento de Jesús, El Cristo* (Quito: Consejo Latinoamericano de Iglesias, 2004), 121.

follow and serve with tenderness and solidarity and in doing so worship God who builds up sanctification in their lives.

Women recover, in their relationship with God, the feminine principle of the divinity that "makes it possible to worship, to believe and love God not only as the strong Father who creates us and liberates us with his powerful arm, but also as a Mother, full of tenderness, grace, beauty and receptivity, who accepts the seed of life and feeds it in her womb, so it may become a full being in the light of day."[182] Focusing on an embodied ministry of love—the salvation of Jesus—women search for alternatives that are in tension because life promised is also negated.

To enlighten realities of death, women pay attention to Jesus' ministry based on inclusion, service, and mercy. Friend of the poor and outcasts, Jesus overcomes traditional depictions of structures and male-female relationships. In their contextual experience of the message, women transgress in the *"caminata"* [183] what patriarchal structures have promoted and rooted. Women promote sacred spaces through experiences of freedom to accept persons as they are, not only as women, but they also accept other minorities and marginalized people who embody the suffering of the cross.

God, acting through the gospel message, the life and ministry of Jesus, builds up sanctification in a relational and liberating manner. Even more, Jesus allows women to enter in dialogue and to engage in active faith. In relationship with Jesus, women felt courageous to make decisions, to "argue, to discuss theology, transgress, sit at Jesus' feet, touch him, confess their faith and recognize him as the Messiah."[184] Along with the examples of women in the gospels, their tenacity and courage demonstrates the valid struggle to be admitted

---

[182] Bingemer, "La Trinidad desde la Perspectiva de la Mujer: Algunas Pautas para la Reflexión," in *El Rostro Femenino de la Teología*, ed. María Pilar Aquino (San José: Departamento Ecuménico de Investigaciones, 1986), 67.

[183] The long walk where women became aware of themselves happened by being part of Jesus' ministry of solidarity. See Elsa Tamez, "The Power of Nudity," in *Faith Born in the Struggle for Life*, ed. Dow Kirkpatrick (Michigan: Eerdmans Publishing, 1988), 188.

[184] Wanda Deifelt, "The Recovery of the Body: Jesus in a Feminist and Latin-American Perspective," in *Discovering Jesus in our places—Contextual Christologies in a Globalized World*, ed. Sturla J. Stålsett (Dehli: ISPCK, 2003), 35.

into the presence of grace.[185] It is in the presence of grace that women are encouraged to live daily life in consecration to God and to their neighbor.

C. On the Contextualization of the Lutheran Heritage

The theology of the cross cannot be read without considering God's action in and through the incarnation. A merciful God who decides to indwell in a hostile world was possible and continues to be possible. The cross methodology for theology starts there, where God becomes human in the person of a very vulnerable and dependent being in the baby Jesus. God speaking out to the world through the Son (Heb. 1:2) is the most powerful message of presence given to connect the being God and the lovely creation.

The incarnation is the way God has chosen to be close to the creation, attending to the specific needs of humanity. In this approach, the Word is the presence of God who becomes active. The divine activity promotes justice and accompaniment among followers from different social, cultural, and religious backgrounds. The caring divine wisdom builds bases toward a message that liberates from dualities preserved institutionally as the body/soul, purity/impurity, rich/poor, men/women, slave/free, sane/insane, earth/heaven, etc. From that liberation, God helps followers to recover their wholeness and integrity. It is in the process of restoration of humanity that restoration of the relationship with the self and among human beings, called communion, is possible.

The relationship is holy because the person is accepted in her/his totality. The relationship is built upon the life of a close God, not under the reign of one governing from a place of glory. The relationship is nourished by a God who comes close until the point of revealing the extent of love and compassion on the cross. The cross is then a methodology based on the history of God walking on the paths of the people. In this sphere, the cross reveals not only the vulnerability of God but also the power of love. It is never a power to impose or to control others; it is a power to build up freedom and to liberate. As Senkbeil noted, "There God hid on lowly weakness to

---

[185] Nelly Ritchie, "Mujer y Cristología," in *El Rostro Femenino de la Teología*, ed. María Pilar Aquino (San José: Departamento Ecuménico de Investigaciones, 1986), 126.

show himself to us, there God humiliated himself to give us glory, and there God died to give us life!"[186]

Recovering the meaning of the cross in a contextual manner means being conscious of the different discontinuities the cross places when we want to find, touch, or feel God, forgetting that God's presence is revealed in each person we know or the ones we do not have the opportunity to meet. For a context where living in community is strong, then communion that overcomes familial barriers can help to strengthen the body of Christ. The unexpected places, such as the rivers of markets in Jesus time, are today places where people eagerly look for a good neighbor. The following of God in sanctification is the invitation to be in relationship and to develop a ministry based on relations. Though such can be seen as foolish or eccentric today, these relations are mediated by the message of the cross.

Wisdom is often expressed in notions the world sees as foolishness, and the revelation of the power of God happens in weakness. Sanctification speaks out of the spiritual growth each person experiences together in acting inspired by Christ. And we, as Christians, live and grow through up-and-down experiences exactly because we learn throughout life "how to live" in consecration. Out of our human experience we can also experience the absence of God in critical situations, as in the loss of beloved ones.

Losses are experienced in diverse ways in life. Mourning and healing are processes that help to find peace and to be nourished by the action and presence of God. In difficulties we continue to see God through the cross, and the same happens from the other side; God sees us from the angle of the cross, too, and gives us meaning with compassion and love that covers our weakness and strengthens us.

In sanctification, our lives are in Christ, and that relationship of identity affirms not only that God takes our sins but that God accompanies us to walk on the difficult and easy paths of life. God is present during distress and joys and celebrates with us in even small endings or beginnings. In reality, there is no evidence of progress in growing in faith or in growing in actions. Sanctification is not a race. It is an invitation to be moved by and to hear the wind of God. It is

---

[186] Harold L. Senkbeil, *Sanctification—Christ in Action* (Milwauke: Northwestern Publishing House, 2005), 126–127.

not only a personal listening to God, it is also the invitation to listen to God as community, because it is in that context that the bread and wine are shared and the water spread for new life. These elements are like a fountain for strengthening relationships in order to be guided to serve the neighbor. It is in sharing and receiving that each person grows humbly. There are many needs prayed for and prayed from the different and small corners of our world. The prayers are present in our communities and families, and they are also our own prayers.

The cross of Christ does not hide human needs to God; rather, they are placed on the cross. The request for daily bread works because we ask faithfully. God answers the prayers that have been placed already in the offering made to us on the cross. The cross continues to be a source of strength for the church formed by saints and sinners. When our ecclesiology accepts this reality, the connection to the cross and the involvement in God's mission recovers sense. In that light sanctification is possible. In that light, the struggles of diverse minorities are our struggles and also the struggle of God. God continues to be on the side of the ones who struggle and faithfully waits for change. When we are able to see God acting in and through people, it is the best way to be affected by holy actions. Even simple actions that happen in daily and ordinary life can nourish our lives. It is in the simple that spirituality takes place. It is the simple that converts us and helps us to be closer to the message of the cross.

5.
How God Wrestles with the Shortcomings of His People on the Ontological Level
by Dr. Leon Harris
Assistant Professor of Theology,
Talbot School of Theology, Biola University
La Mirada, California[187]

Introduction	83
A. Personhood as Onto-relations	84
1. Relations and Personhood	84
2. Personhood and the Human Creature	85
a. T.F. Torrance and Colin Gunton on Personhood	85
b. John Macmurray on Personhood	87
c. John D. Zizioulas on Personhood	90
d. Concluding Personhood and the Human Creature	95
B. Ontological Origins: Trinitarian Foundations of the Church	96
1. Origin of the Church in the Grace of the Triune God	96
2. Community as the People of God: The Elected Church	98
3. Body of Christ: Institution or Instituted	99
4. Temple of the Spirit: Church Constituted	101
C. Ontological Recovery: Restoration of Personhood through Relations	103
1. Discipline through Relational Isolation: The Loss of the Person	103
a. Matthew 18:17 "treat him as you would a pagan or a tax collector."	105
b. 1 Corinthians 5:1–5 "hand this man over to Satan, so that the sinful nature may be destroyed"	105
c. Titus 3:10 "Do not associate with him..."	106
2. Reconciliation through Relational Recovery: Restoration of the Person	108
Conclusion	109

Introduction

The question of how God wrestles with His people's failures can be addressed along many different disciplines and methods. The approach in this paper adopts the onto-relational position of theologians such as T. F. Torrance, Colin Gunton, John Zizioulas, and others.[188] The position is: within the Community of God, God primarily wrestles with His people's failures. The Community is a relational community which constitutes the personhood and therefore the *being* of the individual. This constitution of the individual by the

---

[187] Harris earned his Ph.D., University of Aberdeen: www.biola.edu/directory/people/leon-harris.

[188] "Onto" refers to ontology or the study of "being" itself.

Community of faith allows for a personal relationship by the personal God to deal with His people's failures. This is not by any means the only approach, or even the best approach, but it is an approach that can help us understand the relation between God and His creation, especially in light of salvation history as revealed in the persons of the Father, Son, and Holy Spirit.

A. Personhood as Onto-relations

Before we begin our examination of the Community of God as determining the *being* of the individual, it is necessary to establish the framework for understanding personhood as otherness-in-relation and between God and those individuals within His community. The term "person" in modern thinking has become cemented with the notion of the individual, which has given rise to other problems to the detriment of theological thought overall.

1. Relations and Personhood

The British theologian Colin Gunton states that the doctrine of the Trinity "takes us wider and deeper into the mystery of what it is to be a human being in the world."[189] Gunton is reacting against those who have placed the center of value for being human within the human creature and apart from God. For example, Don Cupitt insists that in order for human beings to be authentic, they must have complete autonomy of their own self-definition.[190] For Gunton, Cupitt has completely misunderstood reality, the scripture, the Triune God, and above all the fallenness of man. So instead of defining humankind properly, humankind is defined without consideration of the state of sin and evil in which it exists, and which ultimately imposes on the finite the burden of infinite divinity. There is such an inward turn that fundamental relations for personhood are lost, as well as relations with the Creator and the rest of the created order. So instead of

---

[189] Colin E. Gunton, *The Promise of Trinitarian Theology* (Edinburgh: T&T Clark, 1991), 29.

[190] Cupitt says, "The principles of spirituality cannot be imposed upon us from without and cannot depend at all upon any external circumstance. On the contrary, the principles of spirituality must be fully internalized *a priori* principles, freely adopted and self-imposed. A modern person not any more surrender the apex of his self-consciousness to a god. It must remain his own." Don Cupitt, *Taking Leave of God* (London: Xpress Reprints, 1980), 9. Notice how Cupitt transposes spirituality: "That is, on our account the religious imperative that commands us to become free spirit is perceived as an autonomously authoritative principle which has to be freely and autonomously adopted and self-imposed" (Cupitt, 98.).

creating an autonomous individual, philosophies like Cupitt's have created an enslavement of the individual who is no longer defined by relations with the other; *enslavement* because there is no accounting to the affects that sin has on the individual.

W. J. Hill states that "the full understanding of creaturehood itself is disclosed in the light of the Trinity, for only thus is it clear that world or universe ... bears a trinitarian imprint."[191] In this way when Gunton discusses personhood, it is in relation to the Creator and the created order as opposed to an individually isolated autonomous self. When personhood is viewed in relational terms, beginning with the Triune God, salvation is no longer a matter of personal redemption from a perishing world, but restoration to true humanity by the Triune God who comes into the world to redeem it.

The economic activity of the Father, Son, and Holy Spirit determines what it means to be human and human in the world. The question of personhood should not be viewed as an opposition of human autonomy against heteronomous oppression. Things must be viewed differently in the light of a God who is Lord, but who also acts personally within our fallen human condition. Because redemption involves "the notion of God's faithfulness to his entire creation," the economic action of the Trinity is at the core of what it is to be human and what it is to be human in the world.[192]

2. Personhood and the Human Creature

a. T.F. Torrance and Colin Gunton on Personhood

T. F. Torrance says,

> This onto-relational concept of 'person', generated through the doctrines of Christ and the Holy Trinity, is one that is also applicable to inter-human relations, but in a created way reflecting the uncreated way in which it applies to the Trinitarian relations in God.[193]

---

[191] William J. Hill, *The Three-Personed God—The Trinity as a Mystery of Salvation* (Washington, D.C.: Catholic University of America Press, 1988), 273. When Hill uses the word "imprint" he is referring to the idea that creation and salvation/redemption are Trinitarian events experienced within the history of the world.

[192] Colin E. Gunton, *The Actuality of Atonement—A Study of Metaphor, Rationality, and the Christian Tradition* (Edinburgh: T&T Clark, 1988), 103.

[193] Thomas F. Torrance, *The Christian Doctrine of God, One Being Three Persons* (Edinburgh: T&T Clark, 1996), 103.

In other words, personhood is perceived univocally in relation to the immanent relations in the Godhead and the human creature; albeit asymmetrically, because the relations in God are absolute, perfect, and uncreated. By viewing "person" as onto-relational, the transition between the respective realities of the Creator and the creature gives the created person the freedom to be individual and particular while simultaneously relying on *relationality* to constitute personhood. This pattern of relational *being* and living is grounded in the very act of creation, in that God created humans relationally, first in relation to Himself as humanity's creator and then in relationship with others (the male and female creation event).

Colin Gunton arrives at his relational view of creation from the doctrine of creation and from Christology, for Christ is the basis of renewal and the goal for creation (cf. Col. 1:15; Rom. 8:29). Gunton uses the "image of God" to ground the human relation in the inner life of the Triune God; he expands his view of personhood and relations back into Trinitarian doctrine. Gunton says that "to be God, according to the doctrine of the Trinity, is to be persons in relation: to be God only as a communion of being."[194] Gunton then moves from the definition of persons as defined by the Father, Son, and Spirit, to the definition of the human person because:

> it is that which is replicated, at the finite level, by the polarity of male and female: to be in the image of God is to be called to a relatedness-in-otherness that echoes the eternal relatedness-in-otherness of Father, Son and Spirit.[195]

Gunton does not want to press the analogy too far and assume that human society should be based on a social trinitarian model. He simply defines what it is to be a human person in a relational way, and the doctrine of creation requires a relational view of the human person. It is not simply a relation with other human beings which Gunton is advocating, but a relatedness-in-otherness with the otherness being on one level vertical and on a second level horizontal. The otherness on the vertical level is the human creature's relation with the Creator which is redeemed through Christ in the Spirit. The

---

[194] Colin E. Gunton, *Christ and Creation, The Didsbury Lectures* (Eugene: Wipf & Stock, 1992), 100.

[195] Ibid., 101.

human creature is created in time and space which is given to it by the Creator, and the human creature is related to the Creator because its very existence is contingent on the free will action of the Creator. The horizontal level for Gunton is the relation between human persons and the created order. Being created in the "image of God" includes the idea that human persons are *persons constituted* by relationships with other human beings and a relatedness to the created order. It is through the various relations between families, friends, acquaintances, and the created order where the "image of God" is recognized: "we are placed on earth to join in mutually loving relations with those whom God gives us to be loved by and to love through the finite time he grants." [196] In this scheme, the human person is constituted by relation because the incarnated Son's personhood is constituted by His eternal relation with the Father. Therefore, the human person is grounded and constituted by mutual relations, albeit in a created and finite manner.

In order to complete the notion of personhood as otherness-in-relation, John MacMurray and John D. Zizioulas can enlighten the discourse.

b. John Macmurray on Personhood

John Macmurray presented two lectures at the Gifford Lectures during the Spring of 1953 and 1954. In the two lectures, Macmurray expounded on what it is to be a "person." Though difficult to do justice to Macmurray's thought, a brief examination will assist with our definition of personhood as otherness-in-relation. The foundation of Macmurray's proposal is a rejection of the Enlightenment's dualism mainly because the "person" is lost to the self, or in Macmurray's usage, lost to the subject. It is the self as subject, as an "I think" which separates the person from the world in which the person lives. Basically, Macmurray's position is that in order for a philosophy to be coherent and relevant, it must have some correspondence to experience, but dualism prefers "thought" or reason over and against experience. Experience does not mean simply

---

[196] Colin E. Gunton, *The Christian Faith—An Introduction to Christian Doctrine* (London: Blackwell Publishers, 2002), 46.

the five senses, but the activity of the person within the world in which he/she lives; the world where "person" takes shape.

Simply stated, Macmurray finds that Kant is the radical departure for philosophy, and that all succeeding philosophies are basically grounded in Kantian philosophy. Even though this is an extravagant or even an overstated claim, Macmurray is only using Kant as the pivotal point in philosophy because he also finds that Descartes' famous *Cogito ergo sum*—"I think, therefore I am"—provides the foundation for Kant. Macmurray believes that Descartes' *"cogito"* is a mistake because it places the theoretical above and over experience, or over the practical. Because of the *"cogito"* takes precedence as the starting point of philosophy in Kant, by way of Descartes, a philosophy of individualism developed. Macmurray explains that,

> For thought is inherently private; and any philosophy which takes its stand on the primacy of thought, which defines the Self as the Thinker, is committed formally to an extreme logical individualism. It is necessarily egocentric.[197]

He then shifts the trajectory of the metaphysical dualism of immaterial/material to a dualism of the theoretical against the practical:

> It is that any philosophy which takes the 'Cogito' as its starting point and centre of reference institutes a formal dualism of theory and practice; and that this dualism makes it formally impossible to give any account, and indeed to conceive the possibility of persons in relation, whether the relation be theoretical—as knowledge, or practical—as co-operation.[198]

In this assessment of Descartes' *"cogito"* as a dualism of practical/theoretical, the theoretical is given priority over against the practical so that Macmurray is able to conclude that Descartes' *"cogito"* results in a challenge to authority and results in a declaration of autonomy. In sum, Macmurray's argument is that Descartes' autonomous philosophy is based on doubt; and for Macmurray, "The method of doubt is the rejection of authority in operation."[199] In other words, "doubt" rejects the authority which is outside of the self and denies the activity of the other.

---

[197] John Macmurray, *The Self as Agent* (New Jersey: Humanities Press International, 1991), 71.
[198] Ibid., 73.
[199] Ibid.

By invoking concepts such as authority, the other, and autonomy, Macmurray lays the groundwork for the development of his view of personhood in relational terms. He continues to explain that Descartes' "*cogito*" simply leads to a tension between existence and non-existence. That is, Descartes' *Cogito ergo sum* means that "I am an agent, and my act is thinking."[200] If Descartes is correct, then our being is grounded in thinking, which is non-existence. The reason is that

> to exist is to be part of the world. Thinking, however, in non-causal; it 'moves nothing' as Aristotle said. If it is an activity, it is an activity which is without effect in the realm of existence.[201]

There must be a causal relation to the material world for the person to exist; it cannot be grounded in mere theoretical thought processes. What Descartes' "*cogito*" proved is that the "I" exists; instead he should have proved that "I exist" as a mind and body. Macmurray does not want the person to exist within itself, as an "I"; he wants a personhood that is grounded in relation to the other, a relation which begins with the Uncreated Other, and also encompasses the created other. He is concerned that the person does not become grounded in the realm of the non-existent thought of "*I think*."

Once it is determined by Macmurray that the self cannot be defined by simple mental processes—a denial of both Descartes and Kant—he defines the "self" as an agent. As noted above, without a causal relation in the world, the self does not exist: as only a mental process it has no effect on the other. The "other" for Macmurray, at least at this point, is simply a term meaning something "other" which exists. Therefore, the only way for the self to know its own existence, and the existence of others, is by participating in existence with others. Macmurray states that the self as agent is an active self, which basically means and necessitates a dynamic relation with others. The basic thesis regarding the self is that "the Self is constituted by its relation to the Other; that it has its being in its relationship; and that this relationship is necessarily personal."[202] Since the self is

---

[200] Ibid., 80.
[201] Ibid.
[202] John Macmurray, *Persons in Relation* (London: Faber and Faber Ltd, 1970), 17.

constituted as an agent in relation to the other—because that is where activity happens—Macmurray says that "persons, therefore, are constituted by their mutual relation to one another."[203] In this way, a person is not an isolated self. To be a person is to be in relation with another person; there must be a participation in existence. That is, construing the person as a "thinker" results in an isolated self-as-subject; and the "thinker" is non-existence. The "self-as-agent" is necessarily in relation to the "other," and it must be personal because the self-as-agent is a human person.

Macmurray is not a Christian theologian, but his position is that "to be a person is to be in communication with the Other."[204] His relational view of the person results in the idea that "the intention to maintain community universally has to be expressed symbolically in the idea of a personal Other to which we are all related."[205] For our purposes, it is both the relational and the community language which moves Macmurray from a philosophical trajectory to a theological one.

c. John D. Zizioulas on Personhood

John D. Zizioulas defines "personhood" in relational and communal terms. Zizioulas begins by asking "what does it mean that someone *is* rather than *has* a person?"[206] Zizioulas does not want the concept of "person" to be grounded in an individual identity which connotes absolute "being" apart from other "beings." Zizioulas' goal is to demonstrate that "person" is grounded in patristic theology and ecclesiology:

---

[203] Ibid., 24.

[204] Ibid.

[205] John Aves, "Persons in Relation: John Macmurray," in *Persons, Divine and Human: King's College Essays in Theological Anthropology*, ed. Christoph Schwöbel and Colin E. Gunton (Edinburgh: T&T Clark, 1991), 128. Aves explains that Macmurray does not like the traditional proofs for God's existence because they fall under the category of the "I think," which cannot prove existence. "But for Macmurray, God the Other is known in the act of existence; we discover our freedom in relationship with others.": in Aves, 129. Aves further explains that this activity, or act of existence, is Macmurray's way to eliminate the spirit/matter, immaterial/material dualism because it is the act of God in the world in which we participate that our conception of reality should take place.

[206] John D. Zizioulas, "On Being a Person. Towards an Ontology of Personhood," in *Persons, Divine, and Human: King's College Essays in Theological Anthropology*, ed. Christoph Schwöbel and Colin E. Gunton (Edinburgh: T&T Clark, 1991), 33.

> The person both as a concept and as a living reality is purely the product of patristic thought. Without this, the deepest meaning of personhood can neither be grasped nor justified.[207]

Zizioulas believes that the question of "person" is ontological, and therefore it should be based on what he considers the basic question of humankind: "Who am I?" This simple question has a rather large burden in Zizioulas' program, because it is with this question that he lays the foundation for "person" to be defined in relational terms. In the question, "who am I?" the interrogative "who" locates the questioner in the world where he/she is in the face of other beings. The "I" is a need for particularity over and against the other—a need for otherness. The "am" is just as important in that it seeks an answer to the question of existence. So, an ontology of personhood must adequately address all three aspects of "who, am, I," especially the particularity of the "I" in relation to the interrogative (i.e., "who") and the "to be" verb.

Zizioulas states that "personal ontology is an assertion of the metaphysics of particularity."[208] The problem is that the "I" seeks an eternal state of being; it wants to transcend to the universal level. Based on Platonic metaphysics, there is not any mechanism which allows for continuation of the particular, and in turn, no grounds for personhood. If personhood exists in the universal "being," then the particular is loss. In other words, for ancient Greeks "particularity is not ontologically absolute; the many are always ontologically derivative, not causative."[209] The *particular* will pass away, but the *universal* continues which is shared by the many.[210]

Zizioulas is searching for a mechanism that will allow the particular to be the ground of the person instead of it being grounded

---

[207] John D. Zizioulas, *Being as Communion—Studies in Personhood and the Church* (London: Darton, Longman and Todd Ltd., 2004), 27.

[208] Zizioulas, "On Being a Person. Towards an Ontology of Personhood," in *Being as Communion*, 35.

[209] Ibid., 36.

[210] Zizioulas explains that the particular person does not survive in Greek ontology; both in Plato and Aristotle. Even Aristotle's particularity answered the 'who' question with universal categories; categories which are shared with other things, or beings. Again, Zizioulas: "participation in being is a condition for the particular's being as much for Aristotle as it is for his master Plato." See "On Being a Person," 36–37.

in a shared universal concept of being. To this end, he theorizes that for particularity to have ontological priority, it is necessary to assume that "being" is caused. If in Platonic and Aristotelian thought the world is eternal and the cause of being, then the particular cannot be the ontologically primary cause of being. In other words, the particular is causative and not derivative. Instead of the particular existing as a participant in the universal being, the particular is caused: or in the theological sense, created by particularity.

In the creation account in Genesis, the ground of human existence is in the *causation* by God, but also grounded in the *particularity* of Adam. Not as a participant in God's or Adam's being, but in a causal relationship between the creator and created. At this point, this does not lead to full "personhood"—if "person" includes the constitutive component of continuity of "human existence." Adam does not complete the picture of personal ontology—human existence—because in his death, Adam proved that he does not contain or maintain the totality of human nature in himself. That is, when Adam died, human nature and existence continued.[211]

Once Zizioulas has secured the grounds for "being" in the particular and then demonstrates the insufficiency of grounding "person" in Adam, he turns to God. By turning to God, he always has in mind the triune God as the eternal relations between the Father, Son, and Spirit. Zizioulas states that "in God it is possible for the particular to be ontologically ultimate because relationship is permanent and unbreakable."[212] Since in the persons of the Father, Son, and Spirit, the totality of the divine nature is always present; and always being present, the particularity that is located within each of the trinitarian persons are the bearers of the totality of the divine nature, thereby eliminating the paradox between the "one" and the "many." Since the relations between the three persons are permanent and unbreakable, and always present, Zizioulas argues that

---

[211] From Platonic to Aristotelian philosophy, the basic problem for Zizioulas is that there is not a continuation for the person; this renders true ontology of the person impossible. For Zizioulas, this is seen in Plato's idea of reincarnation in which the person is not eternally connected with the material body, that is, the 'substance' (*ousia*) of man. The difference for Aristotle is that there is no permanence or eternality at all, because the individual which is form and matter simply ceases to exist at death.

[212] Zizioulas, "On Being a Person. Towards an Ontology of Personhood," 41.

relationship should be introduced into the substance itself, so that "being" can be relational.²¹³

Since "being" is grounded in the particularity of the triune persons, Zizioulas gives ontological priority to the "person" over substance. For Zizioulas, God "exists" on account of a person, the person of the Father; and not on account of an ontologically prior substance. The reason is simple, if the substance is the ground of existence, then freedom is lost because existence becomes "necessary"; freedom is based on ontological existence and not personal. So instead of giving priority to the substance by viewing God's personhood as derived from an "uncreated" substance, God's ontological freedom lies "in His personal existence, that is, in the 'mode of existence' by which He subsists as divine nature."²¹⁴ This is what gives man his hope of becoming an authentic person. This means that the Father freely communes, or is in communion with the Son and the Spirit; it is this free communion, which is an ecstatic existence and is the ground of the Father's freedom, and thereby, His personhood.

This ontological expression is played out in love: "God is love" for Zizioulas and "signifies that God 'subsists' as Trinity, that is, as person and not as substance."²¹⁵ There is no ontological necessity in God, but freedom: "love is identified with ontological freedom."²¹⁶ Since, God's existence is not based on ontological necessity, God has seen fit to reveal Himself as the origin of all ontological reality. In summary, since the relationship is between particulars (and the ontology of personhood is based on the particular and relationship), the particular is raised to the level of ontological primacy,

> it emerges as being itself without depending for its identity on qualities borrowed from nature and thus applicable also to other beings, but solely on a

---

[213] Shults explains that philosophers were already viewing 'relation' as a metaphysical category. Shults says, "notice that Kant explicitly makes "substance and accident" a subcategory of Category III, "Of Relation." See F. LeRon Shults, *Reforming Theological Anthropology—After the Philosophical Turn to Relationality* (Grand Rapids: Eerdmans, 2003), 21.

[214] Zizioulas, *Being as Communion*, 44.

[215] Ibid., 46.

[216] Ibid.

relationship in which it constitutes an indispensable ontological ingredient, since it is inconceivable for the rest of beings to be outside a relationship with it.[217]

Since "person" is grounded in the reality of the Trinitarian persons, Zizioulas contends that Christology fulfills the human drive to personhood.

Because Christology is from above, human personhood finds its subsistence in the Father-Son relationship. The hypostatic union becomes crucial, instead of the *communication idiomatum*; the natures *are* because they are particularized in one person. What Zizioulas means is that in Christ the two natures (divine and human) give their qualities to the identity without having the identity rely on the natures in an ontological primary manner; the cause of being is located in the particular and not the general.

The human person realizes their full potential as a "person" in the new-birth because a new identity is received based on the relationship of the eternal Father and Son through and in the Spirit. This new way of identification is seen as salvation; which is the means for humanity being to become a "person" through the love of God; a person who is in a communication of love with God as a free loving *hypostasis*.

According to Zizioulas, the Greek Patristic Fathers understood this as *theosis*, which should be interpreted as participating in God's personal existence, not his essence. For the human person, the Greek Patristic Fathers understood basically two "modes of existence": a hypostasis of biological existence and one of ecclesial existence. The biological existence is a reliance on the body to determine the person; and simply put, this leads to an individualism which is a mask that hides the true person. This existence ultimately leads to the death of the person as this existence is not out of freedom but out of a natural and ontological necessity.[218] But the *hypostasis* of ecclesial existence is "constituted by the new birth of man, by baptism."[219] In order to

---

[217] Zizioulas, "On Being a Person. Towards an Ontology of Personhood," 41.

[218] The necessity is that the "passion" which preceded the conception of the individual created an ontological necessity which also dictates laws; the ontological freedom is lost – there is a sense of createdness which is another way to say "necessity of existence." In other words, the natural substance has ontological priority over the "person."

[219] Zizioulas, *Being as Communion—Studies in Personhood and the Church*, 53.

avoid the "createdness," that is, the ontological necessity, the person must be born "anew" or "from above."

Christ's *hypostasis* is identified in His relationship with the Father; he is the eternal Son of God. It is not a biological existence, because it would be grounded in an ontological necessity and not freedom. So, it is the *hypostasis* of Christ as grounded in the free and loving relationship between the Father, Son, and Spirit which is the ground for "personhood."

d. Concluding Personhood and the Human Creature

Based on our survey of Macmurray and Zizoulas, several key elements come to light which have an impact on our understanding of God's relation with His creation. Based on the model of personhood that I have chosen to adopt, God is a relational being. His divine substance is constituted by the eternal relations between the Father, Son, and Spirit. There is not an ontological priority given to the substance: in the stupendous words of Gregory of Nazianzus,

> no sooner do I conceive of the One
> than I am illumined by the Splendour of the Three;
> no sooner do I distinguish Them
> than I am carried back to the One.[220]

God *relates* to His creatures, especially His human creatures, in a relational and personal way. The relation has concrete existence from within our creaturely existence in the living Christ as mediated by the Holy Spirit. The Holy Spirit is the divine Person who is the agent of communion, in the divine life of the Godhead, and also in the new Community. This community is the people of God, the body of Christ, and the temple of the Spirit.

Now we will turn to the relational model to see how God relates to His people within the new community known as the Church. It is within God's activity through Christ in the Church where God begins to wrestle with His people's failures.

---

[220] Gregory Nazianzen, "Select Orations of Saint Gregory Nazianzen: Oration 40.41," in *A Select Library of Nicene and Post-Nicene Fathers of the Christian Church*, ed. Philip Schaff and Henry Wace (New York,: The Christian Literature Company, 1894), 375.

B. Ontological Origins: Trinitarian Foundations of the Church

1. Origin of the Church in the Grace of the Triune God

The people of God, as the church of Jesus Christ, discover its very being in the grace of God; the church's "being" does not unfold apart from the act of God. The community of Christ has its origin and existence as a divine fiat which is grounded in the existence and act of the triune God. The church is not merely an assembly of believers who have decided to meet because of a like-minded belief in Jesus Christ; it is called out by the Father through His Word and empowered by the Holy Spirit to respond to the Father's call. The "church" is the community of hearers of God's call to salvation that can become the doers or responders of the Word. Michael Horton explains it as follows:

> Therefore, the visible church is not composed only of the regenerate; it is the covenant community where the Spirit brings to repentance and faith "those who are near" (i.e., "you and your children") and "all who are far off, everyone whom the Lord our God calls to himself" (Acts 2:39).[221]

This means that the Church is not simply an historical organization, or an assembly based on notions of hierarchy. The activity of redemption is developed through the covenant that was initiated by God Himself as witnessed in scripture. The covenant between the Father and the Son to redeem creation eternally exists and is the same covenant which establishes the "community" from the foundation of the world. The community of the saints is an eschatological covenantal community that the Holy Spirit is constituting in the "now" and is also is moving towards the future; that is, the "not yet" has a certain promise in anticipation of the *parousia* at the *eschaton*.

Stanley Grenz says, "Because the coming together of believers in mutual covenant constitutes the church, it is the covenant community of individuals."[222] Instead of a collection of individuals who exist in an autonomous fashion, the church is a community of persons-in-relation; they are in relation to the triune God and then in relation to fellow believers. The church is a community that exists as an

---

[221] Michael Scott Horton, *The Christian Faith—A Systematic Theology for Pilgrims on the Way* (Grand Rapids: Zondervan, 2011), 845.

[222] Stanley J. Grenz, *Theology for the Community of God* (Nashville: Broadman & Holman, 1994).

institution, but an institution that has its origin and continual existence in the historical reality of Christ and His continual presence as mediated by the Holy Spirit. As Otto Weber states: "the Community lives by the will of its Lord which essentially establishes it and determines its structure."[223]

The church is not a plurality, but it is a unity. The scripture uses three metaphors to reveal the nature of the church, which also reveals the intimate relation between the triune life of God and the church:

1. **The People of God,**
2. **The Body of Christ, and**
3. **The Temple of the Spirit.**

According to Berkouwer, "Each image points in the same direction, toward the one mystery of the Church, the origin of which is the love and mercy of God."[224] As believers are called by God into the communion of the saints, they are constituted as true persons because their personhood is grounded in the grace of God. The Holy Spirit liberates the individual from the death of unrealized personhood into a realized personhood which brings life through the redemption won by Christ. It is through proper relations with the Creator that constitutes the church without eliminating the individual. The individual is liberated to be the other in relation; but one that is constituted by the proper relation that is won by Christ and actualized when He pours out His Holy Spirit upon us.

There may be a logical priority given to the church, but the ontological priority is given to the act of the triune God. The Father wills the church into existence, and His Son and Spirit complete His will, in absolutely free obedience and cooperation. The Son completes the Father's will in the incarnation by being the person in whom the union between the Creator and creation is realized. The Holy Spirit opens up creation to accept the union of the Son: "He makes the incorporation of creation in the Son possible by enabling creation to

---

[223] Otto Weber, *Foundations of Dogmatics*, trans., Darrell L. Guder, vol. 2 (Grand Rapids: Eerdmans, 1983), 513.

[224] G. C. Berkouwer, *The Church*, Studies in Dogmatics (Grand Rapids: W. B. Eerdmans Pub. Co., 1976), 77.

open to its incorporation in the Son."[225] The church is constituted by the believers, but the believer(s) is (are) constituted by the church; this paradox is only resolved in that both are actually constituted by the agency of the Holy Spirit. It is the pneumatological aspect of God's divine activity which ensures that the unity does not overshadow the individual. The church is only a community due to what it receives from the Father through His Word, that is, it receives the Holy Spirit. The Holy Spirit creates, perfects, and ultimately constitutes the community towards empowerment, witness, worship, and fellowship, all in anticipation of the final reconciliation with God. In order to complete the relational aspect of the community within the divine life of God, it is necessary to briefly examine the three metaphors for the church in relation to the Father, Son, and Spirit.

2. Community as the People of God: The Elected Church

As stated above, the Triune life of God is the communion in which the church participates, and it is a participation which is initiated by God Himself. It is God who called creation into existence; called forth Adam; called out Abraham; and elected Jesus Christ by whom He finally elected us *in* Jesus Christ (Eph. 1:3–5). Calvin states, "But if we are elected in him, we cannot find the certainty of our election in ourselves; and not even in God the Father, if we look at him apart from the Son."[226] Since it is the agency of the Holy Spirit to mediate the presence of the Son to the community, elected believers are always in fellowship with the community. The elected person is constituted by their new relation; a new person results from our earlier concept of persons-in-relation. The Holy Spirit constitutes the elected person to a new relationship in Jesus Christ, and they develop further through the variegated networks of relationships in the community of faith. It is through the electing grace of God that the church's ontological *being* is to be found as its source and origin.

Otto Weber says, "To be elect means to be elect in and with the Community."[227] The relational model of personhood indicates that the

---

[225] John D. Zizioulas, *Lectures in Christian Dogmatics*, ed. Douglas H. Knight (London: T&T Clark, 2008), 132.

[226] Jean Calvin, *Institutes of the Christian Religion*, trans., Henry Beveridge, 4 vols., vol. III (1581), III.24.5.

[227] Weber, 511.

born again Christian is only a new person as he/she participates in the divine election which radiates from the economic life of God. In other words, to be part of the elect means a proper response to the electing call of the Father, an election mediated by and through the Son, and finally actualized by the Holy Spirit. The Holy Spirit as the eschatological agent of perfection and communion is also the bond of love between the Father and the Son; He is the person who completes the eternal and absolute love between the members of the Trinity.

This same Holy Spirit also brings believers into communion, so that instead of an individual autonomous existence, the individual is now liberated into a new existence as a person constituted by otherness-in-relation. The Father's will to elect takes place *in* Christ; that is, God has chosen us to be "one *in* Christ," instead of merely believing or worshipping *one* Christ. Being *in* Christ is liberation from a non-existent life that will eventually lead to death into a liberated existence of eternal life *in* Christ. The liberation is in the election of God towards an existence of communion, that is, a proper otherness-in-relation existence with God, with others, *in* Christ.

Instead of predestination being viewed in a deterministic fashion, or as a coercive act that is planned in the past, election is construed as a calling by the Holy Spirit into a new relation with Christ and in Christ. Creation is liberated from personal non-existence to a proper personal existence of belonging to Christ's community. For Gunton, "The Spirit respects our liberty, because he is not an internal, immanent causality forcing us into the Church, but a personal "other" coming alongside us to set us free for others, just as the Spirit was alongside Jesus in his temptation in the wilderness." [228] The community is the elected community of individuals who are constituted by their relations-in-communion with the Triune God, with others.

3. Body of Christ: Institution or Instituted

The second metaphor for the church is the Body of Christ. This metaphor also denotes unity, but it is a unity which begins with Christ. The church as the body of Christ is not simply an institution,

---

[228] Colin E. Gunton, *Theology through the Theologians—Selected Essays, 1972–1995* (London: T&T Clark, 1996), 201.

but it is instituted by its relationship to Jesus Christ as mediated by the Holy Spirit. The church is an institution—not by its own initiative—as it was instituted in and by Christ who is ever present. It is Christ's continual presence which prevents the church from becoming another earthly, humanly created organization, and it is a continual institution that was instituted by Christ. Berkouwer puts it this way,

> It can be assumed that the Church as the body of Christ stands in the full light of unity, concord, and fellowship; and all opposition, rivalry, and conflict are out of the question on account of the relatedness of the one body and all its members to Him, Who is the Head of the body, the Church.[229]

As an institution, the church is a unitary body of many members who are in relations with each other. The church as the body of Christ submits itself to the living Christ's rule; this rule of Christ eliminates opposition and conflicts because the Holy Spirit is producing unity-in-relation. Christ is the head of the body, so the body receives its life and personal existence from being *in* relation with Christ, a relation that began by the will of the Father and is actualized by the Holy Spirit.

The body of Christ is not the literal body of Christ, or the replacement for the body of the Christ while he is absent. The church is only the body of Christ when church members are in fellowship with Christ and each other. That fellowship is grounded in the agency and activity of the Holy Spirit by faith. Panneberg says that "the church is a fellowship of believers only on the basis of the participation of each individual in the one Lord."[230] Even though Pannenberg's Lutheran affiliation moves him to rely on the sacraments as a means to participate in the one Lord, his theology is derived systematically. The one God in Christ by the Holy Spirit inaugurates and sustains the church. The participation is one that includes the sacraments, but also includes worship and fellowship; a life that is lived on this earth in relation to and for the other.

Fellowship is not limited to a local or global term. Fellowship in Christ, as His body, transcends notions of visible and invisible, and

---

[229] Berkouwer, 80. Cf. Col. 1:18.

[230] Wolfhart Pannenberg, *Systematic Theology*, trans. Geoffrey William Bromiley, 3 vols., vol. 3 (Grand Rapids, Mich.: Eerdmans, 1993), 102.

transcends the local and global terminologies in reference to the community. Fellowship with Christ is just that: fellowship with Christ is such that the local church is not the entirety of the body of Christ, for that fellowship is global and even extends to heaven. Nor does the global community have an ontological priority over the local church. Where the Holy Spirit gathers people who meet, worship, and proclaim in the name of Jesus there is *the* church of God—for there the Father has gathered His people to be the body of Christ. The local church and other churches are united as they independently meet in Christ's name and declare that He is the head of the Church.

This paper is not concerned with church government—or the sacramental vs. the non-sacramental churches—but rather our focus is that the body of Christ is grounded in the unity of the triune life of God. The body of Christ is a unity because of its constitution by the Holy Spirit as a community-in-relations. Whether the sacramental or non-sacramental traditions be true, we leave that to God.

This metaphor of "body of Christ" for the church depicts the redemptive nature of Christ's work and not merely a symbol pertaining to a gathering of like-minded individuals. Soteriologically speaking, the metaphor "people of God" relates to God's calling and electing, the "body of Christ" relates to the redemptive work of Christ. It is the "body" that explains the redemptive work of Christ as forming a new community through redeemed relations. The metaphor "body of Christ" serves as a metaphor of redemption through Christ, but it is not *the sole* metaphor for the church. Because God is a perfect union of persons, all three metaphors are necessary to complete the picture of God's people.[231]

4. Temple of the Spirit: Church Constituted

There is an order in the economic presentation of redemption, in that the origin is in the will of the Father; then moves to the willing obedience of the Son; and finally, is perfected by the free cooperation of the Holy Spirit. The church as the "people of God" and the "body of Christ" realizes her concreteness by the indwelling Holy Spirit who constitutes the church as the "temple of the Spirit." The individual

---

[231] I have decided to assume the metaphor "Bride of Christ" is contained in or derived from the metaphor "Body of Christ."

believers are indwelled by the Holy Spirit. As believers come together under the urging of the Holy Spirit, the community becomes the "temple of the Spirit." The Holy Spirit is the Spirit of communion, and this is realized in the relations between the members as the presence of the living Christ given to the church. Pannenberg says,

> This immediacy that Christians experience as the work of the Spirit characterizes faith in Jesus, yet not just in the sense of knowledge of Jesus, but as the immediacy of a personal relationship. Believers have immediacy to Jesus because all have individual fellowship with Jesus in faith.[232]

When the immediacy is experienced as a gathering and empowering by the Holy Spirit, which gives believers the freedom to maintain their faith in Jesus Christ, there takes place a liberation from sin to a new and restored relationship with the Creator in Jesus Christ.

This liberation from sin is a liberation from non-existence personhood; in a manner of speaking, a liberation from a personhood grounded in an autonomous existence. The Holy Spirit liberates believers to have *fellowship* with Christ through His body or in the "body of Christ"—the church. It is not the clergy or any other office that is the unity of fellowship, but the Holy Spirit mediating the Son's presence to the church.

The church must guard against becoming an institution, which is defined as having independent existence which gives logical priority to the individuals; the church must maintain a proper pneumatology which allows for a relational aspect. The church as a community "is constituted by its members by virtue of their free relatedness to each other."[233] The local church, or institution, cannot lord itself over the members, because if "relation" is an ontological category, then the church is constituted by the relations brought about by the Holy Spirit. The individual persons are also constituted by the relations which take shape in the community—the "temple of the Spirit." So, both the community and the individual can be described as being a "temple of the Spirit" in such a manner that both have their ontological existence located in the grace of the Holy Spirit.

---

[232] Ibid., 124.

[233] Gunton, *Theology through the Theologians—Selected Essays, 1972–1995*, 198.

Based on the relational model of personhood, the church or the community is only what it is because of the will of the Father, the redemption of the Son, and the perfecting agency of the Holy Spirit. The new community may resemble social norms, current organizational methods, or practices of the non-Christian community. But the church should not be judged by these standards, nor will the church completely be at ease with the individualistic autonomous ontology of these systems, for "even when it is completely incorporated, it is nevertheless completely separate because of the Holy Spirit."[234] The relational model adopted here allows room for God to wrestle on a personal level with His people. The personal triune God deals with the struggles of His people in a personal and dynamic manner in the core of our existence.

C. Ontological Recovery: Restoration of Personhood through Relations

From the previous ontological and existential discussions, we now turn to the more practical side of how God is involved, relates, and helps His people in their failures.

1. Discipline through Relational Isolation: The Loss of the Person

At the end of the Fall in Genesis, God expelled Adam and Eve from the Garden. This is the first indication of how God interacts with His people during their failures. Adam and Eve severed the free relation that God established, thereby ending their true personhood; that is, their intimate and ontological status of being constituted as persons-in-relation with God. Athanasius describes the fall as follows:

> For if, out of a former normal state of non-existence, they were called into being by the Presence and loving-kindness of the Word, it followed naturally that when men were bereft of the knowledge of God and were turned back to what was not (for what is evil is not, but what is good is), they should, since they derive their being from God who IS, be everlastingly bereft even of being;[235]

---

[234] Weber, 523.

[235] Athanasius of Alexandria, *On the Incarnation of the Word*, ed. Philip Schaff and Henry Wace, trans., Archibald T. Robertson, *A Select Library of the Nicene and Post-Nicene Fathers of the Christian Church*, vol. IV (New York: Christian Literature Company, 1892), par. 5.

Athanasius does not view the Fall as a moral or epistemological privation, for there is an ontological impact in the Fall. Since Adam and Eve did not instantly die, something else took place. Athanasius states they were deprived of knowledge of God; which is not an epistemological judgment but Athanasius' way of expressing a loss of their "relationship" with God. What died was the full "person," when personhood is defined according to the relational model that we have adopted in this paper. God elected and called forth creation to be in relation to Himself, and when the human creature responded with a "no" to God's "Yes," God allowed the relationship to be severed. But the severed relationship is an eschatological severing, for God's ultimate goal for creation is to be in relation with Him. But more on this later. For now the question is: how does the lesson from the Fall help us identify the strategy that God enacts to deal with His people's failure?

The Law of Moses is replete with commands for expelling from the Israelite community, one who is found ritually unclean as defined in the Law (Gen. 17:14; Exod. 12:15, 19; 30:33; Lev. 13:46; Num. 5:1–4; 12:14; 31:19, etc.). The purpose of the temporary excommunication is to maintain the covenantal status between God and His people by removing the thing (or in this case, the person) that is causing the disruption. Without going into a detailed exegesis of the Mosaic Law, or the historiographical issues of interpretation and use of the Pentateuch, very few would argue against the idea that God uses a form of excommunication within the Law. Throughout the history of Israel, the Old Testament indicates that God used other nations—especially the Assyrians, Babylonians, and the Persians—to effectively scatter His people. Since Israel as a community is the people of God, this scattering of Israel serves as an ontological disruption of the relationship between God and His people. Israel no longer existed in a proper relationship with God, thereby losing their proper ontological personhood status; in essence, they were dying. God dealt with His community by allowing them to experience a lack of true humanity—a lack of full personhood—if being a true human is defined by our model of persons-in-relation with the triune God.

If God dealt with His people using excommunication, or severing of the relation, we would expect to see the same theological practice in the New Testament. It does appear that in the new community of faith—the church—that God does indeed deal with His people through types of excommunication and a breakdown of relations; we see these as changes in the ontological status of the believer or the community. A few examples from the scriptures demonstrate this. Later, we will review the purpose for severing the relation, thereby, changing the ontological status of the person or community.

a. Matthew 18:17 "treat him as you would a pagan or a tax collector."

Jesus instructs his followers in the method of church discipline that will take place in the new community. One commentator says that, "to treat a person as a 'pagan or a tax collector' means to treat him or her as unredeemed and outside the Christian community."[236] Treating this person as unredeemed means that he/she has lost the true ontological status that comes with being-in-relation with God through the body of Jesus Christ, a status constituted by the Spirit. Not only has the person's status changed, but the relations are no longer intact; the person is no longer orientated to God through Jesus Christ.

b. 1 Corinthians 5:1–5 "hand this man over to Satan, so that the sinful nature may be destroyed"

In his letter to the Corinthian church, Paul engages in an issue of grave importance to the life of the community. Without going into detail regarding the theories behind the identity of the person, the central idea for our purposes is the relaxed nature of the church itself. Paul says that instead of being horrified, the Corinthian church is actually "proud." Gordon Fee says, "Whatever the actual relationship of their pride to the incest, it has blinded them both to the fallen brother's true condition and to their own."[237] The true condition of the community is an impaired relationship with their Creator, and in turn with themselves. The prideful state of the community indicates their struggles with their new-found liberty in Christ and their old conduct as a member of the Corinthian community. The theology of Paul is consistent with the theology of the Old Testament scriptures in that the new community deals with struggles through expulsion. Paul

---

[236] Craig Blomberg, *Matthew, The New American Commentary* (Nashville: Broadman Press, 2001), 279.

[237] Gordon D. Fee, *The First Epistle to the Corinthians, The New International Commentary on the New Testament* (Grand Rapids: Eerdmans, 1987), 202.

mentions in 1 Corinthians 5:2, 4–5, 7, and 13 that the church should expel the immoral person. The theological connection for Paul is found in verse 5:13: "Expel the wicked man from among you." Paul connects Deuteronomy to the current situation. Paul also tells his congregation that when they are assembled in the "name of the Lord" that the "power of the Lord is present," and this is the time when this person is to be handed over to Satan. By invoking the "name of the Lord," Paul is locating the authority of excommunication in Jesus Christ Himself. Based on our relational model, the community's personhood is affected by the impaired relationship which the sin of the individual has created. It is not only the sin itself, but the community's lack of concern which has changed its relational orientation towards the teaching of Christ. The Holy Spirit is no longer ruling the community. Rather, outside forces are ruling the community, which if allowed to continue will eventually damage the community as a whole. Collins says that "the purity of the community is Paul's primary concern. Paul urged the community to act as he did because it was the temple of God."[238] By expelling the individual, the ontological orientation has changed; the individual has lost his true self, because his personhood as otherness-in-relation has changed in relation to God, to Jesus Christ through the Holy Spirit, and also in relation to the local church.

c. Titus 3:10 "Do not associate with him…"

In this passage, instead of the usual banishments due to an egregious sin, the attitude of the person is the impetus for Paul's exhortation. Paul lists a series of offenses (foolish controversies, genealogies, arguments and quarrels about the law) prior to his command of excommunication as the reason for his pronouncement. These problems are not of a sexual nature or egregious sins obvious even to pagan communities. For Paul, these heretics or separatists are false teachers who are forming "dissident groups, thus dividing the body of Christ."[239] Paul included instructions that the church should

---

[238] Raymond F. Collins, *First Corinthians*, Sacra Pagina Series (Collegeville, Minn.: The Liturgical Press, 1999), 208.

[239] John Norman Davidson Kelly, *A Commentary on the Pastoral Epistles: I Timothy, II Timothy, Titus*, ed. Henry Chadwick, *Black's New Testament Commentaries* (London: A. & C. Black, 1986), 256.

give the individual repeated warnings as an indication that the community is involved in the problem. The problem is not simply an individualistic inner struggle. No, the entire community is involved due to the relational make-up of the body of Christ, even to the ontological level which is at the core of Christians' personhood. So, in keeping with the teachings from the Old Testament, and the teaching on discipline from Christ himself, Paul follows the same theological trajectory by injecting excommunication. Again, God deals with the struggles of His people through relational disconnects, which in turn, changes the ontological constitution of the person.

There are other passages, such as 2 John 10 and Romans 16:17, which indicate that those who are causing division or bringing non-Christian conduct within the community should be dealt with via excommunication. Again, the purpose of excommunication is not simply for punitive justice to force a change the person's behavior. Importantly, and part of the major message of this paper, if the person does *not* change or repent, then the excommunication *changes* the person: the person is no longer living *in* the Spirit.

This means that even on a larger scale God wrestles with His people's failure through relational means, and often with an expulsion from the community of faith. We have seen at various points in Church history, from the early church councils of Nicaea to Constantinople, from Luther at Worms to the Synod of Dort, that as the church struggles with doctrine, or other failures, separation takes place. In other words, God, through His divine providence and absolute knowledge, allows certain types of excommunications to take place so that the relational status of the church changes, and, indeed, so the relational status of individuals change. In many cases, the change results in the loss of the true person because the onto-relation status has changed. The same is true of the community; the community is no longer the "people of God" because they have severed themselves from the presence of the living Christ by denying the urging and mediation of the Holy Spirit. This takes place when those in the community give priority to other teachings instead of grounding their authority in the true Word. So instead of allowing the community to maintain this false existence, God allows the community to continue in their choice, but their choice comes with the consequence of no longer being in a relation with Him.

Again, as we will see, the purpose of God in severing the relationship with His people, thereby changing their ontological status, is not simply punitive, it is also eschatological. God wrestles with His people through expulsion so that they can be restored back to Him in a full and complete relationship, a relationship which returns them to their true ontological being.

2. Reconciliation through Relational Recovery: Restoration of the Person

One recurring theme found within the Old Testament prophets is restoration. One of the great restoration passages in the Bible is Ezekiel 37:5: "Thus says the Lord GOD to these bones, 'Behold, I will cause breath to enter you that you may come to life'" (NASB). God does not sever the relationship for punitive purposes alone, but as part of His eschatological goal—God's *telos* for creation is communion with Him through restoration of life and for eternal life. From Adam, to the Law and through the exile of the Israelites, God promised restoration. As any reader of the Old Testament can attest, the Psalms, Lamentations, and the Books of the Prophets offer copious examples of Israel crying to God, yearning for restoration of the relationship with Him. The Holy Spirit allowed the Israelites to experience life without God through the broken relationship, that is, an excommunication from God. That experience caused a breach in their ontological nature and creates a yearning for their true selves, a yearning which could only be fulfilled by divine action. Since God called forth humanity *ex nihilo*, only God can recreate true humanity by restoring the persons-in-relation—a proper relation with *the Other*—with God in Christ.

The same is true in the new community—the church as the body of Christ—where expulsion or excommunication takes place in order to restore the individual and the community. In the passages listed above, there is a sense that the purpose of the punishment is restoration. We see that in Matthew 18:17, Jesus' command to treat the individual as a tax collector "remains rehabilitative rather than retributive in design."[240] Also, notice the eschatological tone of Paul's reason for expelling the sinful individual: "so that the sinful nature

---

[240] Blomberg, 279.

may be destroyed and his spirit saved on the day of the Lord" (1 Cor. 5:5). Theologically speaking, Paul is instructing the church to excommunicate the person so that the "flesh" can give way to the "spirit." Ontologically, that person who is out of relationship with God and headed for destruction is being eliminated; but a new person is being re-created in the Spirit by returning to a proper relationship with God through His community.[241]

Based on the ontology of relation model of this paper, God excommunicates the person or the community, so that through the change in ontology, that is, change in the relations, the person or community will recognize their new, but deadly, nature. Paul says in 2 Thessalonians 3:14–15 that the purpose of disassociation with the disobedient person is in order that he may feel ashamed. Yet do not regard him as an enemy but warn him as a brother. The person whose nature has changed, or whose personhood has changed from life to death, will hopefully regain their connection with the urgings of the Holy Spirit and return to the community of faith. God will restore that person (or that community) by His Holy Spirit who is continually calling out to His lost people.

Conclusion

When the church struggles with failure, God wrestles with those failures by suffering the loss of the relationship, with the eschatological emphasis—and hope—of a complete and restored people. God continues to struggle with the failure of His human creatures by maintaining an ontological and epistemological distance—a hiddenness—so that His creatures can realize their lack of true life and respond to God's "Yes." God continues to pour out His Spirit through His Son on creation in order to redeem it from a non-existence due to its improper relation with the Father, Son, and Spirit. In this way, God has expelled the entire creation with an eschatological view toward redemption and restoration of the true life, which is creation's intended destiny. The church is the community of

---

[241] Raymond F. Collins says, "'Flesh' (*sarx*) and 'spirit' (*pneuma*) are among the more important of Paul's anthropological terms but these terms do not refer to parts of a human being as they would in a Hellenistic anthropology. Rather they refer to aspects or orientations of a person or community. Paul's anthropological dualism is not philosophical; it is soteriological.... Paul's perspective is that of the community." Collins, *First Corinthians, Sacra Pagina Series* (1999), 213.

faith where we see the expression of the eschatological anticipation of Christ's Lordship. The Holy Spirit is the agent who is bringing about this communion, this perfection of creation as the church returns to the Father through the Son in the power of the Spirit to a state of a perfected relationship with God. God wrestles with His people by sending the Holy Spirit as a down payment in anticipation of future glory with Christ. Humanity's "No," becomes God's "Yes" through the death of the old ontology and the renewal towards the new ontology of being-in-communion, a communion with the perfect communion of the Father, Son, and Holy Spirit.

6.
Irrevocable Nature of Salvation as a Basis for Trusting God with the Daily Affairs of Life
by Rev. Christopher D. Surber
Pastor, First Congregational Church, Peru, Illinois
Founder and Exec. Director, Supply and Multiply
Montrouis, Haiti[242]

Introduction—Necessity of the Practical in Theology 111
A. Practice of the Doctrine of Eternal Security 112
    1. Theological Foundations of Eternal Security 112
    2. God's Work in Salvation 113
    3. God's Purpose in Salvation 118
    4. A Workable Understanding of Personal Sin.. 121
    5. A Workable Understanding of Grace and Works.. 123
B. A Word of Caution 125
Conclusion 125

Introduction—Necessity of the Practical in Theology

Evidence abounds of the fall of man into sin. My life's work and calling from God is to spiritually lead a local church. In that capacity I am a shepherd and a practical theologian, though the distinction *practical* as theologian is somewhat unneeded. All theology is validated by the extent to which it is practical; that is, the extent to which it may be applied in the lives of Christians.

Theology must be proven valid in the context of the day-to-day experience of imperfect people living in a fallen world. Everyday followers of Jesus Christ are the true examiners of theoretical theological doctrines. Practitioners of Christian truths apply the litmus test of life to doctrines expounded from the Scriptures, which are developed within the context of the ivory-tower scrutiny of logic and academic endeavor.

The purest test of the validity of a biblical doctrine is not that it passes the test of syllogism or the rigorous examination of the minds of the doctors of the church. If a doctrine, belief, or standard of

---

[242] Supply and Multiply is a mission of the gospel of Christ and resources to Montrouis, Haiti, all to glorify "God in Haiti": www.SupplyandMultiply.com.

Christian theological understanding is not able to pass the test of the daily experience of the believer, then its truth value must be questioned. Such an assertion is not intended as an argument in favor of pure pragmaticism. It is the biblical assertion that revealed truth has been revealed for a *purpose*.

God's activity in this world and in the lives of individuals is not without aim or definition. In the formal study of systematic theology, practical theology is often relegated to a position of academic inferiority, as though practical theology is a lesser discipline than pure theology.

All theology is practical, because the highest aim of theological endeavor is not the production of philosophical dialogue—in and of itself—but the transforming of Christian men and women to be increasingly more confident and obedient in Christ. Theological pursuits that are not inherently beneficial for Christian discipleship or that do not speak to those practical pursuits which benefit the Christian's life become utterly useless. So, it is toward the *practice* of the doctrine of eternal security that we turn our attention.

A. Practice of the Doctrine of Eternal Security

1. Theological Foundations of Eternal Security

Before we can begin a discussion of the irrevocable nature of salvation as a basis for trusting God with the daily affairs of life, we must first establish at least a cursory biblical criteria for what we mean by eternal security and its biblical and theological foundations. The doctrine of eternal security and those doctrines directly related to it are, above all, pastoral doctrines. God has revealed these truths in the Bible so that His children may know the extent and depth of His love for them. These doctrines are intensely practical.

For the purpose of this essay I will limit my preliminary discussion to a succinct explanation of the connection between divine foreknowledge and election as a theological foundation for the eternal security of the believer.

It has been stated that a man cannot lose that which he cannot earn. It is impossible to adequately discuss the practical application of the doctrine of eternal security without a clear definition of why Christians are eternally secure. We must understand the nature of salvation. Sadly, a lack of clear understanding of the nature of salvation disallows many Christians from enjoying the practical daily benefits that come from knowing and applying personal knowledge of the irrevocable nature of salvation.

It is God who saves. Regardless of one's theological persuasion with regard to the nature of the sovereignty of God and the role of God's sovereignty in salvation, serious students of the Bible must concede at least this statement: *Man is the recipient of salvation.* We are saved not merely from something, as from an eternity apart from God, but we are also saved *unto* a life of growing dependence and obedience to God.

God is active in salvation. Salvation is the consequence of God's saving action. Indeed, God works through the faith of the individual receiving His gift. However, faith is an *instrument* of salvation, not the *means*. God saves men and women in Christ. The Holy Spirit draws them to repentance unto salvation. They receive salvation by faith and are born again.

If God reigns supreme in the universe, His plans cannot be thwarted, and salvation is the consequence of His plan and supreme action; it follows that salvation is irrevocable. While we may quibble over the details of the precise nature of divine foreknowledge, election, saving faith, and other related matters, when the nature of salvation is understood as the noncontingent sovereign act of God, then it necessarily follows that salvation is irrevocable. No man or woman may, through wrong activity or blatant inactivity, lose a salvation that was utterly nondependent upon their own action or inaction to begin with.

Salvation is the gift of God. It cannot be earned. Therefore, it cannot be lost. Contrary to the position of some, when this is properly understood and applied as a foundation for the daily lives of Christians, it does not produce slothfulness in righteousness and good works. When applied biblically, this doctrine produces internally secure believers who are able to approach daily life knowing that salvation is God's work, who live out God's purpose in salvation, who have a tenable understanding of personal sin, and who are able to produce good works as a consequence of grace rather than in an effort to attain favor with God.

2. God's Work in Salvation

Our lives are thematically shaped by vast collections of individual moments. Human lives are not given definition by a summary of explanation at the end of life. No eulogy has ever captured even a fraction of the essence of a person's life. Moment by moment our lives are defined, and until believers learn to reside, abide in, and dwell in the satisfying knowledge of the vast implications of the irrevocable nature of salvation, they will not find the peace that is available in each moment in Christ.

The notion that salvation is revocable has the potential of creating or at least exacerbating anxiety in the spiritual life of the follower of Jesus. Confidence in one's salvation is greatly diminished within the context of a system of Christian understanding that neglects, ignores, or rejects the irrevocable nature of salvation. Biblical anthropology clearly identifies the fallen nature of man and his inability to reconcile himself to God. If salvation is revocable and somehow dependent upon humans in any way, there is little hope for genuine internal peace in the life of any believer.

As long as there is the remotest possibility that the saved person could ever be lost, to that extent the door is opened for anxiety. As long as you entertain the possibility that, somehow or somewhere, you could sin so that you sever your relationship with God and risk being sent to hell, you cannot have perfect peace. The whole time you are talking to God you are aware that the same God you are talking to will not be on speaking terms with you should you displease Him. Therefore, at bottom when you are talking to Him, you are aware that you hold the cards, as it were. It is ultimately up to you.[243]

Man has no ability to save himself. Prior to the time of conversion, each person is spiritually dead and lost in their sinful condition. "As for you, you were dead in your transgressions and sins" (Eph. 2:1). The notion that man has any part to play in salvation, other than that of receiving the gift of it, is a spiritual principal that is guaranteed to be a source of anxiety, pride, and spiritual uproar. Confidence in Christ is the outgrowth of an understanding of what Christ has done and is doing in the lives of believers.

---

[243] R. T. Kendall, *Once Saved, Always Saved* (Waynesboro, GA: Authentic Media, 2005), 33.

> God demonstrates his own love for us in this: while we were still sinners, Christ died for us. Since we have now been justified by his blood, how much more shall we be saved from God's wrath through him! (Rom. 5:8–9).

Present-tense trust in God, though, is rooted in more than merely the knowledge of what God has done for us in Christ. Confidence is associated more with action than with knowledge. It is not merely the byproduct of something *known*, but something known *and applied*. A runner who learns proper technique but never spends any time on the racetrack will never know what it means to have confidence in his running. It is in the application of his learned and honed technique that confidence grows. A man is not a boxer who has merely watched thousands of hours of boxing film so that he is able to recount all of the best skill of the greatest prize fighters in history and has never stepped inside a ring. He is merely an observer.

God is active in the lives of believers. He is actively reshaping them into the image of His Son. While there is a point in time when God—working through our faith—saves us in His Son, the total process of salvation and of sanctification is the work of God. They are intrinsically connected in that they are the method of God restoring His image in the elect. Application knowledge of this aspect of biblical truth is crucial to having confidence in the here and now— the present-tense boxing ring of life. Confidence in Jesus Christ and willingness to trust God in the daily affairs of life grow out of the knowledge gained from experiencing and observing the personal transformation that comes as God reshapes us into the image of Christ, restoring the *Imago Dei*. What happens in the daily affairs of this life is the product or byproduct of God's shaping us into the image of His Son.

Humanity is God's special creation. "Then God said, 'Let us make man in our image, in our likeness, and let them rule over the fish of the sea and the birds of the air, over the livestock, over all the earth, and over all the creatures that move along the ground'" (Gen. 1:26). Mankind has a unique place and role in God's economy of creation. Humanity was made in the image of God, and the central theme of God's work or aim in salvation is the restoration of that image in man. We see reflected in the person of Jesus Christ the fullness of the image of God and something of the ideal of the image of God in man.

In John 14:9, John records that Jesus said,

> Don't you know me, Philip, even after I have been among you such a long time? Anyone who has seen me has seen the Father. How can you say, "Show us the Father"?

Jesus is the perfect image of God. In Christ we see the perfection of the *Imago Dei*. This does not relegate Jesus to a status of mere divine messenger. Indeed, He is divine. This points to the manner in which God is at work restoring His image in believers. "The god of this age has blinded the minds of unbelievers, so that they cannot see the light of the gospel of the glory of Christ, who is the image of God" (2 Cor. 4:4). Christ is the perfect image of God, and God is working in the lives of believers to transform them into the image of Christ, who is the image of God.

Salvation is the act of God in restoring His image in us through Christ, who is His perfect image that was lost in the fall. The full range of meaning and nuance of application that this truth entails is impossible to give with a many lifetimes of books, much less in this paper. Suffice here to say that man was created in God's image, with a full range of creative, moral, and spiritual qualities and abilities. Through man's fall into sin, these qualities were disrupted but not destroyed. Gardoski puts it like this:

> God gave of his divine 'life-breath' to man alone. This not only made man a living and breathing creature, but also a thinking, speaking, volitional, moral, and spiritual being. These aspects of God's own nature which God granted to man at creation constitute the *Imago Dei*.[244]

Paul said in his letter to the Romans, "For those God foreknew he also predestined to be conformed to the likeness of his Son, that he might be the firstborn among many brothers" (Rom. 8:29). In his letter to the church at Corinth he wrote, "And we, who with unveiled faces all reflect the Lord's glory, are being transformed into his likeness with ever-increasing glory, which comes from the Lord, who is the Spirit" (2 Cor. 3:18). A central aspect of God's work in redemption through Christ is the restoration of these qualities. Redeemed men and women who have received Christ by faith, according to God's grace, are being *re-created*.

---

[244] Kenneth M. Gardoski, "The Imago Dei Revisited," *The Journal of Ministry and Theology* 11–12, no. 5–37 (fall 2007).

This is not to suggest that salvation is an ongoing process. There is a point in time when men believe, receive Christ, and are saved. At the initial point of salvation men completely change their positional relationship with God. They are no longer at enmity with God. They are in Christ, and the wall of separation between God and men has been demolished through faith, according to God's grace.

> For he himself is our peace, who has made the two one and has destroyed the barrier, the dividing wall of hostility, by abolishing in his flesh the law with its commandments and regulations. His purpose was to create in himself one new man out of the two, thus making peace, and in this one body to reconcile both of them to God through the cross, by which he put to death their hostility. (Eph. 2:14–16)

The process of the restoration of God's image in man is not something that must be completed in order to receive salvation. This process is not a box that must be checked in order to gain entrance into heaven. It is the broader purpose of salvation. The process of restoration is the ultimate aim of salvation as it relates to the human composition. This is the matter of *propositional* transformation of the believer. When taken into consideration, it is potentially a tremendous source of daily confidence in God.

The Lord Most High is at work re-creating His perfect image in believers who are the elect. Salvation is irrevocable because it is the labor of God. One aspect of that labor is that God is in fact working to restore His perfect image in us. As believers see themselves being transformed, confidence in Christ grows, as does the willingness and ability to trust God in the daily affairs of life.

Confidences in living the Christian life increases as believers interact with the world and with God in the manner in which they understand themselves changed toward an increasingly reflection of the image of God reflected in Christ. I am convinced that the apostle Paul was alluding to something similar when he wrote, "Therefore I glory in Christ Jesus in my service to God" (Rom. 15:17). Our ability to glory in God is intrinsically connected to our experiential knowledge of God and the spiritual transformation that is occurring within our own lives. This comes in the form of a "mystical" connection to God through the Holy Spirit. It also comes through the evidence of observable transformation in propositional terms.

In the epistle of James, the Bible records the following:

> In the same way, faith by itself, if it is not accompanied by action, is dead. But someone will say, 'You have faith; I have deeds.' Show me your faith without deeds, and I will show you my faith by what I do. (James 2:17–18).

Remembering that faith is the instrument of the receipt of grace and not the means of grace itself, it may be stated that the evidence of the faith spoken of in James is the evidence of God's grace working through faith in the life of a believer. If there is no observable change—change toward an increase in reflecting the image of God in Christ—one must not question God's faithfulness to transform but question the individual's faithfulness to participate in the process of transformation.

This line of reasoning begs a discussion of the difference between grace and works-based salvation. Good works are the evidence of salvation; in no way are they the means of salvation. We will address that topic in the final portion of the body of this essay. The point here is related though with a slight difference.

God is restoring His image in us. Many believers live as though they are preparing themselves for heaven. The reality is that we are free in the process of transformation, sanctification, and holiness. God is restoring His image in us. The work is His. He most often uses the events that are allowed or purposed in the lives of believers in order to shape and transform us.

Followers of Jesus are free to trust God in the daily circumstances of life, whatever they may be, because God's primary work in every instance, every moment, every single breath we take that He gives us, all comes together as the work of a sculptor who chisels away at a stone, creating a masterpiece. God's tools in this present life are events, trials, joys, struggles, heartache, and rejoicing. All of these things are used by God, either by design or allowance, to shape believers into the image of Christ—to restore His perfect image in His children.

> And we know that in all things God works for the good of those who love him, who have been called according to his purpose. For those God foreknew he also predestined to be conformed to the likeness of his Son, that he might be the firstborn among many brothers. (Rom. 8:28–29).

3. God's Purpose in Salvation

For what purpose did God send His Son to die for humanity? When asked this question, most well-intentioned Christians, having been schooled in a "me-centered" modern church culture, are likely to answer something like "to save sinners." Or they may answer more specifically, "So that we can get to heaven." While salvation does bring with it these and other personal benefits, Jesus' death on the cross had much more to do with God than it does with humanity. Just prior to His journey to the cross, Jesus said, "Now is the Son of Man glorified and God is glorified in him. If God is glorified in him, God will glorify the Son in himself, and will glorify him at once" (John 13:31–32).

Jesus' death on the cross does provide atonement for our sin, but God's purpose in salvation is not primarily our good. His purpose in salvation is essentially to glorify Himself through Christ and ultimately in us. Salvation is irrevocable because it is the act of God bringing glory to Himself through the cross. We are recipients of His grace and instruments of His glory. As such, we are free to delight in His worth as His children and give ourselves over completely to trust in Him.

In the Romans 10:3–4, Paul said,

> Since they did not know the righteousness that comes from God and sought to establish their own, they did not submit to God's righteousness. Christ is the end of the law so that there may be righteousness for everyone who believes.

God's purpose in salvation includes sinful mankind, but the emphasis of salvation is Christ, and its highest aim is the glorification of God. This notion flies in the face of modern constructs of evangelical practice and the most common articulations of the gospel.

Christ did die to save sinners. But that statement is incomplete. Sinners are saved when they receive Christ by faith in order that God's glory may be put on display when the nations of the earth are gathered to sing His praises. Righteousness is extended, as the apostle writes above, to everyone who believes. But the purpose of the righteousness that covers and indwells regenerate men and women is meant to translate them from unrepentant sinners who scoff at God's glory into spiritually reborn saints who glorify God.

This is not to say that man's happiness, joy, security, or peace are not an integral part of the plan of God in salvation. It is only to say that the highest aim of salvation is the glorification of God, and this brings with it the highest state of man. Ultimate happiness, joy, security, and peace within man result of his living in a state of union with and glorification of God. John Piper says, "The key to the coherence between passion for God's glory and compassion for perishing man is that rejoicing in God himself, through Christ, glorifies God."[245]

When salvation is viewed through this lens, from this more completely theocentric perspective, we find a basis for trust in God even in seemingly mundane affairs. Every aspect of every moment of life becomes an opportunity to glorify God. The burden of each moment becomes an opportunity to rest in the strength of God. Anxiety and performance-based pseudo-religion vanish, and we become free to bask in His glory, fully convinced of His grace working in us!

We pervert the gospel when we arrogantly assume that Christ died in order to magnify *our* worth and to increase *our* pleasure. Many believers fail to find a practical basis for trusting God in the daily affairs of life, because they invert God's purpose in salvation. When anyone makes humanity central in God's plan of salvation, they rob themselves of the highest aim of salvation and consequently rob themselves of its chief benefit. As believers glorify God, they *participate* in the present outworking of His glory, and in that participation, they find the peace, joy, and satisfaction that their hearts so desperately long for.

We ascribe to God glory. He blesses us with fulfillment.

If God's ultimate aim is my pleasure, I become the object of His love after the manner of a doting father, fanning the flames of my vanity. My value is fleeting and tarnished at best. It is not a worthy foundation for trusting God.

God's worth is an infinitely more valid premise for trust, and God's work in salvation is the gathering of people to celebrate His worth. All that occurs in life happens either by design or allowance from the sovereign hand of God in order to draw us into a place of deeper trust, increased commitment, and growing dependence upon God—so that His glory can be expressed in us more completely. He is the object of salvation.

---

[245] John Piper, *Let the Nations Be Glad!* (Grand Rapids, MI: Baker Academics, 1993), 212.

God's purpose in salvation is to express His own glory, and believers get to participate in the expression of His glory. "And we, who with unveiled faces all reflect the Lord's glory, are being transformed into his likeness with ever-increasing glory, which comes from the Lord, who is the Spirit" (2 Cor. 3:18). We can trust Him in all things because we are His. In trials we can trust that He is working out His purpose in us. "Endure hardship as discipline; God is treating you as sons. For what son is not disciplined by his father?" (Heb. 12:7).

4. A Workable Understanding of Personal Sin

Even after a sinner has been reconciled to God through faith, he or she will continue to come up short in matters of personal holiness. God is actively restoring His image in believers. He is shaping His children into sanctified vessels of worship. He is putting His glory on display in and through believers.

Personal sin in the life of the believer is a reality. "If we claim to be without sin, we deceive ourselves and the truth is not in us" (1 John 1:8). While the argument is sometimes made that this passage refers to the life of the unregenerate sinner prior to the time of conversion, the context doesn't necessitate such an interpretation, nor does the weight of biblical data. The apostle Paul, at a time in his life when he was plainly a believer, wrote:

> What a wretched man I am! Who will rescue me from this body of death? Thanks be to God—through Jesus Christ our Lord! So then, I myself in my mind am a slave to God's law, but in the sinful nature a slave to the law of sin. (Rom. 7:24–25).

While the argument is sometimes made that Paul wrote in a hyperbolic or euphemistic fashion; again, the context does not necessitate or even strongly imply that he is doing so. The weight of biblical data supports the reality that believers continue to struggle with sin after the time of conversation and regeneration. The day-to-day experience of believers bears this out. Humans fail to maintain a consistent, authentically holy lifestyle. The reality of sin in the life of the believer necessitates the development of a basis for trust in God in light of sin in the life of the believer.

Any system of biblical theology that fails to deal adequately with the fact of God's purpose in salvation (to glorify Himself), God's work in salvation (to restore His image in believers), and the presence of sin in the life of believers is inadequate. God is glorifying Himself in humans through salvation in spite of past, present, or future sin. God is restoring His image in humans because of their inability to maintain that image in any sense. The presence of sin in a believer's life is not abhorrent to the security of their salvation, nor must it be a roadblock to their ability to trust in God.

God saves men and women in spite of past sin. How can present sin affect one's eternal security? Yet anxiety over present sin is often the cause of a diminished capacity of trust in God in the life of the follower of Jesus. Since the work of salvation is solely the work of God, believers are eternally secure. And to the extent that they recognize that they are eternally secure, they will be able to maintain a life of growing dependence on God in the day-to-day affairs of life.

Believers have been plucked out of the world, but much of the world remains in them. While they are positionally holy—that is, set apart for God's usage and service—they remain surrounded by and inundated with temptation to sin and with sin itself. In no instance does the Bible state or imply that believers are free to give into sin. Through the inspiration of the Holy Spirit, the apostle Paul writes,

> What shall we say, then? Shall we go on sinning so that grace may increase? By no means! We died to sin; how can we live in it any longer?" (Rom. 6:1–2).

Followers of Jesus are being transformed by God into the image of Christ. Jesus lived a purely holy life. We are not free to commit sin with no conscience. However, we are freed to trust God with our sin in Christ who soothes our conscience. We are free in Christ to rest in the security of our salvation, trusting God in the daily affairs of life, knowing that while we are utterly unworthy, we are covered by His grace, indwelt by His Spirit, and guided by His sovereign will.

God even uses our sins and mistakes through His redemptive plan. He does not cause or tempt anyone to sin. But when we do, if we are contrite and confess our sin, He uses our brokenness to crush our pride so that He may reign more completely and be glorified more wholly in our lives.

A workable understanding of personal sin is derived from a right understanding of what sin does in the believer's life. There are those who say that sin blocks our connection to God. In what way can this conclusion be derived from Scripture? Sin blocked our access to God prior to conversion, as we were cut off from the knowledge of God.

However, the Bible tells us that "if we confess our sins, he is faithful and just and will forgive us our sins and purify us from all unrighteousness" (1 John 1:9).

For unbelievers there is an initial entrance into the kingdom, which comes at the point of salvation and regeneration. For believers there is an ongoing process of sin, conviction by the Holy Spirit, repentance, forgiveness, and cleansing. This process is an upward cycle. The more we yield to God and experience His forgiveness, grace, and cleansing from sin, the less we will need it. This is where the life of submission to God and His work of restoring His image in believers intersect. The more yielded we are to His work in us, purely as recipients of His grace, the more evidence of His transformative power will be seen in our lives.

The more evident His work becomes in our lives, the more highly evident His trustworthiness becomes. In Hebrews 2:18 the Bible says of Christ, "Because he himself suffered when he was tempted, he is able to help those who are being tempted." We follow a Savior who is not foreign to our experience in this sin-inundated world. The Lord is faithful and just and will forgive the sins of believers (1 Cor. 1:9). God is trustworthy in the sinful and imperfect affairs of the daily lives of all believers.

5. A Workable Understanding of Grace and Works

When salvation is understood as the objective work of God in believers, a basis for trust in God emerges. We are able to view salvation as the work of God alone. Faith becomes a part of the work of God in salvation; His grace is the means. Good works and righteousness are understood as the consequence of the work of God restoring His image in us, and present peace is the immediate consequence. Salvation is the objective work of God of restoring the *Imago Dei*, His image, in the elect. When understood along these terms, a completely theocentric soteriology emerges.

Eternal security means that I am not merely working to please God. We are His creation and He is recreating us in Jesus Christ. Our good efforts and work on behalf of His glory and His kingdom are love offerings to the God who has saved us in spite of ourselves.

Good works often become a sort of counterfeit trust. Believers convince themselves that they trust God as evidenced by all they do for God. This is an imitated form of trust, a forged, inadequate version of trust. There is a radical difference between trust and obedience versus insecurity and working to garner favor.

In Matthew 7:21–23, Jesus said,

> Not everyone who says to me, "Lord, Lord," will enter the kingdom of heaven, but only he who does the will of my Father who is in heaven. Many will say to me on that day, "Lord, Lord, did we not prophesy in your name, and in your name drive out demons and perform many miracles?" Then I will tell them plainly, "I never knew you. Away from me, you evildoers!"

Apparently right action does not necessarily equate to right belief. While the preceding verses do inform us that a way to know a tree is by its fruits, these verses plainly give us the parallel truth that right action often flows from impure motives.

Good works are the consequence of faith, not the means. This is abundantly clear from Scripture. "For it is by grace you have been saved, through faith—and this not from yourselves, it is the gift of God—not by works, so that no one can boast" (Eph. 2:8–9). When believers reside in the reality that good works are the outgrowth of grace working through faith, they are enabled to trust God in their daily tasks, as God has assigned them.

It is common for a sinner to come to Christ by faith and trade in a set of worldly addictions for a set of slightly more sanctified addictions. But is a relationship of trust in Him established by attending every worship service at the local church? Is the Lord pleased when a believer volunteers for every possible committee, board, or project in their local church? In a familiar yet seldom applied passage in the gospels, Jesus says,

> Come to me, all you who are weary and burdened, and I will give you rest. Take my yoke upon you and learn from me, for I am gentle and humble in heart, and you will find rest for your souls. For my yoke is easy and my burden is light. (Mt. 11:28–30).

The test of trust in God is not the amount of good works done. It is the degree to which the believer's heart and mind are secure in the promises of God. The tallest of giants in the faith are not necessarily those who have *done* the most. They are those *in whom* the most has been done. Trusting God in the daily affairs of life is ultimately about resting in His comfort and trusting in His provision for the daily affairs of life. Trust is something to be grasped by the *mind*, enjoyed in the *heart*, and lived out in the *here and now*.

B. A Word of Caution

In embracing a thoroughly theocentric view of salvation as described above and adapting the supremacy of God's role in salvation as a basis for trusting God in the daily affairs of life, there is a high degree of potentiality that a believer may spiritually drift into that most egregious of errors referred to as antinomianism. Briefly, antinomianism is "the doctrine that it is not necessary for Christians to preach or obey the moral law of the Old Testament."[246]

While the New Testament places the emphasis in salvation upon the work of God in humans, this does not contradict the moral teachings of the Old Testament. Biblical ethics must not be viewed as a means to securing favor with God or adding to salvation in any way. Proper life conduct is the right activity that follows the work of God in salvation. It is the natural consequence of the restoration of the *Imago Dei*. Moral law is not nullified by grace. Indeed, only through God's work in salvation and the subsequent process of the restoration of His image in believers are men and women enabled to fruitfully adhere to the ethical code and *spiritual* observance of the highest principals and aims of the Old Testament.

Speaking to the Pharisees, Jesus said, "Woe to you, teachers of the law and Pharisees, you hypocrites! You are like whitewashed tombs, which look beautiful on the outside but on the inside are full of dead men's bones and everything unclean" (Mt. 23:27). The grace of God that comes by faith enables genuinely righteous living. It does not nullify its need. "Do not think that I have come to abolish the Law or the Prophets; I have not come to abolish them but to fulfill them" (Mt. 5:17). As believers rest in grace, they are freed to walk in obedience.

Conclusion

All that occurs in this life happens either by the direct design or allowance of God. This means that everything in life, whether or not it is the perfect and pleasing will of God, is part of the plan of God to conform believers into the image of Christ. God actively uses all of the affairs of this life to transform believers as He works to restore His perfect image in us. This understanding of the revelation of God's will through the truth of Scripture provides a basis for trust in

---

[246] R. D. Linder, "Antinomianism," *Evangelical Dictionary of Theology*, 2nd ed., 2001.

God in the daily affairs of life, because everything that occurs happens according to His intention.

This life is not my own. My present circumstances are instruments of God's ultimate plan for my life.

> Praise be to the God and Father of our Lord Jesus Christ, who has blessed us in the heavenly realms with every spiritual blessing in Christ. He chose us in him before the creation of the world to be holy and blameless in his sight. In love he predestined us to be adopted as his sons through Jesus Christ, in accordance with his pleasure and will—to the praise of his glorious grace, which he has freely given us in the One he loves. (Eph. 1:3–6).

You and I are free to trust Him and respond to His grace, correction, and will—all of which will fill us with confidence and peace. The basis for peace in this life is abiding in the knowledge of God's sovereignty in the universe and the world, in our salvation, and in all things, granting us an eternal security in His salvation.

7.
Pastoral Care Treasures in Prison and the Golden Hour
by Dr. Michael G. Maness
Ret. Senior Clinical Chaplain
Texas Department of Criminal Justice
Managing Editor, *Testamentum Imperium*[247]

A. Pastoral Care Most Needed in Prison 127
     * James V. Bennett Quotes 128
B. Pastoral Care's Vital Issues Aid Entire Prison Mission 130
     * Pastoral Care's Vital Issues 130
C. *Staff* Chaplains—Key to Optimum Level of Care 131
     * Texas Prison Staff Chaplain 2012 Statistics Shortlist 131
D. Hard Fight in 2011 to Preserve Pastoral Care in Prison 132
E. Religion—Greatest Source for Change and Solace in History 133
     * *Staff Chaplain Maxim* 133
F. Pastoral Care Profession in Prison vs. Hospital 135
G. Pastoral Care Facing Death and the Golden Hour 137

A. Pastoral Care Most Needed in Prison

"For where your treasure is, there your heart will be also," recorded Matthew in his Gospel (6:21). Christian pastoral care is needed in prison as air is needed to live: it is the highest form of sociability, the most humane interaction, the least related to the authoritative vagaries between the keeper and the kept, one of the greatest influences for honorable conduct, and in many other ways the very example of grace from the Christian chaplain and thousands of volunteers to the hurting souls in every corner of the prison.

Pastoral care is valued everywhere and has over the last century been detailed by many top theological professors and pastors and has

---

[247] Maness earned a D.Min. at NOBTS and a M.Div. at SWBTS, and is a retired senior clinical chaplain of Texas Department of Criminal Justice (20 years). He is the author of nine books and over 100 articles, including *How We Saved Texas Prison Chaplaincy 2011* (2015; www.PreciousHeart.net/Saved); *Ocean Devotions—From the Hold of Charles H. Spurgeon* (AuthorHouse, 2008); *Would You Lie To Save a Life?—A Theology on the Ethics of Love, Love Will Find a Way Home* (2007); and *Heaven—Treasures of Our Everlasting Rest* (2004). His domain, www.PreciousHeart.net, has over 10k links to resources over the world and hosts the largest collection of papers and data on prison chaplaincy in the world. He has been managing editor and publisher of *Testamentum Imperium* for most of its publication history, www.PreciousHeart.net/ti.

clear connections with the experts on empathy.[248] Every human being has a soul, a spirit, and spiritual needs. Divining between the psychological and spiritual, a potent concern in care, there is no end to refining research, theory, and skill—all in Christian love. As in law and medicine, and, because of its theological moorings and its dealings with unique human-to-human relationships, there will *never* be an end in refining one's skill in pastoral care.

Two penetrating quotes on the gargantuan and exceedingly complicated needs in prison come from James V. Bennett, director of the Federal Bureau of Prisons from 1937 to 1964, the FBOP fostering seismic changes toward more programming and with most states following suit in a variety of degrees. Bennett said,

> Society wants men to be taught to use
> liberty wisely while deprived of it.[249]

> I believe there is a treasure in the heart of every man
> if we can find it — if we can help him find it.
> I believe this is the true way to fight crime.[250]

* James V. Bennett Quotes

From the 1960s, research on in-prison programming skyrocketed, with several laboriously analyzing the studies themselves. Then Lipton and Martinson shocked all proving that "nothing worked." [251] Yet

---

[248] See www.PreciousHeart.net/Saved/Bibliography-Chaplaincy.pdf and a host of links.

Pastoral care: see Seward Hiltner's *Pastoral Counseling* (1949), one of the best who helped shape the meaning of pastoral care; Anton Boisen's *The Exploration of the Inner World* (1955), the undisputed beginning of clinical pastoral education, and *Religion in Crisis and Custom* (1955); William B. Oglesby's *Biblical Themes for Pastoral Care* (1980) and *Referral in Pastoral Counseling* (1978); Howard Clinebell's *Basic Types of Pastoral Care and Counseling Resources for the Ministry of Healing and Growth* (Yale University Press, 1983); and Charles Gerkin's *Living Human Document: Re-Visioning Pastoral Counseling in a Hermeneutical Mode* (1984). The list has no end.

Empathy: Carl Rogers' *Client Centered Therapy* (1951), for many the beginning of the "listening" schools of psychology; see also his *On Becoming a Person* (1951), *A Way of Being* (1980) and his classic definition, "Empathic: An Unappreciated Way of Being," *The Counseling Psychologist* 5 (1975): 2–10, and see www.PreciousHeart.net/Saved/Rogers-Empathy.pdf. Arnold P. Goldstein and Gerald Y. Michaels' *Empathy: Development, Training, and Consequences* (1985); Gerard Egan's *The Skilled Helper* (1st ed., 1980, now in 10th ed.); and Nancy Eisenberg and Janet Strayer's *Empathy and Its Development* (Cambridge University Press, 1987) represent a host on the skill and value of empathy.

[249] James V. Bennett, *I Chose Prison* (Alfred A. Knopf, 1970), 11.

[250] Ibid., 229, the last two sentences of book.

[251] In a 1974, Lipton, Martinson, and Wilks evaluated 231 studies of inmate treatment programs, Martinson declaring his now famous "nothing worked," concluding that one in three returned to crime no matter whether given psychotherapy, group counseling, job training, or no assistance at all. See D.

[Footnote continued on next page]

none of the 1,000s of studies and analyses of studies dealt with the prison chaplains' pastoral care or their religious facilitation.

Thomas P. O'Conner and Byron Johnson helped pave the way on the proving the impact of religion and Christianity on crime, prison, and human health, and *all* of their studies give many more rock-solid proofs of the value of staff chaplaincy services.[252] Complementing those are the massive Oxford and Routledge handbooks and more.[253]

Now then, if you are among the majority looking at prison from the outside, allow me to press a question. Do our healthy and courageous young men and women in the military *need* a chaplain? Sure, they do![254] Likewise, our fine free citizens in the hospitals of our great land need a chaplain. Then, not just for pity's sake but for society's sake, our most disturbed and rattled sons and daughters in our prisons need a chaplain who delivers quality pastoral care.[255] More than the well-funded FBOP, the state prison is the most interpersonally hostile environment legally constituted, a city under constant siege, with human dynamics unique unto itself. By law,

---

Lipton, R. Martinson, and J. Wilks, *The Effectiveness of Correctional Treatment: A Survey of Treatment Evaluation Studies* (New York: Praeger, 1975); and Robert J. Homant, "Ten Years After: A Follow-up of Therapy Effectiveness," *Journal of Offender Counseling, Services and Rehabilitation* 10 (Spring 1986): 51–57. See www.PreciousHeart.net/chaplaincy/Programming_History.htm for the chapter surveying the literature on in-prison programing in my doctoral dissertation in 1997.

[252] See Thomas P. O'Conner, "What Works: Religion as a Correctional Intervention: Part II." *Journal of Community Corrections* 14, no. 2 (Winter 2004–05); Byron R. Johnson, *More God, Less Crime* (2011); Johnson and David B. Larson, *The Inner-Change Freedom Initiative* (CRRUCS Report; 2003); and Sung Joon Jang, Byron R. Johnson, et al, "Prisoners Helping Prisoners Change: A Study of Inmate Field Ministers Within Texas Prisons," *International Journal of Offender Therapy and Comparative Criminology* (2019).

[253] Theo Gavielides, ed., *Routledge International Handbook of Restorative Justice* (Abingdon, UK; NY, NY: Routledge, 2018); Arjan Blokland and Victor van der Geest, eds., *Routledge International Handbook of Life-Course Criminology* (Routledge, 2017); and Michael Tonry, ed., *Oxford Handbook of Crime and Criminal Justice* (Oxford University Press, 2011).

[254] See www.PreciousHeart.net/chaplaincy/Army_Chaplaincy_History.htm for more the several huge volumes of the U.S. Army's fine chaplaincy corps: *From Its European Antecedents to 1791: The United States Army Chaplaincy* (Vol. 1, by Chaplain Parker C. Thompson;, 1978), *Struggling for Recognition: The United States Army Chaplaincy 1791–1865* (Vol. 2, by Chaplain Herman A. Norton, 1977), *Up From Handymen: The United States Army Chaplaincy 1865–1920* (Vol. 3, by Chaplain Earl F. Stover, 1977), *The Best and The Worst of Times: The United States Army Chaplaincy 1920–1945* (Vol. 4, by Chaplain Robert L. Gushwa, 1977), *Confidence in Battle, Inspiration in Peace: The United States Army Chaplaincy 1945–1975* (Vol. 5, by Chaplain Rodger R. Venzke, 1977), *He Was Always There, The U.S. Army Chaplain Ministry in the Vietnam Conflict* (Vol. 6, by Chaplain Henry F. Ackermann, 1989), *Encouraging Faith, Supporting Soldiers: A History of the U.S. Chaplain Corps 1975–1995* (Vol. 7, by Chaplain John W. Brinsfield, 1997).

[255] Yet only 6–9% of are made up of women, a decades-long consistent statistic.

force and necessity, the prisoners are isolated from normal free-world contacts. If our more healthy and honorable citizens and soldiers need a chaplain, then the common good would say the need is much greater for their struggling sons and daughters in prison.

Yet much more is immediately seen when the word *religion* arises, for all in the world knows that religion is the greatest source for change and solace in the history of the world. And while truly respecting every faith and the power of *faith* to change, and to facilitate solace in crises, we also see that Christianity predominates in the West and in the prisons, especially Protestant variants. Though "pastoral care" can be facilitated from every faith, the term has been best defined and refined through the centuries by Christian scholars, pastors, and chaplains. And many have distinguished pastoral care within the vast expertise of psychiatry and psychology.[256] No one is in competition, and all realize the good of science, as well as the roots of "care" in the theological—or *should*—for all the noble religions have cared for the soul since their religion's inception. Protestant Christianity has valued the "soul" as eternal since the beginning, even from Genesis, and through the present unto our eternal rewards.

B. Pastoral Care's Vital Issues Aid Entire Prison Mission

In delicate pastoral care, then, valuing the eternal soul, chaplains facilitate the Vital Issues woven together in our mysterious, wondrous precious hearts—in our souls—all in heated conflict in most prisoners. Inside of the cold, hostile environs of prison, the staff chaplain labors uniquely and co-labors wisely with immeasurably valued volunteers as they together facilitate, nurture, champion, challenge, and walk gently between all these Vital Issues:[257]

Pastoral Care's Vital Issues

God, Supreme Being and/or Spirit	Existence – Being – Non-Being
Life Crises and Goals	Identity and Sexuality
Eternity and Annihilation	Nature of Growth and Death

---

[256] See articles and books in the bibliography, the numerous pastoral care/chaplaincy associations, and several articles on that articles at *Testamentum Imperium*, www.PreciousHeart.net/ti.

[257] See www.PreciousHeart.net/chaplaincy/Chaplain's_Job.htm. For more, see any of the works of Southwestern Baptist Theological Seminary Vice President for Academic Affairs and Professor of Philosophy of Religion John P. Newport (1917–2000; R.I.P. to a good man), especially his *Life's Ultimate Questions: A Contemporary Philosophy of Religion* (Dallas: Word, 1989; 644p.). And, no, that is not a comprehensive list.

Universal Forces	Origin – Beginning – Ending
Purpose of Pain and Pleasure	Purpose of God and Humankind
Derivation and Purpose of Law	Sources of Authority
Destiny of Humankind	Coping with Life and Prison
Scripture Interpretation	Transcendence
Truth – Dignity – Honor – Love	Cycles and Stages of Life
Moral and Social Accountability	Family – Marriage – Separation
Wisdom and Life Skills	Essence of Good – Evil
Essence of Humankind and Principles	Purpose – Meaning in Life

Pastoral care listens and guides in all of these and more, as a light unto the path of life, while respecting and facilitating the faith of the prisoner. Every mission-critical function of the prison agency is aided as the prisoner adapts, grows, becomes more peaceful and honorable, and in the long haul becomes a stronger better man. And, to a lesser degree and as a *staffer* himself, the chaplain aids the staff.[258]

C. *Staff* Chaplains—Key to Optimum Level of Care

Pastoral care and religion in prison are uniquely, optimally, cost-effectively, even exquisitely facilitated by the *staff* chaplain, as he or she cares for the souls of the prisoners, the prison staff, the volunteers, and the families of all three. The awesome task is underfunded and too often simply ignored today. Look at a small shortlist of the *care* Texas prison staff chaplains facilitated in 2012 alone:

Texas Prison Staff Chaplain 2012 Statistics Shortlist

125 TDCJ Chaplains Facilitated and Cared for 99.8% of
- ✓ 20,000 Volunteers in their 418,000 visits with
- ✓ 500,000 hours with an astounding
- ✓ 4,000,000 prisoners in attendance—*plus*
- ✓ 19,602 Critical Illness/Death Notices and more [259]

---

[258] Scanty as is the literature on pastoral care in prison, it is nonexistent on the staff chaplain's work among the staff in prison; by reason and human concern, it should be obvious that a staff chaplain sharing accountabilities has a uniquely valuable place in care and company mission in every institution.

[259] Maness, *How We Saved Texas Prison Chaplaincy 2011: Immeasurable Value of Religion, Volunteers and Their Chaplains* (Authorhouse, 2015; www.PreciousHeart.net/Saved), Item 5, p.72, culled from this report, www.PreciousHeart.net/chaplaincy/RPD-Dunbar-08-2012.pdf, wherein the staff Chaplains reported these, though not obvious and no routing therein.

See www.PreciousHeart.net/Saved/Reports/FY2012-Volunteer-Stats-by-Month.xls, for what was available in 2011, but not used, by those who slated the end of prison chaplaincy, and at that book's site for many of the statistical runs for previous years—outstanding stats!

A lot of *care* and *solace* are taking place in Texas prisons, and if you look at the larger statistical tables on the Texas prison chaplaincy services, you will see a nearly superhuman volume of care in a mind-boggling array of diverse programs.[260]

D. Hard Fight in 2011 to Preserve Pastoral Care in Prison

I wrote the book, *How We Saved Texas Prison Chaplaincy 2011*, on our hard fight and how we won a stupendous victory. Despite decades-old statistics on precious work, chaplaincy was killed in the 2011 Texas budget, and a few us ignited a wildfire that saved it. First time in print, we showed in Austin how the loss of the staff chaplain (1) devalued *care* for religion, (2) devalued *care* for the volunteers, (3) devastated the pastoral care to prisoners and their families, and (4) how chaplaincy recovered its cost at least three times over. Among those four, we thoroughly nailed one point in Austin in 2011: those killing chaplaincy ignored its well-documented entire cost recovery, and then we nailed how *some* staffer would *still have* to care for religion and volunteers (veritable owners of the prison franchise).[261] With a staffer like an already over-worked lieutenant having to facilitate volunteers—what *then* was the cost saving? *None!* Yet, the fight in 2011 exposed those in TDCJ who did not value religion. The only reason for killing chaplaincy given by TDCJ in Austin was "the volunteers can do it all," an abysmal rational countered in Austin by the volunteers themselves saying, "No, we cannot do it." And they *should* not. But we chaplains, the volunteers, citizens, and legislators won—this time—amidst some who truly did not value religion, even in the place where religion is needed most—our prisons!

I cannot express here the 20 years of work behind that heavily referenced book, *How We Saved ... Chaplaincy*. As in the military, the optimum level of pastoral care in prison is facilitated best by a

---

[260] Ibid., and see www.PreciousHeart.net/chaplaincy/Prison_Ministries.htm for a very old and obsolete list of 700-plus providers of programs for chaplains, a list no longer maintained. To date in 2016, there is no readily accessible list, much less database, of the ministries and programs in Texas prisons, and I suspect the same is true nationwide.

[261] The "savings" alleged in cutting chaplains in 2011 was met resoundingly when it was pointed out that some staffer would still *have* to handle religion and all the volunteers in prison—no true cost savings at all. For more on how staff prison chaplaincy recovers its operating costs *several* times over, see *How We Saved Texas Prison Chaplaincy 2011*, 100–110 and 195, a total cost-recovery detailed over ten years earlier. Worse, there was no cost-benefit analysis or written plan of continuity.

seminary educated *staff* chaplain; or, said in another way, without a *staff* chaplain, so many pastoral care "needs" go unmet, even go unseen, and care for the dear citizen volunteers would go south.

E. Religion—Greatest Source for Change and Solace in History

We proved the value of pastoral care in prison to our beloved Texas legislators in Austin with solid support from many religious quarters of Baptists, Methodists, Catholics, Jews, and several religious lobbying groups. Decisively and as if for the first time, we heralded and even highlighted a staff chaplain maxim:

Staff Chaplain Maxim

Chaplains Facilitate the Greatest Source for
Change and Solace in Human History—*Religion*.[262]

Regardless that most hospitals are parochial, chaplains respect faiths and provide pastoral care to all and facilitate local clergy. All military chaplains do the same in a more restrictive setting. And prison staff chaplains see more differing religious adherents more often, primarily because the prisoners have no easy access to free-world persons or internet resources.[263]

Religion—who does *not* value it? Religion in prison *is* the greatest source of change and solace, and, in Texas, Christianity commands the largest percentage of prisoners and of free-world volunteers.[264] One would like to think that the reason so few studies are done is because of the "value" of religion is so obvious, for the vast majority of earth has valued religion since the Neanderthal crafted his first spear. Yet, despite that long history of the great value of religion within most of earth's greatest nations—and the founding of most of their greatest schools—the reality is a *minimalist* investment strategy

---

[262] First articulated in 2000 when I led a coalition of 60-plus chaplains in Texas to secure our first pay raise in 40-plus years for TDCJ, MHMR and TYC, seen most here: www.PreciousHeart.net/chaplaincy/01-Chaplain_Pt_1_Proposal_2000.pdf.
See www.PreciousHeart.net/chaplaincy, one of the largest sites on prison chaplaincy in U.S.

[263] Furthermore, though not aware of any study yet (though useful), it seems that the prison has many more involved with the fringe, radical, and anti-social religions than any other institution.

[264] See www.PreciousHeart.net/chaplaincy/FY2010_Chaplaincy_Faiths.pdf, for the first comprehensive breakdown and longitudinal look at the faiths of prisoners in Texas prisons.

in most state prison chaplaincy departments throughout the U.S. (when it is not killed altogether).[265]

Most of the religious activity in prison is programmatic and facilitated by volunteers, as in worship, study, discipleship, mentor, and 12-step growth/addiction programs. Indeed, the number and diversity of "programs" would take a large book to detail and is long overdue. Yet, few are the volunteer chaplain assistances that engage in deep one-on-one pastoral care. And in Texas, who knows for sure? Sadly, Texas and most states have bad retention strategies and have destroyed the meager statistics they collect after three years, not allowing for any significant longitudinal studies.[266] Though Texas has revised some retention, no longitudinal studies have yet been done.[267]

Why are there no longitudinal studies? Still, are they needed?

Religion is a *right* in prison, and all prisons make allowance, but—*please hear this*—religion is so *needed* in prison. Professor Byron R. Johnson has proven that in his monumental work, *More God, Less Crime*.[268] Thomas P. O'Conner's hefty studies likewise proved the value of religion in prison, and he appears to be only director of chaplains to have contributed *several* academic pieces.[269]

---

[265] That minimalist strategy is documented in several appendices in *How We Saved Texas Prison Chaplaincy 2011* (www.PreciousHeart.net/Saved), especially Appendix 5 "Texas and TDCJ Budget Conundrums Appendix 9," "Chaplain Professional Equity 2001 and Subsequent Cuts and Additions," and Appendix 11 "TDCJ Annual and Statistical Reports and Record Retention of Chaplaincy and Their Volunteers 2000–2015," with all appendices available for view at the book's web site.

[266] Except as one chaplain has archived, www.PreciousHeart.net/chaplaincy. See *How We Saved Texas Prison Chaplaincy 2011*, pgs. 322–336, Appendix 11: TDCJ Annual and Statistical Reports and Record Retention of Chaplaincy and Their Volunteers 2000–2015.

[267] From Open Records requests, the TDCJ's RPD had not done any in the last 10 years.

[268] Byron R. Johnson's *More God, Less Crime* (2011). He initiated studies of faith-based programs. Johnson's *The Inner-Change Freedom Initiative: A Preliminary Evaluation of a Faith-Based Prison Program*, with David B. Larson, International Center for the Integration of Health and Spirituality (CRRUCS Report 2003), 19, noted "IFI graduates are significantly less likely to be incarcerated within two years of release than those IFI members not completing the program (8% vs. 36.3%)."
See www.Baylor.edu/content/services/document.php/25903.pdf.

[269] Thomas P. O'Conner, "What Works: Religion as a Correctional Intervention: Part II," *Journal of Community Corrections* 14, No. 2 (Winter, 2004–05): 4–26, reviewed a host of studies, saying decisively religion helps all aspects of prison, recidivism, coping, and pressing for more: "Perhaps what is needed even more than improved religious correctional interventions and research is for the multitude of religious traditions within the United States to raise their voices to ask that U.S. correctional systems become more loving, and thus, more authentically religious in nature" (p. 23)! At the time he wrote that, he was the Administrator for Religious Services for the Oregon DOC.
See www.Oregon.gov/doc/omr/docs/pdf/rs_whatworks2.pdf.
See his site www.TransformingCorrections.com.

Pastoral care originated from religion, especially Christianity. The greatest maxims are the Golden Rule, seek first the kingdom, love God and love neighbor, and, truly, *love is the greatest*. Those and others are both religious core values and high psychological principles. For those who killed chaplaincy in several states, who tried to kill it in Texas, and who do not value religion—for them, pastoral care is either vain or at best political Play Doe. Wealthy politically powerful religious groups command attention of prison administrators, and the administrators must cater. But chaplains, who facilitate, aid, and love the volunteers and love religion—well—look see in this article's many references. It is true, despite chaplaincy's noble and even hallowed roots in religion, some in authority do not want quality pastoral care in prison? Again, they have killed it a few states and in 2011 *tried* to kill it in Texas.

We must not deny the current milieu. We must not forget that some are *hostile* to religion and quality pastoral care—even today! That is critical to the sensitivity of delivering "care" in prison, knowing that some *are* hostile, just as some were hostile to Jesus.

For 20 years, I and 20,000 volunteers have seen how a prisoner's faith helped. Faith helped him cope, helped him deal with life, while living in hell, and—dearly—helped him reconcile his dastardly felonies with society and often with his precious family. Not just *a* right, but a cherished and *absolute* right—and beyond inherent *rights*—religion is the *deepest* of all human needs, and more than anything else needed in prison. Indeed, religion is not only needed in prison, but it is much more a constitutional "right" in prison than are medical, schooling, and three squares of food a day "rights" in prison! The professional staff chaplain is justified and needed as is any position, and more, as the gentle facilitator of the vast treasure of Vital Issues woven through every prison's human dynamics.

F. Pastoral Care Profession in Prison vs. Hospital

There are a host of chaplain organizations. The American Correctional Chaplains Association (ACCA) was established in 1885 and was the first affiliate of the American Correctional Association (est. 1870) that certifies most prisons nationwide, including Texas.[270]

---

[270] See www.CorrectionalChaplains.org and www.ACA.org.

The Associated Chaplains in California State Service is an organization of *all* the state-employed chaplains in *five* state entities; look at all the places they have *staff* chaplains in California.[271]

Yet, today, prison chaplains are woefully behind their counterparts in the great hospitals that have been continuously developing a large body of professional literature since the 1950s, the dawn of written professional pastoral care.[272]

The Association for Clinical Pastoral Education is the standard-bearer for clinical training for most all professional chaplains, their journal being among the most long-standing and respected.[273] The Hearthcare Chaplaincy Network in New York is a leader in research with a great motto: "Caring for the Human Spirit, Finding Meaning, Bringing Comfort."[274] The Association of Professional Chaplains has a large collegiality and has an excellent journal in ongoing research.[275] Yet, unlike the medical and psychiatric sides in prison, after much research, I know of no state prison chaplaincy that fully funds membership, much less regular travel, for its chaplains in these great organizations. Sadly put, compared to the other degree-bearing professions in state prisons, chaplains are *not* treated equitably.[276]

---

[271] The www.ACCSS.org invites exclusive *staff Chaplain* membership from California Department of Corrections and Rehabilitation (www.CDCR.ca.gov), Division of Juvenile Justice (DJJ), Department of Developmental Services (DDS), Department of State Hospitals (DSH), Department of Veteran's Affairs (CalVet). Unlike Texas' Chaplains I–IIIs for all employed Chaplains, the CDCR positions are for Catholic Chaplain, Jewish Chaplain, Protestant Chaplain, etc. Just like Texas, while slightly higher in pay, there is a similar disparity in pay compared to the *other* degree-bearing professions in California.

[272] See our second footnote for a very short list.

[273] See www.ACPE.edu and http://pcc.sagepub.com, *The Journal of Pastoral Care and Counseling*, est. 1947, is a joint publication of Journal of Pastoral Care Publications, Inc. (www.JPCP.org) and Sage Journals, http://online.sagepub.com. As of June 2015, it is in its 69th volume, running for 69 years, one of the most massive bodies of literature on professional pastoral care, mostly in the hospital setting. Because of the internet, http://pcc.sagepub.com/content/by/year, view *all* volumes and articles to 1968— *phenomenal!* Why would *all* the state Chaplaincy services *not* supply a subscription to this?

[274] See www.HealthCareChaplaincy.org and their *PlainViews: Translating Knowledge and Skills into Effective Chaplaincy and Pallative Care*.

[275] See www.ProfessionalChaplains.org, Association of Professional Chaplains and its *Chaplaincy Today: Journal of the Association of Professional Chaplains*.

[276] In 2000, I led Chaplain Professional Equity in Texas with about 60 chaplains from TDCJ, TYC and MHMR in our successful effort to gain our first pay-group pay raise in 40-plus years: www.PreciousHeart.net/chaplaincy/01-Chaplain_Pt_1_Proposal_2000.pdf and a fact sheet www.PreciousHeart.net/chaplaincy/CPE-2000.pdf. This was the first time professional prison chaplains banded together for a legislative push in the U.S. history.

Perhaps the most significant piece published on the *value* of professional hospital chaplains was the 2001 landmark *Professional Chaplaincy: Its Role and Importance in Healthcare* put together by the five largest and often most esteemed chaplaincy associations in North America.[277] *Value?*—here it is! Several times I suggested we prison chaplains do something comparable.[278]

In 2000, I wrote a defense of prison chaplaincy's contribution to several specific mission-critical functions in a flyer we shared in Austin for our 2001 push for Chaplain Professional Equity.[279] Furthermore, *How We Saved Texas Prison Chaplaincy 2011* is chock-full of *value* that is referenced and linked to the hilt.[280]

Quality pastoral care facilitates the cherished Vital Issues and further credentials the universal value of religion itself, and as such it contributes to every mission-critical function of every agency, be that hospital, prison, military, or corporation. Furthermore, though "cost" alone will always be secondary to the lives changed in prison, staff chaplains recover their *entire* operating cost several times over. We asked in Austin in 2011: where is there a *more* productive or *more* cost-effective program in Texas than chaplaincy?[281] Therefore, given the universal value of religion and the proven cost recovery, and given the gargantuan *human* need so easy to see for those with a heart—instead of killing chaplaincy, why is it *not* the best funded?

G. Pastoral Care Facing Death and the Golden Hour

With eventually thousands of volunteers—each a citizen—all over Texas certifying as they helped us in Austin, part of the heart cry we

---

[277] See www.PreciousHeart.net/chaplaincy/Chaplaincy_Healthcare.pdf, a collaborative effort of the Association for Clinical Pastoral Education, www.ACPE.edu; The Association of Professional Chaplains, www.ProfessionalChaplains.org; The Canadian Association for Pastoral Practice and Education, www.SpiritualCare.ca (*now* Canadian Association of Spiritual Care, celebrating 50 years in 2015 from 1965); The National Association of Catholic Chaplains, www.NACC.org; The National Association of Jewish Chaplains.

[278] See www.PreciousHeart.net/Chaplaincy and in Appendices 9 and 10 *How We Saved Texas Prison Chaplaincy 2011* is the story of 2001 Chaplain Professional Equity.

[279] See www.PreciousHeart.net/chaplaincy/CPE-2000.pdf, a fact sheet 60-plus chaplains and I used in Austin, Texas, in 2000 to defend Chaplain Professional Equity, a synopsis of sorts of www.PreciousHeart.net/chaplaincy/01-Chaplain_Pt_1_Proposal_2000.pdf.

[280] Maness, *How We Saved ... Chaplaincy 2011* (www.PreciousHeart.net/Saved).

[281] Ibid., chapter VI, pgs. 97–123, and VI.B.3, "Composite Savings—Where Is a MORE Cost-Effective Department?" 106–08.

heralded in 2011 was how the chaplains with kindred spirit facilitate the volunteers themselves. Another critical part of the heart cry we heralded was that the *heart* of pastoral care in prison is seen most of all in how the staff chaplain facilitates the grief and the torment prisoners experience in personal crises—and in death!

One last time, the heartbeat and deepest level of "Care for the Soul" is when an educated and trained man or woman full-time *staff* chaplain, especially one who has been in a facility for 10-plus years, sits one-on-one with a prisoner in the loss—in the death—of his mother or grandmother (or auntie), that dear person who raised the often fatherless child. Not the mere *monitoring* of a phone call, that anyone can do, but the chaplain *facilitates* grief and solace and communication before, during, and after such a call. I call it the

Golden Hour of Pastoral Care in Prison.

Terrifying is the notice of a horrific assault and battery on a loved one. Likewise stage-four cancer of a dear father or mother or sister. Or the rape of a dear little one. Rape of a sister. Car accident that cripples a brother. Heart attack of a father-like uncle. Grandmother's house burned down, all is lost, but grandmother is *alive*. Motorcycle accident maims a brother, cripples a child. Gun shot. Knife wound.

Accidents and acts of evil *cripple* many more than the victim.

Crises respect no person's status or schedule.

A 10-year-old little boy broke both legs and pleaded to talk to his father in prison, his *daddy!* A young daughter was raped and wants to talk to her *daddy!* A brother just arrived home from overseas military duty, a wounded warrior, missing an arm and a leg—he wants to talk to his brother in prison. Tell the story. Heart to heart. And the Vital Issues that a wise chaplain facilitates are golden moments of eternal value, and those moments contribute to every facet of prison life.

Yes, 125 Texas prison chaplains facilitated 19,602 Critical Illness/Death Notices in 2012, the very year the entire chaplaincy department was scheduled for execution.[282] Over the course of 20 years, I personally facilitated about 5,000 crisis calls. Value—the staff chaplain's office is the critical hub, or center of care, or the

---

[282] Maness, *How We Saved Texas Prison Chaplaincy 2011* (2015: 412p.), Item 5 (p.72), culled from this report, www.PreciousHeart.net/chaplaincy/RPD-Dunbar-08-2012.pdf.

"heart of the institution" if you please, with much, much more facilitated in 500,000 hours every year through their 20,000 precious volunteers radiating out with thousands of programs, all immeasurably valuable, all administratively aided, tracked, and caringly facilitated by a relatively few extraordinary *staff* chaplains.[283]

Yet, of all the crises, perhaps you already know, *death* hurts the worst of all. Death of spouse. Death of child. Death of a brother or sister. Death of a lover.

Often for a young man—most prisoners are *young*—the death of a loved one is the first time he lost a dearly loved brother or child. Many prisoners are *tough*, but not yet *experienced* in life's crucibles, not yet acquainted with *deep personal grief*. Most normal people are not prepared for the world-shaking *SHOCK* that breaks the heart of the most sensible. That shock is especially brutal for young men in prison—troubled as they already are—who have mostly denied their dearest feelings most of their lives. Then, to encounter the most rocking and explosive of griefs in the death of a dear loved one, then ... then, cut to the quick of their already disenfranchised being—like *never* before—the young man breaks down.

He cries. Stomps feet. Covers face. Looks to heaven. *Cries.*

At the same time, he is ashamed to cry. Often, the conflict swirls like a burning cauldron in his fragile conflicted heart.

In that moment of crushing grief, the prisoner is without anchor and adrift without an oar on the wildest ocean waves. Tears, bitter tears fall from his eyes like he has never shed before, and then he is afraid of his tears, too, as though they are not manly and somehow wrong. And he cannot go to his family. Crises cubed upon grief, each time unique, plumbing the depths of his soul.

Now let me gently nudge you, precious reader to the worst of all.

Death ... death in so many forms, by accident or by evil—*death*—that grim reaper's sharp dark scythe slices fast. For mostly young wild men, the death of their mother (or mother-like granny) while they are in prison hits the hardest, breaks the most hardened and pulls apart the heart. Tears, oh, the tears of the grieving are most precious.

---

[283] Ibid., in Texas, without full-time clerical help. See 2000 Chaplain Professional Equity proposal, www.PreciousHeart.net/chaplaincy/01-Chaplain_Pt_1_Proposal_2000.pdf, several charts comparing TDCJ chaplaincy with the prison school system's independent school system.

I emptied a box of tissue every month for 20 years, thousands of tissues for only God knows how many tears.

That single solitary moment of death's notification becomes the prisoner's most vulnerable hour—the Golden Hour of Pastoral Care, and is—truly—also the chaplain's finest hour. Truly, truly, truly, as most good pastors and priests know so well, and uniquely powerful in prison, when that moment of notification is preceded by *years* of pastoral care in the prison and followed by *years* of pastoral care, that is truly hallowed ground—the

Golden Hour of Care for the Soul.

And some tried to kill that Golden Hour in Texas in 2011.

For the staff chaplain who has been *there* for the prisoner in the city under siege for the past ten-plus years, seen all and managed a good chapel with integrity—the prisoners are *always* watching—that prisoner has seen "his chaplain" exhibit time and again, and *time and again*, a sincere compassion, a consistent integrity, and an authentic "Care for the Soul." Precious. Golden. In that prisoner's most vulnerable and heartbreaking moment of his short, troubled life, that prisoner feels *safe* with his tears. His Vital Issues are laid bare like never before with a skilled chaplain at the helm, perhaps also with a tear, and chaplain helps the young man navigate the storm.

So many precious Vital Issues crash through our tender hearts in death, causing *all of us* to reevaluate, renegotiate and often see what was and is truly valuable in our lives. For most young men, the crashing ignites shocking revelations. What we missed, too, regretted or fell short of, or were angry with—all hit us fast and hard. For our most troubled children in prison, the need for pastoral care seems obvious and even priceless, even a steel key to unlocking the golden treasures within their precious hearts.

8.
Pastoral Care in Public Settings: A Theoretical & Theological Premise with Effective Outcomes of Chaplaincy

by Dr. Keith A. Evans
Senior Manager of Spiritual Care Services
Banner Thunderbird Medical Center, Glendale, Arizona[284]

Introduction 141
A. The Widening Faith Gap 142
B. Spirituality and Soul Care Defined 143
C. Theoretical Premise for Chaplaincy 144
D. Theological Context for Chaplaincy 145
E. Challenge for Conservative Christian Chaplains 148
F. Quality Clinical and Workplace Outcomes 151
Conclusion 156

Introduction

Most people continue to believe that there is a God or universal spirit, but many are unchurched and have a rising skepticism of organized religion.[285] Effective, practical and relevant applications of theology and faith beliefs are needed in our growing pluralistic culture. Religious and cultural research reveals that twenty-five percent of unchurched adults are skeptical of God's existence, labeling themselves as either agnostics or atheists.[286] This skepticism of God's existence is stated to be based upon rejection of the Bible, a lack of trust in the local church, and the cultural reinforcement of a

---

[284] Evans is the author of *Essential Chaplain Skill Sets—Discovering Effective Ways to Provide Excellent Spiritual Care* (Westbow Press, 2017), www.ChaplainSkillSets.com. Evans earned degrees from Parker College of Chiropractic (D.C.), Trinity College of the Bible and Theological Seminary (M.A.), Liberty Baptist Theological Seminary (M.Div.), and Temple Baptist Seminary (D.Min.). He is a board-certified clinical chaplain with specialty experiences in law enforcement and trauma healthcare chaplaincy. He is also on the Adjunct Faculty of Grand Canyon University College of Theology teaching courses on "Spirituality and Ethical Decision Making in Healthcare."

[285] "Most Americans Still Believe in God," *Gallup*, June 29, 2016, accessed May 30, 2017, www.Gallup.com; "U.S. Public Becoming Less Religious," November 3, 2015, www.PewForum.org (accessed May 30, 2017).

[286] Barna Group, "2015 State of Atheism in America," www.Barna.com/research/2015-state-of-atheism-in-america.

secular worldview. This trend is more predominant in younger adults who are more educated and racially and ethnically diverse.

For ministers, this type of data is not a new revelation, but it validates the changing expressions of faith and spirituality in America as well as across the globe. If one holds to the premise that each person,

1. Is spiritual,
2. Possesses an inner spiritual nature or spirituality, and
3. Is consciously or unconsciously searching for meaning and purpose in their lives;

then unique public ministry approaches are of paramount importance. If so, then one approach falls within the realm of skilled chaplain ministers who work in pluralistic marketplaces and organizations. This purpose of this paper is to lay a theoretical and theological premise for workplace and clinical chaplaincy and review the research that reveals the effective outcomes of chaplaincy.

A. The Widening Faith Gap

When people do not attend organized religious groups, ministers should ask, "Is there a need for me to go out to them?" Spirituality is indeed diverse and is being defined and expressed in many ways.

> With so many of the population not active in a local church or organized faith community, there is a great need for effective soul care to be brought to them in their respective places of work by their coworkers and friends.... Chaplains are uniquely qualified to bridge this growing gap in our society, which has pushed back against organized religion yet still strives to find meaning and relevancy in their spiritual selves.[287]

Michael Langston, a retired military chaplain and Columbia International University professor of chaplaincy, said,

> However, in the midst of all this change, religion and spirituality continue to thrive and provide a sense of hopefulness for millions of people around the world. People are buoyed by their faith and continue to seek out avenues to practice that faith.[288]

---

[287] Keith A. Evans, *Essential Chaplain Skill Sets: Discovering Effective Ways to Provide Excellent Spiritual Care* (Bloomington: WestBow Press, 2017), 2.

[288] Ibid., vii.

Observing this trend and the need for practical and relevant ministry applications, Langston continues,

> Today, there is a strong trend and desire to have that spiritual need addressed in the workplace, where people live 30–40 percent of their lives. In the workplace environment, life goes on and people experience all the joys, excitement, successes, heartaches, struggles, and failures that life brings. In an effort to maintain productivity, corporations and institutions search for ways to address workers' specific religious/spiritual needs so that productivity continues to meet expectations of the organization, board of directors, and shareholders. Many of these corporations, health-care systems, and institutions see the importance of providing for the comfort, care, and spiritual nurture of their workforce. If the workforce is healthy in body, mind, and spirit, then the workforce can wholeheartedly focus on the mission at hand and remain productive. This care that is provided by the workforce employer is done through the profession of chaplaincy.[289]

The above and more forms the essential premise and justification for a professional pastoral chaplain ministry.

> While chaplaincy as a whole is not faith specific, it nevertheless reaches out to care for the religious and spiritual needs of the workforce built upon specific skill sets that are imperative in the direct hands-on care provided.[290]

B. Spirituality and Soul Care Defined

Christina Puchalski of the George Washington Institute of Spirituality and Heath proposed a definition of spirituality that is widely accepted by most in health-care chaplaincy:

> spirituality is the aspect of humanity that refers to the way individuals seek and express meaning and purpose and the way they experience their connectedness to the moment, to self, to others, to nature, and to the significant or sacred.[291]

Others perceive that spirituality stems from one's inner consciousness and is the source behind the outward form of defined religious practices.[292] Religion is more strictly defined as how one's spirituality is practiced within a specific doctrinal or theological context.

---

[289] Ibid., vii–viii.

[290] Ibid., viii.

[291] Christina M. Puchalski, et al, "Improving the Spiritual Dimension of Whole Person Care: Reaching National and International Consensus," *Journal of Palliative Medicine* 17:6 (2014): 642.

[292] William A. Guillory, *Spirituality in the Workplace: A Guide for Adapting to the Chaotically Changing Workplace* (Salt Lake City: Innovations International Inc. Publishing, 1997), xi.

In *Care of Souls*, David G. Benner said,

> The soul is the meeting point of the psychological and spiritual. Its care must, by necessity, include both spiritual and psychological aspects.[293]

In the past century, there have been great strides in understanding the human psyche. But at the same time, the experts have tended to dissect the immaterial self of the individual and divide it up into distinct components (psychological, spiritual, and emotional), with each one standing separate and without connection to the other. However, there is a growing understanding that this may not be the case. In fact, a dichotomist view of humanity may have more merit in this context of soul care when you assess how individuals cope with crises in their lives. Benner stated that we should

> understand *soul* as referring to the whole person, including the body, but with particular focus on the inner world of thinking, feeling, and willing. Care of souls can thus be understood as the care of persons in their totality.[294]

Of the many not engaged in a local church or spiritual community, then who assists people in their journeys? Most often, no one.

C. Theoretical Premise for Chaplaincy

The work of psychologist Kenneth I. Pargament has been especially well received within the medical field over the past several decades. Pargament has written extensively on the psychology of an individual's resiliency based upon religion and spirituality as positive coping skills.[295] His behavioral theories and literature reviews can easily be extrapolated to include individuals under any stress.

Attending to a person's spirituality has been shown to help a person's overall resiliency after crisis and stress. A 2011 study noted that individuals who have spiritual and religious resources available to them during a time of crisis, such as critical life situations and nearing

---

[293] David G. Benner, *Care of Souls: Revisioning Christian Nurture and Counsel* (Grand Rapids: Baker Books, 1998), 22.

[294] Ibid., 23.

[295] Kenneth I. Pargament, *The Psychology of Religion and Coping: Theory, Research Practice* (New York: Guilford Press, 1997).

death itself, incur lower overall medical costs.[296] One can infer from this study that the individuals became less anxious and more emotionally and psychologically relaxed when they felt more supported. They felt less vulnerable. As this occurred, there was less need for anxiety or pain medications, which led to the patients' better comfort and rest and even increased healing rates because their immune systems improved. When this occurs, the patient will often have a shorter length of stay and better satisfaction with overall care. Other research supports this general premise, noting that results "may be attributable to chaplain's assistance to patients and families in making decisions about care at the end-of-life, perhaps by aligning their values and wishes with actual treatment plans."[297]

This and other data support the notion that spirituality is vastly important to the resiliency and maintenance of emotional well-being and wholeness for individuals. Even though organized religion is often opposed in the public square, and regardless, the professionally trained chaplain may be the most reasonable public clergy when fully respecting all beliefs in the effort to aid resiliency. For the multitude of people with spiritual needs who are also on quests for their own deeper meaning and purpose in life, the well-equipped and skilled chaplain may prove to be their best spiritual mentor and guide.

D. Theological Context for Chaplaincy

The Judeo-Christian theological basis for public ministry in hospitals or other settings for chaplains can be supported by the scriptural premise of the two great commandments. The first, "You shall love the Lord your God with all your heart, and with all your soul, and with all your mind" (Mt. 22:37 NASB) sets the intention and motivation of one's actions, and the second, "You shall love your neighbor as yourself" (Mt. 22:39 NASB) reveals the level of concern and care to be rendered to others.

---

[296] Tracy Balboni, M. J. Balboni, A. C. Phelps, A. A. Wright, J. R. Peteet, S. D. Block, C. Lathan, T. Vanderweele, and H. G. Prigerson. "Support of Cancer Patients' Spiritual Needs and Associations with Medical Care Costs at the End of Life." *Cancer* 117, no. 23 (May 2011): 5383–91.

[297] Kevin J. Flannelly, Linda L. Emanuel, George F. Handzo, Kathleen Galek, Nava R. Silton, and Melissa Carlson. "A National Study of Chaplaincy Services and End of Life Outcomes," *BMC Palliative Care* 11, no. 10 (2012): 1, accessed Sept. 1, 2013.

These core principles are evident in the biblical parable of the Good Samaritan (Luke 10:30–37). This parable reveals the context of showing empathy and kindness to others of differing cultures, faiths, and status with an impartial and humble attitude.[298] Forrest Kirk poses an interesting term that this love toward strangers and showing hospitality in serving the needs of guests is displayed in the definition of the Greek compound word *philoxenos*. [299] Kirk states that philoxenosology has been proposed to be the logic-based, operations-centered "Theology of Hospitality" which is at the root of the workplace chaplain's identity and scope of practice.[300] Professional chaplains administer soul care that is centered upon *philoxenos*.

A classic biblical example for this theological basis is observed in the Apostle Paul's approach as he spoke to the Athenians at the Areopagus, or Mars Hill, as recorded in Acts 17:16–34. The narrative describes the once Christian persecutor turned missionary-evangelist before the great council by the same name, Areopagus, after a similar less auspicious encounter in the open-air market in Athens. Many of his listeners were not from Paul's culture or Jewish theological understanding, but the Athenians were very interested in religious things. To this group, Paul states,

> Men of Athens, I observe that you are very religious in all respects. For while I was passing through and examining the objects of your worship, I also found an altar with this inscription, "TO AN UNKNOWN GOD." Therefore, what you worship in ignorance, this I proclaim to you (Acts 17:22b–23 NASB).

Paul understood the context and theological position and understanding of his listeners. Achieving this, Paul was able to construct his conversation and vocabulary in a practical way that his listeners would understand.

---

[298] Forrest L. Kirk, *Chaplains as Doctors of the Soul: Navigating Between the Sacred and Secular while Negotiating a Functional and Ontological Ministry Identity* (Ph.D. diss., New Orleans Baptist Theological Seminary, 2011; Proquest, Umi Dissertation Publishing, 2011). Cf., an article abridgement of his diss., http://baptistcenter.net/journals/JBTM_9-1_Spring_2012.pdf.

[299] Kirk, 101. Kirk supports his premise by referencing the *The New Testament Greek-English Dictionary*, Sigma-Omega (1991) s.v. "*philoxenos*" a Greek compound of *phil* "love" and *xenos* "stranger," "the love of strangers or hospitality shown to a guest, suggests both a fondness for and a natural desire to serve the needs of others, given to hospitality."

[300] Kirk, 103.

Paul's speech was before a pluralistic culture much different from his own. From this example, professional and contemporary chaplains can observe two generally observed principles. First, Paul begins with a respect towards his philosophical listeners by connecting his concerns to their inquisitive intellect (Acts 17:17–21). Second, Paul respectfully noted his observations of this pantheistic culture as being very religious as well as his perspective that the unfamiliar listeners desired to know more about themselves and other cultures and faiths (Acts 17:22).

First century Athens was the epitome of Greek hedonism and secular philosophy. Athens worshipped many gods such as Apollo, Jupiter, Venus, Mercury, Bacchus, Neptune, Diana, and Aesculapius.[301] Theologian John Stott describes Athens as possessing "innumerable temples, shrines, statues, and altars."[302] As Paul walked around the city observing its historical and spiritual diversity, it was Paul's own personal experience and faith in Christ and God which caused his heart was to be filled with compassion and have a desire to avail himself to the Athenians (Acts 17:16).

With this sincere consideration of the cultural context of Athens, Paul's unique approach intrigued his listeners as he established an intellectual rapport. From this starting point, Paul begin a very specific and intentional dialogue about what he knew about the "Agnosto Theos" or unknown god of the Greek culture.[303]

Two groups were mentioned, the Epicureans and Stoics (Acts 17:18). The Epicureans were materialistic and atheistic. Founded by Epicurus, they believed that physical matter was the only reality, and the mind was purely material. They believed in chance and denied concepts of life after death. Theologian and religious counselor Jay E. Adams states, "To put their beliefs in the form of a slogan, they said,

---

[301] John R. W. Stott, *The Message of Acts*, The Bible Speaks Today Series, ed. John R. W. Stott, (Downers Grove: InterVarsity Press, 1990), 277.

[302] Ibid.

[303] Pausanias, *Pausanias's Description of Greece: Volume 1*, trans. with a Commentary by J. G. Frazer (London: MacMillan and Co. Limited, 1898), Kindle e-book edition. Location: 1816, 6607. Pausanias conducted very thorough histories and descriptions of the Athenian topography of the mid-second century.

'pleasure is good, pain is evil.'"[304] On the other hand, the Stoics were founded by Zeno and taught that "whatever happens is good and right and [one] must go with the flow."[305] The Stoics did not place much merit in whether or not life after death existed and generally strived for apathy, that is, trying to be not too happy nor too sad. Adams sums up the Stoics as "pleasure is no good, pain is no evil."[306] Adams states these same attitudes are still prevalent today. He asserts,

> All of these beliefs, in one form or another, are abroad in our culture today. Your counselees are influenced by them. You must know how to deal with them. Paul's address deals with the lot. It is a very valuable source from which to glean answers and responses to such beliefs whenever they surface in counseling.[307]

The contemporary relevancy of ancient biblical writings is refreshing in today's culture and can be very effectively used by chaplains and ministers in public situations.

Theologically (and theoretically), the Apostle Paul demonstrated in ancient Athens what workplace chaplains do daily. Stott assesses that as a fellow clergy,

> If we do not speak like Paul because we do not feel like Paul, this is because we do not see like Paul. That was the order: he saw, he felt, he spoke.[308]

Ministers of all types must strive to respectfully yet dutifully observe different and difficult situations, learn about the specific context, and build rapport with others through intentional spiritual conversations.

E. Challenge for Conservative Christian Chaplains[309]

Today's society clearly calls for tolerance in a pluralistic setting for chaplains of all religious traditions. For the conservative Christian Chaplain, and specifically chaplains of evangelical faith, there is a

---

[304] Jay E. Adams, *The Christian Counselor's Commentary: Acts* (Woodruff, SC: Timeless Texts, 1999), 114.

[305] Ibid., 113.

[306] Ibid.

[307] Ibid., 114.

[308] Stott, 290.

[309] Portions of this section have been adapted from Keith A. Evans, *Using Chaplains as Key Leadership in Evaluating and Enhancing Workplace Spirituality for a Rural Hospital Setting*, D.Min. diss. (Winston-Salem: Temple Baptist Seminary, 2015), www.Academia.edu.

great challenge in balancing the biblical mandate to share the message of Jesus Christ (Mt. 18–20; Acts 1:8b; 2 Tim. 4:2; 1 Pt. 5:15) paired with the need to demonstrate love, respect, and compassionate caring to others of any faith or spirituality (Eph. 4:25, 29).

In the same context that the Apostle Paul approached people groups differently based upon their settings and culture, so do chaplains. Spiritual soul care by chaplains often is administered in differing modes than a parish or congregational clergy might consider. Chaplains assist individuals in meaning-making, emotional processing during crisis events, and assist in relational dynamics for workers personally or between peers. In parallel to Howard Clinebell's theory of pastoral care, chaplains use "methods that stabilize, undergird, nurture, motivate, or guide troubled persons – enabling them to handle their problems and relationships more constructively."[310] For evangelical Chaplains, Clinebell's theory is undergirded and enabled by the power of the Holy Spirit working in and upon the lives of hurting souls.

Jesus Christ demonstrated a model of evangelism which conservative evangelical Chaplains may be wise to consider. Jesus often used a form of permission evangelism that would intrigue his listeners to ask more about God, of spiritual matters, and for physical healing. Former atheist Michael L. Simpson speaks to this special form of spiritual conversation and evangelism.[311] Simpson noted that many of the recorded physical and spiritual healings by Christ were initiated and accomplished as a direct response from a direct request by those in need.[312]

Using permission-based spiritual and religious conversations with individuals in need (or crisis) is both a theoretical and theological-based skill for chaplains to consider. Simpson discusses the philosophical differences between the old concepts of evangelism and the new post-modern concepts of being a witness for Christ. Simpson

---

[310] Howard Clinebell, *Basic Types of Pastoral Care and Counseling: Resources for the Ministry of Healing and Growth* (Nashville: Abingdon Press, 1984), 170.

[311] Michael L. Simpson, *Permission Evangelism: When to Talk, When to Walk* (Colorado Springs: Cook Communications Ministries, 2003), 43–63. Simpson references physical and spiritual healings of Jesus Christ in Matthew 8:5–13, 9:27–28; Mark 1:32–34, 5:22–23, 7:31–37, 8:22–26, 10:50–51; Luke 5:12–16, 17:11–19; John 4:46–54.

[312] Ibid., 56.

states that the former mindset for individuals seeking salvation was a definitive "How do I get to God?" versus the current post-modern abstract question of "How do I become a better person?"[313] Many post-moderns possess a negative view of religion and the organized Church but still seek purpose, value, and meaning in their lives. Simpson states that for the post-modern, the path or journey to becoming a better person is now the goal based upon relative trust versus the former quest which resulted in a definitive eternal salvation based upon absolute truth.[314]

The concept of permission evangelism also loosely parallels the general pastoral counseling model in which the counselee is asked open-ended questions to elicit verbalization and expression of their own needs or struggles. This model can produce questions by the counselee in which the counselor is permitted to answer without being perceived as judgmental, hypocritical, prescriptive or presumptuous. In order to do this well, there is a challenge for conservative Christian chaplains to use more neutral theological and religious language in conversations in hopes to not confuse or mislead.

The above correlates with and is indirectly supported by George Everly's work regarding spiritual distress of individuals who experience intense critical incidents. Avoiding overly religious language in these situations is highly recommended. Everly's work in pastoral crisis intervention observes that any crises may manifest in "concerns regarding self-identity, affiliative crises, existential, spiritual, or even theological or theodilitic crises (a crisis of faith)."[315]

The chaplain always attempts to enter a critical situation with a comforting "ministry of presence" offering the availability of scriptural education, intercessory prayer, unifying and explanatory worldviews, and ventilative confession. Other functions which the chaplain brings to the crisis situation are:

- the ability to provide ritual and religious practices,
- belief in life after death,
- viewpoints regarding evil and suffering,
- privileged communications, and

---

[313] Ibid., 38.

[314] Ibid.

[315] George S. Everly Jr., *Pastoral Crisis Intervention* (Ellicott City: Chevron Publishing, 2007), 13.

- the art of helping to instill hope grounded upon scriptural and religious beliefs.[316]

All of these extra functions of the pastoral interventionist help to further stabilize and mitigate "signs and symptoms of distress and dysfunction" and help to "facilitate a return of adaptive functioning" of the one involved in the traumatic event. [317] For Everly, the assistance of properly trained chaplains during crisis is an "added-value" for emergency first responders and healthcare providers.

F. Quality Clinical and Workplace Outcomes

Research findings in healthcare and clinical settings have discovered many parallels for the congregational pastor and minister to consider. Harold G. Koenig is the Director of Duke University's Center for Spirituality, Theology and Health. As a psychiatrist, Koenig has conducted extensive research on the effects of faith and spirituality upon specific health issues as well as well-being in general. A few outcome findings are that individuals with religious beliefs possess a more optimistic worldview,[318] are more hopeful,[319] and have a greater meaning and purpose in life.[320] Koenig brings to light that even Sigmund Freud (1930) had to admit that

---

[316] Ibid., 32.

[317] Ibid.

[318] S. Sethi and M. E. P. Seligman, "Optimism and fundamentalism," *Psychological Science* 4 (1993), 256–259, see www.jstor.org/stable/40062552; and S. Sethi and M. E. P. Seligman, "The hope of fundamentalists," *Psychological Science* 5 (1994), 58.

[319] Ibid.

[320] J. S. Mattis, "Religion and Spirituality in the Meaning-making and Coping Experiences of African American Women: A Qualitative Analysis," *Psychology of Women Quarterly* 26, No. 4 (2002), 309–321, see https://journals.sagepub.com/doi/10.1111/1471-6402.t01-2-00070; S. K. Fletcher, "Religion and Life Meaning: Differentiating between Religious Beliefs and Religious Community in Constructing Life Meaning," *Journal of Aging Studies* 18, No. 2 (2004): 171–185, see www.ScienceDirect.com/science/article/abs/pii/S0890406504000064; Sylvia Mohr, Pierre-Yves Brandt, Laurence Borras, Christiane Gillieron, and Philippe Huguelet, "Toward an Integration of Spirituality and Religiousness into the Psychosocial Dimension of Schizophrenia," *American Journal of Psychiatry* 163, No. 11: (2006): 1952–1959; A. Skrabski, M. Koop, S. Rozsa, J. Rethelyi, and R. H. Rahe, "Life Meaning: An Important Correlate of Health in the Hungarian Population," *International Journal of Behavioral Medicine* 12, No. 2 (2005): 78–85; and K. Soothill, S. M. Morris, J. C. Harman, C. Thomas, B. Francis, and M. B. McIllmurray, "Cancer and Faith. Having Faith—Does It Make a Difference among Patients and Their Informal Carers?" *Scandinavian Journal of Caring Sciences* 16, No. 3: (2002): 256–263, see www.ncbi.nlm.nih.gov/pubmed/12191037, furthermore, of 402 questionnaires, "Not surprisingly, both patients and carers with faith identified a greater need for opportunities for personal prayer, support from people of their own faith and support from a spiritual adviser."

> Only religion can answer the question of the purpose of life. One can hardly be wrong in concluding that the idea of life having a purpose stands and falls with the religious system.[321]

In Koenig's text, *Handbook of Religion and Health*, he gives supportive outcome evidence that forty-two of forty-five studies reveal, "Significant positive relationships between religiousness and purpose or meaning in life."[322] In a review of relevant studies, Koenig reports, "Prior to the year 2000, 81 of 102 quantitative studies (79 percent) reported greater well-being among those who were more religious. Since the year 2000, at least 175 of 224 additional studies (78 percent) found positive associations between greater religiousness and greater well-being."[323]

Clinically, science and spirituality research reveal that individuals want to be asked about their spiritual and faith beliefs. First, patients prefer that their physicians inquire about their religious and spiritual beliefs as part of routine history taking.[324] Secondly, research has noted that two-thirds of surveyed patients say trust in their physician would increase if they were asked about religious and spiritual beliefs.[325] Thirdly, patients reveal their desire for spiritual interaction with their physician increases with severity of illness.[326] And lastly,

---

[321] Sigmund Freud, 1930, "Civilization and its Discontents," in *Standard Edition of the Complete Psychological Works of Sigmund Freud*, ed. and trans. by J. Strachey (London: Hogarth Press (1962), 25, 36.

[322] Harold G. Koenig, Dana King, and Verna Benner Carson, *Handbook of Religion and Health*, 2nd ed. (New York: Oxford University Press, 2012), 131.

[323] Koenig, 144.

[324] Christina M. Puchalski, et al., "Improving the Quality of Spiritual Care as a Dimension of Palliative Care: the Report of the Consensus Conference," *Journal of Palliative Medicine* 12, No. 10 (2009): 885–904; D. E. King, and B. Dushwick, "Beliefs and Attitudes of Hospital Inpatients about Faith Healing and Prayer," *Journal of Family Practice* 39, No. 4 (1994): 349–352; and Gary McCord, Valerie J. Gilchrist, Steven D. Grossman, Bridget D. King, Kenelm F. McCormick, Allison M. Oprandi, Susan Labuda Schrop, Brian A. Selius, William D. Smucker, David L. Weldy, Melissa Amorn, Melissa A. Carter, Andrew J. Deak, Hebah Hefzy, and Mohit Srivastava, "Discussing Spirituality with Patients: a Rational and Ethical Approach," *Annals of Family Medicine* 2, no. 4 (July 2004): 356–361, see www.ncbi.nlm.nih.gov/pmc/articles/PMC1466687/.

[325] J. W. Ehman, B. B. Ott, T. H. Short, R. C. Ciampa, and J. Hansen-Flaschen, "Do Patients Want Physicians to Inquire about Their Spiritual or Religious Beliefs if They Become Gravely Ill?" *Archives of Internal Medicine* 159, no. 15 (August 1999): 1803–1806. See www.ncbi.nlm.nih.gov/pubmed/10448785.

[326] D. C. MacLean, Beth Susi, Nancy Phifer, Linda Schultz, Deborah Bynum, Mark Franco, Andria Klioze, Michael Monroe, Joanne Garrett, and Sam Cykert, "Patient Preference for Physician Discussion and Practice of Spirituality," *Journal of General Internal Medicine* 18, no. 1 (January 2003): 38–43.

surveys reveal that physicians should inquire about beliefs in a thoughtful, rational and ethical manner, while respecting differing perspectives and worldviews.[327] If these are the desires of individuals under medical care, would not it be reasonable that these same desires hold for individuals in any life crisis and situation of stress?

Individuals have noted that they are more pleased with overall care when their spiritual or faith-based needs are recognized. Health care satisfaction surveys show that patients who had a chaplain visit are significantly more likely to endorse positive responses.[328] A specific survey of 1.7 million patients asked those patients if the "staff addressed my emotional and spiritual needs." The results noted that this need is one of the three main drivers of patient satisfaction with hospital experiences.[329] When spiritual needs are unmet, satisfaction is notably lower; unmet spiritual needs affects end-of-life experiences in quality of life, costs of health care, and whether one dies either in an intensive care unit or with hospice care.[330]

One study noted that seventy-eight percent of decision-making surrogates of patients consider religion important, but only sixteen percent of family medical care conferences ever discuss the topic with surrogates. For the family medical care conferences that did offer a spiritual discussion, it was the surrogates who initiated it sixty-five

---

[327] S. G. Post, Christina M. Puchalski, and D. B. Larson, "Physicians and Patient Spirituality: Professional Boundaries, Competency, and Ethics," *Annals of Internal Medicine* 132, no. 7 (April 2000): 578–583; Alan B. Astrow, Christina M. Puchalski, and D. P. Sulmasy, "Religion, Spiritual, and Health Care: Social, Ethical, and Practical Considerations," *American Journal of Medicine* 110, no. 4 (March 2001): 283–287; and Harold G. Koenig, "MSJAMA: Religion, Spirituality, and Medicine: Application to Clinical Practice," *JAMA* 284, No. 13 (2000): 1708.

[328] D. B. Marin, et al, "Relationship between Chaplain Visits and Patient Satisfaction." *Journal Health Care Chaplaincy* 21, no. 1 (2015): 14–24, a survey of 8,978 patients, they said, "Chaplains' integration into the healthcare team improves patients' satisfaction with their hospital stay."

[329] P. A. Clark, M. Drain, and M. P. Malone. "Addressing Patients' Emotional and Spiritual Needs." *The Joint Commission Journal on Quality and Patient Safety* 29, no. 12 (December 2003): 659–670, see www.ncbi.nlm.nih.gov/pubmed/14679869.

[330] Alan B. Astrow, et al, "Is Failure to Meet Spiritual Needs Associated With Cancer Patients' Perceptions of Quality of Care and Their Satisfaction With Care?" *Journal of Clinical Oncology* 25, No. 36 (2007): 5753–5757; Tracy A. Balboni, et al., "Provision of Spiritual Support to Patients with Advanced Cancer by Religious Communities and Associations with Medical Care at the End of Life," *JAMA Internal Medicine* 173, No. 12 (2013): 1109–1117; Tracy A. Balboni, et al., "Support of Cancer Patients' Spiritual Needs and Associations with Medical Care Costs at the End of Life," *Cancer* 117, No. 23 (2011): 5383–5391; and Tracy A. Balboni, et al., "Provision of Spiritual Care to Patients with Advanced Cancer: Associations with Medical are and Quality of Life Near Death," *Journal of Clinical Oncology* 8, No. 3 (2010): 445–452.

percent of time and providers only six percent of time.[331] While physicians see the value of spirituality and religious discussions in medical decision-making and offering social support to patients, they recognize that deleterious effects of religious positions may occur when beliefs conflict with their medical recommendations.[332]

Research has also revealed several barriers. Physicians do not believe they,

1. Have the time to discuss spiritual and religious beliefs with patients;
2. Have the adequate training to provide competent spiritual care;
3. Possess the education to address diverse faith beliefs and spiritual systems; but,
4. Physicians do feel more comfortable when the patient begins spiritual conversations.[333]

In data gathered from workplace chaplain ministries noted in one survey by Cornell University's Roper Center for Public Opinion, Bryan Feller observed that eighty-seven percent of employees said they would work harder for a company willing to help them with their personal problems.[334] For organizations, the inclusion of a workplace minister can offer a huge savings to the bottom-line as a worker's emotional-spiritual issues can dramatically affect performance, job satisfaction and job continuity/turn-over rates. One group cited that in general, "Estimates vary, but most agree that the costs associated with employee turnover are at least 50% to 150% of an employee's annual

---

[331] N. C. Ernecoff, et al, "Health Care Professionals' Responses to Religious or Spiritual Statements by Surrogate Decision Makers During Goals-of-Care Discussions," *JAMA Internal Medicine* 175, no. 10 (October 2015): 1662–1669.

[332] F. A. Curlin, et al, "How Are Religion and Spirituality Related to Health? A Study of Physicians' Perspectives," *Southern Medical Journal* 98, no. 8 (August 2005): 761–766, see www.ncbi.nlm.nih.gov/pubmed/16144169; B. R. Doolittle, et al, "Religion, Spirituality, and HIV Clinical Outcomes: A Systematic Review of the Literature," *AIDS Behavior* 22, no. 6 (June 2016): 1792–1801; and N. Reynolds, et al, "Spiritual Coping Predicts 5-year Health Outcomes in Adolescents with Cystic Fibrosis," *Journal of Cystic Fibrosis* 13, no. 5 (2014): 593–600; A. C. Sherman, et al, "A Meta-analytic Review of Religious or Spiritual Involvement and Social Health Among Cancer Patients," *Cancer* 121, no. 21 (2015): 3779–3788, "In total, 78 independent samples encompassing 14,277 patients were included in the meta-analysis. Social health was significantly associated with overall R/S [Religion and Spirituality]"; and C. L. Park, et al, "Spiritual Peace Predicts 5-Year Morality in Congestive Heart Failure Patients," *Health Psychology* 35, no. 3 (March 2015): 2003-201, see conclusion, "Spiritual peace ... were better predictors of mortality risk ... than were physical health indicators."

[333] Balboni (2013, 2014), Astrow (2001), and Post (2000).

[334] Bryan Feller, "A Business Care for Corporate Chaplaincy" (2011), 2.

salary."³³⁵ Organizations that utilize chaplains in their workforce have cited substantial cost savings to employee turnover. Home Banc reduced turnover from a banking industry average of twenty percent down to fourteen percent.³³⁶ A Taco Bell franchise reduced turnover (from the fast food industry average of three hundred percent) to one hundred twenty-five percent.³³⁷ Allied Holdings reduced turnover (from the trucking industry average of one hundred percent turnover) to below ten percent.³³⁸ And one American LubeFast owner described their chaplain employee assistance provider as *"an employee assistance plan on steroids"* citing dramatic decline in turnover and product loss.³³⁹

In general, Department of Health and Human Services data reveal that employees who utilize employee assistance providers (EAP) file less health claims due to less sickness and accident benefits, mental healthcare costs, less absenteeism, reduced lost wages, reduced medical costs, less turn-over, less worker's compensation costs (up to forty-one percent savings), and less disability costs (up to forty-nine percent savings).³⁴⁰ Feller also noted several intangible benefits for companies who utilize a workplace chaplain:

- Saving employee marriages and relationships,
- Improved customer service,
- Reduced employee conflicts,
- Increased management effectiveness,
- Decreased risk of litigation, and
- Decreased risk of workplace violence.³⁴¹

---

[335] PricewaterhouseCoopers. "Driving the bottom line: improving retention" Saratoga, PricewaterhouseCoopers LLP, 2006.

[336] Tracy McGinnis, "Business Has a Prayer," *Forbes* (June 2006).

[337] Ibid.

[338] Harriet Hankin, *The New Workforce: Five Sweeping Trends That Will Shape your Company's Future* (New York: American Management Association (AMACOM, 2004).

[339] Garrett McKinnon and Tim Embrey; "2007 Fast Lube Operator of the Year," *National Oil & Lube News* (December 2007).

[340] T. C. Blum, and P. M. Roman, *Cost-effectiveness and Preventive Implications of Employee Assistance Programs*, U.S. Department of Health and Human Services (Rockville, MD: SAMSA, 1995).

[341] Feller, 6–7.

Conclusion

Theoretically and theologically, research regarding spirituality and health reveals strong anecdotal and empirical evidence for the practical need of spiritual care services to workers and patients. The evidence also reveals that chaplains bring an 'added-value' (holistically and economically) to organizational systems. For chaplains, the mode of caring and counseling may appear vastly different from parish ministry. The many functional roles which a chaplain might fill in an organization may range from advocate-liaison, counselor, bioethicist, professional educator, comforter, priest, to even liturgist.[342] The effective Christian chaplain will search for areas where they are embedded within pluralism and inject their Christian influence without undue judgement while not compromising their own faith tradition.

---

[342] Larry VandeCreek, and Laurel Burton, "Professional Chaplaincy: Its Role and Importance in Healthcare," *Journal of Pastoral Care* 55, no. 1 (Spring 2001): 86–88. See www.ProfessionalChaplains.org/chaplaincy_importance, for this extraordinary joint statement of the five largest chaplaincy bodies representing 10,000-plus members.

9.
Use of the Concept of New Identity in Christ in Counseling Sexual Addiction in Young Men

by Dr. Alan M. Martin
Dean Emeritus, Oklahoma Christian University
Edmond, Oklahoma, USA, and currently
Vice President of Academic Affairs, African Christian College
Eswatini (Swaziland), Africa

Introduction 157
A. Struggle with Identity.. 158
B. Nature of the Sexual Addiction Struggle 161
C. Use of the Concept of New Identity in Christ to Help the Sexual Addict 163
    1. Restoring the Environment of Sonship: I am loved.. 163
    2. Restoring the Environment of Community: I am not alone 164
    3. Restoring the Environment of Assurance: I am saved 165
    4. Restoring the Environment of Grace: I am favored 166
    5. Restoring the Environment of Forgiveness: I am free.. 166
    6. Restoring the Environment of Victory: I am Destined to Overcome 167
Conclusion 169

Introduction

Glen Whitehouse (2004) draws on the works of H. Richard Niebuhr (1963) that dealt with issues pertaining to the "Responsible Self." His conclusive notion is that a consistent or unified identity through time becomes the crucial precondition for ethical and responsible behavior. Fully living out such responsible behavior means that the individual grows into respecting and enhancing the life of integrity (consistency in claimed identity with actions) in all personal and relational interactions and behaviors in the sight of God. Is "Responsible Selfhood" not the creational mandate for every human being? Was "Responsible Selfhood" not the undermining target of the Adversary from the beginning of time?

Sexual addiction in young men is one such indication of a "Responsible Self" having been undermined through the dissection and division of an individual's integrity and thus his God-like identity. Sexual addiction is in essence an inordinate desire for "what is not rightfully" within the prescribed identity for human, moral, and spiritual behavior. From the beginning of time, man has had the struggle of competing "selves." The Genesis (Gen. 2–3) account bears testimony to the struggle and clearly shows what happens when the "Responsible Self" succumbs to the pressure of inordinate desires. It is clear that human beings are created with built-in tensions between the physical and the spiritual (Cohen, 1995). And so, like our primordial ancestor Adam, human beings struggle to live with the tension between our God-like potential and our created human natures. A huge part of the human being's struggle with sin can be analyzed to also be an integral struggle with "identity."

A. Struggle with Identity

Since the fall of humankind, man has had the quest for the full integration of self. The search for "human wholeness" is really a search for the integration of the physical with the spiritual selves. Daniel Helminiak (1996) posits that "Spirituality is supposed to relate to the deepest meaning of humanity." There are several diverse contemporary approaches to spirituality that acknowledge that spirituality is in essence a quest for personal integration in the face of forces of fragmentation and depersonalization. The identity struggle, therefore, is a much greater struggle than merely a struggle to restore one's personal self. It is fundamentally a struggle for the restoration of the "whole self"—that is, the personal self (man with his body, emotions, psyche, and mind) restored to the spiritual self (man with body, soul, and spirit fully connected to his Maker). Sandra Schneiders (1986) informs that "spirituality refers to the experience of consciously striving to integrate one's life in terms, not of isolation and self-absorption but of self-transcendence toward the ultimate value one perceives" (p. 266).

The struggle with sexual addiction is a struggle for completeness. It is a desire to have increasingly more of some type of physical fulfillment, which fundamentally could not be totally achieved in the physical realm. When subjected to sexual addiction, the "Responsible Self" is therefore fragmented and becomes depersonalized to the degree that the individual's identity remains in a state of struggle. A biblical reminder of such a struggle is evident in Romans 7:15:

> For that which I am doing, I do not understand; for I am not practicing what I would like to do, but I am doing the very thing I hate.

The identity struggle, in the main, is the struggle and quest for spirituality—the ultimate search for God and the restoration of the creation-mandated "image" (Gen. 1:26–27). Stanley Grenz (2002) reminds us of Augustine's "Confessions" in which he said: "Thou hast made us for thyself. Therefore, our hearts are restless until they find rest in thee, O God" (p. 96).

Charles Taylor (1989) in a seminal work, *The Sources of the Self— The Making of Modern Identity*, stresses that if we wish to explore the topic of identity then we must essentially examine the topic of selfhood and morality. His emphatic notion is that selfhood and morality are so inextricably linked: to do otherwise would result in skewed outcomes. Others have argued similarly that moral understanding and moral behaviors are embedded in the structures of a person's perception of "self" (Grenz, 2002). With Christianity, therefore, known as a religion that shapes an individual's thinking (mind), and hence behavior (moral actions), it would behoove us to consider the impact of Christian identity on the ever-perplexing phenomenon known as "sexual addiction."

Numerous scholars have wrestled with the question of identity and have asked whether identity is not perhaps shaped by more than just the "individual self." The quest is for a deeper and more systemic understanding of all the forces that go into the formulation of an individual's identity. Some have postulated that one's identity is not merely, and only, formed by the dependency on one's personal experiences and memory, but that it must of necessity have deep roots in the realm of one's social construction and shaping. William L. Wardekker and Siebren Miedema (2001) have presented lucid thoughts on this aspect of identity formation that is worth noting:

> On this view, identity is the way we explain, in the form of a life story (autobiography), the choices we make in our commitments, and their consistency, to others and to ourselves. The advantage of this model over others is that it does not posit the individuals the sole creator of its own self-concept. Individual stories are created through the use of story schemata, genres, motives, metaphors, examples, and other elements that are found in culture. (It is exactly the use of such cultural elements that makes an individual's story comprehensible to others and to the self.). Moreover, other people play a role in the construction process: as audience, as people to relate the story to, as co-constructors.

The Wardekker and Miedema (2001) view seems to hinge on the crucial impact that social relationships have on the shaping of "self," and how those influences engender and enhance understanding of one's identity. This second aspect becomes crucial in formulating an approach to counseling young men trapped by sexual addiction, because it does follow the biblical notion of the importance of the individual's mature development of a Christ-like identity, not only as an individual "self," but crucially as "self in community" within the body of Christ. In essence, a person's Christian identity as a believer should serve as the compass to give direction to all other parts of the self (cognitions, affective domain, and behaviors). And, since all humans are made in the "image of God," it follows that any fragmentation of that image (and identity) through alienation from God needs restoration through God's primary image bearer, Jesus Christ. Romans 8:29 (NASB) states: "For whom He foreknew, He also predestined to become conformed to the image of His Son, that He might be the firstborn among many brethren." But more than that, the Father has clearly designed for the Son to be His image:

> And He is the image of the invisible God, the first-born of all creation. For by Him all things were created, both in the heavens and on earth, visible and invisible, whether thrones or dominions or rulers or authorities—all things have been created by Him and for Him. And He is before all things, and in Him all things hold together. He is also the head of the body, the church; and He is the beginning, the first-born from the dead; so that He Himself might come to have first place in everything. For it was the Father's good pleasure for al the fullness to dwell in Him, and through Him to reconcile all things to Himself, having made peace through the blood of His cross; through Him, I say, whether things on earth or things in heaven. And although you were formerly alienated and hostile in mind, engaged in evil deeds, yet He has now reconciled you in His fleshly body through death, in order to present you before Him holy and blameless and beyond reproach—if indeed you continue in the faith firmly established and steadfast, and not moved away from the hope of the gospel. (Col. 1:15–23, NASB).

The ordering of a believer's identity is, therefore, not without a divine blueprint and the definitive promises of obtaining fullness, reconciliation, holiness, and blamelessness (freedom of guilt and reproach). The full realization of the intention for humans is to be found in the clothing or re-clothing of the fragmented human self and identity with the *Imago Dei* (Glanzer & Ream, 2005). Before we embark on the explication of the influence of the *Imago Dei* on moral behavior, it would be to our advantage to have a cursory understanding of sexual addiction and its seeming indomitable power over young men.

B. Nature of the Sexual Addiction Struggle

As I am writing this journal article, the news media is having a feast over the Penn State University coach's alleged paraphilic sexual indiscretions. He had been arrested on alleged charges of about fifty counts of sexual assault with 10 minor boys over a period of 15 years. If all of this is true and verified, where would this have started? Most professionals who work in the field of sexual addiction counseling believe that it grows from seeds planted in childhood. During adolescence, the indicators of this penchant may be accepted as normal sexual development. However, from young adulthood, the disorder may grow progressively worse if it goes undetected and untreated (Laaser, 2004). For young men (and the same is also true of adult men) then, being trapped in the sexual addiction cycle has some etiology established during the early developmental years of life.

Leanne Payne (1991) highlights a quote from a Roman Catholic philosopher-theologian, Roman Guardini who wrote:

> The act of self-acceptance is the root of all things. I must agree to be the person who I am. Agree to have the qualifications which I have. Agree to live within the limitations set for me.... The clarity and the courageousness of this acceptance is the foundation of all existence (p. 31).

The foundation for a young man's identity and sexual security and fulfillment is rooted in a healthy measure of "self-acceptance and self-love." This was the kernel of Jesus' response to a Pharisaic lawyer in Matthew 22:37 (NASB):

> "You shall love the LORD your God with all your heart, and with all your soul, and with all your mind." This is the great and foremost commandment. The second is like it, "You shall love your neighbor as yourself." On these two commandments depend the whole Law and the Prophets.

Structuring Jesus' response from the personal to the divine would sound something like this: "Loving and accepting yourself correctly first will lead to loving and accepting your neighbor correctly next, and then most importantly loving and accepting God correctly." John says:

> for the one who does not love his brother whom he has seen, cannot love God whom he has not seen. And this commandment we have from Him, that the one who loves God should love his brother also (1 John 4:20–21, NASB).

There is, therefore, something to be said for the love of "self and neighbor" which will reflect on a person's love for God. There is a clear linkage, according to Jesus and John with respect to loving self, neighbor, and God. And that linkage, according to Jesus, has much to do with the core status of an individual's love and acceptance of self. The way the neighbor (which could be an image of the opposite sex or even same sex for that matter) will be treated or viewed depends on the deep psychological schemata of an individual's *own view of self and personal acceptance.*

The literature is replete with categorical elements that comprise the dynamics and characteristics of sexual addiction. According to Laaser and Gregoire (2003), the dimensions of healthy sexuality—in order of priority—are spiritual, personal, behavioral, relational, and physical. The core element is the "spiritual," that gives direction and value to all the connecting elements. An exploration, therefore, of the person's spiritual life (how his life is connected and committed to things divine or God-directed) and commitment must be dealt with first. The "seeking the kingdom first" principle (Mt. 6:33) and practice is what will give direction to all the "other needs" that an individual may have. Furthermore, the assessment of the person's willingness to "surrender" his life and passions to the authority of Jesus Christ then becomes paramount to embarking on the fulfillment of perhaps a spiritual and emotional thirst that may exist within. The paradoxical "dying to self to find life" is no less true with respect to a person's physical, emotional, and psychological illicit passions and desires.

In the realm of the personal and behavioral, exploration must involve checking if there are any wounds in the areas of sexual abuse, emotional and psychological abuse, and loneliness and issues of isolation (Laaser & Gregoire, 2003). Issues of a loss of control over life or circumstances may also contribute largely to a person wishing to feel a sense of control over "something" (which in this case is sexual activities). The person may have the illusory sense that he is exercising control during such times, but it is merely the feeding into the same cycle of "being controlled" by the addiction (Garcia & Thibaut, 2010). Therefore, the greater the secret feeling of being in control, the deeper the dominance of the private and addictive behaviors with the individual.

In the realm of the relational, assessment must involve checking for difficulties at a person-to-person level (Levine, 2010). The relational disconnect(s) usually have their origins in the parent-child attachment/abandonment issues. Unavailable and sexually punitive spouses may trigger the historical, childhood abandonment issues which will then in turn compel the addict to retreat into his comfortable, secret place (Marcus, 2010). This re-experiencing of abandonment further enhances the addict's drive to avoid growth in the actual person-to-person intimacies. The addictive, sexual behavior with unknown people or objects, therefore, becomes an outlet for intimacies without the threats of the person-to-person abandonment. How then will we use the knowledge about the nature of the sexual addiction struggle at the intersection with the young addict's new identity in Christ?

C. Use of the Concept of New Identity in Christ to Help the Sexual Addict

Young men who are caught in the trap of sexual addiction roam around in a private world of shame and guilt. Outwardly they may manifest confidence, self-control, and psychological normalcy, but inwardly there is a raging war with foes that want to undermine their newfound identity and standing in Jesus Christ. We, therefore, want to recalibrate their personal views of their spiritual environments which, for sure, have been demolished by the Evil One to keep them in the cycle of sexual addiction. Their personal and spiritual identities have been undermined and are in need of serious restoration. A healthy, spiritual systemic approach to dealing with their sexual addiction will affect much more than just the cessation of the addictive behaviors. It will restore spiritual confidence and reestablish the person's walk in his designated and pre-ordained *Imago Dei* identity.

1. Restoring the Environment of Sonship: I am loved

The believer who is caught up in the cycle of sexual addiction perennially lives with untold guilt and shame. It is the nature of guilt and shame to drive a person towards isolation and a sense of feeling "unworthy" (White & Kimball, 2009). The words of the lost son in Luke 15:21 ring true to the life of the person who is experiencing the cycle of guilt, shame, and unworthiness: "Father, I have sinned against heaven and against you. I am no longer worthy to be called your son." The lost son's father recognized that restoration had to start with an immediate reminder that this lost son was still "this son of mine" (Luke 15:24). At the heart of the celebration was not only the fact that the son returned, but a reaffirmation of his place and position in the family.

Sexual addicts feel psychologically, emotionally, and even sometimes physically isolated from those who are "in the family." They need the genuine embrace of the Father and His reassurance that they are still "His sons." Here it behooves the counselor or minister to represent the heavenly Father's actionable embrace with the accompanying words: "Quick! Bring the best robe and put it on him. Put a ring on his finger and sandals on his feet" (Luke 15:22). The reconfirmation of sonship is the foundational platform for the start of the sexual addict's rehabilitation work. Those caught in the cycle of sexual addiction need to be reminded that the heavenly Father desires their existence and position to be that of "sons" and not that of "slaves to addiction." The fresh realization of "sonship" with all its divine privileges and power will instill a sense of hope, confidence, and gratitude. The reminder and reconfirmation of "sonship" will also begin to eliminate feelings of guilt and shame, and will initiate the process of restoration of the personal and spiritual identities.

2. Restoring the Environment of Community: I am not alone

In multiple case studies of Christians who are caught in the cycle of sexual addiction, the major issue for them is "how they would be seen as individuals ... if their problem was revealed within the church" (White & Kimball, 356). The stigmatization, labeling, and the fear of enhanced isolation are sure realities for the sexual addict. Some have suggested the sharing of stories, publications, and books with the addict to let him know that "he is not alone in his struggle" (Bridges 2003). Several churches have programs that cater for the support of people who are caught in the cycle of some type of addiction. The sexual addict should be connected with such programs in addition to personal counseling and accountability partnership.

Bentley (2005) found that 60% of young men (aged 19–22 years) in a Christian denomination have accessed pornographic sites more than 25 times. That is not unusual across denominations nowadays, which clearly is a red flag warning to the church that we need to be in the "ready mode" to deal appropriately with this surging dilemma within our church communities.

We have done well to alert people to the Christian websites that could block access to pornographic sites, but we have not done well in educating our church communities in addressing the dilemma "in church." The reality is that cybersex addiction is spiraling out of control among our young adults with little to no concrete, spiritual help being offered within our church communities. This writer is of the conviction that the church community (as a collective) and not merely a side program (e.g., Celebrate Recovery) must be the fountain of healing, embrace, and support to the young men in our midst who are enslaved to sexual addiction.

To fully restore the sexual addict's personal and spiritual identity, he has to feel and experience the sense of attachment to his spiritual community. And that sense of attachment is not merely experiencing corporate worship with the affiliation group, but it must be the integral daily connection that the sexual addict must have after his spiritual dilemma has been revealed to the church community. It would be prudent for the counselor or minister to provide avenues for such connection(s) for the sexual addict. The connections (a small group or couple of individuals) could then serve as mentors and accountability partners to the sexual addict. The mentors could also be used to guide the sexual addict through a period of exercising several spiritual disciplines like praying, bible study, fasting, meditation, confession, and the like.

3. Restoring the Environment of Assurance: I am saved

The believer who has succumbed to sexual addiction must be reminded that his ultimate destiny is not determined by the addiction. There will be times when the sexual addict's struggles will be so overwhelming that he will "feel" totally unsure about his salvation. The reminder of assurance can bolster the person's faith in the purpose of salvation—ongoing redemption, reconciliation, and healing. The sexual addict must be given a fresh reminder of John 10:27–29:

> My sheep listen to my voice; I know them, and they follow me. I gave them eternal life, and they shall never perish; no one can snatch them out of my hand. My Father, who has given them to me, is greater than all; no one can snatch them out of my Father's hand.

The voice of Jesus is definitely *the* voice of assurance when it comes to sheep who listens to His voice. Hurting and struggling sheep are never bashed and made to feel unworthy during their struggles. They are continually called to "keep following and listening to His voice." They are tenderly shepherded to find rest and healing.

The voice of the counselor or minister must resemble and echo the voice of the Good Shepherd during the addict's struggle. The sexual addict must walk out of every session of counseling with a sense of reassurance and hope that he is still saved and in God's fold. The counselor's voice must be a directive one, but it must simultaneously be a voice of total healing, empathy, genuineness, acceptance, and reassurance (Steffen, 1998). Wounded people have an extraordinary sixth sense for discerning judgementalism. Beware of the judgementalism that will crush any hopes of the sexual addict gaining any traction on the pathway of assurance.

4. Restoring the Environment of Grace: I am favored

Human strength and will are not enough to carry the sexual addict through the valley of recovery. What is needed is a fresh realization of the power of God's grace in the midst of the struggle. The reminder of grace will restore the person's vision of hope, and grace will reignite the realization that divine salvation or any type of spiritual healing has never been based on pure human effort alone. The environment of grace—the pouring forth of God's undeserved favor—is the healing balm that every sexual addict needs for the removal of disordered layers of guilt, shame, and sense of unworthiness (Arends, 2010).

It is the environment of grace that will provide the believing sexual addict with the confidence of his secure position in Jesus Christ and his place in the body. Peter admonishes believers to

> be on guard so that you may not be carried away by the error of lawless men and fall from your secure position. But grow in the grace and knowledge of our Lord and Savior Jesus Christ. (2 Pet. 3:17–18, NIV).

The counseling process must, therefore, provide opportunities for the sexual addict to *grow in the grace of Christ.* Such an environment is not one of totalitarian control and legalism, but it is clearly an environment of understanding, nurturing, and compassionate guidance into the will of God.

5. Restoring the Environment of Forgiveness: I am free

No sin (except for blasphemy) can keep the sexual addict separated from God while the blood of Jesus Christ is available. The reminder of forgiveness and its depth and height will restore the person's trust in God and Christ's work on Calvary. Most, if not all human beings despise and loathe any type of enforced bondage. The struggle, therefore, under a self-imposed bondage for most human beings is physically, psychologically, emotionally, socially, and spiritually gigantic. Sometimes the worst part of the sexual addict's struggles is that of accepting and believing that he has been forgiven (Wagner, 2009). While the struggle exists, which will be the case even during the healing process, the person may feel bound, pulled, and even "unforgiven." It is, of course, Satan's ever-prevailing task to keep the sexual addict under the umbrella of "guilt and shame," so that he can fall back into the old pattern of feeling unworthy and condemned.

The pivotal role of the counselor or minister here is to take the sexual addict back to the power and efficacy of the cross of Jesus Christ. Paul's words in Ephesians 1:7–8 (NIV) can be very helpful at this stage of the process:

> In him we have redemption through his blood, the forgiveness of sins, in accordance with the riches of God's grace that he lavished on us with all wisdom and understanding.

Emphasis must be laid on the biblical doctrine that the blood of Jesus Christ has perpetual cleansing powers (1 John 1:9) available to believers, irrespective of their struggles. Submission and obedience to the will of God even during difficult struggles are clear signs and indicators of faith and trust in Him Who loves and forgives.

6. Restoring the Environment of Victory: I am Destined to Overcome

In this final, essential, environment for restoration, it will be important for the counselor to remind and emphasize the fundamental premise of the Christian faith—*victory!* Believers have the promise of victory through Jesus Christ. The reminder of victory will *empower* the person to *fight* to overcome, rather than surrender to the subtle and drenching power of the Evil One. Once the sexual addict has confessed his sinful pattern—of being trapped in the vicious cycle of sexual addiction—it is easy to begin the process of wallowing in the pit of victimization (Reed, 2000). This is a very important juncture in the therapeutic process; because although all the above-mentioned environments may be in place, the psychological underpinning of victory is what will take the sexual addict into the "I can do this" mindset. A huge part of this victory reformation for the sexual addict, though, is to be reminded of the basis of his victory.

John Coe (2008) has some helpful reminders of what this basis is all about:

> The moral temptation is the attempt to deal with our spiritual failure, guilt and shame by means of spiritual efforts, by attempting to perfect one's self in the power of the self. It is the attempt of the well-intentioned believer to use spiritual formation, spiritual disciplines, ministry, service, obedience—being good in general—as a way to *relieve the burden of spiritual failure, lack of love and the guilt and shame that results. It is the temptation to try to relieve a burden that Christ alone can relieve* (pp. 55–56).

Important in this reminder is the notion that the sexual addict needs to know that former acts of moral failure can never be made up for by positive deposits of numerous good deeds. Redemption is only possible through the blood of Jesus Christ and not earned goodness. Coe (2008) posits that

> the Christian has the possibility of being the most "moral" in the fullest and best sense of the term. That is, it is possible for the believer to be good and grow in virtue not as a way to deal with failure, guilt and shame in the Christian life but to do so in freedom, on the basis of the cross and in the Spirit (p. 56).

The environment that merges all the restorative elements within this process of counseling the sexual addict is rock solid on the foundation of the achievements of Christ on the cross, and the continuing work of empowerment and victory that the Spirit will provide to all of God's children, irrespective of their idiosyncratic struggles.

It is also pivotal to help the sexual addict to develop an "inward rather than an outward" focus on the struggle. Too many counselors and ministers set up their counselees for failure by merely focusing on the behavioral transformations that need to happen. A major part of the believer's new identity is his revision or renewal of perspective. As the apostle Paul would say:

> For our struggle is not against flesh and blood, but against the rulers, against the authorities, against the powers of this dark world and against the spiritual forces of evil in the heavenly realms. (Eph. 6:12, NIV)

Preston (2010) would remind us that "what matters most for how life goes and ought to go is what we are on the inside. This 'within' is the arena of spiritual formation and, later, reformation" (p. 217).

Conclusion

Sexual addiction among young men is growing in our world, and the community of faith must be ready to serve the wounded. The restorative environments of

> Sonship,
> Community,
> Assurance,
> Grace,
> Forgiveness, and
> Victory

are essential for the holistic and systemic rehabilitation of the sexual addict. As noted earlier, the sexual addiction cycle is vicious, pernicious, and powerful, and all the spiritual strongholds that God has placed at our human disposal for healing must be brought into full view and use during such a struggle.

At the heart of the sexual addiction struggle is the issue of clarifying the true self. Part of that clarification involves the verification that the self is accepted—by God as His child—*attached* to the family of God and not cut off because of the struggle, and *assured* of a continuing eternal salvation as the sexual addiction battle is fought, a certain recipient of God's grace and forgiveness—all with the promise of victory over the sexual addiction struggle.

10.
New Identity in Christ—Counseling Women Who Have Been Sexually Abused or Raped
by Dr. LaVerne Bell-Tolliver
Associate Professor Emeritus, School of Social Work
University of Arkansas, Little Rock[343]

Introduction 171
A. Emotions and Behaviors of Victims.. 172
B. Influence of Sexual Assault on Women from a Spiritual Standpoint............. 174
C. New Identities in Christ... 176
D. Therapeutic Methods of Counseling Women Victims 179
Summary 183

Introduction

When I was asked to write this article, I thought of two possible ways of handling the material: I could either write it from a totally professional and objective standpoint, or I could also disclose that I too have been a victim of this type of trauma. The reason that I ultimately chose to write from the latter position is the fact that so many people have been sexually traumatized and find it extremely difficult to reveal the information to anyone. Unfortunately for many of them, the pain, fears, shame, and other emotions may remain locked within. These feelings may well influence future decisions and behaviors these women make, as well as the thoughts they have about themselves, others, and life in general. I therefore chose to model the behavior that I would like for readers who may have experience the trauma of being raped or sexually assaulted by briefly sharing information concerning my assault. It is hoped that by sharing a little of my story, readers will become more understanding of and compassionate to the needs that other victims may have in order to help them appropriately move forward on the path of healing.

I was a victim of date rape at the age of 19 while I was away from home for the first time and in college. I was unaware that I had to be

---

[343] Bell-Tolliver holds a MSW, MABC, Ph.D., LCSW, and prior to retiring was Assistant Professor and Coordinator of the Post-Masters Marriage and Family Therapy Certificate Program, University of Arkansas at Little Rock School of Social Work.

concerned about being harmed by someone I knew and thought I could trust. Because I was a virgin at the time, I believe that this act affected me even more profoundly because of what I saw as the loss of my dreams and hopes for a happy marriage to a loving husband and followed by the birth of healthy and happy children. I learned firsthand of the emotions that many victims experience and that are discussed in this article.

Since that time and in my professional life, I have also provided therapy to many girls and women who were sexually abused as children or raped or assaulted as adolescents or adults. I understand and can directly identify with the questions that women may have concerning their identities—who they are after experiencing the trauma, and more importantly, who they are in Christ.

According to the Bureau of Justice Statistics (2010), one in every 1,000 ages 12 and over in the United States were victims of rape or sexual assault. Rape was defined as "forced sexual intercourse including both psychological coercion as well as physical force." Although violent crime rates (including murder, rape and sexual assault, robbery, and assault) have decreased since 2000 (Truman & Rand, 2010), and are down by 39% according to this report, the emotions that victims of these crimes experience are profound.

I describe the emotions and possible behaviors that females may display as result of experiencing the trauma. I then explore the impact of the crimes of rape and sexual assault on women from a spiritual standpoint, consider the victims' new identities in Christ, and discuss therapeutic methods of counseling those women who have been traumatized by rape and sexual assault. Throughout, I identify persons from the Bible who may have suffered from the trauma of rape and sexual assault. For the purpose of this article, the terms "rape," "sexual abuse," and "sexual assault" will be used interchangeably unless otherwise specified.

A. Emotions and Behaviors of Victims

Females of all ages have been raped and sexually traumatized (Pratt, 2005). When they experience some form of sexual assault, their feelings of emotion may range from shame, to fear of negative social repercussions or guilt (Fontes, 2007). When Amnon raped his half-sister Tamar (2 Sam. 13:1–20), she may have experienced many feelings ranging from shock, betrayal, grief, and despair. Feelings of grief and loss are common during such situations (Miller, Cardona, and Hardin, 2006). Tamar knew how she would be treated by others within her culture at the time, and therefore pleaded unsuccessfully with Amnon to cease his attack on her. The fear of what others might say is all too often based on reality, in that perpetrators, parents, relatives, friends, or community members might blame the victim for the assault (Webster & Dunn, 2005). Unfortunately, after the rape, Tamar lived in despair and never again saw herself as someone of worth, dignity, or worthy to be loved (2 Sam. 13:20).

Victims, even children, might be told that they invited the assault, because they either dressed too provocatively, looked at the perpetrator in a sexual manner, or otherwise engaged in some type of sexually inviting behavior. As a result, some victims are afraid to let anyone know that they have been abused (Crisp, 2007; Fontes, 2007). Victims may change their appearance or behavior in various ways in order to prevent a recurrence of the same situation (Crisp, 2007). All too often, women suffer from such clinically classified disorders such as Post-traumatic Stress Disorder (Whetten et al., 2006), anxiety, depression; that includes a lack of psychological well-being in general, and they often report having poor physical health (Murray-Swank & Pargament, 2005).

Victims of sexual assault may subsequently engage in self-destructive behaviors such as substance abuse, high-risk sexual behaviors, and some even become abusive toward others (Kim & Williams, 2009; Whetten et al., 2006). Others may engage in self-injurious behaviors that might result in bringing significant harm to themselves (Wagner & Rehfuss, 2008). Many times these women are unaware of the reasons for employing such practices. Unfortunately, the behaviors are frequently used as a psychological defense to cover the pain they are feeling, and those defenses tend to bring their own set of negative complications, e.g., drug addiction, sexually transmitted diseases, or further loss of integrity and esteem.

Consider the possibility that Rahab, "the harlot" (Josh. 2:1–21; 6:22–25), may have been a victim of an assault. Scripture does not inform us how Rahab arrived at the decision of becoming a prostitute. It simply proclaimed that as her occupation. Certainly, the occupational options for women who could not marry were limited in that day, although people belonging to nations other than Israel may have had a wider range of choices. Nevertheless, Rahab chose, as do many women who have been sexually abused or raped, to become a harlot, a profession and set of behaviors that eventually lead to a cycle of degradation, despair, and possibly even death. Thanks be unto God, that He chose to rescue her from this life, to redeem her of her sins, and to rebirth her and her family to a different nation that would eventually yield the Savior of the world.

B. Influence of Sexual Assault on Women from a Spiritual Standpoint

Victims of sexual assault frequently suffer damaging blows to their senses of self. They may wonder who they are and whether they are considered as persons of worth or dignity after the occurrence of the incident. As mentioned earlier, their perceptions may well be complicated by the messages they receive from such persons as the perpetrator, family members, friends, or the community in general (Greenspun, 1994). During normal phases of development, children and adolescents look to some of these same people for affirmation of their self-worth. Depending on the age of the person when the assault or *assaults* happened, the victim might still be in their formative stages of psychosocial development (Kim & Williams, 2009). Such a trauma, along with the messages they receive, have a great potential to heavily influencing the outcomes of them successfully mastering their current and future developmental stage crises; and it is hard for anyone to successfully develop after such trauma.

For example, adolescents in general must answer such major questions for themselves as:

> Who am I?
>
> What do I believe in?
>
> What is my purpose in life?'

Later, into young adulthood and the subsequent stages, a sense of self-worth may be reaffirmed or maintained internally as they learn how to navigate social, career, religious, and intimate relationships (Zastrow & Kirst-Ashman, 2010). A person who is victimized by trauma may experience both a distorted sense of self-worth from both the internal and external messages they receive. As a result of that trauma, victims tend to react both positively and negatively to religiosity, to spirituality, and to God.

The term "religiosity" describes the practices that are utilized to build and strengthen one's relationship with God. Some of those practices include church attendance, prayer, reading the Bible, and other types of religious literature, including watching and listening to some types of religious information and music (Chatters & Taylor, 1998). "Spirituality" describes the personal beliefs that give meaning to existence and provides a sense of a connection to the universe and a higher power (Wilkerson, as cited in Bell-Tolliver & Wilkerson, 2011). While these terms are frequently used interchangeably in literature, as they will be used in this manuscript, they are also frequently used separately.

A Christian believer has taken a step beyond mere *religiosity* and *spirituality* in that he or she has placed a deeper trust in the Redeemer. This step transcends religious practices and a general sense of belief in a higher power and the universe. Indeed, this profession of faith moves the individual into the beginning stages of a personal relationship with Christ.

Several studies have proposed that victims of childhood sexual abuse have been found to subsequently have negative opinions toward God and religion (Finkelhor, Hotaling, Lewis, and Smith, as cited in Kim & Williams, 2009; Hall, as cited by Murray-Swank & Pargament, 2005; Russell, as cited in Crisp, 2007). Some child victims of incest found it difficult to see their Heavenly Father separately from their earthly fathers who sexually abused them, and therefore distanced themselves from God.

"Who we are and our relationships to others, including God, are tested in the light of our experiences" (Crisp 2007, p. 302). The "experiences" of being sexual traumatized brings victims face to face with the test of determining how to move forward in a totally different world and with a different self. For many victims, their response is to leave the church, to distance themselves from religious practices, and decrease spiritual beliefs. Unfortunately, decreased physical and mental well-being are also associated with people who select this option (Murray-Swank & Pargament, 2005). This makes sense: to whom would a victim turn for hope if he or she no longer sees a loving and saving God as an option to run for refuge?

C. New Identities in Christ

While it is not difficult to understand the reasons that many victims of such violent crimes as rape and assault would question the safety of world as they know it, or turn from God as they know Him, it is important for the body of Christ to have a response for those who are still in the questioning phase of their journeys after having been assaulted. It is also important to recognize that there might be at least three categories of victims. Those categories are separate from the developmental stages that are mentioned earlier in this article.

> **First**, there are victims who are unsaved, and as such do not know Christ, or have a relationship with him. This group can also include those who attend church, but have not gone far beyond that point.
>
> **Second**, there are believers who have accepted Christ as their Savior, but have not matured very much in the faith.
>
> **Finally**, there are believers who are spiritually mature, who are studying, living, and learning about God on a daily basis, and who are committed to leading Godly lives (Mt. 13:3–9).

The *horror*—it is *imperative* for us to note certain facts as we address the horror of sexual assault. We who are believers realize and acknowledge that we live in a fallen world (Gen. 3). As a result, we recognize that all manner of sinful and evil acts occur (Rom. 1; Gal. 5:19–21). As a matter of fact, we are all sinners, both as a result of being born in the family of Adam (Rom. 6:12–14) and because of our own sinful works (Rom. 3:23). We also confess that, although we are sinners and certainly deserving of death (Rom. 6:23), Christ Himself provided the solution for us by becoming the propitiation for our sins, both Jew and Gentile (Eph. 3:14–18).

There is another issue, however, that is critical for women who are victims of sexual assault to realize and accept: they are not to bear the burden of guilt for being raped or abused. This world will continue to have people who commit crimes because, as humans, we have free will. Many victims have taken on the unnecessary guilt for having been attacked and doubt their previous course of actions: some will say, "I should have?" or "If only I hadn't." As mentioned earlier, these statements are often compounded by the messages victims receive from friends, family, perpetrators, and even the legal system.

These horrendous feelings or emotions often carry victims into bottomless pits of anger and depression. While it is of critical importance to help women victims arrive at the point of understanding that all of us have sinned and are in need of a Savior, it is also crucial to help them to understand that they should not take on the responsibility of bearing someone else's guilt and sin. That point of awareness and acceptance can prepare victims for the opportunity to establish a new and real identity in Christ on the basis of

1. Needing Him to forgive them of their personal sins (Rom. 10:9–10), and
2. Because they need His healing and total cleansing power (Mark 6:53–56).

There is a freeing power in discovering that they are new creatures in Christ.

> Therefore, if anyone is in Christ,
> he is a new creation;
> old things have passed away;
> behold all things have become new
> 2 Cor. 5:17 NKJV

As a result of becoming a daughter of God (John 1:12), the victim no longer has to bear the marks of shame, guilt, or uncleanliness.

> Healing of shame begins when a woman identifies and confesses the lies she has believed about herself. She then must begin to replace those lies with biblical truth about who God is and who she is as His beloved child—a person of immeasurable worth, righteous and uncondemned (*The Woman's Study Bible*, 1995, 1933).

This healing process helps victims begin to establish their new identities. Indeed, they no longer have to remain in the role of "victim." For many who have been abused, the shame and guilt that is involved may bind victims in an emotional bondage or prison. As they heal by understanding *who they are in Christ*, they become aware, first, that God is with them and that they do not have to fear the workings of the world, no matter how strong the challenge may be (Heb. 13:5–6). Second, as they heal, they are being increasingly transformed by the renewing of their mind to live according to the truths of God, and not according to the messages of the world (Rom. 12:1–2). Third, they realize that they actually have spiritual power, given to them by God, even the mighty power to fight the fears within and the outside worldly messages they receive.

> For though we live in the world, we do not wage war as the world does. The weapons we fight with are not the weapons of the world. On the contrary, they have divine power to demolish strongholds. We demolish arguments and every pretension that sets itself up against the knowledge of God, and we take captive every thought to make it obedient to Christ. (2 Cor. 10:3–5, *Today's New International Version*)

Imagine how excited Mary Magdalene must have felt when Jesus healed her from the demons within (Mark 16:9). Although she may or may not have been sexually assaulted, Mary was traumatized in ways that few of us can imagine in the U.S., though some do suffer similar injustices today in countries that legalize abuse of women. After being healed by Jesus, however, Mary faithfully served Him in ways that still allow us to think of her and to thank God for her service to the Kingdom (John 20:11–18).

A huge dilemma for women victims is the belief that God could have prevented the act of sexual assault from occurring to them. Given the fact that He is all-powerful and sovereign, they might reason, He *should have* prevented this horrendous tragedy from occurring. Such thinking can, and indeed has brought many to the point of leaving the church (Murray-Swank & Pargament, 2005). What tends to happen is that these women may have developed a form of distorted thinking.

Instead of recognizing that humans are responsible for their willful acts of disobedience to God, many victims choose to blame God Himself. Instead, the Bible holds "men responsible for their voluntary actions alone, or more strictly for their choices alone" (Finney, 1992, p. 184). In this case, the perpetrators are responsible for the trauma they wrought upon the victims. Finney reminds us of the scripture from James 1:14–15 (NKJV):

> But each one is tempted when he is drawn away by his own desires and enticed. Then when desire has conceived, it gives birth to sin; and sin, when it is full-grown, brings forth death.

Tragically, this death is spread not only to the perpetrator, but also to the victim. For the perpetrator, the consequence is separation from God because of his willingness to engage in the voluntary act of disobedience. For the victims this could potentially mean, as it did once to me, death to beliefs, dreams, hopes, plans, etc. God, however, has not failed to provide the victim with the opportunity to be healed, strengthened, loved, and transformed, even in spite of the terrible circumstances (1 Cor. 10:13). Women have been able to move past the anger and confusion, and they have been able to discover the great truth that God truly does love them.

Although studies have demonstrated that women victims distance themselves from religion after being attacked, other studies have also found that God's love, or one's relationship with God, has been found to serve as a protective factor for victims (Kim & Williams, 2009; Murray-Swank & Pargament, 2005). These findings were explained by virtue of the fact that those who have identified God as their internal source for esteem were not as significantly affected by what occurred to them on an external basis. In other words, their personal relationships with Christ seemed to protect them from the powerfully negative and traumatic attacks of the world (Eph. 6:12).

D. Therapeutic Methods of Counseling Women Victims

The church and counseling community must prepare a therapeutic response for women who have been sexually assaulted. Crisp (2007) reports that the church has a negative history to overcome; in previous years, victims have reported their abuse to the church and have frequently been rejected, not believed, or even placed in harm's way by being told to obey one's parents or authority figures. As members of the body of Christ we are equipped to meet the needs of the body (1 Cor. 12). Fouque and Glachan reported that many people who participated in Christian counseling that was "directive and authoritative" (2000) spoke negatively of it, explaining that they felt blamed for having committed sins related to being sexually abused. The authors argued that this approach could "violate boundaries, repeat an abusive situation or use the survivor client to meet the counsellor's own unrecognized needs for power and control." Unfortunately for victims, it is quite possile to re-experience the abuse in a variety of settings, including the counseling environment. This serves as a caution for persons who are not licensed or who have not received education in counseling; particularly in the area of sexual abuse, unskilled helpers should strongly consider referring victims to the appropriate sources for help in order to prevent the possibly of well-intentioned re-victimization. (Fouque & Glachan, 2000).

Only a few studies exist currently that focus on spiritually or biblically therapeutic interventions that have been developed for women victims of sexual trauma. One is *Solace for the Soul*, and below a few others approaches are given.

Solace for the Soul was developed by Murray-Swank (2005). This "non-denominational" spiritual intervention utilizes seven themes during individual therapy: "images of God, abandonment and anger at God, spiritual connection, shame, the body, and sexuality" to help victims focus on the spiritual challenges they experience and to utilize spirituality as a coping resource (Murray-Swank & Pargament, 2005, p. 192). Although the article identifies this approach as non-denominational and spiritual, as opposed to being Bible centered or strictly Christian in nature, *Solace for the Soul* actually refers to various types of religious beliefs including "Judaism, Christianity, Islam, Zoroastrianism, and Sikhism" (Murray-Swank & Pargament, 2005, p. 192). Nevertheless, participants have found this approach to be effective for them. The fact that spirituality is used within a therapeutic setting is a significant step forward in working with clients. One participant made a favorable comment, "Although I haven't let go of the anger completely, I am working towards God" (Murray-Swank & Pargament, 2005, p. 201).

Within the secular therapeutic community, Narrative Therapy has been utilized with victims of sexual assault, and more particularly with childhood sexual abuse victims (Miller, Cardona, & Hardin, 2006). Narrative Therapy is an intervention that allows clients to tell their stories and assign their own meanings to those stories, before moving forward and co-constructing, with their therapists, a strong, more empowering resolution to their future lives (Nichols, 2010). This approach can be quite helpful to women who have been victimized, as many experience feelings of powerlessness or helplessness after having been assaulted on several levels. This approach also allows them to externalize their problem, so that, instead of internalizing the guilt, blame, shame, etc., the victim is able to verbalize these emotions and to then move to a new role beyond that of "the victim" (Miller, Cardona, & Hardin, 2006).

This type of therapeutic approach could be helpful within the Christian community. Victims can become greatly empowered as a caring a professional, a pastor, or a fellow church member listens and models a spirit of servanthood to a victim.

> I waited patiently for the Lord, and He inclined to me, and heard my cry. He also brought me up out of a horrible pit, out of the miry clay, and set my feet upon a rock, and established my steps. He has put a new song in my mouth—praise to our God. Many shall see it and fear and will trust in the Lord. (Ps. 40: 1–3).

That short passage contains similar elements to Narrative Therapy: (1) God is listening to individual's story or complaint. He does not try to stop the person or to place blame on him. (2) God not only listens and hears, but as He hears the person, and the individual is taken out of the pit—in this case, a pit depression or despair. (3) The individual is moved from having shifting emotions and negative thoughts to a new place with a different type of foundation—a solid rock. (4) During this process of being moved to a new construction, the person is transformed. He has a new direction in which to go, a new story or "song," and a sense of hope and thankfulness, "praise to our God."

One victim described that pit as being so deep that she could not see the light of day. However, later, she was able to accomplish much more than she ever thought possible. Imagine what Dinah, Jacob's daughter, may have accomplished with her life if she had received help of this sort to deal with the trauma of rape (Gen. 34). Although some of her brothers avenged the act that was taken against her, she did not have many options to be comforted or healed.

Rather than offering a therapeutic model of treatment, Crisp (2007) provides several suggestions to consider as interventions with victims who are seeking spiritual therapy. As she identifies potential pitfalls of therapy for women of faith because of their relationships with the church, she also provided these interventions: (1) Help victims to renegotiate their images of self and God by encouraging them to see God as resurrected, and therefore a God of hope; (2) Encourage victims to break the silence of abuse in order to begin the healing process. This includes the silence they may have maintained as they refrained from praying; (3) Educate victims about the emotions of anger and forgiveness from a Biblical perspective (Eph. 4:26, 31–32), by encouraging them to recognize Christ also demonstrated times when He was angry, yet He did not sin (Mark 11:15–17). It is important to allow appropriate expression of these emotions by equipping victims with skills that allow them to effectively manage their emotions, thoughts, and behaviors.

> Some survivors will come to the point when they have thought about killing their abuser or even wanting to.... Provided such thoughts remain just that and are not enacted, this energy of anger and resolution to move forward should not be stifled. Too often, there are stories of Christians who didn't feel they could express their anger to God, and hence didn't. (Crisp, 2007, p. 307)

The focus should be on allowing the Holy Spirit to move victims past the negative emotions and into a future of safety and healing. If such emotions are repressed, victims remain stuck in the past.

In the case of child sexual abuse, various forms of family therapy have also been found to be helpful for each member of the family, particularly if the perpetrator is out of the home and the home is found to be safe for all members. Non-offending members need to have as much therapeutic intervention as the victim (Fontes, 2007). The fact that abuse may have occurred to only one person does not lessen the influence of the act on the entire family. Frequently, each member will also need to be involved in individual therapy prior to, or simultaneously, with receiving family therapy in order to resolve their own feelings of guilt, shame, anger, even denial, or blame against the perpetrator, the non-offending parent, or the victim.

Although it is not unusual to involve the perpetrator in the therapy process, therapists and pastors must be very cautious in introducing that person into family therapy. Just as in the case of domestic violence, new instances of sexual abuse could be occurring without the professional becoming aware of the incidences until much later in the therapy process, that is, if the family continues to be engaged in therapy (Greenspun, 1994).

Movement from the *holding on* of these emotions is promoted when victims are able to recognize and accept that God's love for them is not conditional (Kim & Williams, 2009), and that their self-worth is not connected to the violent assault that fell upon them. If the family is not physically or emotionally available to victims, a supportive church congregation may be the best measure of support. The church, or a group of members from the church, could model unconditional love toward victims as they move forward in their journey, exchanging their role of "victim" for their new identity as "Victorious in Christ."

Summary

This article described various emotions and behaviors that females may display as result of experiencing the trauma—or, rather, the horror of sexual and other assaults. It is not uncommon for women victims to engage in self-destructive and injurious behaviors as a result of experiencing a traumatic injury, such as sexual abuse or rape. Whether the individual is a child, a teen, or an adult, this attack has the potential for creating major problems with identity and self-esteem. Biblical models provided examples of some of the pain that is experienced by women who have been raped and sexually abused.

From a spiritual standpoint, some victims tend to lose faith in God or to turn away, erroneously believing that God failed to protect them. Unfortunately, other victims may have encountered people within the church, even counselors or pastors, who provided a message that indicated the victims were responsible for allowing the attack. Those powerfully negative messages only serve to reinforce the shame, guilt, and anger that may be building within the individual.

Rather than to remain steeped in the shameful experiences brought on by an assault, we discussed the need to help victims discover their identities in Christ. Taking on a new identity provides the opportunity to discover that they are new creatures in Christ, that remaining in him and growing in Him will renew them and transform their minds, and that they will become victorious rather than victims, as they become equipped to defeat thoughts of fear, anger, shame, and more with spiritual weapons (2 Cor. 10:3–5; Eph. 6:10–18).

Among the very few evidence-based Biblical counseling theories that are available to women in the Christian therapeutic community, I described one of them: *Solace for the Soul.* This method provides spiritual-based therapy that focuses on seven themes to address with victims: "images of God, abandonment and anger at God, spiritual connection, shame, the body, and sexuality." Areas addressed by other therapeutic interventions for victims of sexual abuse and rape include:

1. Allowing victims to tell their stories of the abuse, and thus break the silence of what happened;
2. Encouraging victims to view their images of self and to cast off the distorted view that they may have taken on as a result of the abuse; and

3. Encouraging them to see God as resurrected, and therefore a God of hope.

The article cautions the use of family therapy in situations of incest. It is extremely important to make sure that the victim, other family members, and the perpetrator work on individual issues sufficiently for all parties, including the therapist, to ensure the safety of the victim. Although healing, and even though the process of forgiveness can take place within the context of family therapy, make no mistake, a great deal of work would need to be accomplished by all before all are ready to move forward to this therapeutic venue.

A gap exists in therapeutic models that are specifically designed to provide evidence-based biblical counseling for victims of sexual abuse. Although there are some models of Christian counseling available, some studies report negative results in that participants leave feeling as if they are responsible and therefore guilty, of having been abused.

Yet, there is hope, as we have shown, for several studies report that participants who have a strong faith in God are able to recover from horrible traumas. Therefore, it is critically important for scholars to continue to explore effective methods of helping victims resolve traumas.

11.
Justification through Union with Christ with His Faith Becoming Our Own into New Creation
by Dr. John DelHousaye
Associate Professor of New Testament
and Spiritual Formation
Phoenix Seminary[344]

Introduction	185
A. Justification	186
1. Messianic Basis of Justification	187
2. Act of Justification	189
3. Already / Not Yet	189
B. Faith(fullness) of/in Christ	191
C. New Creation	193
D. Union with Christ	195
1. Faith and Love	197
2. Love and Suffering	197
Conclusion	198

Introduction

I remember as a child taking in a mosaic and discovering, to my fascination, that many of the shards came from the same plate. The colors and lines of the plate, now broken apart and cemented at different angles, still contributed to the new form of art. Many of us get the same impression from Paul's letters. We see behind his occasional writings a unified vision of God's salvation in Jesus Christ—an icon of the crucified yet resurrected Lord. But this way of seeing comes to us in fragments, albeit as parts of letters with their own coherent structure and beauty.

What follows is my attempt to correlate three shards of this vision—justification, faith, and new creation—with the "mystery" of

---

[344] DelHousaye is the author of several books and articles, including *Scripture and the People of God—Essays in Honor of Wayne Grudem* (co-editor; Crossway, 2018), *Engaging Ephesians—An Intermediate Reader and Exegetical Guide* (GlossaHouse, 2018); "John's Baptist in Luke's Gospel," in *Christian Origins and the Establishment of the Early Jesus Movement*, ed. Stanley E. Porter and Andrew W. Pitts (Leiden: Brill, 2018); "Jesus and the Meaning of Marriage: A Close Reading of Mark 10:1–12," *Journal for Biblical Manhood and Womanhood* 21, no. 1 (2016); "Jewish Groups at the Time of Jesus," in *Understanding the Big Picture of the Bible: A Guide to Reading the Bible Well*, edited by Wayne Grudem, C. John Collins, and Thomas R. Schreiner (Wheaton: Crossway, 2012).

being in Christ. Without confusing one shard with another, I hope to show that all three are part of God's singular act of redemption.

Jesus Messiah is the head of this plan, whose faith and justification are confirmed by God at his resurrection, the beginning of a new creation. The Spirit of Christ comes to us in the hearing of faith, so that we no longer live outside of him. We die with him in baptism, and, enlivened by the Spirit, continue to perform his mission of reconciliation, as members of his body, the church. Who we are in Christ, which is presently hidden from us, is already justified and glorified at the right hand of the Father; but until we are found in him at our resurrection, the consummation of the new creation, our saving faith in Christ should become the faith of Christ, as we pick up our own crosses and follow him. We shall focus on Paul's argument in Galatians, with some referencing to other letters.

A. Justification

The Hebrew prophets warned that God will judge nations and individuals at the end of the present age.[345] God will justify ("declare righteous") or condemn ("declare guilty") in response to human righteousness or wickedness.[346] The "righteous one" (Hebrew, *tsadīk*) obeys the will of God, thereby demonstrating "faith" or "faithfulness."[347] Daniel relates this judgment to a resurrection of the dead:

> Many of those who sleep in the dust of the earth shall awake, some to everlasting life, and some to shame and everlasting contempt. (12:2, ESV)

He also introduces a mysterious "son of man," who shares in the judgment of God:

---

[345] See, e.g., Isa. 3:10–11; 24–27; Zech. 14; Joel 3; Mal. 4. Ezekiel emphasizes individual accountability (ch. 18). Peter Stuhlmacher provides a good summation of the evidence in his *Revisiting Paul's Doctrine of Justification: A Challenge to the New Perspective*, with an essay by Donald A. Hagner, trans. Daniel P. Bailey (Downers Grove, Ill: IVP, 2001), 14–16.

[346] This was the basis for the salvation of Noah and his family from the flood (Gen. 6:9; 7:1). Abraham makes it the basis for assuaging God's judgment of Sodom (Gen. 18:23, 24). See, e.g., Gen. 18:25; Exod. 23:7; Ps. 1:5, 6; 7:9; 11:5; 37:17. God is "a righteous judge" (Ps. 7:11). Note also human judges who are to justify the righteous and condemn the wicked (Deut. 25:1; Prov. 17:15).

[347] See Ezek. 18:5–9; Gen. 38:26. The Torah is righteous (Deut. 4:8). On the correlation between righteous and faithful, see Neh. 9:33. On the correlation between obedience and righteousness, see Deut 28:1. In contrast, the Exodus generation habitually disobeyed and died in the wilderness because of their faithlessness (Num. 14:33; Deut. 32:20; 32:51).

> As I looked, thrones were placed, and the Ancient of Days took his seat...the court sat in judgment, and the books were opened.... with the clouds of heaven there came one like a son of man, and he came to the Ancient of Days and was presented before him. And to him was given dominion and glory and a kingdom, that all peoples, nations, and languages should serve him; his dominion is an everlasting dominion, which shall not pass away, and his kingdom one that shall not be destroyed. (Dan. 7:9–14, ESV)

Jesus appropriates, but also universalizes Daniel's vision:

> Amen, amen I say to you that the hour is coming and now is when those who are dead will hear the voice of the son of God. And the ones who hear will live. For as the Father has life in himself, in the same way he also gave life to the Son to have in himself. And he gave authority to him to practice judgment, because he is the son of man. Do not be astonished by this. For an hour is coming in which all who are in tombs will hear his voice, and will come out—those who did good deeds to the resurrection of life, but those who practiced evil deeds to the resurrection of judgment. (John 5:25–29, my translation)

The first Christian hermeneutic allows Jesus himself to determine the meaning of Scripture.[348] Whereas Daniel may have had a partial resurrection in view,[349] now "all who are in tombs" will be judged by the "son of man." Their justification or condemnation is based on their behavior.

1. Messianic Basis of Justification

Paul assumes the necessity of righteousness for justification, but attributes it to faith, not "works of the Torah," using Genesis 15:6 as a proof text: "Abraham believed in God, and it was reckoned to him for righteousness" (3:6; see also Rom. 4:3).[350] The apostle reads the verse through the lens of God's promise to bless all people in Abraham's seed, Jesus, the Messiah. He maintains that Abraham did nothing to earn this righteousness, except to trust that God would keep his promise.

From this messianic presupposition, the apostle maintains that Jesus "gave himself (over to death) in place of (Greek, *huper*) our

---

[348] See, e.g., Luke 24:27.

[349] John J. Collins, *The Apocalyptic Imagination—an Introduction to* Jewish *Apocalyptic Literature.* 2nd ed. (Grand Rapids: Eerdmans, 1998), 112–13. We find a parallel vision in *1 Enoch* (ch. 104).

[350] Wright, 2009, 116.

sins" (1:3).[351] The claim would have been meaningful to both a Hellenistic and Jewish mindset.[352] Greeks and Romans venerated the "good death"—the noble performance of actions for the sake of others, which transcends selfishness.[353] Hyperides notes that Athenian soldiers "gave their lives in exchange for (*huper*) the freedom of the Greeks."[354] Paul claims Jesus' death provides "freedom" from the enslavement of sin (2:4; 5:1, 13). The Hellenistic-Jewish work, *4 Maccabees* (AD 19–72), presumes that a righteous individual, who suffers undeservedly, merits righteousness for others in his community by suffering the consequences of their sin. Eleazar, one of the martyrs, prays:

> You have known, God, [that] while being able to save myself I am dying with burning tortures because of the Torah. Be merciful to your people. Let our punishment suffice on behalf of them. Make my blood their purification, and take my life in exchange [or as a ransom] for theirs. (16:27–29, my translation)[355]

The prayer appears to be ultimately grounded in Isaiah's song of the Suffering Servant (52:13–53:12):

> He bears our sins, and because of us he suffers greatly.... He was wounded because of our acts of lawlessness.... The Lord gave him over for our sins... He did not practice lawlessness, nor was guile found in his mouth.... And the Lord wants to remove [him] from the suffering of [his] soul and to show him the light and to form [him] with understanding, to justify the just one, who serves many well. And he will bear their sins. (53:4–11 LXX, my translation)

The prophet claims the chosen servant of God helps the "many" to obtain a new right to their existence before God through his innocent,

---

[351] The Greek preposition *huper* should be translated "in the place of," with the sense of "representation": Daniel B. Wallace, *Greek Grammar Beyond the Basics: An Exegetical Syntax of the New Testament* (Grand Rapids: Zondervan, 1996), 383–89.

[352] See Jarvis J. Williams, *Maccabean Martyr Traditions in Paul's Theology of Atonement: Did Martyr Theology Shape Paul's Conception of Jesus' Death?* (Eugene, OR: Wipf & Stock, 2010).

[353] Theon, *Prosgymnata* 9.25.

[354] *Funeral Speech*, 9, 16.

[355] The author adds: "They, having become, as it were, a ransom for the sin of our nation. And through the blood of those devout ones and their death as an atoning sacrifice, divine Providence preserved Israel that previously had been mistreated" (17:21–22). See also 1 Macc. 6:44; 9:10; 13:4; 2 Macc. 8:21.

vicarious suffering.[356] Jesus correlates the visions of Isaiah and Daniel: "The son of man did not come to be served, but to serve and to give up his life as a ransom in exchange for many (Greek, *lutron anti pollōn*)" (Mark 10:45). As the Suffering Servant—Son of man, Jesus associates himself with a sinful people, and dies in their place, thereby securing their forgiveness. Yet we find in the Jesus Tradition and Paul's letters the same universalism as with the resurrection: the Messiah's people are both Jews and the Nations (Gentiles).

2. Act of Justification

As Jesus unites resurrection with justification, so does Paul: Jesus Messiah was "delivered over (to death) because of our wrongful actions, and was raised from death because of our justification" (Rom. 4:25).[357] Jesus came from death, the judgment of sin, into the presence of God the Father, who bestows life to the righteous. The Father resurrects and justifies through his word—a divine "speech act" or "performative utterance," to appropriate the work of J. L. Austin (1911–1960).

3. Already / Not Yet

The resurrection and justification of Jesus Christ is a past event. He is presently glorified at the right hand of God the Father. The early church, including Paul, is therefore able to understand justification as *already* realized in Jesus Christ. Yet G. E. Ladd (1911–82) notes: "the resurrection of Christ is the beginning of *the* resurrection as such, and not an isolated event."[358]

Paul and the Galatians had yet to follow Jesus in what we may call "embodied resurrection."[359] The apostle presupposes the empty tomb in his restatement of an earlier confession ("that he was buried, that he

---

[356] Peter Stuhlmacher, *Revisiting Paul's Doctrine of Justification: A Challenge to the New Perspective*, trans. Daniel P. Bailey (Downers Grove, Ill: IVP, 2001), 17.

[357] J. V. Fesko, *Justification—Understanding the Classic Reformed Doctrine* (Philipsburg, NJ: P&R Publishing, 2008), 264; J. R. Daniel Kirk, *Unlocking Romans—Resurrection and The Justification of God* (Grand Rapids: Eerdmans, 2008), 222; Eberhard Jüngel, *Justification—The Heart of the Christian Faith* (Edinburgh: T&T Clark, 2001), 210–11.

[358] Ibid., Fesko, *Justification*, 264.

[359] Consistent with biblical and contemporary Jewish thought, the apostle appears to have held to a "psycho-somatic" view of human nature. The body does not merely house a soul, but is essential to the nature of a person, who is part of creation.

was raised," 1 Cor. 15:4), and goes on to affirm that, like a sown seed, our buried bodies will be raised as "spiritual bodies" (15:35–44).

The extended stay of our bodies in a tomb, in contrast to Jesus' resurrection on the third day, requires a *not yet* to Paul's vision of salvation (Gal. 2:17; see also 6:5, 8,). Defending his table fellowship with Gentile sinners, the apostle rhetorically asks: "But if *while seeking to be justified* [Gr. *zētountes dikaiōthēnai*] in Christ we ourselves are also found to be sinners [by some other Jews], then is Christ a servant of sin?" (2:17). In Philippians, he uses the verb "found" in reference to his resurrection:

> And I regard [all things to be][360] excrement, so that I might gain Christ and be found[361] in him not having my righteousness, the (kind) by the Torah, but the (righteousness) through the faith of Christ,[362] the righteousness (granted) by God because of faith, so that I might know him and the power of his resurrection and the fellowship of his sufferings, being conformed to his death, so that, if possible, I might attain to the resurrecting-out from those who are dead. (Phil. 3:8–11, my translation)

It would seem that Paul is contrasting the human court of his opponents in Galatians with the divine court of his future. He later speaks of "the hope of righteousness" (Gr. *elpida dikaiosunē*, Gal. 5:5).[363] If justification is part of resurrection, it makes sense that Paul would look forward to a future verdict.

Yet Paul can speak of already being justified (Rom. 5:1, 8:30). This is so because Jesus Messiah has gone ahead of his people to save them from their sins. Paul does not look forward to his own justification, apart from Christ, but hopes to share in the very justification and resurrection of Christ. From a human perspective, this may appear like two different events. But from a divine point of

---

[360] Several MSS, including the most likely reading of papyrus 61, provide the infinitive.

[361] We find the same verb with an eschatological sense in Epictetus' teachings (*Discourses* 4.10.11–12). But the philosopher hopes to be justified before the divine because of his faithfulness to reason (14–15). Closer, yet still importantly different, are anecdotes about rabbis and desert fathers approaching death fearful of God's displeasure.

[362] For this reading, see below.

[363] The substantive shares the same root as the verb "to justify" in Greek, which occurs in the previous verse.

view, there is only one resurrection and justification, with Christ at the beginning of the activity.[364]

B. Faith (fullness) of/in Christ

New Testament scholarship is trending toward reading *pistis Christou* as a subjective or plenary genitive.[365] The faith of Christ, expressed in obedience to the will of God the Father, makes salvation for his people possible. Unlike his sinful community, Jesus Messiah is righteous. He is the righteous one, who trusts God for his vindication. He is able to accomplish what all previous (and subsequent) generations of God's people could not—a good death before a righteous God. Jesus did not force God's will; but God's very righteousness would not tolerate the injustice. Death could not win. Jesus dies trusting the righteousness of God.

The main argument against this reading is that Paul does not explicitly mention Jesus' faith.[366] But this ignores the correlations with obedience and righteousness and is ultimately question-begging: the phrase under discussion could be an *explicit* reference to Jesus' faith. Paul's expression "the message of faith" may refer to Jesus' fidelity to God's will by dying on the cross.[367] Paul uses the same

---

[364] The present righteousness of the believer is "an *eschatological* reality," notes N. T. Wright, "inaugurated indeed in the Messiah but awaiting its full consummation" (emphasis his). Wright, *Justification—God's Plan & Paul's Vision* (Downers Grove: IVP, 2009), 138.

[365] On "plenary," there is the possibility of a "full" or "plenary" genitive, which convey both and objective and subjective sense. See Mark Reasoner, *Romans in Full Circle—A History of Interpretation* (Louisville: Westminster John Knox Press, 2005), 31. My argument allows either sense.

On "genitive," see Gal. 2:16 (x2), 20; 3:22; Rom. 3:22, 26; Phil. 3:9. The same ambiguity persists in the Apostolic Fathers (Ignatius, *To the Romans*). The subjective reading goes back to at least Origen (Reasoner, *Romans in Full Circle*, 24). Richard B. Hays is largely responsible for stirring up the present debate in his *The Faith of Jesus Christ—An Investigation of the Narrative Substructure of Galatians 3:1–4:11*, 2nd ed. (Grand Rapids/Cambridge: Eerdmans; Dearborn: Dove Booksellers, 2002, 1st 1983). He claims Paul presents Jesus as the subject of our salvation—specifically, his *pistis*, "the power or quality which enables him to carry out his mandate" (115). He summarizes his position: "God is the sender whose purpose to convey blessing to humanity is carried out through the action of a single 'Subject,' Jesus Christ" (160). The faithful obedience of Christians continues the story of Jesus' faithfulness. Yet faith itself is not a human work (120).

[366] Moisés Silva claims the subjunctive reading "faces the insuperable linguistic objection that Paul never speaks unambiguously of Jesus as faithful." Silva, *Philippians*, 2nd ed. (Grand Rapids: Baker Academic 2005; 1st 1992), 161.

[367] For this translation, see Hays, *The Faith of Jesus Christ*, 129.

Greek to describe "the faith of our father Abraham" (Rom. 4:12; see also 4:5).[368] Some also miss the semantic force of *pistis* as trust.[369]

We are justified by the faith of Jesus Messiah. If we appropriate the subjective or plenary reading, Paul claims:

> Knowing that a human is not justified (before God) from works of the Torah, except through the faith of Jesus Christ, we believed in Christ Jesus, so that we might be justified (before God) by the faith of Christ and not from works of the Torah, because from works of the Torah *no* flesh[370] *will be justified.* (2:16, my translation)[371]

Jesus obeys the will of God by dying in the place of Paul and the Galatians (1:4; 2:21). He "became obedient to the point of death—even death on a cross" (Phil. 2:8). As Luke makes clear, he dies with faith: "Father, *into your hands I entrust my spirit*" (Luke 23:46). God responded to his obedience by resurrecting, justifying, and glorifying him (v. 9).

While the Messiah's faith makes justification possible, the hearer of the gospel must also believe "in Christ Jesus."[372] Indeed, the faith of Jesus Christ has become the apostle's mode of being: "what I now live in flesh, I live in faith—the (faith) of the son of God" (Gal. 2:21). Paul extends this reality to all "those who are faithful" (Gal. 3:22, 26). The Galatians believed after seeing the faith of Jesus Christ displayed on the cross: "O you foolish Galatians! Who cast the evil eye on you, before whose eyes Jesus Christ was publicly depicted crucified?" (Gal. 3:1; see also 1 Cor. 1:23). This conforms to the biblical pattern of salvation: people witness God's righteous activity and believe. God demonstrated his righteousness at the cross (Rom. 1:17; 3:21–26). We learn what faith before God must look like in Jesus Christ.

Immediately after the question, Paul rhetorically asks: "Did you receive the Spirit by works of the Torah or by the message of faith?"

---

[368] Many scholars have noted this: see Hays, *The Faith of Jesus Christ*, 149. Paul also mentions the "the faithfulness of God" (Rom. 3:3; see also Col. 2:12).

[369] For example, Thomas Aquinas (1224–1274) argues Jesus did not have faith, because faith involves divine reality beyond human sight, and Jesus could see everything (*Summa Theologiae* 3a.7.3).

[370] The Psalm as we have it reads "living thing." Jesus was not justified in the flesh, but in the Spirit—following his resurrection. "No flesh" is justified because all flesh is under the curse.

[371] See also Rom. 3:21–26.

[372] The Greek clearly makes "Christ Jesus" the object of faith.

(Gal. 3:2). The Spirit comes in the proclamation of the gospel and inhabits those who believe the message.

Martin Luther (1483–1546) maintains "Christ is present in the faith itself," *in ipsa fide Christus adest*.[373] In *The Liberty of the Christian* (1520), the Reformer writes: "Faith does not merely mean that the soul realizes that the divine word is full of all grace, free and holy: it also unites the soul with Christ."[374] Paul later refers to "the Spirit of Christ" (Gal. 4:6), lending credibility to the reformer's insight. Yet Jesus teaches that Father and Son are also present in the Holy Spirit (John 14:15–31), so that, despite the notional distinction the Lutheran tradition makes between justification and regeneration, with Christ comes the author and another agent of new creation.

C. New Creation

Paul claims Jesus "gave himself" over to death in our place, "so that he might deliver us out from the present evil age (or realm)" (Gal. 1:3–4; see Col. 1:13). He recapitulates the exodus at letter's end:

> But may it not be that I would boast, except because of the cross of our Lord Jesus Christ, through whom the world has been crucified to me, and I (through him) to the world. For neither circumcision is anything nor un-circumcision, but new creation. (Gal. 6:14–15, my translation)

We find numerous claims in Scripture and Second Temple literature that "the present evil age" would transition into "the age to come" (Heb. 6:5), when God's righteousness would prevail.[375] Reality would return to ideal, primeval conditions.[376]

---

[373] Carl E. Braaten and Robert W. Jensen, eds., *Union with Christ—the New Finnish Interpretation of Luther* (Grand Rapids: Eerdmans, 1998), viii; Tuomo Mannerma, *Christ Present In Faith—Luther's View of Justification* (Minneapolis: Augsburg Press, 2005), 27.

[374] Translation by Alister E. McGrath, "Newman on Justification: An Evangelical Anglican Evaluation" in *Newman and The Word*, edited by Terrence Merrigan and Ian T. Kerr (Louvain; Paris, Sterling; Virginia: Peeters, 2000), 91-108, specifically 99. McGrath references *D. Martin Luthers Werke: Kritische Gesamtausgabe*, vol. 7 (Weimer: Böhlaus, 1897), 25.26–26.9.

[375] Paul's most immediate influence is the final vision of the Prophet Isaiah (Isa. 65:8–25 LXX). See also 1 En. 91:15–17; 2 Esd. 7:50, 113; Jub. 23:23–31.

[376] In a Jewish context, see Jub. 1:29; 4:26; 1 En. 72:1; 1QS 4:25; 2 Bar. 32:6; 44:12; 4 Ezra 7:75; for the broader motif, Virgil's *Fourth Eclogue* and the Sumerian myth of Dilmun.

The need for new creation goes back to a curse imposed because of Adam's sin: "Cursed[377] is the ground (or earth) because of you (Adam); in pain you shall eat of it all the days of your life" (Gen. 3:17). After presenting Jesus as the antitype of Adam (ch.5), Paul writes:

> For I consider that the sufferings of the present season are not worthy (in comparison) to the coming glory to be revealed to us. For the yearning of creation waits for the revelation of the sons of God (at the resurrection). For creation was subjected to futility—not of its own free will, but through the one who subjected (it) in hope. For the creation itself also will be set free from the slavery of decay into the freedom of the glory of the children of God. For we know that the whole creation is groaning and is co-suffering until now—but not only (creation), but also we ourselves, who have the first-fruits of the Spirit—we ourselves also are groaning within ourselves, waiting our adoption, the redemption of our body. (Rom. 8:18–23, my translation)

The apostle presents the human body as part of the suffering creation, awaiting its redemption at the resurrection. While believers are resurrected with Christ in Spirit, our bodies still suffer under the curse. This is not to equate the pre-resurrection body or creation with evil. It frames evil, suffering, and death as a contamination of the good.

The grounding for Paul's gospel is not simply hope in what God might or will do in the future but follows on what God has already done in Jesus Christ—raising, justifying, and glorifying. *Jesus, the last Adam, went ahead of us into new creation.* Yet Christ unites himself to us in faith, so that "if anyone is in Christ, (he is) new creation. The old things passed away; new things have come into being" (2 Cor. 5:17, my translation). The apostle understands Jesus' resurrection as a metamorphosis, the transition from one mode of being to another. Both the inner and outer dimensions of Jesus, the God-man, were resurrected, as evidenced by the empty tomb. Paul hopes that while he is already in union with the inner dimension of the resurrected Christ, enjoying "newness of life" in fellowship through the Spirit of Christ, he may also someday share in the outer dimension of the resurrection, thereby entering fully into new creation.

---

[377] The LXX as we have it employs *epikataratos*. Paul uses the same word at Gal. 3:10, citing Deut. 27:26 and 28:58.

If the resurrection of Jesus Christ marks the beginning of new creation, his crucifixion reflects the "birth pains" at the end of the present age. The maternal image is common in Jewish apocalyptic literature for the sufferings accompanying the new creation.[378] The divine judgment is an expression of the curse, directed towards the woman: "I will greatly multiply your sufferings and groaning. With sufferings you will bear children" (Gen. 3:16 LXX, my translation). Jesus describes these birth pains in the Olivet Discourse:

> There will be earthquakes in various places. There will be famines. These things are the beginning of the birth pains (Mark 13:44, my translation).

The Messiah underwent these sufferings himself, becoming a curse in our place.[379] Yet these contractions will continue until new creation.

D. Union with Christ

The realities of resurrection, justification, and new creation impact the believer through union with Christ. John Calvin (1509–64) provides this context for his discussion of justification and sanctification in the *Institutes*:

> How do we receive those benefits which the Father bestowed upon his only-begotten Son—not for Christ's own private use, but that he might enrich poor and needy men? First, we must understand that as long as Christ remains outside of us, and we are separated from him, all that he has suffered and done for the salvation of the human race remains useless and of no value to us. (3.1.1)[380]

Through the obedience (faith) of Jesus Christ, many "will be made righteous" (Rom. 5:19; see 1 Cor. 1:30). Paul claims: "On our behalf, he made him to be sin who knew no sin, so that we might become the righteousness of God *in him*" (2 Cor. 5:21, emphasis mine). We are so because of our union with Christ. Yet to be outside Christ, the embodiment of new creation, is to remain under the curse of the present order (Gal. 1:8–9).

---

[378] See Isa. 13:8, 26:17; Mic. 4:9f.; Hosea 13:13; Jer. 4:31; 1 En. 62:4; 4 Ezra [= 2 Esdras] 4:42; Targum Psalms 18:14; 2 Apocalypse of Baruch 56:6; Rev. 12:2; 1 Thess. 5:3.

[379] See Brant Pitre, *Jesus, The Tribulation, and The End of The Exile* (Tübingen: Mohr Siebeck; Grand Rapids: Baker Academic, 2005).

[380] Commentators rightly point out that this claim undergirds the reformer's discussion of justification and sanctification: See, e.g., Lewis Smedes, *Union With Christ—A Biblical View of The New Life in Jesus Christ*. Second Edition (Grand Rapids: Eerdmans, 1983, 1st 1970), 10.

Paul often uses the phrase "in Christ" (Gr. *en Christō*).[381] Scholarship appears to be moving toward the interpretation of being incorporated "into Christ," which is another metaphor for entering the Kingdom of God.[382] Yet Paul seems to make an ontological claim: "I am crucified together with Christ. Now I myself no longer live, but Christ lives in me" (Gal. 2:19–20). He interprets the union between a husband and wife, when the two "become one flesh" as a type of Jesus and the church (Eph. 5:31–32). Calvin refers to a *unio mystica*, but never defines it (3.11.10). He probably shares the concept of a union of wills, with Bernard of Clairvaux (1090–1153).[383] In Sermon 74 on the Song of Songs, the abbot gives a first-person account of experiencing Christ's presence:

> When the Word and Bridegroom entered into me from time to time, his coming was never made known by any signs—by word, or appearance, or footstep. I was never made aware by any action on his part, nor by any kinds of motions sent down to my most inward parts. As I have said, it was only from the motion of my heart that understood he was present. I recognized the power of his might from the way vices were banished and how carnal desires were repressed.[384]

Like most Christian mystics, Bernard stops short of a union of essence. We are not absorbed into God or become God, just as a wife is not absorbed into her husband. But we can share the will and power of God, through a union of Spirit (*unitas spiritus*), which Bernard McGinn defines as "a uniting of willing and loving in which the infinite Divine Spirit and the finite created spirit nonetheless always maintain their ontological distinction" (2006, 428). To use Paul's words, in Christ we are able to "walk by" his Spirit (Gal. 5:16).

---

[381] The phrase occurs 13 times in Romans, 13 times in 1 Corinthians, 7 times in 2 Corinthians, 7 times in Galatians, 10 times in Philemon, and 3 times in 1 Thessalonians. The phrase plays a major role in Eph, occurring 13 times—more than any other Pauline letter close to its size. Yet the phrase and concept is not unique to Paul. We find it in 1 Peter 3:16, 5:10, 14 and 1 John 5:20. John also relates the call of Jesus to "abide" in him (John 15:4, 6, 7, 9, 10; see 1 Jn. 2:27–28; 4:13).

[382] See, e.g., Charles H. Talbert, *Ephesians and Colossians* (Paideia; Grand Rapids: Baker, 2007), 44. We are combined into one body or unit, like an incorporated town.

[383] Dennis E. Tamburello, *Union with Christ—John Calvin and the Mysticism of St. Bernard* (Louisville: John Knox Press, 1994), 103–106.

[384] *Sancti Bernardi Sermones in Cantica*, Sermo LXXIV, in PL 183:1141–42. I follow the translation of Bernard McGinn's *The Essential Writings of Christian Mysticism* (NY: The Modern Library, 2006), 223–24.

1. Faith and Love

Jesus expressed his faith through love—dying on the cross in our place (Gal. 2:21; see 1 Cor. 13:2). Paul writes: "in Christ Jesus neither circumcision nor un-circumcision is able to accomplish anything, but faith working through love" (Gal. 5:6). This fulfills what the apostle calls the "Torah of Christ" (Gal. 6:2). For Paul, love is not a merit, but a divine manifestation—a fruit of the Spirit (Gal. 5:22). If love is the ground of Christian living, then the ultimate agent behind every good work is God. The pattern is Jesus Christ.

2. Love and Suffering

To be filled with the love of God is to suffer with Christ. Before Paul's calling (conversion), he played the role of the antagonistic Pharisee, attempting to destroy Christ's body, the church (Gal. 1:13–14). Yet now his opponents from Jerusalem have taken that role against him! Before, Paul was zealous about preserving national purity. Now he eats with Gentiles. The Gospels relate that Jesus became friends with "sinners and tax collectors," sharing his meals with them, and was persecuted by Pharisees who had come down from Jerusalem.[385] Paul came to the Galatians suffering, and they received him as Jesus Christ (4:12–20). He bears the "stigmata of Christ" (Gal. 6:17).

Suffering with Christ is not restricted to the apostle. Mentioning their reception of the Spirit, Paul wrote: "Did you suffer so much without reason, if indeed (it was) without reason?" (3:4; see 2 Cor. 1:5). God sent out his Spirit into our hearts crying *"Abba"* (Father) (Gal. 4:6). The Aramaic "abba" evokes Jesus' prayer in Gethsemane, where the Son asks the Father for an alternative to suffering and death. Paul seems to be aware of this context—here and in the parallel in Romans 8:15. Jesus says: "Whoever does not receive his cross and follow after me is not worthy of me. The one who finds his life will lose it, and the one who loses his life because of me will find it" (Mt. 10:38–39). To find life in Christ is to join his mission.

---

[385] Mark 3:22; Mark 7:1 par.; Mt. 11:19 par.

Conclusion

Like shards from the same plate in a mosaic, I propose that justification, faith, new creation, and being in Christ are all part of a unified vision of salvation in the crucified yet resurrected Lord. Jesus and Paul view justification as part of the general resurrection of the dead, which is part of new creation. The resurrection and justification of Jesus Christ is the beginning of new creation. We are brought into this singular divine activity through faith in Christ. We are already justified in Christ but have yet to enter fully into his resurrection. Although forgiven, our bodies are not yet free of the curse. Paul grounds our justification in the faith of Jesus Messiah, which, through the sharing of the Spirit, becomes our own. We find ourselves loving with God, which leads to suffering with Christ.

12.
A Non-legalistic Doctrine of Sanctification: Refuting Recent Controversy in the Reformed Church Christian Failure and Christian Growth

by Rev. Dr. Enrique Ramos
President, Evangelical and Education Ministry
Addiction Counselor, VA Hospital, San Juan, Puerto Rico
Theologian in Residence at Reforma Dos Ministry at Center Church
Iglesia del Centro, Arecibo, Puerto Rico[386]

Introduction 200
A. Main Theoretical Argument 201
B. Overview of Reformed Church's View of Justification and Sanctification..... 202
C. Federal Vision: New Perspective on Paul? 203
   1. The Gospel 204
   2. The Righteousness of God 204
   3. Final Judgment According to Works 205
D. Justification in the Federal Vision 206
   1. Works of the Law 207
   2. Covenant and Election 208
   3. Imputation 208
   4. Nature of Union with Christ 209
E. FV Disagrees with the Westminster Shorter Catechism,
   Confession of Faith, and Larger Catechism 209
F. Arguments Against the Federal Vision... 210
   1. Righteousness 210
   2. Works of the Law 211
      a. Covenantal.. 212
      b. The Law Court.. 212
      c. Present and Future Justification 212
G. Summary Against the Federal Vision 213

---

[386] Ramos currently works as an Addictions Therapist at the V.A. Hospital in San Juan, Puerto Rico. He is a Theologian in Residence with Reforma Dos Ministry of the Iglesia del Centro, Arecibo, Puerto Rico; Chaplain in the Naval Reserve having served at Roosevelt Rhoads in Ceiba, Puerto Rico; and a former theology professor at the Inter-American University in San Germán, Puerto Rico. He has a M.Div. from Westminster Theological Seminary, a M.S.W. from the Universidad de Puerto Rico, an M.Th. from North-West University, South Africa; a Ph.D. from Seminario Campbell Morgan, Argentina; a Ph.D. from Seminario Mayor Escuela de Teologia y Ciencia de la Religion from Colombia; and a Th.D (Hon.) from Faculdade Teologica, Missao, Macedonia, Republica Federativa, Brasil. He is an ordained minister in the General Lutheran Church serving as its International Coordinator and Resident Theologian. He is also Professor at the Reforma Dos Escuela de Ministerios (School of Ministry) in Caguas, Puerto Rico, and at the Seminario Reformado students, Latinoamericano of Colombia teaching Systematic Theology and Apologetics, as well as in charge of guiding the doctoral students in their dissertations. He is an ordained minister in the General Lutheran Church serving as Deputy Dean, International Coordinator, Director of Chaplaincy Services, and Resident Theologian.

H. The Lordship Controversy	213
1. The Lordship Doctrine	213
2. Summary of Errors in the Lordship Position	218
Conclusion Against the New Positions on Paul and Sanctification	221

Introduction

The focus of this article is on recent challenges to the central tenet of the classic Reformed theology of mainstream Protestantism, namely the doctrine of *justification* by faith and its corollary, continuing growth though *sanctification* in the life of the Christian believer. Among the sources of schism in the Reformed Church is the repeated appearance of new disputes regarding this doctrine and the truth of the orthodox Protestant interpretation of justification and sanctification.

Over the last four decades, mainstream Reformed Protestantism has seen a series of what are termed "controversies," from the Shepherd Controversy (1974–81), leading to the Federal Vision Controversy (ca. 2002–2010), down to the current Lordship Controversy, all of which have adherents claiming to draw inspiration and authority from the early Reformed Church. Among the many subjects of recent debate have been such central doctrines as justification by faith, works of the law, covenant, election, Christ's human and divine nature, and the nature of the believer's unity with Christ.

The focus of this study is on the traditional Protestant doctrine of justification by faith, and the imputation that through grace, the Christian believer grows in sanctification over the natural course of life. The author's position is that this traditional understanding of sanctification as the product of God's grace is correct, and that the challenges that have been advanced in recent years—the Federal Vision and Lordship Controversies—are false in their reasoning and problematic in their implications. This study therefore attempts to diagnose the errors of these "controversies" through the use of exegetical analysis and a point-by-point review of the claims of their adherents , in order to show the way back to the classical or "orthodox" Protestant approach to sanctification and justification by faith.

The author's personal theological position is in disagreement with these recent "controversies," including Lordship Salvation and the

Federal Vision, which he believes can be described as a radical theology taking up heretical positions on the teachings of Paul. The core of the author's belief is akin to the doctrine of Sonship as traditionally espoused, although this might better be referred to as Christian grace. From this position, a son or daughter of God receives grace and salvation through Christ's righteousness, a total dependence in the Holy Spirit for his or her sanctification, and the believer constantly "preaching of the Gospel to himself" on the doctrines of repentance and faith.

A. Main Theoretical Argument

The most basic assumption of this article is that Scripture is the sole basis for determining the revealed word of God, and that new doctrines should therefore be evaluated in the light of Scripture's exclusive authority on the Biblical matters to which they relate. The study further assumes the fundamental premise of Reform Protestantism, that of justification by faith rather than works as the true path to sanctification and salvation. The theoretical framework of the study is comprised of the Reformed Doctrine, held in the Three Forms of Unity (Heidelberg Catechism, Belgic Confession, and the Articles of the Synod of Dort), as well as the Westminster Confession of Faith and its catechisms. The author believes that the Reformed Faith has a universal standing in all Reformed churches in the world; thus, he believes correct interpretation may benefit all who hold to the Reformed Faith, regardless of their national or cultural identities.

The theoretical foundation for this investigation is the extensive body of exegetical analysis and theological speculation available today. This research method calls for scholarly comparative study of theological doctrine and speculation with Scripture and the Reformed tradition, with the use of the tools from linguistic analysis, historiography, and philological criticism of the texts. Literary criticism classifies texts according to style and attempts to establish authorship, date, and audience; legalism argues for a strict literal interpretation of dogma and law as the key to salvation, without regard to faith. Legalism is not therefore a proper critical method for the analysis of doctrine.

The other sound basis for methodology is tradition criticism, which seeks the sources of Biblical materials and traces their development; correct exegetical analysis always takes the Gospels and Scripture as their authority and starting point. This research design includes investigation of primary and secondary literature regarding the specific doctrinal positions. This includes a comparative analysis of the positions of Federal Vision, Lordship, and Shepherd Controversies in the light of the biblical revelation, and an assessment of the points of similarity. At the same time, we attempt to identify any common features among their differences that would benefit from a more scripturally valid interpretation. Although the author's personal religious background is one that finds most sympathy with the Sonship position regarding sanctification, he is aware of the potential for bias that such a background affords. In order to avoid the potential distortions and prejudices resulting from such a bias, therefore, he proposes to give a balanced recognition to sources of information that offer evidence in support of each of the controversial propositions. These sources are primarily periodicals, journal articles, and privately published pamphlets. The validity and reliability of such a literature-based research methodology is supported by the special requirements of theological scholarship in areas of contemporary controversy.

B. Overview of Reformed Church's View of Justification and Sanctification

Before summarizing the Federal Vision (FV) view, we may here briefly state the Reformed view of the two central issues in question, namely justification and sanctification. In the Reformed view, justification is by definition a one-time act of God, never to be repeated. In contrast, sanctification is the ongoing process that removes the pollution of sin and gradually conforms the sinner to the image of Christ (Eph. 4:20–24). The sinner's justification definitively sets the believer apart from the world of sin, and God always looks upon the believer as holy because of the imputed righteousness of Christ. If the believer's standing before God were to hinge upon sanctification, the believer's status would always be in question because of its imperfect nature (Gal. 5:16–26) (Fesko, 2010).

As the Westminster Divines characterize sanctification:

This sanctification is throughout, in the whole man; yet imperfect in this life, there abiding still some remnants of corruption in every part; whence arises a continual and irreconcilable war, the flesh lusting against the Spirit, and the Spirit against the flesh (13:2).

Calvin writes that justification "is the main hinge on which religion turns" and that apart from it, we do not have a foundation upon which to establish our salvation nor one on which to build piety toward God (Shepherd, n.d.).

Justification is founded only on the work of Christ, and thus sanctification will always be imperfect. Calvin powerfully defends justification as the first blessing and sanctification as the second, for the free pardon of justification provides the indispensable context for the second blessing of our sanctification (Billings, 2007). First, the believer is sanctified by Christ through Spirit and not through himself. That sanctification does not come about in moving away from sin but comes about through union with Christ. Second, sanctification is by faith alone through Christ. Believers are sanctified through the work of Christ through Spirit rather than by their own obedience (Fesko, 2010). The believer is completely dependent on Christ and Spirit for sanctification; there is no perfection until death and resurrection. Therefore, the believer must rely on Christ for his sanctifying power.

C. Federal Vision: New Perspective on Paul?

In the 1970s, the Rev. Norman Shepherd, then a professor of Systematic Theology at Westminster Theological Seminary, proposed that sinners are justified by "faith and works." This doctrine created considerable opposition and ultimately led to Mr. Shepherd's dismissal from the seminary. Over the course of the controversy in the 1970s, Shepherd modified his language to teach justification through "covenant faithfulness" but without discernable change to the substance of his theology. Since that time he has openly rejected the Reformed doctrine of the imputation of the active obedience of Christ (i.e., that all of Christ's obedience was not for himself but for us, and that all that he did—and not just his death on the cross—is imputed to believers). Along with this proposed revision of justification by faith alone came proposed revisions of the doctrines of covenant, election, and baptism.

In the 1990s, after a series of conferences at Auburn Avenue Church, a number of theologians deeply influenced by Shephard and by the insights of other scholars writing extensively on the New Perspective on Paul (NPP) gave themselves the name The Federal Vision (FV). They claimed to be recovering authentic Reformed theology, and that American Reformed theology had been corrupted by revivalism. Thus, the Federal Vision movement is associated with N. T. Wright, Norman Shepherd, James Jordan, and Douglas Wilson, among others, who subscribe to a revisionist impulse that significantly recasts the Reformed tradition (Evans, 2010). These NPP authors interpret Paul's message to advocate for a redefinition of the doctrines of justification and imputed righteousness. Mr. Wright and others who advocate for the FV view have an alternate understanding of Paul's message, including the gospel, the righteousness of God, final judgment according to works, justification, and works of the law (*Joint Federal Vision Profession*).[387]

1. The Gospel

According to Jordan (2007),

> The gospel is the theocratic message that whereas in the old time only one nation was baptized and discipled under the loving teaching of Yahweh, now all nations are to be baptized and discipled under the enthroned Incarnate Yahweh. That's clear in Matthew and Acts and everywhere else. Ordo salutis is not the gospel; it's been around since Genesis 3. The gospel is the message that history has changed, that Satan has been defeated, that now all nations, every single one, is destined for transformation. Not just white nations. All nations. That's the new good news. Sometimes the gospel is called postmillennialism. They are synonyms.

Hence in the FV view, Paul is not referring to a system of salvation when he speaks of "the gospel." Paul's use of the term is not a set of instructions about how to be saved; instead, the gospel is the message "Jesus Christ is Lord." When Paul preached the gospel that Jesus is Lord and listeners were moved to believe in Jesus, Paul knew that the announcement itself functioned as the vehicle of Spirit, the means of grace. The gospel is a summons to obedience, which takes the form of faith (Wright, 2003).

2. The Righteousness of God

Paul used this phrase to denote the "righteousness of God himself" rather than the status that God's presence bestows on his people. God's righteousness is not an attribute that is imputed to his people. For God's people, righteous status is the result of God's action in

---

[387] Federal Vision. 2011. *Joint Federal Vision Statement*. Accessed April 18, 2011, www.Federal-Vision.com/joint_statement.html, now moved to http://federal-vision.com/uncategorized/joint-federal-vision-statement.

Christ and by Spirit. Ignoring the distinction between God's righteousness and the status of righteousness in his people leads one to a misunderstanding of justification (Wright, 2003). Wright uses the metaphor of the law court (legalism) to explain forensic justification. When a judge rules on the part of one party, that party gains the status of "righteous." This status is not a moral statement about the vindicated party; nor does it have anything to do with the righteousness of the judge. The judge's righteousness is not imputed to the defendant or the plaintiff; only the status of "righteous" (Wright, 2003).

This view of righteous status versus imputed righteousness argues that the "reckoning of righteousness" in Romans 5:14–21 refers to the individual who has heard the gospel and responded with the obedience of faith, thus gains the status of "covenant member" accredited to those in Christ. This righteousness is neither God's nor Christ's own (Wright, 2003). The FV meaning of covenant, as defined by Jordan, is "a personal-structural bond which joins the three persons of God in a community of life, and in which man was created to participate" (Fesko, 2004).

3. Final Judgment According to Works

Wright (2003) suggests there has been "a massive conspiracy of silence" regarding Paul's teaching that the believer's final judgment is according to works. He finds Romans 2:13 positively to teach that "the doer of the law will be justified." At the end of life a believer is justified, Wright says, drawing from Romans 8:3–4, "because the Spirit is at work to do, within believers, what the Law could not do—ultimately, to give life." Wright is not saying that works are a necessary consequence of justification, or that justification must necessarily be joined to sanctification, or that saving faith is never alone without works. He is saying that at the end of a believer's life, the basis of his justification is good works. As he says in his commentary on Romans 2:13, "Justification, at the last, will be on the basis of performance, not possession." Paul's message is that God's final judgment will be in accordance with works of the believer's entire life; that good works produced over one's life due to Spirit's indwelling will lead the Christian to completion on the day of Jesus Christ. This future positive verdict can be denoted with the verb "justify." Wright says that "justification by faith ... is the anticipation in the present of the justification which will occur in the future, and gains its meaning from that anticipation" (Wright, 2003).

D. Justification in the Federal Vision

According to Wright (2003), justification is:

> God's declaration a) that someone is in the right (their sins having been forgiven through the death of Jesus) and b) that this person is a member of the true covenant family, the family God originally promised to Abraham and has now created through Christ and the Spirit, the single family which consists equally of believing Jews and believing Gentiles.

Wright notes that while traditional Reformed theology understands justification as comprising both forgiveness and the imputed righteousness of Christ (see Westminster Confession of Faith XI.1), the New Perspective categorically denies the latter. In his discussion of "the righteousness of God," Wright specified that while God "does indeed 'reckon righteousness' to those who believe ... this is not, for Paul, the righteousness either of God or of Christ." As he wrote in *What St. Paul Really Said*, "It makes no sense whatever to say that the judge imputes, imparts, bequeaths, conveys or otherwise transfers his righteousness to either the plaintiff or the defendant. Righteousness is not an object, a substance or a gas, which can be passed across the courtroom." This follows through when he focuses on justification, for while Wright affirms that the believer is reckoned as righteous, this is as a member of God's covenant people and not by an imputation of Christ's righteous achievement. He says, "Paul does not say that he sees us clothed with the earned merits of Christ."

Wright further specifies that justification occurs twice. "It occurs in the future... on the basis of the entire life a person has led in the power of the Spirit—that is, it occurs on the basis of 'works' in Paul's redefined sense. And, near the heart of Paul's theology, it occurs in the present *as an anticipation of that future verdict*." In this New Perspective scheme, faith is not an instrument of justification but rather "it is the anticipation in the present of the verdict which will be *reaffirmed in the future*." The present possession of faith indicates that one will go on to do good works, and it is by virtue of those good works that the believer may be ultimately justified.

From Wright's statements we may conclude that the FV view is a particular interpretation of *Ordo Salutis*, the chronological order of events beginning with the individual's position outside of God's community of people, through the finally saved sinner. Paul referred to the moment of belief and obedience not as "justification" or "conversion," but calling. The step after calling is justification. God does not grant a new status or privilege based on a person's faith (Wright, 2003). Norman Shepherd argued, "Since faith, repentance, and good works are intertwined as covenantal response, and since good works are necessary to justification, the 'ordo salutis' would better be: regeneration, faith/repentance/new obedience, justification" (Schwertley, n.d.).

Justification, or vindication, in Wright's law-court imagery, follows the call. The call summons the sinner to reject sin and turn to God, to follow Christ and believe in God and Jesus' resurrection. Wright maintains that justification is God's declaration that the individual's sins have been forgiven, and that the individual has become a member of the covenant family (Wright, 2003). Wright further states that justification means "membership in God's true family" (Wright, 2009).

As was seen above, this view holds that justification occurs twice: first in the present as an anticipation of that future verdict, which will be reaffirmed in the future. Wright notes: "Justification is not 'how someone becomes a Christian'; it is God's declaration about the person who has just become a Christian." The present declaration consists of the believer's anticipation of final resurrection and manifests as baptism. Second, the final declaration will consist of the believer's resurrection. We are justified by faith by believing in the gospel that Jesus is Lord and resurrected by God, rather than believing in justification by faith (Wright, 2003).

Sanders refers to justification essentially as not how one gets into God's people, but rather about God's declaration that someone is in God's people. Salvation is by grace, but judgment by works. So, one receives the status of "righteous" by God's election and maintains righteous status by obedience (Sanders, 1977).

1. Works of the Law

The Federal Vision denies the historic Protestant distinction of law and Gospel. It says:

> We deny that law and gospel should be considered as hermeneutics, or treated as such. We believe that any passage, whether indicative or imperative, can be heard by the faithful as good news, and that any passage, whether containing

gospel promises or not, will be heard by the rebellious as intolerable demand. The fundamental division is not in the text, but rather in the human heart. (Federal Vision, 2011)[388]

This would seem to be a latent denial of the law/Gospel distinction.

James Dunn holds the view that the Jews did not practice works to earn God's favor or attain salvation, but instead practiced their boundary markers (circumcision, food laws, sabbath) to keep themselves within the boundary of God's people (Dunn, 2008).

2. Covenant and Election

Among several key issues for FV proponents are:

> An unease with the idea that Adam could "merit" eternal life through his perfect and perpetual obedience to God's command;
>
> Covenant established with Adam was fundamentally gracious, not legal; and
>
> God's dealings with humankind must be understood by way of covenant, rather than his decrees.

For FV proponents, the elect are identified by their association with the church; in other words, those people who are in covenant with God. Without emphasizing the necessary response of faith to the covenant promise, a faith that savingly unites the believer to Christ and His benefits affirms that all covenant members are individually elect and true beneficiaries of Christ's saving work with all of its benefits. The FV of the elect is, perhaps, one of the clearest declarations of the fundamentally legal interpretation of those who argue the FV view.

3. Imputation

This term historically refers to believers being made just before God by having Christ's righteousness imputed (credited) to them by a judicial declaration of a gracious God. FV questions the correctness of this understanding, especially in regard to the imputation of Christ's active obedience. The consequence is that the believer's obedience, in addition to faith, becomes responsible for justification, and not simply the evidence that one's faith is genuine. As Lusk says:

---

[388] A Joint Federal Vision Statement. Accessed April 18, 2011, from www.federal-vision.com/joint_statement.html, moved to: http://federal-vision.com/uncategorized/joint-federal-vision-statement/.

> The resurrection is the real centerpiece of the gospel since it is the *new* thing God has done.... It is not Christ's life-long obedience per se that is credited to us. Rather, it is his right standing before the Father, manifested in his resurrection. His resurrection justified us because it justified him. Again, it is not that his law-keeping or miracle-working are imputed to our account; rather, Christ shares his legal status in God's court with us as the One who propitiated God's wrath on the cross and was resurrected into a vindicated, glorified form of life. (Lusk, 2010, p. 142).

The essential point for FV proponents is their agreement that union with Christ's resurrection life, rather than the imputation of Christ's earthly obedient works, is how sinners are justified before God.

4. Nature of Union with Christ

According to FV proponents, when individuals are baptized, they are united to the church, which is Christ's body (hence, they are united to Christ). As a result of this "covenantal union," individuals receive many of the benefits of Christ's mediation: election, justification, adoption, and sanctification. Joseph Minich (who claims not to be an FV advocate) writes,

> Baptism is not a 'work' performed, after which one can have full assurance. It is not another 'instrument' of justification alongside faith. Rather, it is a visible act of God (especially apparent in the case of infants) that is to be seen as the locus of Christian certainty. It is the place where God promises to meet His own. To look to baptism for assurance is not to look for salvation in 'water,' but to cling to the place where God promises to meet His people and bless them.

While baptized individuals receive a number of benefits through their "covenantal union," they do not receive the gift of perseverance. This they receive as they live in "covenantal faithfulness," obeying God's law throughout their lives. Wright justifies his view of covenantal faithfulness using Habakkuk 2. However, the emphasis in Habakkuk 2 is on the faithfulness of God's people (Makidon, n.d.). Some have suggested that the paradigm of covenantal faithfulness ends up resting our justification upon our sanctification; others wonder if this is the best solution to the problem of apostasy (abandoning one's faith).

E. FV Disagrees with the Westminster Shorter Catechism, Confession of Faith, and Larger Catechism

Before moving to the author's criticisms of the FV position, a number of short quotations may serve to make the points of disagreement clear as seen in quotes from the Westminster Shorter and Larger Catechism:[389]

1. "Justification is an act of God's free grace, wherein he pardoneth all our sins, and accepteth us as righteous in his sight, only for the righteousness of Christ imputed to us, and received by faith alone" (WSC, 33).

2. "Those whom God effectually calls, he also freely justifieth; not by infusing righteousness into them, but by pardoning their sins, and by accounting and accepting their persons as righteous; not for anything wrought in them, or done by them, but for Christ's sake alone; nor by imputing faith itself, the act of believing, or any other evangelical obedience to them, as their righteousness; but by imputing the obedience and satisfaction of Christ unto them, they receiving and resting on him and his righteousness by faith; which faith they have not of themselves, it is the gift of God" (WCF, 11.1).

3. "Faith, thus receiving and resting on Christ and his righteousness, is alone the instrument of justification: yet is it not alone in the person justified, but is ever accompanied with all other saving graces, and is no dead faith, but worketh by love" (WCF, 11.2).

4. "Although sanctification be inseparably joined with justification, yet they differ, in that God in justification imputeth the righteousness of Christ; in sanctification his Spirit infuseth grace, and enableth to the exercise thereof; in the former, sin is pardoned; in the other, it is subdued: the one doeth equally free all believers from the revenging wrath of God, and that perfectly in this life, that they never fall into condemnation; the other is neither equal in all, nor in this life perfect in any, but growing up to perfection" (WLC, 77).

F. Arguments Against the Federal Vision

1. Righteousness

The term righteousness cannot mean "covenant membership," as various theologians associated with the NPP maintain. Such a definition is untenable in the face of texts such as Genesis 18:24–25, where Abraham negotiates the deliverance of Sodom and Gomorrah on the premise that there might be fifty righteous men within its confines. Given that God was only in covenant with Abraham, it is impossible here to define righteousness as covenant membership. Clearly, righteousness is moral equity. When one considers the term righteousness as it is applied to God, it cannot universally mean his

---

[389] See https://thewestminsterstandards.com/table-of-contents/.

covenant faithfulness. What, for example, of God's righteousness towards those who are outside the covenant? Is God righteous in his dealings with unbelievers? The Scriptures affirm that God is righteous with both those inside and outside the covenant. To understand righteousness as covenant membership and God's covenant faithfulness is exegetically indefensible.

Furthermore, there are two aspects to the work of Christ: namely, his *passive* and his *active* obedience. Christ's passive obedience is his suffering obedience, his bearing of the penalty of the curse of the law throughout his life and especially in his crucifixion. By this work, our sins are forgiven. Christ's active obedience is his keeping of the commands of the law throughout his life. By this work, we are reckoned to have kept the law perfectly, as originally demanded of Adam in the covenant of works. Thus, the demands of God's justice are satisfied, and the glorious riches of his grace are displayed. This righteousness of Christ must be applied to believers if it is to be of benefit to them. This application of Christ's benefits comes by means of imputation. That is, Christ's righteousness is judicially reckoned or credited to sinners so that their sins may be forgiven and the perfect obedience of Christ may be accounted as their own.

FV proponents reject the idea of Paul's teaching that Christ's righteousness is credited to us. In other words, they deny the clear Gospel message that Christ's perfect obedience is credited to believers so that they stand before God as perfect law keepers themselves.

2. Works of the Law

It has proven exegetically unsustainable to define the "works of the law" as only referring to circumcision, food laws, and the Sabbath. This definition has now been modified by James D. G. Dunn, for example, to include the entire law functioning as a boundary marker, though Dunn has left his overall understanding of justification unchanged. When Paul quotes Deuteronomy 27:26 in Galatians 3:10, the reference cannot be only to boundary markers; but it is to the entire law, which is evident from the broader context of Deuteronomy 27–30. Moreover, to argue that there was an absence of legalism in first century Judaism ignores indisputable primary source evidence to the contrary.

Focusing on Wright's understanding of justification by works, his view has been particularly influential within Reformed circles; he argues that justification is covenantal, forensic, and eschatological. Wright also maintains that there is a present and future justification. Let us briefly examine Wright's argument.

a. Covenantal

Wright is correct to say that justification is covenantal, though he understands "covenant" in terms of first century Judaism. Paul's understanding of covenant, however, is much broader than the first century, evidenced by the absence of any citation of first century literature in his writings. Rather, justification is covenantal in terms of the broken covenant of works and the covenant of grace, or as Paul explains it—the first and second Adams.

b. The Law Court

First, Wright is correct to argue that justification is forensic, though his understanding hinges upon a declaration before the world of who is in the covenant and therefore "in the right." In other words, justification is a forensic declaration of vindication before the world. Paul, however, does not place the law court before the world but before the presence of God.

Second, Wright rejects the doctrine of imputation on the basis of his understanding of the Jewish law court. The judge does not transfer anything to the one who stands accused. Wright, however, imposes his understanding of the Jewish law court upon the Scriptures. Wright misunderstands the heart of the gospel by imposing an earthly human court and its proceedings upon the heavenly court. What judge, for example, sends his own son to die in the place of the accused?

c. Present and Future Justification

Wright clearly affirms that there is a present justification, which one receives by looking to Christ in faith, understood as faithful submission to his lordship, and a future justification, based upon one's Spirit-produced works. The Reformed church has historically rejected such a construction because of its similarity to the Roman Catholic understanding of justification, where one is declared righteous on the basis of his sanctification. Historically, when Reformed theologians have spoken, they have done so not in terms of a future justification, but in terms of an open acknowledgement and acquittal on the Day of Judgment (cf. LC, 90; SC, 38). In other words, our justification occurs in secret now, but that same justification will be open or public on the Day of Judgment.

G. Summary Against the Federal Vision

The general conclusions of this critique mean that the following points of the Federal Vision are out of accord with Scripture and our standards:

1. "Righteousness" defined as covenant membership rather than moral equity, or adherence to a moral standard.
2. "Works of the law" for justification understood as boundary markers identifying Israel as God's covenant people.
3. Justification only as vindication.
4. A second or future justification that has a different ground from one's justification by faith.
5. Shifting the ground of justification from the finished work of Christ to the Spirit-produced works of the believer.
6. Denial of the imputation of the active and/or passive obedience of Christ.
7. Compromising the self-authenticating and self-interpreting nature of the Scriptures by giving the literature of Second Temple Judaism undue interpretive weight.

H. The Lordship Controversy

1. The Lordship Doctrine

The Lordship Theology is probably the most widely accepted of the dissident views among Reformed thinkers. Those who hold to Lordship Theology believe that if a person is truly a Christian, they *must* live a righteous, obedient life. Without this practical righteousness, there is no reason for a person to think that they are a Christian. In the long run, however, the Lordship position compromises the Biblical and Reformed position of Salvation *sola fide, sola gratia*—justification by grace through faith in Christ *alone*.

In his commentary on the Sermon on the Mount, Martyn Lloyd-Jones says, "Nothing is more dangerous than to rely only upon a correct belief and a fervent spirit, and to assume that, as long as you believe the right things and are zealous and keen and active concerning them, you are therefore of necessity a Christian" (Lloyd-Jones, 1976).

According to Lordship Salvation, saving faith includes submission and obedience. Richard Belcher (1990) says, "True saving faith includes in it a submission to the Lordship of Christ." Another

Lordship proponent says, "Saving faith is trust in Christ Himself. It is a commitment of self in submission to all of Christ that is revealed." John MacArthur (2006) says, "Saving faith, then, is the whole of my being embracing all of Christ. Faith cannot be divorced from commitment." He also says, "The true test of faith is this, does it produce obedience? If not, it is not saving faith." In the same vein, Bailey Smith (1991) asserts, "Saving faith is not mere intellectual assent, but it involves an act of submission on our part."

Those who hold to the Lordship view would say that true Christians live a life characterized by obedience to all that the Father has commanded. John MacArthur wrote,

> Hell is undoubtedly full of people who did not actively oppose Jesus Christ, but simply drifted into damnation by neglecting to respond to the gospel. Such people are in view in Hebrews 2:1-4. They are aware of the good news of salvation provided by Jesus Christ but aren't willing to commit their lives to Him." (MacArthur, 1986, p. 80)

Why does he say these people are not believers? What do they lack? The answer is clear: Commitment! MacArthur gives this story to illustrate his point:

> I will never forget a particular lady who came into my office and informed me that she was a prostitute. She said, "I need help; I'm desperate." So I presented the claims of Christ to her. Then I said, "Would you like to invite Jesus Christ into your life?" She said, "Yes, and she prayed." I said, "Now, I want you to do something. Do you have your book with all your contacts?" She said she did. I said, "Let's light a match to it and burn it." She looked at me and said, "What do you mean?" I said, "If you want to live for Jesus Christ, and you've truly accepted His forgiveness and met Him as your Savior, then you need to prove it." She said to me, "That book is worth a lot of money. I don't want to burn it." She put it back in her purse and looked me right in the eye and said, "I guess I don't really want Jesus, do I?" Then she left. When it came down to counting the cost, she wasn't ready. I don't know what the outcome of that poor woman has been. I do know that she knew the facts and believed them, but she was not willing to make the sacrifice. (MacArthur, 1986, p. 84)

MacArthur (1988) further discusses questions he received in response to his book, *The Gospel According to Jesus*. He quotes Zane C. Hodges from Hodges' *Absolutely Free!*

> What faith really is, in biblical language, is receiving the testimony of God. It is the *inward conviction* that what God says to us in the gospel is true. That—and that alone—is saving faith. (Hodges, 1989)

MacArthur then rebuts Hodges' argument: "By emphasizing the words inward conviction and underscoring them with the phrase 'that—and that alone,' Hodges is explicitly rejecting the concept that faith inevitably produces righteous behavior" (1988).

The question MacArthur raises in response to Hodges are:

> Is Hodges adequately characterizing what it means to believe?
>
> Do people know on an intuitive level whether their faith is real?
>
> Can someone belief in his belief, yet not truly believe?
>
> Is there no such thing as spurious faith?

MacArthur maintains that the NT writers answered these questions repeatedly, and that they saw imitation faith as a very real danger. The debate over Lordship Salvation must ultimately answer the question of whether assenting to the facts of the gospel, and holding an inward conviction that the truths apply, is enough to guarantee eternal life if the individual never shuns sin or submits to Christ? What MacArthur terms "mental assent" is dead faith (n.d.).

Sam Storms (2006) takes up the question of what is at stake in the Lordship Theology debate. He characterizes those who affirm "Lordship" salvation as those opposing the idea that we can possess saving faith in the absence of submission to the Lord Jesus in daily obedience. He maintains, "We are saved by faith alone, but not by the faith which is alone (*sola fides iustificat, sed non fides quae est sola*)." Faith is not saving in the absence of submission to the lordship of Jesus. He argues that Lordship Salvation does not teach that Christians cannot sin; rather that they cannot be complacent in sin. Lordship Salvation insists that Christians will sin less. If they sin, they will suffer for it. Complacency and contentment in sin, Storms maintains, are the hallmarks of an unregenerate soul (Storms, 2006).

Lordship Salvation distinguishes between acknowledgement of the principle of Christ's authority over the convert's life and the practice of progressive submission to Christ. Lordship advocates recognize:

> First, that Christ died for sinners and that eternal life waits for those who believe in Christ's death;
>
> Second, that we know we are God's children because the Holy Spirit awakens our hearts to this confirmation; and
>
> Third, one's profession is borne out by loyalty, love, and obedience (Storms, 2006).

Another Lordship proponent, Ernest Reisinger (1993), says that one of the major points of disagreement in the Lordship controversy concerns the role of repentance in salvation. Teachers of both viewpoints believe in repentance, but the Lordship teaching is that "faith alone is not the kind of faith that justifies." Repentance and saving faith cannot be separated in the application of God's salvation. Temporary or delusive faith, implicit faith and historic faith are all spurious. Lordship gospel is different from non-Lordship gospel, and only one is biblical gospel.

Repentance is important because Jesus said if we do not repent, we will perish. Reisinger finds the following errors in the non-Lordship position:

1. Repentance is not an essential part of salvation.
2. The forgiveness of sin offered by non-Lordship teaching is not necessarily connected to repentance.
3. Repentance is a call to God's fellowship and is not connected with eternal life.
4. Repentance and rejecting sin in coming to Christ have nothing to do with each other.
5. Repentance has been redefined in a way that removes its association from the idea of turning away from sin.

The non-Lordship position does not recognize the inseparable connection between repentance and faith. However, in Reisinger's view, evangelical repentance and true saving faith are "Siamese twins—inseparable in their application." Reisinger writes that repentance is spurious when it dwells not on sin itself, but on the consequences of sin. Repentance and faith are sacred duties and inseparable graces (1993).

Tom Nettles (1991) discusses the term "easy-believism" and "cheap grace" as terms with pejorative overtones that non-Lordship followers resist. Nettles, however, believes that certain aspects of these terms have some truth attached. Saving faith involves both assent and intellect. True faith is hard work because of all the evil we must conquer as a demonstration of genuineness.

In his critique of the non-Lordship position, Tom Ascol (1991) begins with a quote from J. I. Packer:

> If, ten years ago, you had told me that I would live to see literate evangelicals, some with doctorates and a seminary teaching record, arguing for the reality of

> an eternal salvation, divinely guaranteed, that may have in it no repentance, no discipleship, no behavioral change, no practical acknowledgment of Christ as Lord of one's life, and no perseverance in faith, then I would have told you that you were out of your mind. Stark, staring, bonkers, is the British phrase I would probably have used. (Packer, 1991, cited in Ascol, 1991).

The fundamental questions are whether it is possible to believe in Christ without submission to his Lordship, and secondly, whether the reception of Christ as Lord and Christ as Savior are two distinct and separate experiences in a believer's life. The answers to these questions reveal one's position, and the gospel itself is at stake. Faith is a duty and must involve the will. Nor can faith be restricted to the intellect. Saving faith involves the whole man (Ascol, 1991).

In his discussion of the Carnal Christian theory, Earnest Reisinger (1994) holds that the "carnal Christian" teaching is in error when it separates justification and sanctification, thereby making optional the act of submission to Christ. Reisinger preaches that non-Lordship teachers have invented a category of "carnal Christian" to explain the lives that have not been changed by the power of the Holy Spirit. The separation of conversion, in which the decision is made to accept Christ as a personal Savior, from the decision to make Christ Lord, is in error because no human can make Christ Lord. Christ's status as Lord is independent of sinners' thoughts and actions. Only God can make Christ Lord.

Reisinger goes on to say of the "carnal Christian" teaching that in between conversion and the decision to make Christ Lord the believer may continue to live as if he were an unbeliever. This second blessing teaching he says is in error, because it sends Christians to search for holiness that is received by a single religious crisis experience as opposed to the daily submission to God's will; carnal Christians will comfortably go to hell; lordship teachers believe and instruct that Christians are sometimes carnal in some parts of their lives at some times, and spiritual in others; otherwise they are not Christians at all (Reisinger, 1994).

John MacArthur defines the carnal person as one who places himself on the throne, rather than putting Christ in charge. Thus, the carnal person still lives a life of chaos, because his life has not changed. Carnal Christians believe in Jesus for the purpose of salvation, but do not want to submit their lives to Christ (MacArthur, n.d. Bible Bulletin Board).

2. Summary of Errors in the Lordship Position

Christian Temple (1999) presents the case for faith alone as a condition for eternal life, which is in opposition to the Lordship position of faith based on knowledge of the facts, assent to this knowledge, repentance, and submission to Christ as conditions of eternal life. He asks if simple faith is "dead faith," and answers with a quote from the *Wycliff Bible Dictionary* (1998):

> A proper definition of faith must take into consideration its complexity, for while the exercise of it may be said to be simplicity itself, it involves the whole personality.... Saving faith, therefore, involves active personal trust, a commitment of oneself to the Lord Jesus Christ. But it is not the amount of faith that saves, it is the object of faith that saves. Great faith in the wrong object does not alter man's lost estate one iota. Little faith (so long as it is faith) in the right object [Christ] must result in salvation.

Temple notes that speaking of a free gift that costs more in terms of giving us something to do in order to achieve salvation is not consistent; gifts only need to be accepted and are not earned. Nor do gifts require repayment. Temple goes on to discuss other potential errors in the Lordship position. These errors seem to arise from the desire to have Christians engage in behavior that is Christian-like. The greatest error, as he sees it, is that the Lordship position puts individuals in a Catch-22. "You must make Christ Lord in order to be saved, but you must first be saved in order to make Christ Lord."

Additionally, the Lordship position holds that the meaning of the New Testament use of the word "lord" (*kurios*) denotes "sovereign master," to whom submission is required. However, the Greek *kurios* is almost always used to denote "deity." Christ, as a deity, carries the authority to administer salvation to believers (Temple, 1999). Submission thus implies a cost to the believer. Packer's supposition that "free forgiveness in one sense will cost [the forgiven] everything" brings up the question of how a free gift can cost anything (Packer 1991).

Temple's next issue with Lordship is that the believer must have some knowledge of biblical principles to submit to Christ's Lordship. He asks,

> How is a new believer to have had prior knowledge of biblical knowledge at the moment when salvation is at hand? How much does a believer have to know in order to be saved? Along the same lines, how much submission is enough

submission? How much willingness to submit to Christ is enough? (Temple, 1999).

The Lordship position also leaves Christians in the unfortunate position of having to judge others' commitment to submission (Temple, 1999).

Temple ends his analysis with his position that the Lordship Salvation view "presents an inadequate (rigid) view of the salvation process." What of the non-believer who is not witnessed to, or has no church or bible study to help? What of those who know *only* that they are seeking mercy and the *gift* of forgiveness and salvation? How is this non-believer supposed to obtain the knowledge of Christ's requirements? The *free gift* carries too many qualifications if one must submit to Christ's lordship in order to obtain it (1999).

Zane Hodges weighs in on the matter by observing that "Salvation, of course, is not earned." Therefore, it can be said to be "by grace ... through faith" and "not of works" (Eph. 2:8–9). Our works have nothing to do with whether we go to heaven or hell. Salvation is a gift, and it is absolutely free. Faith in Christ is the means by which this gift is received (Hodges, 1991).

John's Gospel often says that believers in Jesus have eternal life; conversely, John does not suggest that lack of good works in a believer's life disqualifies him from the guarantee of eternal life. The notion that a believer in Christ can go for years and not be affected by its miraculous nature is bizarre (Hodges, 1990). Hodges further maintains that the issue is assurance, and that this belief that assurance depends on good works reinforces and breathes new life into man's boastful inclinations (Hodges, 2009).

The Lordship view teaches that assurance comes from obedience, from holy living, from your works. Martin Luther said, "For certainty does not come to me from any kind of reflection on myself and on my state. On the contrary it comes solely through hearing the word, solely because I cling to the word and its promises."

John Calvin wrote, "From one's work conscience feels more fear and consternation than assurance." John Calvin taught that assurance was of the essence of faith (Calvin, 1536). If good works are the basis of assurance, then the believer's eyes are distracted from the sufficiency of Christ and His work to meet his eternal need. His eyes are focused on himself. If I seek assurance through examining my good works, one of two things must necessarily result: (1) I will minimize the depth of my sinfulness; (2) I will see my deep sinfulness as hopelessly contrary to any conviction that I am saved. Our assurance is to be based upon God's Word; His promise that He would give eternal life to all who believe on His Son. Assurance does not come from our works.

Saving faith is accepting the testimony of God. Do you believe that Jesus is the Christ? If you do, then on the testimony of scripture, you are saved, you possess everlasting life. Benjamin Warfield, the Presbyterian who probably would not have put himself in the Lordship camp, said, "The saving power resides exclusively, not in the act of faith, or the attitude of faith, or the nature of faith, but in the object of faith." The truth is, technically, that we are not saved *by* faith but *through* faith. Faith is the instrumental means; grace is the efficient means of our salvation. We are saved by Jesus Christ. We are saved by His grace. We are saved through faith. You would understand what I meant if I said to you, "I put the fire out with the hose." Now hoses do not put out fires. But hoses are the channels for water that puts the fire out. The hose is the instrumental means; the water is the efficient means. Faith is the instrumental means by which we are able to access our salvation through Jesus Christ.

The Lordship view teaches that in order to be a Christian, you must do more than believe the gospel. I see this as adding to the gospel; indeed, it is totally unbiblical! The Grace view teaches that a person becomes a Christian when they understand and believe the gospel of Jesus Christ. At that moment they are placed into the body of Christ, given Christ's righteousness, indwelt by God, and are as sure of heaven as if they were already there. They are "in Christ."

Because God permanently indwells, His power is constantly available to the believer. That power will not operate in the Christian's life, however, unless he personally appropriates it by faith. Moment by moment the believer must trust God rather than himself to give him power for victory in daily life.

What if the Free Grace view is not correct? If it is wrong, what damage could this view possibly cause? If the Free Grace view is wrong, it could cause people to think that they are saved when they are really not; it would be giving false hope to unbelievers. What are the consequences of false hope? Do you believe in election? Will the elect of God ever be lost? No. Will the reprobate ever be saved? No.

So, in the author's opinion, the worst that the Free Grace view will do is give false hope to the reprobate.

If the Lordship teaching is wrong, what harm can it do? It can cause a believer to think that they are not redeemed because of sin in their life. This view can bring the elect to despair under guilt and condemnation. It can cause a believer to give up on Christianity by making them doubt that they really are saved.

Conclusion Against the New Positions on Paul and Sanctification

The new positions on Paul, the Federal Vision, and the Lordship views of justification and sanctification have been briefly described above in a fair and adequate manner. These views, the author contends, share a common fallacy: they make Christianity something to be achieved by following doctrines from men who do not properly understand the plan of salvation. Those views affirm that salvation comes by obedience, keeping commandments, and by following rules or rituals of practice. We refer to such views as "legalism," and these Christian legalists take certain passages of scripture to imply that the Bible says something that really cannot be supported in inside the full light of the Gospel of the Bible.

With regard to the Federal Vision, it has been argued that their definition of righteousness as covenant membership, rather than moral equity or adherence to a moral standard, is a legalistic interpretation that offends a proper reading of the scriptures. The law was given to show that we are imperfect and condemned to be separated from God unless God Himself did something to bridge that gap. The Law of Faith is belief that only God is righteous and merciful, and only He can provide the way of salvation for mankind. This plan of salvation from God was carried out when God the Son, Jesus Christ, paid the requirements of the law for all on the cross. Those who, by faith, believe God and accept the sacrifice He provided for mankind's sins will be saved. As Don Koenig (2005) says:

> God is interested in saving people who truly trust in Him.... He is not interested in having people in His presence who think they got there by their own righteousness through following the letter of the law or by rituals of obedience.

Furthermore, the FV upholds the view that "works of the law" are to be understood, in terms of justification, as boundary markers identifying Israel as God's covenant people. That is legalistic and offends the accepted Reformed view where justification is by definition a one-time act of God, not dependent on works, indeed and truly, not dependent upon any legalistic boundaries.

In closing, we may reaffirm that since the Reformation, the core Protestant Reformed doctrine holds that salvation is "by Christ alone, by grace alone, and by faith alone" (Williams, 2002, p. 1). The logical consequence of which is that sanctification, too, comes by and through faith in Christ. As we are justified by faith, so are we sanctified by faith, which can only be achieved and demonstrated by spiritual union with Christ. By splitting the law of obedience from the life of faith, these new legalists indulge in a Pharisaic observance of outward forms and rituals. However, true sanctification can only come through God's grace and the faith that receives it through the intercession of Christ. This constitutes Paul's "gospel of grace" and the correct understanding of the role of sanctification in the life of the Christian believer.

13.
How Does the Doctrine of Justification by Faith Impact Christian Counseling?

by Sabrina N. Gilchrist
Director, Right Moves For Youth
North Carolina[390]

Introduction	223
A. Problem of Humanity—a Fallen People	224
B. Theological Need for Justification	225
C. Christian Counseling and Justification by Faith	227
D. Doctrine as Platform for Healing	228
Conclusion	229

Introduction

The conflicts and tensions that people experience have their root in the paradox of human nature. Our intended place at the pinnacle of creation is in stark opposition to how we actually are in our fallen state. For fellowship with God to be restored, guilt and tension experienced in our human conscience must be diminished. The pursuit of justification is one's attempt to resolve inner-tensions and be reconciled with oneself in order to have inner-peace. It is at the point of forgiveness and grace that self-justifications must diminish in order for one to take responsibility, love self, and embrace God's love, all of which I argue are closely tied to the idea of justification by faith. In my view, the doctrine of justification by faith is a launch pad for growth and healing in the work of counseling.

It could be stated that while Martin Luther was one of the most influential pioneers of the Protestant Reformation in Europe, he was at one time a troubled soul with looming symptoms of depression and anxiety. One scholar writes that Luther "felt himself tempted to believe that he was a castaway and a child of destruction, that he

---

[390] Gilchrist holds a MDiv, MA, NCC, and LPMHC, is the Director, Right Moves for Youth, NC, founder of Sabrina Nichole LLC, is the first African-American woman to graduate from Wake Forest University with the prestigious dual degree of Master of Arts in Counseling and Master of Divinity.

could never be redeemed. God loved everyone but him."[391] Luther finally found peace through a new understanding of Paul's Epistle to the Romans. Evidenced by his lectures between 1513 and 1518, Luther developed a growing sense of clarity and maturity concerning Paul's writings. Luther "suddenly felt the force of the words 'The just shall live by faith'" as he sat in the tower studying the biblical text.[392] Kenneth W. Allen quotes Luther:

> I grasped the truth that the righteousness of God is that righteousness whereby, through grace and sheer mercy, He justifies us by faith. Thereupon I felt myself to be reborn... and whereas before "the righteousness of God" had filled me with hate, now it became unto me inexpressively sweet in greater love.[393]

A standard edition of Luther's lectures and writings consists of over one hundred volumes with about seven hundred pages each.[394] With that alone, it is easy to see how, through Luther's efforts, the Reformation commenced as "the greatest revival since Pentecost."[395] Luther's new understanding of Paul's exquisite writings spurred what we now refer to as the Doctrine of Justification by Faith.

A. Problem of Humanity—a Fallen People

William E. Hulme expounds on the fallen state of humanity and suggests that the four basic needs of troubled personalities have counterparts within what he refers to as the three major doctrines of Christian faith:

> Doctrine of Man,
> Doctrine of the Priesthood of the Believer, and
> Doctrine of Christian Liberty.

For the purposes of this paper, it is important to note Hulme's thoughts concerning the doctrine of man, which is that the conflicts

---

[391] Owen Chadwick, *The Penguin History of the Church vol. 3: The Reformation* (New York, NY: Penguin, 1990), 40–75.

[392] Ibid., 45.

[393] Kenneth W. Allen, "Justification by Faith," *Bibliotheca Sacra* 135, no. 538 (April 1978), 109.

[394] Helmut T. Lehmann, "Luther on the study of Luther," *Word & World* 3, no. 4 (September 1, 1983), 398. See also Concordia Publishing House's massive work on Luther's writings.

[395] Allen, 109.

and tensions that people experience have their root in the paradox of human nature.[396]

Likewise, in his article "Christian Counseling: A Synthesis of Psychological and Christian Concepts," Stanley R. Strong argues that the fallenness of humanity includes the person's proclivity toward the misuse of free will, the desire to make oneself the center of existence, and the inevitable result of cutting oneself off from God; ergo, fallenness is at the root of human problems.[397] In other words, what we were intended to be in creation is in opposition to how we actually are as fallen and sinful people. In order for fellowship with God to be restored, thereby enabling "confidence and security to personality" to form, the guilt and tension experienced in the human conscience must be diminished.[398] Constant and prolonged feelings of anxiety, guilt, insecurity, etc., undoubtedly impair one's ability to function, causing sufferers to feel helpless, hopeless, and meaningless. As in Luther's case, these feelings can certainly lead to self-condemnation, self-hatred, and indignation.

B. Theological Need for Justification

Stanley Strong suggests society is in hot pursuit of self-justification, a way to fight the void and angst of meaninglessness.[399] The pursuit of justification is one's attempt to resolve inner-tensions and be reconciled with oneself, to have inner-peace, and to move from feelings of wretchedness to self-esteem (from Rom. 7:24 to Ps. 139:14).

In the opening chapters of Romans, Paul begins to state his case for humanity's need for justification before God. According to Paul, there is the universal law written within the hearts of humans, and there is also universal accountability for a lack of adherence to the law. This accountability is most notably present through the human conscience. Because human beings do not live up to the universal

---

[396] William E. Hulme, "The Theology of Counseling," *Theology Today* 9, no. 2 (July 1952), 191.

[397] Stanley R. Strong, "Christian Counseling: A Synthesis of Psychological and Christian Concepts," *The Personnel and Guidance Journal* 58, no. 9 (1980), 589–592.

[398] Ibid., 193.

[399] F. W. Dillistone, "The Recovery of the Doctrine of Justification by Faith," *Theology Today* 11, no. 2 (July 1954), 205.

law, and our conscience reminds us that we have "fallen short"—we are thereby universally guilty. Humanity's guilt renders us in dire need of justification before God which cannot be obtained through works.[400] F. W. Dillistone describes two Old Testament views of justification. In the first view, justification is seen as God's vindication of God's honor and people before his adversaries. In the second view, justification is the process of bringing an offender into right-standing within the Old Testament covenant, which reconciles the offender to their neighbor.[401] In essence, the theological need for justification is reconciliation of humanity to God and to others. He quotes Tillich as stating that one's "bad conscience" is defeated by accepting Jesus as God's self-sacrificing Christ, and thereby reconciling with God:

> God, so to speak, subjects himself to the consequences of his wrath, taking upon himself, thus re-establishing unity with us. The sinner is accepted as just in spite of his sinfulness.[402]

Allen sums it up like this:

> [Through] His one great propitiatory offering, Christ turned away the wrath of God, provided an objective basis for mercy, and made it possible for God to justify the believing sinner while still vindicating His own righteousness.[403]

The response to the void of meaninglessness is a fresh proclamation of the Pauline doctrine of justification by faith by modern-day seers and prophets.[404] One way to put Reform theology's premise of justification by faith is that it is

> the quintessential experience that ... God has accepted [human] life by taking it into God's self and changing it. The alienated person is justified before God only through faith in God.[405]

---

[400] Allen, "Justification by Faith," 110.

[401] Dillistone, "The Recovery of the Doctrine of Justification by Faith," 201.

[402] Ibid., 208.

[403] Allen, "Justification by Faith," 112.

[404] Dillistone, "The Recovery of the Doctrine of Justification by Faith," 205.

[405] Gerhard Sauter, et al., "God Creating Faith: The Doctrine of Justification from the Reformation to the Present." *Lutheran Quarterly* 11, no. 1 (March 1, 1997): 17.

Dillistone writes, "It seems to me that this doctrine has taken on new relevance and even meaning through the witness of modern psychological studies."[406]

C. Christian Counseling and Justification by Faith

As the Christian counseling movement has continued to mature, there has been an increased attempt to integrate psychology and Scripture.[407] This attempt to integrate seems logical since both arenas attempt to understand and answer the problem of humanity, but from very different vantage points. According to William Hulme, "Both psychology and theology are concerned with the same basic problem, namely, human nature."[408] Likewise, Dillistone suggests that the psychological professional, theologian, and existential philosopher find common ground in the attempt to relieve the angst of human life resulting from one's desire for justification and the inadequacies of "self-justification."[409]

According to Stanley Strong, despite the particular approach that one may use, Christian counseling espouses three basic tenets pertaining to creation, fallenness of humans, and forgiveness and grace. The tenet of creation holds that humans are good, have free will, are intelligent, are lovable, and are in need of a close relationship with God. Fallenness refers to how persons misuse free will, desire to make themselves the center of existence, and cut themselves off from God. Problems take root in our fallen nature and bear unhealthy fruit in our lives. The principle of forgiveness and grace suggests that the person who is well—whole—accepts their inner self as loved by God, owns their flaws, and gives love responsibly.[410]

In psychoanalytical terms, people begin to develop defense mechanisms to protect a fragile ego from contrary feelings, such as

---

[406] Dillistone, "The Recovery of the Doctrine of Justification by Faith," 204.

[407] George G. Konrad, "Responsible Christian Counseling," *Direction* 7, no. 2 (April 1978): 23–32, https://directionjournal.org/7/2/responsible-christian-counseling.html.

[408] Hulme, "The Theology of Counseling," 189.

[409] Dillistone, "The Recovery of the Doctrine of Justification by Faith." 204.

[410] Stanley R. Strong, "Christian Counseling: A Synthesis of Psychological and Christian Concepts," *The Personnel and Guidance Journal* 58, no. 9 (1980): 589–592.

anxiety, hopelessness, and despair.[411] Another way of putting it is that we sometimes create and embrace self-justifications, or excuses, in an attempt to justify our actions and state of being when we are experiencing anxiety or angst. The field of Christian counseling is wide and varied; however, many scholars and practitioners seem to agree that for the counselee to find wholeness they must come to accept responsibility for their own actions. This requires that the counselee desist from placing blame on others for their plight, and recognize that they are responsible for their spiritual destiny.[412] It is at the point of forgiveness and grace that self-justifications must diminish in order for one to take responsibility, love self, and embrace God's love, all of which I argue are closely tied to the idea of justification by faith. In my view, the doctrine of justification by faith is a launch pad for growth and healing in the work of counseling. One scholar quotes David Augsburger as stating:

> I discover that as I own [faults/flaws/state of being], accepting full responsibility, I am then able to respond in new ways. I become response-able.[413]

D. Doctrine as Platform for Healing

The doctrine of justification by faith is therefore a critical platform upon which the counselee finds healing and wholeness. From this doctrine, one sees the paradox of inherent goodness as God's creation side by side the sinfulness of human nature resulting from the fall. The doctrine points to the existence of feelings of guilt leading to anxiety, and the inevitable belief that one should be punished; yet the doctrine provides an explanation for how God's love has provided Christ as a propitiation to remove guilt and to take punishment in proxy of the wrongdoer. Hulme suggests that one gift of theology is the doctrine of atonement which satisfies the need for justice and meets humanity's desire for forgiveness and inner-peace. He states:

---

[411] William E. Hulme, "Theology and Counseling," *Christian Century* 68, no. 8 (February 21, 1951): 239.

[412] Konrad, "Responsible Christian Counseling," 28.

[413] Ibid, 28.

Through the receptivity of faith [man] has forgiveness and freedom. Theologically, this is the doctrine of justification by grace through faith.[414]

Sauter, et al, also suggest that God not only reveals definitively who He is through His acts of salvation and justification, but that the act of justification causes the person to inquire into their current identity and who they will come to be.[415] The process of change and transformation can begin with justification by faith.

Gladding discusses the developmental and wellness approach to counseling, noting that this approach emphasizes "the positive nature and health of human beings."[416] One of the strengths of the counseling profession is that it helps clients identify their strengths and coping resources, build upon those strengths, and that helps them to solve their own problems. This is called a strengths-based approach to counseling, and "refers to utilizing the positive attributes of a group of people, community, or society, and building on these strengths as a way to implement change and forge progress."[417]

The principles of Carl Rogers' person-centered counseling method have been a good influence on pastoral counseling, because they teach respect for the image of God in man and give us a fresh understanding of the priesthood of every believer.[418] According to Howard Stone, the counselor must understand that the counselee has strengths that should be explored and built upon, for the counselee is the expert on their experiences and life.[419]

---

[414] Hulme, "Theology and Counseling," 239.

[415] Sauter, et al., 18.

[416] Samuel Gladding, "Personal and Professional Aspects of Counseling," in M.D. Fossel & P.D. Bennett (Eds.), *Counseling—A Comprehensive Profession*, 6th Edition. (Upper Saddle River, NJ: Pearson Education, Inc., 2009), 47.

[417] D. A. Harley, "The Black Church: A Strengths-based Approach in Mental Health," in *Contemporary Mental Health Issues Among African Americans*, ed. D.A. Harley & J. M. Dillard (Alexandria, VA: American Counseling Association, 2005), 196.

[418] Hulme, "Theology and Counseling," 238.

[419] Howard W. Stone, *Strategies for Brief Pastoral Counseling* (Minneapolis, MN: Fortress Press, 2001).

Conclusion

One scholar states, "After we accept ourselves as sinners—even as God does—we can begin to understand ourselves."[420] We believe the doctrine of justification by faith provides a platform from which the process of healing for the counselee can be certainly launched. The doctrine speaks to a deep, theological underpinning of human dysfunction, especially to the fallen nature of humanity and our need for righteous vindication by and restoration to God and neighbor. Another scholar puts it like this: "The doctrine of justification by faith keeps ever before [our] conscience [that] ... [God] justifies the ungodly, he loves the unlovely, he accepts the unacceptable."[421]

While this paper considers the impact of the doctrine of justification by faith on Christian counseling, it is important to note that the umbrella of Christian counseling is broad, wide, and extremely diverse. Seegobin, et al, state that "a variety of counseling approaches, faith assumptions, and definitions of healing fall under the rubric of Christian counseling."[422] In similar fashion, Konrad states that approaches to Christian counseling vary greatly and can lend themselves to the "pastoral counselor" being at a loss for which approach to take when helping others.[423]

It is also important to note that there is a gap in the literature regarding the theological stance on justification by faith in counseling. Much of the literature that points to theological discourse in this regard seems to have been written in the 1950s and 1960s.

As such, the author suggests that more research be done in the area of justification by faith and the impact that embracing this doctrine could have on the effectiveness of treatment and the counselee's experience in therapy. Within that research, operational definitions should be offered regarding the type of therapy or counseling that is being offered (i.e., pastoral counseling, spiritually-integrated psychotherapy, nouthetic counseling). Offering a more specific

---

[420] Hulme, "The Theology of Counseling," 195.

[421] Dillistone, "The Recovery of the Doctrine of Justification by Faith," 209.

[422] Winston Seegobin, Mark R. McMinn, Ryan C. Staley, and Kurt C. Webb, "Just What Is Christian Counseling Anyway?" *Professional Psychology, Research and Practice* 41, no. 5 (October 2010): 391.

[423] Konrad, "Responsible Christian Counseling," 23.

description of the counseling involved could help to narrow the focus with regard to the umbrella of Christian counseling and its related but often confused therapeutic counterparts.

Overall, justification by faith remains a critical component to wholeness.

14.
Christian Spirituality of Eschatological Hoping (*Promissiology*): Towards a Theological Hermeneutics of Human Anticipation and the Quest for Meaning in Suffering

by Professor D. J. Louw
Head of the Department of Practical Theology
Stellenbosch University, South Africa[424]

Introduction and Paradigm Shift 233
A. Eschatological Dimension in a Theology of Hopeful Suffering: *Eschatologia Crucis* (Significance of the Cross from the Perspective of Hope & Future) 238
B. Trinity Reformulated within the Paradigmatic Framework of a Hermeneutics of Suffering (Divine Forsakenness) 239
C. Towards a Theology of the Resurrection (*Theologia Resurrectionis*): Divine Dimension of Salvific Hope and Illustration of the Faithfulness of a Living God 248
D. Zig Zag Pattern of Hope within the Paradox of Frailty/Weakness/Sinfulness and Quest for Meaningful Living: Wherefore God? 252
E. Spiritual Framework of Meaning: Realm of the Fulfilled Promises of God as Indication of Divine Faithfulness (Promisiology & Promisio-therapy) 257
Conclusion 263

Introduction and Paradigm Shift

The article probes into the theological dimension of Christian hope.[425] In order to differentiate hope from merely an affect or a positive attitude based on future speculation (future as *futurum*) or wishful optimism, an *eschatologia crucis*—hope and future as theologically founded by the interplay between the cross and resurrection of Christ—is proposed as the guarantee for our future hope (future as *adventus*).[426] The fulfilled promises of God as

---

[424] Louw is former dean of the faculty of theology and head of the Department of Practical Theology, University of Stellenbosch; president of the International Academy for Practical Theology (2003-2005); and president of the International Society for Pastoral Care and Counselling (2011-2015). For more detail, see djl@sun.ac.za and www.sun.ac.za.
[425] "Promissiology" refers to the notion of divine promises that promote a trustful and sustainable future connected to the faithfulness of *Jahwê* and to all the fulfilled promises as illustrated and realised in the gospel narratives of the cross of Christ (*theologia crucis*) and resurrection (*theologia resurrectionis*).
[426] Latin is used in order to step into the tradition of the early Christian Church and to help forward Christian theological categories with grammar and research paradigms that distinguish Christian theology from other disciplines and sciences. It is hoped to stimulate the interdisciplinary discourse. Distinctions

[*Footnote continued on next page*]

displayed in the faithfulness of *Jahwê* (the *promissio*-character of hope) and not *fortigenetics* (merely positive psychic and mental energy; inner strengths) determines the character of the Christian hope. Hope is then described as a new state of being and mindset in order to instill meaning in suffering. The Christian hope correlates with an attitude of joy and gratitude in the present that is fueled by the anticipation of the coming of Christ as expressed in the notion of the New Testament's understanding of *Parousia*: the future as *adventus*.

Christian hope does not by-pass the inhumane suffering of human beings in the present. It wrestles with the theodicy question, namely, how to link the justice, grace, and goodness of God to evil, destruction, and the frailty of life. Instead of the notion of the impassibility of God, or positivistic explanations that probes speculatively into the possible causes for human suffering, Christian hope is based on the *passio Dei*: the compassion of God as expressed in the suffering of the Son of God (a *theologia crucis*). God suffers with us, on our behalf. Thus, the choice is to link the theological founding of hope to theopachitic theology: God suffers with us (God as the co-suffering God). In this respect Jürgen Moltmann's theology of hope makes a substantial contribution towards a hermeneutical approach that tries not to *explain* suffering (explanatory model) but to *understand* suffering as a challenge to reach out (the service of *diakonia*) to suffering human beings and to demonstrate God's compassionate being with human brokenness by means of pastoral caregiving.[427] In this regard, pastoral hermeneutics illustrates the image of a "vulnerable God." With reference to the place of God-images in a pastoral hermeneutics of suffering, a paradigm shift from the immutability of God towards the *derilictio* of God (the vulnerable power of God as exposed in total forsakenness) is proposed.

The article deals with the following basic research question: wherein resides the unique, spiritual, and theological character of Christian hoping in pastoral caregiving?

---

are needed so that it becomes clear that Christian theology refers to a religious background and written tradition that differs from other sciences. For example, pastoral caregiving is a theological science and not merely psychology covered with a Christian caster sugar.

[427] References will be made in the original languages (mostly German texts) because translations cannot represent the precise meaning. Due to difficult nuances, the German will be given, either in brackets or in footnotes, in order to enhance clarity for those who know the languages.

The basic presupposition is that hope is a many-layered concept. Hope operates in a systemic and relational dynamic of several interacting dimensions.

1. **Corporate Dimension** is the most basic dimension within the act of hoping and related to human health, well-being, including the physical and neurological conditions of the human body. Ill health diminishes hope. Well-being enhances health and contributes to a positive disposition.
2. **Psychic Dimension** includes personal wishes, ideas, dreams, and expectations that envision human flourishing and better life conditions.
3. **Social Dimension** of hope refers to the quality of human relationships and social interaction. The social dimension includes public issues and the quest for human rights. It promotes human dignity.
4. **Structural Dimension** implied in Hope refers to communication systems, technology, and general human development.
5. **Environmental Dimension** of hope is built on preservation and conservation measurements that safeguard a sustainable earth (green hoping).
6. **Existential Dimension** of hope includes the phenomenon of anticipation and the striving for a better future and a sense of happiness and need-satisfaction. It includes the philosophical dimension of wisdom thinking and ideas that bring about change and future orientation.
7. **Spiritual Dimension** of hope deals with the transcendent dimension of life as connected to the quest for meaning in suffering (theodicy question) and the religious perspectives that link belief systems and God-images to a sense of courage and trust that can face human vulnerability, frailty, helplessness, despair, anxiety, and death.

Therefore, the article views hope as a systemic and networking phenomenon. Hope should promote human wholeness (spiritual humanism) (Louw, 2016, pp. 483–566). The main focus will be on the character of Christian hope and its connection to a theology of hope.

In order to clarify the complexity of a Christian interpretation of hope and a hermeneutics of sustainable hoping and a meaningful future-life orientation, the following paradigm shift is most needed:

> The paradigm shift: from inner strength and positive thinking (fortigenetics) (psychic dimension) to positive being and compassionate trusting (parrhesia: spiritual dimension).

There is a huge difference between hope and wishful thinking, between the anticipation of the future in terms of an eschatological understanding of life and the manipulation of the future in terms of optimistic speculation and aggressive planning as often projected by information technology and the social media (Castells, 2004, p. 181).

Christian hope is not the opposite of a pessimistic life view. Hope deals with the painful reality of suffering and should be understood as an ontological category. Christian hope points in the direction of a new state of mind and being (ontic dimension[428]), thus the proposed paradigm shift is from hope as a principle (philosophy of hope) and hope as an affective positive mode (psychology of hope) to hope as a new identity and mode of being—the Christian spirituality of hope. This shift is of paramount importance in terms of constructive approaches regarding processes of stigmatisation and discrimination within the current HIV & AIDS discourse (Van Dyk, 2005, pp. 92–94) and the quest for new prevention strategies in the present in order to deal with "future hope."

In the light of the above, this article poses the following critically important theological questions:

- What differentiates the Christian spiritual understanding of hope from wishful thinking, speculative optimism, and merely a psychology of hope?
- Why is the anticipation of the future in a theological understanding of hope, not futuristic imagination (*futurum*), but the certainty of ontological trust (*adventus*)?
- Is hope merely a philosophical principle derived from cosmic developments (Ernst Bloch, 1959) or an indication of a total new creation (*novum*), way and mode of being and existence?

The argument will be that a Christian spiritual understanding of hope implies more than a positive attitude. It differs from, for example, current developments in psychology with the emphasis on fortigenetics.[429]

Fortology represents a movement away from pathology and towards constructive enforcement and encouragement. Strümpfer, for example, points out the importance of *fortigenesis* in adult life (2006, pp. 11–36). Fortigenesis (*fortis* = strong) refers to a strength perspective, which relates human wellness to the positive components

---

[428] "Ontic" and "ontology" refer to "being" and one's existence in the world.

[429] The differentiation between the psychic dimension and the spiritual dimension does not mean that a psychology of hope and a theology of hope are two opposing, dualistic categories. In a hermeneutical approach they are in fact complementary and supplementary.

in human behaviour. This approach concentrates on those components in human wellness that create strength, courage, and a positive approach to life demands.

The background to a "science of strength" is to be found in the meaning dimension of life. Interpersonal flourishing and subjective well-being are closely related to one another. Research applications in the field of positive organisational behaviour are developing as part of the paradigm of fortology. Both *psychofortology* and *positive psychology* support the development of human strengths and their role in motivation and constructive performance.

In a spirituality of hope the emphasis is on *parrhesia*—Greek for "bold speech"—which is forwarded as the New Testament's equivalent of Paul Tillich's "courage to be," as the embodiment of a theology of the cross and a theology of the resurrection.[430]

The equivalent in Scripture for fortigenesis is the *parrhesia*, i.e., a courage that is not a human quality but a quality that emanates from God and Christ (1 Thess. 2:2[431]), which is a stance and ontic position in Christ due to the eschatological reality as founded by the cross and resurrection of Christ. *Parrhesia—boldness* is a pneumatic function and part of the fruit of the Spirit. Due to the indwelling presence of the spirit in our bodily existence (ensouled embodiment), inhabitation theology is about the charismatic reality of the fruits of the Spirit of God within the realm of our daily existence and life experiences. This inhabitational presence creates a "spiritual noetics" of understanding and interpreting life events (wisdom, *sapientia*). Pneumatology then becomes the concrete embodiment and exhibition of an *eschatologia crucis* (eschatology of the cross), i.e., the theological foundation of the Christian hope and ontic guarantee of certainty within the realm of eschatological hope.

This hope refers to the theological dimension of trust. It should be sustainable in order to deal with two existential realities, namely human vulnerability and the unpredictability of life events. Thus, the plea and argument is for a "theological sustainability" residing in the *passio Dei* (divine suffering as identification with human pain and

---

[430] See Strong's #3954 & 3955, where *parrhesia* is "to be frank in utterance, or confident in spirit." See Paul Tillich, *The Courage to Be*, 2nd ed. (New Haven: Yale University, 2000; 1st 1952).
[431] *Parrhesia* appears 31 times in the N.T., plus 8 more times in a bolder form as in 2 Thess. 2:2.

fear) and not in the *passio hominem* (human suffering within painful emotions).

A. Eschatological Dimension in a Theology of Hopeful Suffering: *Eschatologia Crucis* (Significance of the Cross from the Perspective of Hope & Future)

According to Moltmann (1995, p. 12; Louw 2016, pp. 318–338), a Christian eschatology should not be reduced to apocalyptic solutions regarding the end of creation. The primary theme and formula of an eschatology is not "the end" but "the essence" (the new beginning) of everything. It is about the new creation through which all beings received a new quality: the dawn of a radically new life (resurrection)—hence the reason for hope.[432] Christian hope is an ontic reality that opens up new avenues for—and new ways of—*being*. This ontic reality is closely connected to a theology of the cross and the interconnectedness between God and the Messianic suffering on the cross.

Moltmann's theology of the cross is based on the premise that, if the suffering on the cross is, in fact, a Messianic suffering, then God Himself is involved in the suffering. To Moltmann, this means that the Christian faith stands or falls by the confession of the crucified One—on the admission of God in the crucified Christ. Moltmann joins Luther in saying even more emphatically: God was crucified. Hence the notion of the crucified God.

By this premise, Moltmann breaks away from Aristotle's metaphysical theistic view of God as being immovable, apathetic, and unchanging (the immutability of God). A theology of the cross means a radical change in Western Christianity's concept of God. The God-concept inspired by the Greeks is one of apathy, with immutability as a static-ontic category. In contrast, a theology of the cross is a "pathetic theology" in which God's *pathos* is emphasized, not his *apatheia*.[433] It is in *pathos* that God reveals Himself in such a way

---

[432] Eschatology and hope are essentially about a new ontic stance. Hope is a new mode of being. Hence Moltmann's remark (1995, 12): "In the resurrection of Christ, the beginning of the whole of the cosmos is already comprised in *the end* (the victory over all forms of destruction and death)."

[433] Moltmann, 1972a, 256: Apathy is in fact a metaphysical category stemming from Platonic philosophy. "Seit Plato und Aristoteles wird die metaphysische und ethische Volkommenheit Gottes mit *apatheia* beschrieben."

that He becomes involved in loving solidarity with human suffering. An apathetic God moulds a human being into a *homo apatheticus*; a pathetic God moulds a human being into a *homo sympatheticus*. God is *with* us—Immanuel.

B. Trinity Reformulated within the Paradigmatic Framework of a Hermeneutics of Suffering (Divine Forsakenness)

Moltmann's attempt to design a theology of the cross should be assessed in terms of his basic intention: to reframe our traditional understanding of a Triune God as merely a metaphysical speculation. The Trinity should, therefore, be redefined in terms of the most essential component of, and element in, suffering: *derelictio* (rejection, forsakenness, and loneliness). In order to deal with the dialectics of both life and death, triumph and defeat, hope and despair, the Trinity should not be described and understood in isolation of the cross (death) from the resurrection (life). This basic theological assumption implies a radical change in existing God-images in the vocabulary of Christian thinking and systematic reflection.

With an attempt to establish an *eschatologia crucis*, the following theological indicators should be considered:

- An *eschatologia crucis* portrays God's faithfulness and steadfast love and grace in terms of the resurrection: the living God who raises the dead (the notion of the covenantal and living God) and conquered all forms of evil and destructive death.
- In terms of the cross, an *eschatologia crucis* portrays the suffering God in solidarity with human being's pain and misery (the notion of the compassionate God) in order to instil a sustainable hope that transcends the barriers of meaningless despair.

Moltmann's argument is that in Jesus' resurrection God is the *God in action*; in the crucifixion, He is the *God in passion*. The latter is not a static God, but a dynamic God, who is actively involved in the God-forsaken cry of Christ on the cross: "My God, my God, why have you forsaken me?" Jesus' cry from the cross (*dereliction*, forsakenness) outlines a Trinitarian theology of the cross. This cry defines God's "how?" in suffering.

Several critical Trinitarian questions arise:

- Does suffering only affect the Son?
- Are the Father and the Spirit involved in suffering as well?

- How far can a theology of the cross explain the "how?" of God's involvement in suffering?

The theological understanding of the link between God and suffering is important for both the theodicy question as well as for the question for the "certainty of our future hope." How "sustainable" is the Christian hope?

In his book *Menschwerdung Gottes*, Hans Küng (1970, pp. 660–631) pays particular attention to this question. He sees this as a challenge to dogmatic orthodoxy. The incarnation already challenges the concept of an apathetic God. Küng, therefore, bases his theory of the suffering God on the incarnation which involves a dynamic *Selbstentäusserung* (self-condescension, self-abandonment) of the Logos. The latter must not be interpreted as an *apotheosis* of the flesh, but as an *ensarkosis* of the Logos (enfleshment): God is not "static," but "pathetic" in the events surrounding the incarnation. Küng views God's suffering as a consequence of the fact that the God-Logos, as subject of the incarnation, is also intimately involved in the Son's suffering. We can thus speak of the death and suffering of the God-Logos.

Hans Küng emphasizes God's identification with suffering but insists that suffering does not define or constitute God. Küng views the cross as a demonstration of God's solidarity with a suffering humanity: his love expressed as co-suffering.[434]

In *Christ Sein*, Küng (1978, p. 529) asserts that God's suffering is not merely an affect (emotion), but an existential event; i.e., God is *there for others* who suffer (*Dasein für*; God being there for others, with them). The cross does not display (as in the case of Moltmann's theology of the cross) a dialectic between God and God, in which God is pitted against God in an inner-trinitarian event of suffering on the cross. To Küng, God *in Christ* experiences suffering *indirectly*, not directly. This implies not a frightening, theocratic God "from above," but a human-friendly co-suffering God, "with" us here "below."

Herebert Mühlen (1969, p. 16) is also reluctant to go too far in answering the question: "Did God Himself suffer?" However, he rejects the Platonic interpretation that God did not suffer. God's

---

[434] Küng, 1978, 530: Against an apathetic God "one can revolt, however over against a pathetic, compassionate God, one can surrender and start to trust."

mutability is a category of identity that presupposes the Trinity which should be interpreted in terms of personal categories. Hence the notion of a dynamic I-you relationship, the divine Being is actually a very dynamic entity which represents a relational event in which God's love gives something of Him-self away (*Weggabe*). This giving away describes a loving act, manifested in the cross as a way in which God places his very Being at stake for the purpose of salvation (*Dahingabe* = giving away towards; surrender and delivery). God's suffering is restricted to this "giving away towards" and is not completely identical to the suffering of the Son. Mühlen does not want to go beyond a *Dahingabe*. God Himself does not utter the God-forsaken call from the cross. In the debate between the Father and Son, God stands close by, but nothing more.

In *Theologie des Schmerzes Gottes*, the Japanese theologian Kazoh Kitamori takes up the notion of a suffering God, but describes His unique suffering as God's grief, which he views as a dialectic between wrath and love. God overcomes his wrath towards sin through his love for humankind. God's grief is wrath conquered by love. Through loving human beings (who are actually unlovable), God contradicts the fundamental justice which is part of his inner nature. This contradiction is the origin of his inner grief and self-abnegation. God's grief is a negative expression of his love that does the impossible. In the cross, wrath battles with love, all within the same God. The fact that the Father allows the Son to die expresses this grief.[435]

God hides Himself in the Person of the Son and goes through death without Himself being annihilated. God, Himself, does not die. He dies in the Person of the Son and remains in the events of the cross—"I am that I am," and thus, immutable. This is possible in the sense that God dies in the person of the Son but remains alive in the person of the Father (Kitamori, 1972, p. 113). Because God lives in the Person of the Father, the death of God's Son can be described as God's grief: i.e., God's love which conquers his wrath. Therefore, God's grief is not the result of sin that wounds Him to the heart. Sin elicits God's wrath. God's grief is unloosed when He looks upon us as

---

[435] Kitamori, 1972, 44: "The God of the gospels suffers painful grief in the mode of fatherly love; the act of letting his Son dying our place."

the object of his wrath, but nevertheless directs his love to us (1972, p. 114).

Moltmann's theology of the cross goes further than Küng's view of God's dynamic co-suffering and his indirect suffering. Moltmann also goes further than Mühlen's personal *Dahingabe* and Kitamori's grief of God. For Moltmann, God's suffering on the cross is not merely a revelation of God's compassion, involvement, or grief, but is an inter-Trinitarian event that becomes a constituent element in God's very Being.[436] Immanent Trinity (the inner relationship of the Triune God) and economic Trinity (the function of the Trinity in terms of our salvation) are replaced by a staurological Trinity within which immanence and economy alternate compatibly.[437] The economic Trinity does not merely reveal the immanent Trinity, but reflects back to the immanent Trinity and initiates suffering in God. The grief and suffering of the cross determines and even defines the inner Being of the Triune God from eternity to eternity (Moltmann 1980, p. 177). Via the cross, the immanent Trinity participates in the eschatology. The economic Trinity will complete itself in an immanent Trinity as displayed in the eventual kingdom of glory (God all in all). In the meantime, the economic Trinity defines the immanent Trinity as a dynamic entity of suffering: i.e., God's pathos.

Moltmann's Trinitarian theology of the cross is construed by Christ's cry: "My God, my God, why have you forsaken me?" Forsakenness (*derelictio*) becomes the primary issue for a hermeneutics of the cross (staurology) which tries to reframe the God-metaphors in terms of suffering. Moltmann makes use of the method of dialectic in order to develop his Trinitarian formula. God could only be understood properly as a suffering God if forsakenness is applicable to his very Being? Only the God who can be recognized in the face of the crucified One is the true God. This is a God who is truly there in the real abyss and anguish of history, in the God-forsakenness of the God-less. In Jesus' cry to God, "My God, my God," not only is Jesus under threat, but also God the Father. Because,

---

[436] On this point, Moltmann's theology of the cross should be assessed against the background of Hegel's dialectic philosophy.

[437] Moltmann, 1980, 176ff, explores this concept in his *Trinität und Reich Gottes*. The economic Trinity is the immanent Trinity and vice versa.

if God the Father forsakes Jesus, this forsakenness means that God hands over His Son, thereby forsaking Himself too—generating "my God, why have you forsaken Yourself?" (*'mein Gott, warum hast du Dich verlassen?'*).[438] The forsakenness of the cry when dying must be seen as happening between Jesus (the Son) and God (the Father); thus, it is an event taking place between God and God *within* God.[439]

Moltmann believes that we cannot say patripassionistic that the Father suffered and died. The Son's suffering differs from the Father's suffering. Jesus' death cannot simply be understood theopaschitic, as God's death (1972, p. 230). It can only be understood intertrinitarially as a patricompassionism. The death on the cross is a Trinitarian event between God and God: the suffering of the Father as the One who suffers forsakenness while forsaking his Son by giving Him over and away (*hingebendes Verlassen*), and the suffering of the Son as the One who suffers forsakenness, because of the very fact that He has been forsaken by the Father through this act of being given over and away (*verlassende Hingeben*).

The events of the cross exist within God's Divine Being. It occurs within God as a dialectic event between Father and Son.

Jesus suffers God-forsakenness; the Father suffers too as a result of this God-forsakenness. The Father's suffering is not unto death, but is a compassionate suffering arising from his love (patricompassionism). *Deus crucifixus* means that in the crucified Son, the Father humiliated Himself by means of a death cry—by God-forsakenness. The crucifixion is, thus, an event between God and God, not between a forsaken human being and a silent God. From a Trinitarian perspective, a theology of the cross thus means a dynamic, inter-Trinitarian event between a Father who gives over and away (*hingebende Vater*) and the forsaken Christ. The forsaken Son (*verlassenen Sohn*) is within the powerful act of being given away (*Hingabe*); i.e., the Holy Spirit who justifies the ungodly and fills the forsaken with love. The Holy Spirit is thus an ongoing, future-

---

[438] Moltmann, 1972, 144.

[439] Moltmann, 1972, 144: Forsakenness becomes a divine event within the very being of God despite the fact that the suffering of the Father differs from the suffering of the Son: "Die Verlassenheit am Kreuz, die den Sohn vom Vater trennt ist ein Geschehen in Gott selbst, ist stasis in Gott—'Gott gegen Gott.'"

revealing and liberating agent of the interaction between the Father and the Son.[440]

Moltmann's theology of the cross is a radical theology. God is not only at work in suffering and history: suffering and history are also in God and occur within Him. God not only reveals his compassion; in the suffering, God identifies with the suffering (God's pathos). At the same time, this identification is also a definition of the Being of God, Himself.[441] And exactly this divine mode of suffering constitutes the Christian hope to the ontic event of the new creation: our new being as a mode and condition of hope is the guarantee for the certainty of our future, not as *futurum* (speculation), but as *adventus* (founded expectation). Theologically speaking, the Christian hope is related to passionate humanity and compassionate divinity.

The value of Moltmann's theology of the cross resides in the fact that he indicates how God, through the suffering of the Son, timely identifies Himself with the suffering of humankind. In this, Moltmann shares the theopaschitic views of Barth, Küng, Mühlen, and Kitamori.

Without doubt, there is a link between God and suffering. God's suffering is indeed revealed in the grace and love (compassion) of the God who "loved the world so much that He gave His only Son" (John 3:16). Compassion and dynamic grace become a message of Godly pathos, especially when the father sees the prodigal son, is moved to compassion, runs towards him, embraces and kisses him (Luke 15:20). The father is described as a compassionate person, who *grieves* for his lost son in the depths of his inner being, thus disregarding Middle Eastern protocol when he runs to greet his returning son. Romans 8:32 is full of pathos: "He who did not spare his own Son but gave him up for us all." God's anger over sin is not merciless punishment, but wounded love. He punishes sin because, in terms of his compassion, He hates sin.

---

[440] See Moltmann, 1980, 140, for a discussion of the question whether the Holy Spirit can be seen as a power or as a person. It depends on the working of the Spirit as to "whether the Holy Spirit is seen dynamically, as a Person. For Moltmann, the Holy Spirit is the subject in so far as He is the acts of the Father and the Son are concerned. The Holy Spirit is a subject as far as He is the *verherrlichende Gott* (the God who glorifies) and the *vereinigende Gott* (the God who unifies). The Holy Spirit, as subject, is, thus, concerned with the glorification and unification of the Father and the Son."

[441] Moltmann, 1972, 179: "God is therefore identified and defined by the suffering of God the Son."

However, it becomes a burning theological question whether such a theological construction of the cross really represents the salvific meaning of God's intervention, identification, and involvement. Indeed, one must admit that in some or other way God suffered on the cross—a mystical element—hence the notion of the suffering God.

On the other hand, to establish a theology of the cross in terms of a Hegelian dialectic (God against God; death as a constitutive component within God's inner Trinitarian Being) could become very speculative. Note the following Hegelian construction:

> **Thesis:** The Father forsakes the Son (thesis);
> **Antithesis:** The Son has been forsaken and experiences forsakenness;
> **Synthesis:** The ongoing work of the Spirit facilitates the message of God's identification with the forsakenness of suffering humankind is constantly being proclaimed.

The above philosophical construction is in danger of becoming an artificial and rational construction *without* reckoning enough with the mystical-spiritual dimension of the cross—the inter-Trinitarian dialogue. Nevertheless, Moltmann's systematic and philosophical construction helps us to link hope in suffering to the divine component of compassion.

According to Kreck, the distinction between Father and Son is overshadowed in Moltmann's theology of the cross by an inter-Trinitarian unity. This distinction is threatened by a monophysitic tendency: suffering functions as a unifying unit which dominates our understanding of God to such an extent that the richness of the different ways in which the Triune God operates becomes dominated by one main theme—God's passion.[442]

Patricompassionism has the following direct consequence: the negative, the death, the suffering, and the rejection are becoming constituent components and ingredients of God. Miskotte regards the statement "the suffering and death are in God" as grave indeed, and thus become constitutive elements of the inner Being of God.[443] God's solidarity with suffering and his identification with suffering

---

[442] Kreck, 1977, 290: The notion of God on the cross does not necessarily imply the cross within the very being of God himself. There should be a distinction between subject and predicate.

[443] Miskotte, 1973, 42: This construction of Moltmann sounds more like pan-entheism than pantheism.

could lead to the conclusion that access to Him is no longer via guilt, conversion, and faith; but, rather, access to Him has already been achieved through suffering.

On the other hand, one cannot avoid the difficult question: How does suffering affect the Being of God? In one way or another, the theme of a "suffering God" has consequences for our understanding of God and the unique character of an ontology of hope as an expression of a theology of hope. Indeed, suffering touches the very heart of God-images.

Fretheim (1984, p. 106) acknowledges the importance of an understanding of God in terms of vulnerability. Hence, the notion of a divine lament in the Old Testament. The human cry becomes God's cry. God takes up the human cry and makes it his own.

Fretheim (1984, p. 108) arranges the variety of texts and the language associated with the divine suffering according to a threefold schema in conjunction with the reasons for God's suffering.

- God suffers because of the people's rejection of Him as Lord.
- God suffers with the suffering people.
- God suffers for people.

According to Fretheim (1984, p. 123), God is revealed in the Old Testament, not as one who remains coolly unaffected by people's rejection, but as One who is deeply wounded by a broken relationship—rejection by Israel. Our understanding of God always remains metaphorical. Therefore, the theme, "a suffering God," must not lead to a speculation or the construction of a philosophical ontology about God. Suffering is, rather, a metaphor to say in symbolic language that Israel's world and experience have been internalized by God. He has absorbed his people's rejection and affliction. However, one must still reckon with the fact that God's grief does not entail being emotionally overwhelmed or embittered by Israel's barrage of rejection. "Through it all, God's faithfulness and gracious purposes remain constant and undiminished" (Fretheim 1984, p. 111). God's salvific will does not waver; His steadfast love endures forever (1984, p. 124).

The "suffering God" indicates that He does not look at suffering extraneously, but from within: God is internally related to the suffering of his people. Jeremiah 31:20 and Isaiah 63:15 are excellent examples of the expression of divine compassion.[444] Indeed, suffering puts the very Being of God at stake. Therefore, Fretheim (1984: 148) asks the following question: What did suffering mean to God? In some way it meant the expending of God's life, expressed primarily in the image of weariness. Even in Old Testament sacrifices it may be said that God gave of Himself to make forgiveness possible. God's life was expended for the sake of sinners' lives. One can even speak of divine humiliation: God immersed Himself in the depths of Israel's troubles in order to make deliverance possible. In a sense, God subjects Himself to a humiliating situation for the purpose of salvation. He does precisely this to prove his faithfulness. Therefore, faithfulness and compassion become two key concepts for an understanding of the metaphorical meaning of the notion of "the suffering God."

In a theological debate regarding the function of a theology of the cross (*theologia crucis*), two dynamic perspectives should always be considered and held together: (1) the salvific meaning of God's identification with our suffering, as well as (2) the demonstrative and convincing effect of his identification, namely, to prove his faithfulness. "God in our suffering" becomes a pastoral metaphor for consolation, certainty, and hope.

The message of God's faithfulness is inextricably linked to the transformative reality of the cross and to the victorious event of the resurrection. Being "saved in hope" makes us more than conquerors. Particularly during times of suffering the church calls out loudly: *maranatha*. In calling for the coming of the Son of God (future as *adventus*), the sufferer asks "When?" This victory that refers to the salvific reality is confessed by faith as an eschatological reality. It expresses the yearning for God's kingdom to break through in all its fullness.

When will this victory finally breakthrough in its complete form? A meaningful reply to this question points towards those events which provide final proof of God's power over death: the resurrection of

---

[444] Jeremiah 31:20, "Is not Ephraim my dear son, the child in whom I delight? Though I often speak against him, I still remember him. Therefore, my heart yearns for him."

Isaiah 63:15, "Look down from heaven and see, from your lofty throne, holy and glorious. Where are your zeal and your might? Your tenderness and compassion are withheld from us."

Jesus Christ. The resurrection, which eliminates the sting of death, points back to the *perfectum* of the cross and forward to the *promissio* of the *parousia*. *Perfektum* and *promissio* are two elements of the eschatological reality. These are the new acts of God's salvation which introduces the "end times" as a qualitatively new creation and point forward to the *eschaton* as an act of God's final and decisive kingdom rule. In its doxological form, the *eschaton* refers to the *shalom* and wholeness of humankind and creation: The God-all-in-all perspective of 1 Corinthians 15 (pan-entheism). The history of salvation is concerned with unlocking the perspective of the *eschaton*. It concerns itself in the act of salvation with eschatological events, with God's new deeds at the turn of time, in the last days, in the revelation of the great mystery.

On the cross Christ fulfilled God's promises. As our substitute, He cancelled the guilt of sin and broke the curse by which God condemned humankind to death and transience. A new covenant is made possible by the blood of the Mediator. This victory becomes a high priestly reality. The fact that this high priestly act of the Mediator is indeed a victory, and that the Word of the Cross is the Gospel, the victory finds its final expression in the resurrection as an act of God and an action of Christ. The resurrection triumphs over the despair of death and replaces it with a victorious faith.[445] The victory of the resurrection becomes a kingly reality within this history, with consequences for the whole of creation and the healing of humankind.

C. Towards a Theology of the Resurrection (*Theologia Resurrectionis*): Divine Dimension of Salvific Hope and Illustration of the Faithfulness of a Living God

As symbol, the cross is often a more powerful symbol in Christian liturgy than the open grave. In many Christian denominations the emphasis is more on human sinfulness, confession of sins and absolution, than on hopeful empowerment and enhancement of human dignity.

Hendrikus Berkhof (1973, p. 332) attributes the diminished role of spiritual empowerment as accredited to the resurrection in many

---

[445] Berkhof, 1973, 324: The resurrection of Christ is the most fundamental, convincing, and final event in the history of salvation: "Daarom. mag de opstanding van Jezus het beslissende heilsgebeuren heten."

confessions, to the fact that Western sobriety ensured that the resurrection, as a central tenet of salvation, nevertheless always stood in the shadow of the cross. Resurrection becomes a kind of aftermath. It does not feature as a central legitimation of the divine dimension of salvation, namely that Christ did not die as a martyr but as a mediator. This diminution of the resurrection also is concomitant with the way in which Western theology concentrated on the works of Christ, in contrast to the Eastern Church's focus on the person of Christ.

Lekkerkerker (1966, p. 134) believes that the Eastern Church saw Christ's suffering and death more in terms of a victory over the powers of evil and could, thus, sense the triumph of the resurrection. In its doctrine of atonement, the Western church concentrated more upon the juridical and forensic dimensions of the cross as liberation for the sinner. Another factor which could have contributed towards an under emphasis on the resurrection is the so-called process of secularization and technological development. Within a very rationalistic and positivistic model it seems that there is little scope for a gospel of resurrection.

De Jong (1967, p. 71) refers to the role of the historical-critical model, the intellectual emphasis of which left little scope for the miracle of the resurrection. The *Formgeschichte* also relativized the gospel of resurrection. Although the new approach followed by the German theologians Käsemann, Fuchs, Bornkamp, and Ebeling made it conceivable that more historical facts were concealed in the interpretation of the message of resurrection than had hitherto been admitted, for many the resurrection still remains more a truth about the cross and a legitimization of the proclamation of the Gospel, rather than a fact that is linked to the open grave.

From a traditional and doctrinal perspective, it would appear as if the doctrines of soteriology and the incarnation headed the theological agendas of the different councils. After the Arian controversy and the emphasis placed on the Divinity of Christ by the Council of Nicaea, the resurrection tended no longer to be in the forefront of theological discussion. The resurrection frequently had to serve as a final proof of the Divinity of Christ. Ultimately, the resurrection became a necessary consequence of the cross, within the successive phases of humiliation and exaltation. According to Gesche (1973, pp. 275–324), the resurrection played the role of an additional legitimizing factor. The resurrection served as proof either of the mission of Christ, of the truth of the Scriptures, of the Divinity of Christ, or of the effectiveness of Jesus' work of salvation.

Goppelt (1980, p. 56), in his theology for the New Testament, argued that the message of the resurrection forms the heart and core of New Testament theology. From the perspective of the resurrection, the existing situation of the early church could be analysed in view of its transformation and its focus on the future. The resurrection message forms the basis of New Testament theology. In view of the central role of hope in theology, Guthrie (1981, p. 389) asserts, "The reality of the resurrection is, therefore, an indispensable basis for Christian hope in the future." According to him, the resurrection is not only important for the theme of hope, but it also has a Christological significance. It focuses particularly on Christ's person and work.[446] For Guthrie, faith in the resurrection provides the necessary continuity for the notion that Jesus is truly God and truly human. As an act of God, the resurrection also has implications for traditional God-images. The message of the resurrection is also decisive for the preaching of the Gospel.[447]

A number of other authors are also conscious of the important role which the resurrection plays in theology. Jonker (1983) believes that the resurrection plays an important role in the panorama of God's salvific deeds. In the gospel of salvation, the message of the risen Christ stands alongside the outpouring of the Holy Spirit. Redemption is an eschatological reality and has a victorious perspective.[448]

Berkouwer (1961, p. 246) regards Paul's ministry as a symbol of a resurrection hope. He considers the resurrection as fundamental for the eschatological perspective of the Gospel.[449] A distinction needs to be made between the resurrection as a salvific reality and the resurrection as a future reality where the mortal will be clothed with

---

[446] Guthrie, 1981, 390: "The major significance of the resurrection is the contribution it makes to our understanding of the person and work of Christ."

[447] Guthrie, 1981, 460: "It makes greater sense to regard the resurrection narratives as providing the link between the historical events of the passion and the apostolic proclamation of the meaning of Christ's death, than to suppose that the interpretation was entirely the church's own construction."

[448] Jonker, 1983, 139: "En deze overwinning maakt nu juist de kern uit van het opstandingsgeloof der eerste Christenen." Victory is the core message of the resurrection.

[449] Berkouwer, 1961, 231: Without the perspective of the resurrection, the whole of life is expsoed to the overwhelming powers of destruction and death. Resurrection constitutes a certainty that guarantees a hopeful future.

immortality. The latter forms part of the former, so that both become determining factors in the dynamic of Christian hope.

The resurrection plays a major role in Karl Barth's work (1953, p. 329ff). He views the resurrection as an act of God. While the cross is the judgement of grace, the resurrection is the grace of the judgement. Any human achievement falls away in the resurrection. Barth regards the resurrection as being so important that he describes the act of resurrection as an act of salvation from which everything else needs to be understood; it is an unique, absolute revelation (*überhaupt*) (1953, p. 332). Barth stresses the resurrection in such a way that God the Father becomes the complete subject of the resurrection. It is exclusively a work of God, without any co-operation from the Son. The resurrection is thus not a consequence of Jesus' death on the cross, but as a sovereign act of God the resurrection indicates God's gracious compassion and trustworthiness (Barth 1953, p. 335).

Barth states that the *theologia resurrectionis* is an independent, new work of God, which confirms the validity of Christ's suffering. The cross and the resurrection is one historical act in which God proclaims and finally confirms his "Yes" of reconciliation to the sinful world. The cross and resurrection form such an indivisible unity within the history of salvation that only one form of theological reasoning can be derived from the uniqueness of the cross and the historicity of the resurrection: forward from the resurrection, not backwards from the *parousia*. The time in which the community lives is always determined qualitatively from the resurrection as *parousia* that is focused on Jesus, the eschaton: the One who has already come and the One who is coming.

Resurrection and suffering are two themes that cannot exist separately. In *A Theology of Auschwitz*, Simon (1967) does not regard the resurrection as an easy way out of suffering and pain, but that the resurrection incorporates them into a new perspective on life. Resurrection faith does not retreat from the reality of suffering but confirms the tragedy of suffering, and at the same time summons human beings to a mode of resilience and constructive engagement.[450] Resurrection moulds being into the paradox of acceptance and resistance.

---

[450] Simon, 1967, 101: "Resurrection is not the easy way out, but the validation of the tragic itself."

In Jürgen Moltmann's theology of hope (1966), the resurrection plays a crucial role in revealing the meaning and gospel of the cross. Within Moltmann's *eschatologia crucis*, the cross is not limited to Christ's reconciliatory work, but becomes a symbol for the *eschaton* of Christ: the resurrection from the perspective of salvific anticipation and victory. The resurrection opens up a future perspective in such a way that the resurrection obtains an eschatological primacy over the cross. Eschatology, derived from the resurrection, reveals the hope principle embedded in the cross. Hope is actually resurrection hope (Moltmann).

To an extent following Moltmann's view, Schütz (1963, p. 351) considers the resurrection to be the most original ontic event in life (*Urereignis*) which forms the basis and norm of all discussion about the future. Heinrich Ott (1958, p. 18) believes the Easter events ensure that the message of Jesus' resurrection became the foundation and source of Christian eschatology and hope.

D. Zig Zag Pattern of Hope within the Paradox of Frailty/Weakness/Sinfulness and Quest for Meaningful Living: Wherefore God?

The cosmic fact of life is that life is frail and human beings are constantly being exposed to the reality of frailty, vulnerability, and the unpredictability of life events without any direct causative factor or explanation. Wisdom in Hebrew thinking has to deal constantly with the factuality of weakness, powerlessness, and helplessness. Meaninglessness is a kind of existential phenomenon. To probe for a rational explanation is essentially fatal. Not even God or the fact of human failure and sinfulness could be introduced as a reasonable explanation for loss, destruction, dying, and death.

The Old Testament perspective on suffering makes a positivistic causal explanation of suffering unacceptable. To use the notion of the fall as a reasonable explanation for human frailty and weakness is to introduce a mechanistic paradigm of cause-and-effect that delivers life to fate and an extreme fatalism and pessimistic worldview. The Old Testament's life view is neither pessimistic nor optimistic. It is about sheer realism within the kaleidoscope of often paradoxical life experiences, wavering between courage and despair.

Sinfulness, disobedience, punishment, wrath, grace, forgiveness, and reconciliation weave a networking dynamic of interactional happenstances and responses that should be interpreted as the realism of life: as existential events subjected to pain, illness, fraud, disappointment, anxiety, and despair. In fact, the narratives in the Bible oscillate between these existential experiences as hermeneutical accounts on human failure; humans attempt to bounce back; stories about the engagement of God within graceful, divine interventions instil hope, courage, faith, and trust.

The challenge is: not to explain life in terms of a causative positivism (rational and reasonable answers and explanations) but to inspire and empower faithful people to face life in terms of the "courage to be." The challenge is to summon believers to respond with boldness—*parrhesia*—with hope and meaningful anticipation of renewal, healing, wholeness, and to display God's grace and compassion within the parameters of obedience and lawful direction.

According to the Old Testament, God punishes sin. Suffering, therefore, as part of the broken reality is associated with admonishment and punishment. Suffering as such is not evil and sinful. However, suffering reveals, inter alia, the factuality of disobedience, unbelieve, failure, the making of wrong choices, and the destructive impact of evil on the meaning and destiny of life. This does not mean that one has to investigate every incident of personal suffering in search of a specific sin as an explanation of that particular situation of suffering. One has not to try to decipher behind life events the so called "punishment and wrath of God." It only means that suffering makes one sensitive to self-examination and the possibility of guilt. Should sufferers become aware of a personal sin, or some other irresponsible transgression which has a bearing on their suffering, then it is their task to repent and to confess their sin.

Coping with suffering, especially in the Old Testament, is often linked to the process of confession of sins and repentance. However, the intention was not to explain suffering and to reveal a rational explication. Suffering's function was to reveal suffering as a relational issue within a covenantal as well as therapeutic paradigm: to bring about change and to foster spiritual growth.

In the Old Testament, suffering is discussed with ambivalence. On the one hand, God is involved in suffering; on the other, the person is held responsible for their own suffering. Human guilt and divine wrath cannot be separated (Ps. 78:21–22, 106:40; 2 Kings 17:18–20; 1 Sam 12:9; Jdg. 2:14). This link between guilt and wrath must be seen against the background of the Old Testament image of God and the cultural world view. For the Israelites, their world was an integrated whole, in which they felt secure. They were supported by their faith in a personal God. The framework of the covenant created a sense of security. Linked to the covenant were God's blessings (life-force/vitality, communal life, productivity, material prosperity), as well as the curse (isolation from the covenantal community, equivalent to death and humiliation). The covenant's character of promise-in-fulfilment created a frame of reference in which suffering could be interpreted. The believer could always count on God's faithfulness. In this way, evil and disaster could be linked to God in terms of his divine grace and loving care.[451]

Isaiah prefaced his declaration that the Lord created disaster with an objective fact: God's salvific acts of faithfulness and covenantal grace. On this fact, Israel's faith either stood or fell. God identified Himself as "I am the Lord, and there is no other; apart from me there is no God." The God "behind" disaster is always Yahweh in his grace and compassion. Disaster exists within the context of divine salvation, punishment within divine grace, and wrath within divine love.

The relationship between wrath and love does not lead to a diminution of wrath as a result of love. Both wrath and love are two interconnected aspects of God's revelation: they are modes of the encounter between God and humankind. Both exist within the unity of the Person of God, in an inseparable relationship with one another. The motive underlying his wrath always remains God's mercy towards the preservation of the sinner. God's heart is involved in the suffering in which He is at work, which reveals his compassion.[452] Suffering in the Old Testament thus needs to be interpreted against the background of the unique covenantal relationship between Yahweh and Israel. Breaking the covenant implied isolation and

---

[451] See Jer. 18:8, "And if that nation I warned repents of its evil, then I will relent and not inflict on it the disaster I had planned." Jer. 18:11, "Now therefore say to the people of Judah and those living in Jerusalem, 'This is what the Lord says: Look! I am preparing a disaster for you and devising a plan against you. So turn from your evil ways, each one of you, and reform your ways and your actions.'" Isa. 45:7, "I form the light and create darkness, I bring prosperity and create disaster; I, the Lord, do all these things."

[452] Ridderbos, 1966, 390: It "refers to the fact that dealing with difficult threats in life, does not imply to introduce a kind of abstract principle of predestination as explanatory cause for what befalls one. More fundamental is the connection faith and grace."

estrangement which can result in suffering and eventually place the covenant people under a curse.[453]

What makes the interpretation of meaning in suffering so difficult is that, throughout the Bible, reference is made to the principle of evil. Concomitant to the involvement of God in suffering, there is also the power of evil (Job 1:6–12).[454] God's involvement in suffering is clearly not evil. God's involvement implies wrath and punishment in order to bring about the sinner's salvation and preservation; its purpose is life to the glory of God; salvation as the transformation and conversion of the sinner; care, healing, transformation in opposition to the powers of annihilation and chaos. The involvement of evil implies a disturbance of the covenantal relationship resulting in disintegration, annihilation, unbelief, and spiritual death.

According to the Bible, finding meaning cannot be sought along the lines of determinism or indeterminism, but rather within the paradoxical zig zag realism of a covenantal relationship of grace and obedience within the awareness of human frailty and failure, even despite the threat of death. Within the dynamics of this relationship, the providence question no longer becomes an abstract dogma and doctrine, but a faith issue, which takes seriously God's righteousness as its point of departure. His omnipotence thus becomes a pastoral category instead of a fatalistic and deterministic category of violent force.

Scripture does not offer a logical explanation to suffering. A logical answer, in any event, offers very little consolation. It provides only a temporary quieting of our rational thinking. God does not give solutions to our logical "Why?" But in the midst of our questions, He inserts the *"therefore"* of the cross and the exclamation mark of the resurrection. God does not provide a solution, but redemption—His Son, Jesus Christ. Through this action, God reveals His trustworthiness. A search for the interpretation of meaning in suffering should start with the presupposition of God's faithfulness, otherwise it is doomed to despair and anxiety right from the start.

---

[453] Thus, Gerstenberger wrote in *Leiden*: "disobedience to God's will leads inevitable to different kinds of suffering" (Gerstenberger & Schrage, 1977, p. 60).

[454] In Gerstenberger & Schrage, 1977, 64–65, Gerstenberge points out that human beings are often their own cause for painful suffering.

God's presence in suffering, by virtue of his mediatory and vicarious suffering, raises a new question. The most important question in suffering is not, in the first instance, "Why?" Because of God's compassion and faithfulness, the believer should rather learn to ask the question, "Wherefore God? For what purpose?" For the believer, the question mark behind "For what purpose?" is actually an exclamation mark which challenges the believer to face suffering, rather than to avoid or become resigned to suffering. The exclamation mark sets an invitation before the believer to seek an opportunity to praise God in suffering and, in the manner in which they suffer, to demonstrate something of the trustworthiness of God's presence with the sufferer and His pathos in suffering. In this way the believer no longer views God's will as an explanatory principle, but as an accompanying and empowering principle. Suffering, as such, is not seen as God's will. His will is rather manifested in that which can happen during suffering in the sufferer's heart, aptitude, and attitude.

The core of the question of finding meaning in suffering is not in what happens *to* us, but what can happen *in* and *through* us. Pastoral care needs to help supplicants to discover how to suffer; it attempts to build a new disposition towards suffering as well as a new perspective on suffering. Suffering becomes a task and a calling through which one embodies God's presence and comfort—his identification with our suffering in Christ and through his Spirit. What interests God is our reaction to that which befalls us (Aggebo 1959, p. 265). The challenge and opportunity of suffering lies in answering the question: "To what purpose is God using suffering in the life of the believer?" The sufferer has to make the following choice in faith between fate and God:

- **Either Fate Rules**—then there is only a last zero point in creation to which no person can pray and appeal. You can only shout, scream, and curse. In fate, a person cannot say "Thou" to fate.
- **Or God Rules**—the other possibility is that God is there; his compassion and grace are in control (Köberle, 1970, p. 25).

With God, suffering can be processed in the form of a complaint or a lament; yes, even as an accusation. A complaint indicates that the complainant expects something from the person against whom the complaint is lodged. In suffering a complaint is expressed in the mode of hope. Knowing the "suffering God" yields real hope!

E. Spiritual Framework of Meaning: Realm of the Fulfilled Promises of God as Indication of Divine Faithfulness (Promisiology & Promisio-therapy)

The question regarding meaning in suffering is about the purpose and direction of one's life. Meaning, as the totality of answers to all questions, does not exist as such. Meaning is about the purpose of human life and its movement within a particular direction, within a specific relation.[455] Theologically speaking, discovery of true meaning can take place only within a living relationship with God and in a loving relationship with fellow-human beings. For this to take place, the believer needs the security that is outlined in God's covenantal promises and the eschatological reality of salvation that is evidenced in the cross and the resurrection. Then the believer will come to know that God, Himself, is not as such the meaning of life. God is more than the totality of meaning. Meaning, rather, is the discovery of a God whom one can trust and who can bring meaning to life due to actual involvement and engagement with those existential realities which threaten humans in the very core of their being.

The fact that God's faithfulness to his covenant promises provides the direction for the "For what purpose?" question, means that the processing of meaning is focused on a God who identifies with our suffering and understands our most basic existential needs: our anxiety for death; our helplessness and hopelessness due to doubt and despair; and our guilt and need for liberation. The purposefulness of the Christian faith within the eschatological horizon of meaning outlines the telic dimension of Scripture. "Telic" is derived from the Greek *teleion*, which implies purposefulness, and is used in Scripture in connection with direction and maturity of faith. Telic implies that a mature faith is directed by values and norms that bring a sense of purpose to existence and which unlock a future which is not dependent solely on human achievement but on God's faithfulness. Such believers are able to integrate suffering as a task and calling through which they can grow towards maturity. "Maturity" implies an overcoming of inflexibility, rigidity, and resignation which enables the internalization of suffering. Furthermore, maturity entails the

---

[455] Gollwitzer, 1974, 20 and 28: Meaningful living is embedded within the dynamic of relational interaction and the service of sacrificial love.

dynamics of anticipation, prospective action, and openness towards the future.

The dynamics of a mature faith imply more than a dialectical approach towards suffering. The danger of such a model is that suffering, in one way or another, becomes a necessary presupposition for the discovery of meaning. Suffering can even be seen as a necessary prerequisite for access to God. It can also happen that suffering becomes a prerequisite for the revelation of grace and the discovery of God's love. Ultimately, suffering becomes a constitutive factor for God's presence and, in the light of a dynamic God-image, is seen as an antithetical factor in God's very Being. Dialectics, as the process of negation of the negative, remains linked, almost like a Siamese twin, to anxiety and death. Despite the value of dialectics in theology, hope is more than a dialectic entity which exists as the antipole of doubt and despair. Hope is a category *sui generis*; it exists due to God's fulfilled promises, despite nothingness and death.

In order to discover meaning in suffering, the theology of pastoral care needs to make use of a dialogical model. God then is seen as an acting God who, in terms of his faithfulness, is always present. As a result of his act of salvation, the believer learns to recognize God's mode in suffering: forgiveness, compassion, and loving kindness. His presence calls us humans, through his Word, to respond within the dynamics of a God-human encounter and continual process of dialogue and communication. Dialogue and encounter within covenantal communication demand faith and obedience on the part of human beings.

There is room within this dialogical mode for the doxological paradox of the "already not yet," despite ambiguity and ambivalence. Precisely this paradox creates space for a process of discovering meaning which expresses itself in the praise and worship of the Lord. A dialogical model is, essentially, a promissiological model within a teleologically directed eschatology. Within the promissiological structure of the dialogical covenant model, the challenge of suffering becomes a meaningful opportunity with therapeutic value for a person in crisis. Therefore, one can conclude that meaning and significance is not "something" or an "achievement." It is rather a relationship and a process within the parameters of faithfulness and hope.

Viktor Frankl was convinced that suffering could be meaningful. He believed that values play a decisive role in the process of dealing with suffering and the discovery of meaning. People possess the ability to adjust themselves to suffering and to take responsibility for their suffering.[456] This is why Frankl's logotherapy makes use of the technique of value identification and goal formulation.

In his logotherapy, Frankl (1969; 1977) distinguishes between an anthropology which views a human being as *homo faber*, committed to the success ethic and threatened by the factor of failure, and an anthropology which views a human being as *homo patiens*. While *homo faber* operates within an achievement ethic, *homo patiens* is prepared to bear testimony in suffering to those values that give life a particular direction. A sufferer should not ask, "What, to me, is the meaning of suffering?" but rather, "What meaning can I give to suffering?" Suffering becomes an invitation to create meaning.

According to Frankl, the highest form of finding meaning can take place in suffering because love is an aspect of human existence. Love, as commitment, means that one can create distance between realizing one's own values in order to respond in a responsible manner to other and higher values. The capacity to distance oneself from one's innate values is already a form of suffering, which can extend one's disposition far beyond one's own selfish ideals. With a devoted and committed will to find meaning, the person discovers in suffering the answer to the challenging question: Why?

Frankl's logotherapy places the emphasis on finding meaning in suffering through love in the light of internalized values. The Gospel's promissio-therapy—the compassionate healing and empowering effect of God's fulfilled promises—goes even further. Our task in suffering is not only to impart meaning. To impart meaning presupposes receiving meaning. In order to discover meaning, a person must have an empowering source from which one receives meaning. If meaning is not received from some other source, then dispensing meaning becomes a wearying task which is dependent solely on one's own potential. Ultimately, one is easily exposed to the possible threat of futility.

The phenomenon of suffering, as such, is meaningless and can become a painful experience; therefore, one should not speak of the

---

[456] See Böschemeyer, 1977, 105ff, for a discussion of this aspect of Frankl's thought.

"meaning *of* suffering." In the process of attempting to discover meaning, suffering can only become meaningful in the sense of imparting meaning. Hence, it is better to speak of discovering "meaning *in* suffering." The solution to the questions "Why?" and "For what purpose?" is, therefore, not a clear-cut answer, but a process and task which challenges one's basic attitude, value system, belief, and philosophy in life. Suffering becomes meaningful within the process of acceptance and taking responsibility. In the light of Christ's vicarious suffering and his high-priestly compassion (God's pathos), a person can discover and impart meaning in suffering. Meaning does not follow automatically. Wishful thinking is pointless in suffering. People can reject the offer of meaning through an attitude of doubt and scepticism, or they can accept the challenge by making a purposeful decision.[457]

On the one hand, the fellowship with Christ brings the death of the sinner in the cross of Christ (*mortificatio*), and on the other, life emanates from fellowship with the risen Christ (*vivificatio*). This participation-in-Christ initiates a process of anticipation that places the believer's existence within the eschatological tension between the already and the not yet. This is the tension of resurrection life lived within the limitations of the eschatological condition. In Victor Frankl's terms, we can speak of the "noödynamics" of hope, whereby the believer remains teleologically orientated towards the future (the *parousia* of Christ) and the dawning of God's doxological kingdom.

Hope prevents rigidity, and brings a teleological orientation which, in turn, can initiate a new process of transcendence and anticipation in a person's faith. The goal or intention of pastoral care to those who are suffering is to encourage hope in a future which, in principle, is already realized—and accessible to faith but which also refers to a process of ultimate completion and fulfilment. The God of the paraclete is the God of hope through the Holy Spirit. As Paul said in Romans 15:5, "May the God who gives endurance and encouragement give you a spirit of unity among yourselves as you

---

[457] Küng, 1978, 527: The challenge for human beings is to respond and to make fundamental decisions regarding meaning, "Wohl aber ein freibleibendes Sinn-Angebot: Der Mensch hat zu entscheiden."

follow Jesus Christ." So, in suffering our hope "becomes even stronger through the power of the Holy Spirit" (Rom. 15:13).

In conclusion, we can say that an *eschatologis crucis* constitutes a founded and enduring hope that safeguards a future. It operates from the perspective of the resurrection and anticipates a promised future.[458] Hope as *promissio*-instigated action into the future. Hope creates endurance and longsuffering; it challenges one to live fully, even in the midst of terminal illness.

The root of the Hebrew word for hope has the connotation of an interrelated web of meaningful connections.[459] It is the vibrating string of God's grace, stretched taut by the resonance of his promises that undergirds the believer during suffering. The bowstrings are taught, and the arrow is directed towards a goal! It is this vivid hope that orientates one towards the web of a meaningful future.

While hope undergirds life, the following question surfaces: How is this resurrection life expressed in people's relationships and in their concrete situations of their daily experience in the present? The certainty of Christian hope emanates in thanksgiving; it reflects and presents the festivity of grace. The embodiment of hope in human existence is the existential condition of a joyful life in celebration and gratitude.

According to Barth, the Holy Spirit is the Spirit of Christ, which edifies and builds up the community. Barth calls the power of the Holy Spirit the Life principle of the Christian church (1953, p. 167). In reality, the joyous life of Christian hope is thus an ecclesial matter which determines the character of the community of believers. Therefore, everything that the community does ought to be done liturgically with joy and festivity.[460]

In a culture which is committed to avoiding suffering, Paul's word in Colossians 1:24 sounds strange: "Now I rejoice in what was

---

[458] Thurneysen, 1964, 13, confirms that true pastoral caregiving is in essence hope care and determined by Christian eschatology: "Alle echte Seelsorge ist als solche Seelsorge der Hoffnung, sie hat eschatologischen Charakter oder sie ist keine Seelsorge."

[459] Haller, 1969, 9: Hope is like the sail of a boat, giving direction and speed despite a stormy sea: "Das hebraïsche Wort '*kiwwah*' stammt dies einer Wurzel 'kw,' die den gespannten Faden im Spinnetz bezeichnet oder das gespannte Seil, den "Stang" an dem man sich helfen kann oder der etwas festhält."

[460] Barth, 1953, 167: The whole communal existence, its liturgies and sacraments, displays the festivity of celebration and glorification.

suffered for you." The idea that suffering should not be avoided and resisted, but can also be accepted, certainly does sound strange to contemporary humans who, driven by their obsession with success, are determined to eliminate all forms of suffering. In a culture that detests wrinkles and blemishes, suffering is a hampering factor. Our contemporary society demands that all opposition, conflict, and tension disappear and be replaced by relaxation, ease, and progress.

Van Ruler is convinced that joy is an essential part of the biblical message.[461] In *"Ik geloof"* ("I believe"), Van Ruler asserts that joy about God's grace and salvation is the highest form of expression of Christian existence. Christian faith is geared towards the enjoyment of God.

The biblical concept for "feast" is directly related to God's salvific acts in the history of his covenant people. When Israel commemorated God's salvific acts in its festivals, such as the pascha and mazzot feast, it was doing more than merely performing a drama for the Israelites. It was not only God's acts of salvation which summoned Israel to commemorate—the feast was not just a commemorative feast—but through the celebrations, the believers actually share in the reality of God's salvific acts. The festival allowed the Israelites to share in Yahweh's living and creative salvific works; it helped them to return to their everyday life with the knowledge: God has overcome the surrounding destructive powers. In the *pascha*, the Israelites obtained a portion of Yahweh's victorious and liberating Exodus power; this empowered them for their daily life. The feast became a deposit for a glorious future, so that the present reality could be transcended in a victorious way.[462]

In the feast, the everyday experience was interrupted by the salvific experience of the past, thereby opening up a new future. Life was carried onwards and forwards by the feast. God's faithfulness towards his covenantal promises awakened an attitude of joy and gratitude. In Scripture, happiness is linked to God's salvific acts, through which his victory is clearly revealed. Joy emanates from the knowledge that the alienation which separates humans from

---

[461] Van Ruler, 1971, 120: Joy is much closer to the heart of God than love.
[462] Otto and Schramm, 1977, 35: Festivity and liturgical events open up a horizon of spiritual joy and entertainment in the presence of God.

themselves, from God, and from their fellow humans has been eliminated through God's salvific work.

The value of this festival joy for pastoral care lies in the way that caregivers orientate the believer towards the Lord's vivid presence. The sacraments of communion and baptism are particularly important here. Through the commemoration of the Eucharist, believers are empowered to face the threat of chaos and death.

Joy is not about cheap optimism or a *theologia gloriae*. Within Israel's faith, the realized salvific reality was linked to the sacrificial and atonement ritual. The festival confronted Israel radically with guilt and sin. The theme of sin forms the core of the atonement ritual within Israel's cult in linking them with the reality of reconciliation. In the same way, the Eucharist urges people towards self-examination and confession. In the New Testament the festive joy is determined by the high-priestly suffering of Christ. In Him, "joy" means sin and death overcome by grace (Otto & Schramm 1977, p. 130).

In New Testament terms, joy refers to the celebration of Christ's death and in the Eucharist. In the celebration of Holy Communion, believers' actual fellowship with the crucified and risen Lord is once more affirmed. Actual participation in this victory motivates believers to live their daily life victoriously.

The resurrection makes us "excited" in the present: resurrection hope contributes to resistance in the present. Resurrection hope instils a new kind of "spiritual fortigenetics": patience as courageous resistance of unjust suffering. There is a moment in hopeful joy and joyous hope wherein one transcends reality, without actually forsaking the reality. It is characteristic of the *homo festivus* that it recalls the past, without betraying the present. At the same time, joy is a creative moment which surpasses the present towards new possibilities. The not-yet in joy is not euphoria, which ousts the painfulness of reality, but the creative vitality of a faith that resists inhumane forms of human suffering and embraces pain in hope.

Conclusion

In a nutshell: The certainty of our future hope is theologically linked to an *eschatologia crucis* that constitutes hope as a founded guarantee and ontological state of being. The certainty does not reside in mere fortigenetics (positive effects and constructive behaviour), but in God's faithfulness as demonstrated by a *theologia resurrectionis*. Due to the event of the *parousia*, our future in Christian hoping is about *adventus*. *Derelictio* (divine forsakenness) as a divine event and compassion as an expression of God's pathos, constitute a mode of enduring faithfulness that is not fuelled by either pessimism or optimism, nor by masochism, but by *promissio* (the future of divine fulfilled promises) and God's faithfulness, the guarantee for our future hope.

15.
Divine Forgiveness and Freedom from the Shame of Past Mistakes: A Communitarian Perspective
by Kevaughn Mattis
Founder and Director of *Testamentum Imperium*[463]

Introduction 265
A. The Gravity of Shame 266
B. God as Most Real Being and Divine Forgiveness 267
C. The Depth and Beauty of Forgiveness 269
D. The Will of God for the Church: Enacting the Forgiveness of God in Community 272
Conclusion: Enacting Forgiveness in the Community of God 273

Introduction

Reflecting on the Protestant Reformation 500 years on, it is beyond a shadow of doubt that the main predicament addressed by this theological tradition from its inception was the problem of sin experienced as guilt. In other words, the Reformation sought to answer the question, "How can a sinner stand justified before a Holy God and have the assurance that he is forgiven?"

Dealing with the vertical relationship between God and man, the Reformation deeply engaged the question of guilt as a forensic category. One can argue that this emphasis came to some extent at the expense of specifically addressing the profundity of the existential angst of shame that many believers feel despite their acceptance of the gospel's promise that their sins are forgiven. The Reformation also dealt less with grace as a unique, qualitative experience of life in the *communio sanctorum*, the *communion of the saints* in the sacred fellowship of all living believers in Christ.

In this article, I wish to briefly address the gravity of shame that many believers feel and how such shame makes it impossible to truly experience the grace of divine forgiveness. Secondly, I will present

---

[463] Mattis founded *Testamentum Imperium* in 2005 to bring scholars together from around the world to discuss the security of the Christian believer, the Great Testament: see www.PreciousHeart.net/ti. He holds a LLB (Hons), University of London, UK, and a LPC from BPP Law School, Manchester, UK, and practices law in Trinidad, Tobago.
    See destinyfromthebeginning@hotmail.com.

theological arguments in favour of disregarding such feelings in the hearts of believers (which will include looking at forgiveness itself as healing and cleansing). Finally, I argue that while divine forgiveness occurs on an individual basis between oneself and God, it was in fact meant to be mediated experientially through the community of the church as the presence of God in the world here and now and what we must do as a church to make that experience real.

A. The Gravity of Shame

Oxford Dictionary defines shame as "a painful feeling of humiliation or distress caused by the consciousness of wrong or foolish behavior."[464] Bernard Golden refers to shame as, "negatively judging ourselves when we believe we've failed to live up to either our own standards or the standards of other people." He distinguishes between healthy and toxic shame referring to healthy shame as guilt: "Guilt can be healthy in moving us toward positive thinking and behavior. It is specific in its focus." Golden quotes Brené Brown:

> Shame, however, when toxic, is a paralyzing global assessment of oneself as a person. When severe, it can form the lens through which all self-evaluation is viewed. As such, some words used to express the emotion of shame include feeling insecure, worthless, stupid, foolish, silly, inadequate or simply less than.[465]

Extreme forms of shame can be associated with depression and even suicide.[466] For example, in Eastern, honour/shame based cultures, suicide was known to be a common antidote to shame. It was more honourable to die than to live in a community where one had been disgraced. Gershen Kaufman, one of the foremost affect

---

[464] See https://en.oxforddictionaries.com/definition/shame.

[465] Bernard Golden, "Overcoming the Paralysis of Toxic Shame: An essential step for Cultivating Healthy Anger," *Psychology Today* (April 27, 2017): www.PsychologyToday.com/us/blog/overcoming-destructive-anger/201704/overcoming-the-paralysis-toxic-shame. Golden references Michael Lewis' *Shame and Guilt in Neurosis* (International Universities Press, 1995) and Brené Brown's *Shame—The Exposed Self* (Free Press; www.TED.com/talks/brene_brown_listening_to_shame). See Golden's article here: www.Psychologytoday.com/us/blog/overcoming-destructive-anger/201704/overcoming-the-paralysis-toxic-shame. Cf., Helen Block Lewis, *Shame and Guilt in Neurosis* (Madison, CT: International Universities Press, 1971.)

[466] Brené Brown "Self-Conscious Emotions and Depression: Rumination Explains Why Shame But Not Guilt is Maladaptive," *Personality and Social Psychology Bulletin* 32, no. 12 (Dec. 2006): 1608–1619.

theorists on shame and how deeply feelings of shame can cut into the core of our basic schemas of the self, made this observation:

> Shame itself is an entrance to the self. It is the affect of indignity, of defeat, of transgression, of inferiority, and of alienation. No other affect is closer to the experienced self. None is more central for a source of identity. Shame is felt as an inner torment, as a sickness of the soul. It is the most poignant experience of the self by the self ... a wound felt from the inside, dividing us both from ourselves and from one another.
>
> Shame is the affect which is the source of many complex and disturbing inner states: depression, alienation, self-doubt, isolating loneliness, paranoid and schizoid phenomena, compulsive disorders, splitting of the self, perfectionism, a deep sense of inferiority, inadequacy or failure, the so-called borderline conditions and disorders of narcissism. These are the phenomena which are rooted in shame.... Each is rooted in significant interpersonal failure....
>
> The binding effect of shame involves the whole self. Sustained eye contact with others becomes intolerable ... speech is silenced. Exposure itself eradicates the words, thereby causing shame to be almost incommunicable to others.... The excruciating observation of the self which results, his torment of self-consciousness, becomes so acute as to create a binding, almost paralyzing effect upon the self.[467]

Returning to shame in the spiritual context, believers suffering with extreme shame over past sins may withdraw from the church community with debilitating feelings and negative self-talk. Common beliefs held in such circumstances are denials that we are forgiven, holy, and loved. Other common beliefs deny the reality of forgiveness altogether—forgiveness is not real—or worse, making forgiveness a lie.

Oftentimes, we project onto God the way we feel about ourselves, creating a dysfunctional God image which leads to perceiving God as judgmental, abusive, and unloving. When this occurs, hearing the message of the gospel and forgiveness of sins may not result in feelings of hope and joy at all.

B. God as Most Real Being and Divine Forgiveness

In tackling the feeling of shame within believers over past sins, it is important to have a clear understanding of who the God that forgives us truly is. The true depth and beauty of God and His forgiveness is seen explicitly in the New Testament.

---

[467] Gordon Wheeler, "Self and Shame: A Gestalt Approach," *Gestalt Review* 1, no. 3 (1997): 224.

Who is this God who forgives?

In Acts 17, in seeking to evangelize the Greeks, the Apostle Paul made consensual reference to the philosophy of the Greek poets that the true God was the One, "in whom we live and move and have our being," said Saint Paul to the Athenians in Acts 17:28. The expression was advocated by the poet Epimenides of Cnossos who "flourished" in the sixth century BC.[468] J. A. Crabtree said of Acts 17:28:

> The most real being (*ens realissimus* or, more typically, *ens realissimum*) is one of several titles that medieval philosophers and theologians used to denote God. The fact that God exists on a higher level of reality than we do—that is, he is more real than we are.[469]

Not only is God the Father through Christ the ground of all being, but all things were created by Him, are sustained in Him, and were made for Him. As Colossians 1:15–17 tells us, Jesus *is*,

> the image of the invisible God, the first-born [*prototokos*] of all creation; for in him all things were created, in heaven and on earth, visible and invisible, whether thrones or dominions or principalities or-all things were created through him and for him. He is before all things, and in him all things hold together." In other words, everything in creation was made by and for God and in the end, everything will serve His ultimate purpose.

These ideas play no small role in our understanding of God's redemptive acts towards us.

Geurt Hendrik Van Kooten made it clear that God, Christ, and the cosmos are closely intertwined in Pauline thought. The scriptures refer to our redemption as God gifting us with a new identity in Christ that belongs to the age to come (God's re-created order of the cosmos). God saves us in His capacity as the most real being, as the author and telos of human history. Consequently, there could never be anything more real and enduringly true in the entire cosmos than what God is doing for creation in Christ. Resultantly, while the shame that seizes our hearts may tell us that we are worthless, foul, and disgraced, there can be no truer reality of ourselves than who we are in Christ and no more authentic and enduring reality in the world than

---

[468] Note from the *Jerusalem Bible* (London: Darton, Longman and Todd, 1966), 231.

[469] J. A. Crabtree, *The Most Real Being—A Biblical and Philosophical Defense of Divine Determinism* (Gutenberg College Press, 2004).

that which is in Christ our Lord. This is why when Paul wrote about the grace we receive from God, he has on occasions done so from a cosmological perspective (see Colossians and Ephesians in particular).[470]

In spite of what our shame may tell us, the truth of the matter is that the forgiven transgressor is in the truest sense possible a pure, beautiful, and cherished person in space and time because of *Who* it is that saves us.

C. The Depth and Beauty of Forgiveness

It is commonplace for many believers to understand divine forgiveness much like a judicial document declaring that our sin debt has been cancelled. However, the Scriptures also speak of our forgiveness as a cleansing phenomenon that is part of the divine act of new creation. Seyoon Kim, in his preliminary considerations on Paul's theology of new creation in 2 Corinthians 5 stated as follows, "At this point Paul may have in mind the Rabbinic idea which compares forgiveness and atonement for sin on the New Year's Day or on the Day of Atonement with a new creation."[471] Sometimes forgiveness in general without any connection with the New Year's Day or the Day of Atonement is compared with a new creation.[472]

Divine Forgiveness not only cleanses us but also affirms our beauty, dignity, and God given majesty (Zech. 3:1–5; Eph. 1:6, 2:5–6).

Finally, divine forgiveness is not only a judicial pardon but an act that draws us into a deep perichoretic union with the God-self.[473] British Theologian T. F. Torrance often reminds us that it is mistaken to separate the gift of salvation from the gift giver. In his *Theology in Reconstruction*, Torrance said,

---

[470] Geurt Hendrik Van Kooten, *Cosmic Christology in Paul & the Pauline School: Colossians & Ephesians in the Context of Graeco-Roman Cosmology, with a New Synopsis of the Greek Texts, Wissenschaftliche Untersuchungen Zum Neuen Testament* 2 (Tübingen: Mohr Siebeck, 2003), 171.

[471] Seyoon Kim, *The Origin of Paul's Gospel* (Wipf & Stock Pub, 2007), 17. Cf. Str.-Bill. ii, 421; iii, 519; Moore i, 334; Ekik Sjöberg, "Wiedergeburt und Neuschopfung im palastinischen Judentum (Rebirth and new creation in Palestinian Judaism)," *Studia Theologica – Nordic Journal of Theology* 4, no. 1 (1950): 45ff.

[472] E.g., Lev.R. 30.3 (to Lev. 23.40); Midr. Ps. 18.6 (str.-Bill. iii. p. 519). See Sjoberg, 58 and 67.

[473] "Perichoresis" refers to the relationship between the three persons of the triune God in Father, Son, and Holy Spirit, particularly that one God has three distinct persons that commune.

> Grace is to be understood as the impartation not just of something from God but of God Himself. In Jesus Christ and in the Holy Spirit God freely gives to us in such a way that the Gift and the Giver are one and the same in the wholeness and indivisibility of His grace.[474]

It follows that believers cannot be anything but holy as forgiven children of God. For God cleanses us by making us participate in the righteousness of His Son (1 Cor. 1:30; 2 Cor. 5:21). The cleansing work of God is therefore too unfathomable to be disregarded in the wallow of our shame. In the present moment, what we truly are in Christ is unseen; furthermore, what is unseen here and now is more real and enduring than what can in fact be seen (2 Cor. 4:18; 1 John 3:1–3).

Who is it that God forgives?

Now, one may think that they are simply too sinful for the glorious redemptive of God to be applicable to them. But the message of scripture is quite the opposite. The salvation of God is for the "least of these." Two biblical lessons suffice.

The first is the gracious message to be found in the genealogy of Jesus in the Gospel of Matthew (Mat. 1:1–17). It tells about much more than who Jesus' ancestors were. The genealogy of Jesus was an abridged tribute to God's grace throughout redemptive history. Matthew wants us to see that Jesus, the king of Israel, is like no other king on earth. Genealogies served as cultural indicators of authenticity, nobility, and honor. And perhaps it is exactly for that reason that the genealogy of the King of grace includes persons you least expect to be included in a genealogy: women and sinful outcasts.

John MacArthur says of this,

> The first outcast was Tamar, the Canaanite daughter-in-law of Judah. She gained notoriety in Genesis 38 by resorting to deception, prostitution, and incest when she couldn't get a child any other way. Tamar disguised herself as a prostitute and tricked Judah into having sexual relations with her. From that illicit union were born twin sons, Perez and Zerah, and thus Tamar and her son Perez joined Judah in the Messianic line. Despite prostitution and incest, God's grace fell on all three of those undeserving persons, including a desperate and deceptive Gentile harlot.

---

[474] Thomas F. Torrance, *Theology in Reconstruction* (Grand Rapids: Eerdmans, 1975; Eugene, OR: Wipf & Stock, 1996), 246.

The second outcast was also a woman and a Gentile, but she made prostitution her livelihood. Rahab was no paragon of virtue, but she put her faith in the God of Israel and demonstrated it by protecting the two men Joshua sent to spy out her city. God spared her life and the lives of her family when Jericho was besieged and destroyed (Josh. 2:1–21; 6:22–25), and, brought her into the Messianic line. She became the wife of Salmon and the mother of the godly Boaz—David's great-grandfather.

Ruth, the wife of Boaz, was the third outcast. Though she was a Moabitess and former pagan, having no right to marry an Israelite, God's grace brought Ruth into the family of Israel, and through Boaz, into the royal line. She became the grandmother of Israel's great King David.

The fourth outcast was Bathsheba. She entered the Messianic line through adultery with David. The son of their sinful union died in infancy, but the next son born to them was Solomon (2 Sam. 11:1–27; 12:14, 24), successor to David's throne and continuer of the Messianic line. Once again, by God's grace Bathsheba became the wife of David, the mother of Solomon, and an ancestor of the Messiah.[475]

What does their inclusion in the genealogy of God incarnate tell us? It shows that God truly demonstrates His pedigree as a savior by his ability to redeem the *least of these*. The people whom God chose to be part of the Messiah's lineage reveal that the grace of God provides hope for every sinner.

The second lesson comes from the story of the Israelite prophet Jonah and the salvation of the city of Nineveh. Oftentimes we focus on the disobedience of Jonah without trying to understand the painful emotional and existential realities the prophet was enduring. What immediately comes to mind are the many socially debilitating ethnic conflicts that have ravaged many countries in our modern time and the difficult process of reconciliation, healing, and transitional justice. Jonah's ill feelings toward warning the city of Niveheh can be easily understood once we understand the intensity of the conflict between Israel and Niveheh. Nineveh was an ancient Assyrian city of Upper Mesopotamia. Nineveh had long been an enemy of Judah and Israel. In 722 BC, the Assyrians defeated the northern kingdom of Israel, destroying its capital, Samaria. In 701 BC, the Assyrians nearly conquered Jerusalem, the capital of Judah. In the book of Nahum, we see God judging Niveheh harshly and are given clues regarding the

---

[475] John MacArthur, "Genealogy of Grace: Matthew 1:1–17," *Grace to You* (Oct. 14, 2009), www.gty.org/library/articles/A287/the-genealogy-of-grace.

kind of experiences the people of Israel had with the Ninevites. Of the Ninevites, Nahum 3:1 says, "Woe to the city of blood, full of lies, full of plunder, never without victims!" Nineveh was a city of violence, known for its brutal treatment of those it conquered. The Assyrians were notorious for amputating hands and feet, gouging eyes, and skinning and impaling their captives. The following verse of Nahum's book emphasizes the violence of the Assyrians in the form of a rhetorical question: "Who has not felt your endless cruelty?" (Nah. 3:19). One could only imagine the kind of angst that Jonah felt about giving such a people an opportunity to be preserved when his memory was haunted by the suffering of his own people at their hands.

But the lesson we learn from this is clear. Israel was the chosen people of God. Consequently, what God was willing to do by showing mercy to the Ninevites was like the parent of a family that had suffered death and unspeakable atrocities sending their one surviving son to give the perpetrators an opportunity to live in spite of their crimes.

God forgives any who come to him no matter the sin. Shame has no power at the throne of grace (Heb. 4:16). In the end we can conclude that God's grace is even for us, the worst of sinners.

D. The Will of God for the Church: Enacting the Forgiveness of God in Community

In the midst of fierce theological rivalry with the Roman Catholic Church, the pioneers of the Reformation placed emphasis on the salvation of the individual. However, it is my contention that while the Reformers were essentially correct in their views on *sola gratia*, *sola fide*, and the assurance of salvation, the relationship between the *communion sanctorum* and these cardinal doctrines was relatively left underdeveloped. One work that has gone a long way to address that lacuna is James M. Howard's *Paul, the Community, and Progressive Sanctification: An Exploration into Community Based Transformation within Pauline Theology*. Therein, Howard briefly outlines one of the definitions of "imago dei" developed by the Reformation movement which will be key to developing a main point of this article. Howard gives three basic views on the understanding of the term "imago dei" and says of the third view:

> Third, the "dynamic view" understands the image of God in eschatological terms. This view also has its roots in the Reformation. Rather than seeing the

divine image as the restoration of something that was lost, it is seen as something toward which all believers are progressing which is higher than what was lost. It includes eternal life and conformity to Christ, neither of which was guaranteed as part of the garden experience. In this regard, to understand image-bearing it shifts the focus from the past and the present to the future and toward what the redeemed are becoming, rather than what they lost at the fall. Divine image studies reflect a growing discussion and understanding of how believers reflect God's image. As defined by Stanley J. Grenz,

> At the heart of the divine image ... is a reference to our humanity as designed by God. We are the image of God insofar as we have received, are now fulfilling, and one day will fully actualize a divine design. And this design—Gods intent for us—is that we mirror for the sake of creation the nature of the Creator.[476]

The gifts we receive from God are part of an overarching grant design of Imago Dei. Union with Christ is both an individual and corporate blessing. Consequently, the spiritual gifts we receive as individuals were meant to be organically expressed and nurtured in the community of the church which is the spiritual body of Christ with diverse physical and institutional manifestations.

To put it summarily, God, the Father, bestows spiritual blessings which express the Trinity (God as an ontologically communal unity). These spiritual blessings, being founded in the communal being of God are naturally nurtured and expressed in community through the church. This process involves both individual and collective human effort in a mystical union between God and the church mediated by the Holy Spirit. The collective expression of these spiritual gifts by the church, as mediated by the spirit, becomes a communal witness to the world of who God is. Good works are therefore a natural expression of our spiritual blessings which are—by their very nature—Trinitarian, communal, and perichoretic expressions of the divine nature.

Conclusion: Enacting Forgiveness in the Community of God

But how are we to enact the spiritual gift of divine forgiveness in community? This can be done in many different ways, and no formula is to be rigidly applied in this regard. However, such enactment must

---

[476] James M. Howard, *Paul, the Community, and Progressive Sanctification: An Exploration into Community Based Transformation within Pauline Theology* (NY: Peter Lang Publishing, 2006), 62.

entail discipling the church as a safe place for sinners to confess their sins in the knowledge that the dominant response to such confession is prayerful support and declaration of the gospel message of forgiveness and transformation. It would also entail developing new songs of worship that specifically address the problem of shame (Kirk Franklin's, "Imagine Me" comes to mind) and newly focused sermons that teach forgiveness and gracious accountability as the way of the church. Finally, the church would need to be discipled into basic human responses that affirm those who are suffering with shame with the simple understanding that friendship and physical presence is one of the most powerful forms of evangelism and transformation.

Bibliography

Ackermann, Henry F. *He Was Always There, The U.S. Army Chaplain Ministry in the Vietnam Conflict*, Vol. 6 of 7 of history of Army Chaplaincy (see U.S. Army ref. for all 7 vols.). U.S. Army, 1989.

Ackerman, Susan. "The Personal Is Political: Covenantal and Affectionate Love in the Hebrew Bible." *Vetus Testamentum* 52 (2002): 437–458.

Adams, Jay E. *The Christian Counselor's Commentary: Acts*. Woodruff, SC: Timeless Texts, 1999.

Adeney, Frances S. "*Sources of the Self: The Making of the Modern Identity* by C Taylor, Book Review." *Theology Today* 48, no. 2 (1991): 204–210.

Aggebo, A. *De kunst van siek sijn en van het omgaan met zieken*. s-Gravenhage: Boekencentrum (1959).

Athanasius of Alexandria (AD 296–373). *On the Incarnation of the Word*. Translated by Archibald T. Robertson. Vol. 4. *A Select Library of the Nicene and Post-Nicene Fathers of the Christian Church*. Edited by Philip Schaff and Henry Wace. New York: Christian Literature Company, 1892.

Allen, Guenther R. *Hosea, Amos—Believers Church Bible Commentary*. Pennsylvania: Herald Press, 1998.

Allen, Kenneth W. "Justification by Faith." *Bibliotheca Sacra* 135, no. 538 (April 1978): 109–116.

Alsdurf, Jim. "The Secret Sin: Healing the Wounds of Sexual Addiction." *Christianity Today* 37, no. 1 (1993): 68–22.

American Association of Pastoral Counselors. "About Us," accessed in 2016, www.aapc.org/Default.aspx?ssid=74andNavPTypeId=1157.

———. "Brief History on Pastoral Counseling." Accessed in 2916, www.aapc.org/Default.aspx?ssid=74andNavPTypeId=1158.

———. "Pastoral Counseling Today." Accessed in 2016, www.aapc.org/Default.aspx?ssid=74andNavPTypeId=1159.

American Counseling Association. "ACA Code of Ethics." Accessed in 2014, www.counseling.org/docs/ethics/2014-aca-code-of-ethics.pdf?sfvrsn=4.

———. "Definition of Psychology." Accessed in 2016, www.apa.org/about/.

American Psychological Association. "Ethical Principles of Psychologists and Code of Conduct." Accessed in 2010, www.apa.org/ethics/code/index.aspx.

Amundsen, Darrel W. *Medicine, Society, and Faith in the Ancient and Medieval Worlds*. Baltimore: The Johns Hopkins University Press, 1996.

———. "Did Early Christians 'Lust After Death'?" in *Suicide—A Christian Response*, edited by Timothy J. Demy and Gary P. Stewart. Grand Rapids: Kregel, 1998.

Anderson, Francis I., and David Noel Freedman. *Hosea: A New Translation with Introduction and Commentary, Anchor Bible*. Garden City: Doubleday, 1980.

Aquinas, Thomas (1225–1274). *Summa Theologica*. AD 1265–1274. Translated by Fathers of the English Dominican Province (1947), https://dhspriory.org/thomas/summa/. Download 6,805-page pdf, www.CCEL.org/ccel/aquinas/summa.pdf.

Arends, Carolyn. "Can't Get No Satisfaction: Addiction Is the Spiritual Disease of Our Time." *Christianity Today* 54, no. 12 (2010): 60–22.

Aristotle (384–322 BC). *Nicomachean Ethics*. c. 340 BC.

Army, U.S., Chaplaincy Histories in 7 volumes, each 600-plus pages. *From Its European Antecedents to 1791: The United States Army Chaplaincy*. Vol. 1, by Chaplain Parker C. Thompson, 1978; *Struggling for Recognition: The United States Army Chaplaincy 1791–1865*, Vol. 2, by Chaplain Herman A. Norton, 1977; *Up From Handymen: The United States Army Chaplaincy 1865–1920*, Vol. 3, by Chaplain Earl F. Stover, 1977; *The Best and The Worst of Times: The United States Army Chaplaincy 1920–1945*, Vol. 4, by Chaplain Robert L. Gushwa, 1977; *Confidence in Battle, Inspiration in Peace: The United States Army Chaplaincy 1945–1975*, Vol. 5, by Chaplain Rodger R. Venzke, 1977; *He Was Always There, The U.S. Army Chaplain Ministry in the Vietnam Conflict*, Vol. 6, by Chaplain Henry F. Ackermann, 1989; and *Encouraging Faith, Supporting Soldiers: A History of the U.S. Chaplain Corps 1975–1995*, Vol. 7, by Chaplain John W. Brinsfield, 1997.

Ascol, Tom. "Old Error Rediscovered." *The Founders Journal* 6 (Fall 1991).
Association for Clinical Pastoral Education. *The Journal of Pastoral Care and Counseling*, est. 1947. See www.ACPE.edu and http://pcc.sagepub.com. This is a joint publication of Journal of Pastoral Care Publications (www.JPCP.org) and Sage Journals, http://online.sagepub.com. As of June 2015, it is in its 69th volume, running for 69 years, a massive body of literature on professional pastoral care, mostly in the hospital setting. View all volumes http://pcc.sagepub.com/content/by/year, view *all* volumes and articles to 1968—*phenomenal!*
Association of Professional Chaplains. See www.ProfessionalChaplains.org, and its *Chaplaincy Today: Journal of the* Association *of Professional Chaplains*.
Astrow, Alan B., A. Wexler, K. Texeira, M. K. He, and D. P. Sulmasy. "Is Failure to Meet Spiritual Needs Associated with Cancer Patients' Perceptions of Quality of Care and Their Satisfaction with Care?" *Journal of Clinical Oncology* 25, no. 36 (December 2007): 5753–5757. See www.ncbi.nlm.nih.gov/pubmed/18089871.
———, M. E. Paulk, M. J. Balboni, A. C. Phelps, E. T. Loggers, A. A. Wright, S. D. Block, E. F. Lewis, J. R. Peteet, H. G. Prigerson. "Provision of Spiritual Care to Patients with Advanced Cancer: Associations with Medical Care and Quality of Life Near Death." *Journal Clinical Oncology* 28, no. 3 (January 2010): 445–452. See www.ncbi.nlm.nih.gov/pubmed/20008625. Note conclusion: "Support of terminally ill patients' spiritual needs by the medical team is associated with greater hospice utilization and, among high religious copers, less aggressive care at EoL. Spiritual care is associated with better patient QoL near death."
———, C. M. Puchalski, and D. P. Sulmasy. "Religion, Spiritual, and Health Care: Social, Ethical, and Practical Considerations." *American Journal of Medicine* 110, no. 4 (March 2001): 283–287. See www.amjmed.com/article/S0002-9343(00)00708-7/fulltext.
———, M. J. Balboni, A. C. Phelps, A. A. Wright, J. R. Peteet, S. D. Block, C. Lathan, T. Vanderweele, and H. G. Prigerson. "Support of Cancer Patients' Spiritual Needs and Associations with Medical Care Costs at the End of Life." *Cancer* 117, no. 23 (May 2011): 5383–91. See www.ncbi.nlm.nih.gov/pmc/articles/pubmed/21563177.
———, M. E. Paulk, M. J. Balboni, A. C. Phelps, E. T. Loggers, A. A. Wright, S. D. Block, E. F. Lewis, J. R. Peteet, and H. G. Prigerson. "Provision of Spiritual Care to Patients with Advanced Cancer: Associations with Medical Care and Quality of Life Near Death." *Journal of Clinical Oncology* 28, no. 3 (January 2010): 445–452. See www.ncbi.nlm.nih.gov/pubmed/20008625.
———, M. J. Balboni, A. C. Enzinger, K. Gallivan, M. E. Paulk, A. Wright, K. Steinhauser, T. J. VanderWeele, H. G. Prigerson. "Provision of Spiritual Support to Patients with Advanced Cancer by Religious Communities and Associations with Medical Care at the End of Life." *JAMA Internal Medicine* 173, no 12 (June 2013):1109–1117. See www.ncbi.nlm.nih.gov/pubmed/23649656.
Athanasius of Alexandria (AD 296–373). *On the Incarnation of the Word.* Translated by Archibald T. Robertson. Vol. 4. *A Select Library of the Nicene and Post-Nicene Fathers of the Christian Church.* Edited by Philip Schaff and Henry Wace. New York: Christian Literature Company, 1892. See www.CCEL.org/ccel/athanasius/incarnation.pdf.
Augustine (AD 345–430). *City of God.* AD 426. See version by Philip Schaff (1819–1893), www.CCEL.org/ccel/schaff/npnf102.pdf, in *Nicene and Post-Nicene Fathers.* Grand Rapids: Christian Classics Ethereal Library.
———. *Confessions.* AD 397–400. See www.CCEL.org/ccel/augustine/confess.pdf, Grand Rapids: Christian Classics Ethereal Library.
Aurelius, Marcus (AD 121–180). *Meditations.* c. AD 170.

Barna Group. "2015 State of Atheism in America." Accessed at www.Barna.com/research/2015-state-of-atheism-in-america.
Barth, Karl. *Die Lehre von der Versöhnung.* Zollikon-Zürich: EVZ. Die Kirchliche Dogmatik IV/1; IV/3, 1953.
Baym, Nina. "The Head, the Heart, and the Unpardonable Sin." *The New England Quarterly* 40, no. 1 (March 1967): 31–47.
Belcher R. P. *A Layman's Guide to the Lordship Controversy.* Southbridge MA: Crowne Publications, 1990.
Bell-Tolliver, L., and P. Wilkerson. "The Use of Spirituality and Kinship as Contributors to Successful Therapy Outcomes with African American Families." *Journal of Religion and Spirituality in Social Work: Social Thought*, 30, no. 1 (2011): 48–70.

Benner, David G. *Care of Souls: Revisioning Christian Nurture and Counsel.* Grand Rapids: Baker Books, 1998.
———. *Strategic Pastoral Counseling, a Short-term Structured Model*, 2nd ed. Grand Rapids, MI: Baker Academic, 2003.
———, and P. C. Hill, eds. *Encyclopedia of Psychology and Counseling* 2nd ed. Grand Rapids, MI: Baker Academic, 1999.
Bennett, James V. *I Chose Prison.* NY: Alfred A. Knopf, 1970.
Bentley, John. "The Problem of Internet Pornography." Freed-Hardeman University Lectureships in 2005. Results of 2005 survey of 4,210 analyzed. See www.PreciousHeart.net/ti/Guest/Bentley_2005_Problem_Internet_Pornography.pdf.
Berkhof, Hendrikus. *Christelifk geloof.* Nijkerk: Callenbach, 1973.
Berkouwer, G. C. *The Church Studies in Dogmatics.* Grand Rapids: Eerdmans, 1976.
———. *De wederkomst van Christus I.* Kampen: Kok, 1961.
Billings, J. T. *Calvin, Participation, and the Gift—The Activity of Believers in Union with Christ.* Oxford: Oxford University Press, 2007.
Bingemer, María Clara Lucchetti. "La Trinidad desde la Perspectiva de la Mujer: Algunas Pautas para la Reflexión." In *El Rostro Femenino de la Teología*, edited by María Pilar Aquino. San José: Departamento Ecuménico de Investigaciones, 1986.
Bingham, D. Jeffrey. "Development and Diversity in Early Christianity." *Journal of the Evangelical Theological Society* 49 (2006): 45–66.
Bloch, E. *Das Prinzip Hoffnung. Band I. Wissenschaftliche Sonderausgabe.* Frankfurt am Main: Suhrkamp Verlag, 1959.
Blokland, Arjan, and Victor van der Geest, eds. *Routledge International Handbook of Life-Course Criminology.* UK and NY: Routledge, 2017.
Blomberg, Craig. *Matthew. New American Commentary.* Nashville: Broadman Press, 2001.
Blum, T. C., and P. M. Roman. *Cost-effectiveness and Preventive Implications of Employee Assistance Programs.* U.S. Department of Health and Human Services. Rockville, MD: SAMSA, 1995. See www.ncjrs.gov/App/Publications/abstract.aspx?ID=160889.
Bock, Darrell L. *Luke 1:1–9:50. Baker Exegetical Commentary on the New Testament.* Grand Rapids: Baker Books, 1994.
Boisen, Anton. *The Exploration of the Inner World: A Study of Mental Disorder and Religious Experience.* Willett, Clark, 1936.
———. *Religion in Crisis and Custom: A Sociological and Psychological Study.* Harper and Brothers, 1955.
Bonhoeffer, Dietrich. *The Cost of Discipleship.* Trans. R. H. Fuller. NY: Macmillan, 1959.
Book of Concord. The Confession of the Lutheran Church, http://BookofConcord.org.
Böschemeyer, Uwe. *Die Sinnfrage in Psychotherapie und Theologie. Die Existenzanalyse und Logotherapie Viktor E. Frankls aus theologischer Sicht.* Berlin and New York. Walter de Gruyter, 1977.
Bridges, William, and Susan Bridges. *Managing Transitions—Making the Most of Change.* New York: Da Capo Lifelong, 2003.
Brinsfield, Chaplain John W. *Encouraging Faith, Supporting Soldiers: A History of the U.S. Chaplain Corps 1975–1995*, Vol. 7 of 7 of history of Army Chaplaincy (see U.S. Army ref. for all 7 vols.). U.S. Army, 1997.
Braaten, Carl E., and Robert W. Jensen, eds. *Union with Christ—New Finnish Interpretation of Luther.* Grand Rapids: Eerdmans, 1998.
Brown, R. Khari, Robert Joseph Taylor, and Linda M. Chatters. "Religious Non-involvement Among African Americans, Black Caribbeans and Non-hispanic Whites: Findings from the National Survey of American Life." *Review of Religious Research* 55, no. 3 (March 2013): 435–457.
Bureau of Justice Statistics. *Rape Trends.* Washington. D.C.: DOJ, 2010. Accessed Dec. 16, 2010 (original site listed no longer active); www.bjs.gov/glance_redirect.cfm.

Calvin, Jean/John (1509-1564). *Institutes of the Christian Religion.* 4 vols. 1546. Translated by Henry Beveridge. CreateSpace Independent Publishing Platform, 2009 (1st published Latin 1536, French 1541). See www.CCEL.org/ccel/calvin/institutes.pdf, for Beveridge translation, 1,268 pages with impressive Scripture index linked in PDF.
Castells, M. *The Power of Identity. Volume II. The Information Age: Economy, Society and Culture.* Malden: Blackwell Publishing, 2004.

Chadwick, Owen. *The Penguin History of the Church vol. 3: The Reformation.* New York: Penguin, 1990.
Chatters, Linda M., and Robert Joseph Taylor. "Religious Involvement among African Americans." *African American Research Perspectives* 4 (1998): 83–93.
Chopra, Deepak, ed. *The Love Poems of Rumi* (1207–1273). NY: Harmony Books, 1998.
Christiansen, Ellen Juhl. *The Covenant in Judaism and Paul—A Study of Ritual Boundaries as Identity Markers.* Arbeiten zur Geschichte des Antiken Judentums und Des Urchristen, vol 27. Leiden: Brill Academic Publishers, 1997.
Clark, P. A., M. Drain, and M. P. Malone. "Addressing Patients' Emotional and Spiritual Needs." *The Joint Commission Journal on Quality and Patient Safety* 29, no. 12 (December 2003): 659–670. See www.ncbi.nlm.nih.gov/pubmed/14679869.
Clinebell, Howard J. *Basic Types of Pastoral Care and Counselling: Resources for the Ministry of Healing and Growth.* Nashville, TN: Abingdon Press, 1966.
Cobb, Mark R., Christina M. Puchalski, and Bruce Rumbold, eds. *The Oxford Textbook of Spirituality in Healthcare.* Oxford, UK: Oxford University Press, 2012; 520p.
Coe, John H. "Resisting the Temptation of Moral Formation: Opening to Spiritual Formation in the Cross of the Spirit." *Journal of Spiritual Formation & Soul Care* 1, no. 1 (2008): 54–78.
Cohen, Norman J. *Self, Struggle & Change—Family Conflict Stories in Genesis and Their Healing Insights for Our Lives.* Woodstock: Jewish Lights Publishing, 1995.
Collins, John J. *The Apocalyptic Imagination—an Introduction to Jewish Apocalyptic Literature.* 2nd ed. Grand Rapids: Eerdmans, 1998.
Collins, Raymond F. *First Corinthians Sacra Pagina Series.* Collegeville, MN: The Liturgical Press, 1999.
Conners, Kenneth Wray. "The Awakened Heart: Living Beyond Addiction." *Christian Century* 109, no. 4 (1992): 103–104.
Cooper-White, Pamela. *Shared Wisdom: Use of the Self in Pastoral Care and Counseling.* Minneapolis, MN: Fortress Press, 2004.
———. *Braided Selves: Collected Essays on Multiplicity, God, and Persons.* Eugene, OR: Wipf and Stock Publishers, 2011.
———. *Many Voices: Pastoral Psychotherapy in Relational and Theological Perspective.* Minneapolis: Augsburg Press, 2011.
Copeland, M. "Executable Outlines." Accessed online July 2, 2010, www.executableoutlines.com/textserm.htm.
Crabtree, J. A. *The Most Real Being—A Biblical and Philosophical Defense of Divine Determinism.* Gutenberg College Press, 2004.
Crisp, B. R. "Spirituality and Sexual Abuse: Issues and Dilemmas for Survivors." *Theology and Sexuality* 13, no. 3 (2007): 301–314.
Cupitt, Don. *Taking Leave of God.* London: Xpress Reprints, 1980.
Curlin, F. A., C. J. Roach, R. Gorawara-Bhat, J. D. Lantos, and M. H. Chin. "How Are Religion and Spirituality Related to Health? A Study of Physicians' Perspectives." *Southern Medical Journal* 98, no. 8 (August 2005): 761–766. See www.ncbi.nlm.nih.gov/pubmed/16144169.

Dallas Theological Seminary Catalog 2011–2012.
Davis, Stephen T., ed. *Encountering Evil: Live Options in Theodicy.* Atlanta: John Knox Press, 1981.
Day, Laura. *Welcome to Your Crisis: How to Use the Power of Crisis to Create the Life You Want.* NY: Little, Brown and Co., 2006.
De Jong, J. M. *De opstanding van Christus.* Gravenhage: Boekencentrum, 1967.
Dearman, J. Andrew. *The Book of Hosea.* Grand Rapids: Eerdmans, 2010.
Deffinbaugh, Bob. "The Woman at the Well." Accessed September 27, 2010, www.bible.org/page.php?page_id=2357.
Definition of Chalcedon (AD 451). Accessed November 6, 2010, www.iclnet.org/pub/resources/text/history/creeds.chalcedon.txt.
Deifelt, Wanda. "The Recovery of the Body: Jesus in a Feminist and Latin-American Perspective." In *Discovering Jesus in Our Places—Contextual Christologies in a Globalized World*, edited by Sturla J. Stålsett. Dehli: ISPCK, 2003.
DelHousaye, John. "Jewish Groups at the Time of Jesus." In *Understanding the Big Picture of the Bible—A Guide to Reading the Bible Well*, edited by Wayne Grudem, C. John Collins, and Thomas R. Schreiner. Wheaton: Crossway, 2012.

———. "Jesus and the Meaning of Marriage: A Close Reading of Mark 10:1–12." *Journal for Biblical Manhood and Womanhood* 21, no. 1 (Spring 2016).

———, Jeff T. Purswell, and John J. Hughes, eds. *Scripture and the People of God—Essays in Honor of Wayne Grudem.* Wheaton: Crossway, 2018.

———. *Engaging Ephesians—An Intermediate Reader and Exegetical Guide.* Wilmore, KY: GlossaHouse, 2018

———. "John's Baptist in Luke's Gospel." In *Christian Origins and the Establishment of the Early Jesus Movement*, edited by Stanley E. Porter and Andrew W. Pitts. Leiden: Brill, 2018.

Demy, Timothy J. "Feel Trapped? A Biblical Perspective on Suicide." *Kindred Spirit* (Autumn 1999): 10–12. Also, *DTS Magazine* 23, no. 3 (Fall 1999), https://voice.dts.edu/article/feel-trapped-a-biblical-perspective-on-suicide-dallas-theological-seminary/.

———, and Gary P. Stewart, eds. *Suicide—A Christian Response*, Grand Rapids: Kregel, 1998.

———, and Gary P. Stewart. *101 Most Puzzling Bible Verses.* Eugene, OR: Harvest House Publishers, 2006.

Didymus the Blind (c. AD 313-398). *On Genesis.* Fathers of the Church Patristic Series. Translated by Robert Hill. Catholic University of America Press, 2016.

Dillistone, F. W. "The Recovery of the Doctrine of Justification by Faith." *Theology Today* 11, no. 2 (July 1954): 199-209.

Doolittle, B. R., A. C. Justice, and D. A. Fiellin. "Religion, Spirituality, and HIV Clinical Outcomes: A Systematic Review of the Literature." *AIDS Behavior* 22, no. 6 (June 2016): 1792–1801. See www.ncbi.nlm.nih.gov/pubmed/28004218.

Downey, Michael. *Understanding Christian Spirituality.* New York: Paulist, 1997.

Droge, Arthur J., and James D. Tabor. *A Noble Death: Suicide and Martyrdom among Christians and Jews in Antiquity.* San Francisco: HarperCollins, 1992.

Dunn, James D. G. *The New Perspective on Paul: Revised Edition.* Grand Rapids: Eerdmans, 2008.

Egan, Gerard. *Encounter: Group Processes for Interpersonal Growth.* Belmont, CA: Brooks/Cole Pub., 1970.

———. *The Skilled Helper: A Problem-management Approach to Helping,* 10th Ed. Cengage Learning, 2013, 1st 1980.

Erickson, Millard J. *Readings in Christian Theology*, vol. 2. *Man's Need and God's Gift.* Grand Rapids: Baker Book House, 1992.

Ehman, J. W., B. B. Ott, T. H. Short, R. C. Ciampa, and J. Hansen-Flaschen. "Do Patients Want Physicians to Inquire about Their Spiritual or Religious Beliefs if They Become Gravely Ill?" *Archives of Internal Medicine* 159, no. 15 (August 1999): 1803–1806. See www.ncbi.nlm.nih.gov/pubmed/10448785.

Eisenberg, Nancy, and Janet Strayer. *Empathy and Its Development.* NY: Cambridge University Press, 1987.

Eisenberg, Nancy. "Empathy-Related Emotional Responses, Altruism, and Their Socialization." Chap. 7, in *Vision of Compassion: Western Scientists and Tibetan Buddhists Examine Human Nature.* Edited by Richard J. Davison and Anne Harrington. NY: Oxford University Press, 2001.

Ernecoff, N. C., F. A. Curlin, P. Buddadhumaruk, and D. B. White. "Health Care Professionals' Responses to Religious or Spiritual Statements by Surrogate Decision Makers During Goals-of-Care Discussions." *JAMA Internal Medicine* 175, no. 10 (October 2015): 1662–1669. See www.ncbi.nlm.nih.gov/pubmed/26322823.

Evans, Keith A. *Using Chaplains as Key Leadership in Evaluating and Enhancing Workplace Spirituality for a Rural Hospital Setting.* D.Min. diss. Winston-Salem: Temple Baptist Seminary, 2015.

———. *Essential Chaplain Skill Sets: Discovering Effective Ways to Provide Excellent Spiritual Care.* Bloomington. West Bow Press, 2017. See www.ChaplainSkillSets.com.

Evans, William B. "Déjà vu All over Again? The Contemporary Reformed Soteriological Controversy in Historical Perspective." *Westminster Theological Journal* 72, no. 1 (Spring 2010): 135–51.

Everly, Jr., George S. *Pastoral Crisis Intervention.* Ellicott City: Chevron Publishing, 2007.

Farstad, A. L. "We believe in Sanctification. Part 1. Introduction." *Journal of the Grace Evangelical Society* 5, no. 2 (Autumn 1992), https://faithalone.org/journal/1992b/Farstad.htm.

———. "We believe in Sanctification. Part 5. Future Sanctification Future Sanctification: Perfect, or Ultimate, Sanctification." *Journal of the Grace Evangelical Society* 8, no. 14 (Spring 1995).

Federal Vision. A Joint Federal Vision Statement. Retrieved from www.Federal-Vision.com/joint_statement.html, accessed April 18, 2011; no longer available, now here: http://federal-vision.com/uncategorized/joint-federal-vision-statement/. Cf. https://en.wikipedia.org/wiki/Federal_Vision.

Fee, Gordon D. *The First Epistle to the Corinthians. The New International Commentary on the New Testament*. Grand Rapids: Eerdmans, 1987.

Feller, Bryan. *A Business Care for Corporate Chaplaincy*. Los Angeles: Chaplains Inc., 2011. See www.yumpu.com/en/document/view/4730933/a-business-case-for-corporate-chaplaincy-chaplains-inc.

Fesko, J. V. *Justification—Understanding the Classic Reformed Doctrine*. Philipsburg, NJ: P&R Publishing, 2008.

Finney, C. G. "Accounting for Moral Depravity." In Millard J. Erickson, *Readings in Christian Theology*, vol. 2. *Man's Need and God's Gift*. Grand Rapids, MI: Baker Book House, 1992.

Flannelly, Kevin J., Linda L. Emanuel, George F. Handzo, Kathleen Galek, Nava R. Silton, and Melissa Carlson. "A National Study of Chaplaincy Services and End of Life Outcomes." *BMC Palliative Care* 11, no. 10 (July 2012): 1. Access www.researchgate.net/publication/228099405_A_national_study_of_chaplaincy_services_and_end-of-life_outcomes. See www.ncbi.nlm.nih.gov/pubmed/21563177.

Fletcher, Susan K. "Religion and Life Meaning: Differentiating Between Religious Beliefs and Religious Community in Constructing Life Meaning." *Journal of Aging Studies* 18, no. 2 (May 2004): 171–185. See www.ScienceDirect.com/science/article/abs/pii/S0890406504000064.

Fontes, L. A. "Sin Verguenza: Addressing Shame with Latino Victims of Child Sexual Abuse and Their Families." *Journal of Child Sexual Abuse* 16, no. 1 (2007): 61–83.

Fossel, M. D., and P. D. Bennett, eds. *Counseling—A Comprehensive Profession*. 6th ed. Upper Saddle River, NJ: Pearson Education, 2009.

Fouque, P., and M. Glachan. "The Impact of Christian Counselling on Survivors of Sexual Abuse." *Counselling Psychology Quarterly* 13, no. 2 (2000): 201–220.

Frankl, Viktor. *Man's Search for Meaning—An Introduction to Logotherapy*. Boston: Beacon Press, 2006 (1st 1946).

———. *The Doctor and the Soul*. London: Souvenir, 1969.

———. *Der unbewusste Gott: Psychotherapie und Religion*. München: Kösel, 1977.

Frazer, J. G. *Pausanias's Description of Greece: Volume 1* (London: MacMillan and Co. Limited, 1898), Kindle e-book edition. Location: 1816, 6607.

Freedman, David Noel. "Divine Commitment and Human Obligation: The Covenant Theme." In *Divine Commitment and Human Obligations—Selected Writings of David Noel Freedman*, edited by John R. Huddlestun. Grand Rapids: Eerdmans, 1997.

Frend, W. H. C. *Martyrdom and Persecution in the Early Church*. Oxford: Blackwell, 1965.

Freud, Sigmund. "Civilization and Its Discontents." In *Standard Edition of the Complete Psychological Works of Sigmund Freud*. Trans. and edited by J. Strachey. London: Hogarth Press, 1962.

Fretheim, Terence E. *The Suffering of God*. Philadelphia: Fortress, 1984.

Garcia, Frederico Duarte, and Florence Thibaut. "Sexual Addictions." *The American Journal of Drug and Alcohol Abuse* 36, no. 5 (2010): 254–260.

Gallup. "Most Americans Still Believe in God." *Gallup*, June 29, 2016, accessed May 30, 2017, www.Gallup.com; cf. PewForum. "U.S. Public Becoming Less Religious," November 3, 2015, www.PewForum.org, accessed May 30, 2017.

Gardoski, Kenneth M. "The Imago Dei Revisited." *The Journal of Ministry and Theology* 11–2, no. 5–37 (Fall 2007).

Gavielides, Theo, ed. *Routledge International Handbook of Restorative Justice*. Abingdon, UK; NY, NY: Routledge, 2018.

Genzen, Gary C. "Counseling for Substance Abuse and Addiction." *Concordia Theological Quarterly* 54, no. 2–3 (1990): 231–232.

Gerkin, Charles V. *Living Human Document: Re-Visioning Pastoral Counseling in a Hermeneutical Move*. Nashville, TN: Abingdon Press, 1984.

Gerstenberger, Erhard S. *Suffering*. Nashville, TN: Abingdon, 1980.

Gerstenberger, G., and W. Schrage. *Leiden*. Stuttgart: Kohlhammer, 1977.

Gesche, A. *Die Auferstehung Jesu in der dogmatischen Theologie*. Theologische Bericht 2. Zürich: Benziger, 1973.

Getz, Hildy G., Ginger Kirk, and Lisa G. Driscoll. "Clergy and Counselors Collaborating Toward New Perspectives." *Counseling and Values* 44, no. 1 (October 1999): 40–54. See https://onlinelibrary.wiley.com/doi/abs/10.1002/j.2161-007X.1999.tb00151.x.

Gladding, Samuel T., and Deborah W. Newsome. *Clinical Mental Health Counseling in Community and Agency Settings* 3rd ed. Upper Saddle River, NJ: Merrill/Prentice-Hall, 2010.

Gladding, Samuel T. "Personal and Professional Aspects of Counseling." In *Counseling—A Comprehensive Profession*, 6th ed., edited by M. D. Fossel and P. D. Bennett. Upper Saddle River, NJ: Pearson Education, 2009.

Glanzer, Perry L., and Todd Ream. "Whose Story? Which Identity? Fostering Christian Identity at Christian Colleges and Universities." *Christian Scholar's Review* 35, no. 1 (2005): 13–27.

Gleuck, Nelson. *Hesed in the Bible*. Jersey City: KTAV Publishers, 1978.

Golden, Bernard. "Overcoming the Paralysis of Toxic Shame: An Essential Step for Cultivating Healthy Anger." *Psychology Today* (April 27, 2017): www.PsychologyToday.com/us/blog/overcoming-destructive-anger/201704/overcoming-the-paralysis-toxic-shame.

Goldstein, Arnold P., and Gerald Y. Michaels. *Empathy: Development, Training, and Consequences*. Mahwah, NJ: L. Erlbaum Associates, 1985.

Gollwitzer, H. *Over de zin van het leven*. Kampen: Kok, 1974.

Goold, William, ed. *Works of John Owen*, Vol. 6. Edinburgh: Banner of Truth, 1967 (repr. 1827).

Goppelt, L. *Theologie des Neuen Testaments*. Göttingen: Vandenhoeck & Ruprecht, 1980.

Gordon, Tom, Ewan Kelly, and David Mitchell Radcliffe. *Spiritual Care for Healthcare Professionals: Reflecting on Clinical Practice*. London, UK: Radcliffe Publishing, 2011.

Gostenik, Christian, Tanja Repi, Mateja Cvetek, and Robert Cvetek. "Hidden Mission of the Psyche in Abuse and Addiction." *Journal of Religion and Health* 49, no. 3 (2010): 361–376.

Graham, Elaine L. *Transforming Practice: Pastoral Theology in an Age of Uncertainty*, Eugene, OR: Wipf and Stock 1996.

Greenspun, W. S. "Internal and Interpersonal: The Family Transmission of Father-Daughter Incest." *Journal of Child Sexual Abuse* 3, no. 2 (1994): 1–14.

Gregory I the Great (590–604 A.D.). *The Book of Pastoral Rule*. Trans. George E. Demacopoulos. NY: St. Vladimirs Seminary, 1994. Accessed at www.documentacatholicaomnia.eu/01p/0590-0604,_SS_Gregorius_I_Magnus,_Regulae_Pastoralis_Liber_[Schaff]_EN.pdf.

Grenz, Stanley J. "Christian Spirituality and the Quest for Identity: Toward a Spiritual-Theological Understanding of Life in Christ." *Baptist History and Heritage* 37, no. 2 (2002): 87–105.

———. *Theology for the Community of God*. Nashville: Broadman & Holman, 1994.

Grudem, Wayne. *Systematic Theology—An Introduction to Biblical Doctrine*. Grand Rapids: Zondervan, 1994.

———. *Christian Ethics—An Introduction to Biblical Moral Reasoning*. Wheaton, IL: Crossway Books, 2018; 1,296p.

———, C. John Collins, and Thomas R. Schreiner, eds. *Understanding the Big Picture of the Bible—A Guide to Reading the Bible Well*. Wheaton: Crossway, 2012.

———, J. P. Moreland, Stephen C. Meyer, Christopher Shaw, and Ann K. Gauger. *Theistic Evolution—A Scientific, Philosophical, and Theological Critique*. Wheaton, IL: Crossway Books, 2017; 1,008p.

Guillory, William A. *Spirituality in the Workplace: A Guide for Adapting to the Chaotically Changing Workplace*. Salt Lake City: Innovations International, 1997.

Gunton, Colin E. *The Actuality of Atonement—A Study of Metaphor, Rationality, and the Christian Tradition*. Edinburgh: T&T Clark, 1988.

———. *The Promise of Trinitarian Theology*. Edinburgh: T&T Clark, 1991.

———. *Christ and Creation—The Didsbury Lectures*. Eugene: Wipf & Stock, 1992.

———. *Theology through the Theologians—Selected Essays, 1972–1995*. London: T&T Clark, 1996.

———. *The Christian Faith—An Introduction to Christian Doctrine*. London: Blackwell Publishers, 2002.

Gushwa, Robert L. *The Best and The Worst of Times: The United States Army Chaplaincy 1920–1945*, Vol. 4 of 7 of history of Army Chaplaincy (see U.S. Army ref. for all 7 vols.). U.S. Army, 1977;

Guthrie, D. *New Testament Theology*. Leceister/Illinois: IVP, 1981.

Haller, E. *Seelsorge in Zeichen der Hoffnung*. Theologische Existenz heute 155. München: Kaiser, 1969.

Hankin, Harriet. *The New Workforce: Five Sweeping Trends That Will Shape your Company's Future.* NY: American Management Association, 2004.

Hannah, John D. *Our Legacy—The History of Christian Doctrine.* Colorado Springs: NavPress, 2001.

Harley, D. A. "The Black Church: A Strengths-based Approach in Mental Health." In *Contemporary Mental Health Issues Among African Americans*, edited by D.A. Harley and J. M. Dillard. Alexandria, VA: American Counseling Association, 2005.

Hawthorne, Gerald F. *Philippians, Word Biblical Commentary.* Logos Library System. Dallas: Word, 1998.

Hawthorne, Nathaniel (1804–1864). *The Snow-Image, and Other Twice-told Tales* (Boston: Ticknor, Reed, and Fields, 1851).

———. "Ethan Brand—A Chapter from an Abortive Romance, the Snow-Image, and Other Twice-told Tales." Accessed April 1, 2011, www.ibiblio.org/eldritch/nh/eb.html.

Hays, Richard B. *The Faith of Jesus Christ—An Investigation of the Narrative Substructure of Galatians 3:1–4:11.* 2nd ed. Grand Rapids: Eerdmans, 2002, 1st 1983.

Health Care Chaplaincy. See www.HealthCareChaplaincy.org and their magazine, *PlainViews: Translating Knowledge and Skills into Effective Chaplaincy and Pallative Care.*

Heitink, Gerben. *Practical Theology: History, Theory, Action Domains.* Grand Rapids: Eerdmans, 1999.

Helminiak, Daniel A. "A Scientific Spirituality: The Interface of Psychology and Theology." *International Journal for the Psychology of Religion* 6, no. 1 (1996): 1–19.

Hill, William J. *The Three-Personed God—The Trinity as a Mystery of Salvation.* Washington, D.C.: Catholic University of America Press, 1988.

Hiltner, Seward. *Pastoral Counseling.* Nashville, TN: Abingdon Press, 1949.

———. "Pastoral Care and Counseling." *The Journal of Religious Thought* 13, no. 2 (1956): 111–122. Retrieved from www.howard.edu/academics/publications.

———. *Preface to Pastoral Theology: The Ministry and Theory of Shepherding.* Nashville, TN: Abingdon Press, 1958.

Hodges, Zane C. *Absolutely Free!—Biblical Response to Lordship Salvation.* Grand Rapids MI: Zondervan, 1989.

———. "We Believe in Assurance of Salvation." *Journal of the Grace Evangelical Society*, 3, no. 2 (Autumn 1990), https://faithalone.org/journal/1990ii/Hodges.html.

———. "We Believe in Rewards," *Journal of the Grace Evangelical Society* 4, no. 2 (Autumn 1991), https://faithalone.org/journal/1991b/Rewards.html.

———. "Assurance and Works: An Evangelical Train Wreck." *Journal of the Grace Evangelical Society* 22, no. 42 (Spring 2009), https://faithalone.org/journal/2009i/Zane-2%20Assurance%20and%20Works%20An%20Evangelical%20Train%20Wreck.pdf.

Holifield, E. Brooks. *A History of Pastoral Care in America: From Salvation to Self-Realization.* Eugene, OR: Wipf and Stock, 2005.

Holmes, Kristin E. "23rd Psalm Holds Answers to Many of Life's Questions." *The Riverside Press-Enterprise* (Oct. 25, 2005): B12.

Homant, Robert J. "Ten Years After: A Follow-up of Therapy Effectiveness." *Journal of Offender Counseling, Services and Rehabilitation* 10 (Spring 1986): 51–57.

Horrell, Joseph. "Milton, Limbo, and Suicide." *The Review of English Studies* 18, no. 72 (Oct. 1942): 413–427.

Horton, Michael Scott. *The Christian Faith—A Systematic Theology for Pilgrims on the Way.* Grand Rapids: Zondervan, 2011.

Howard, James M. *Paul, the Community, and Progressive Sanctification—An Exploration into Community Based Transformation within Pauline Theology.* New York: Peter Lang Publishing, 2006.

Hulme, William E. "Theology and Counseling." *Christian Century* 68, no. 8 (Feb. 21, 1951).

———. "The Theology of Counseling," *Theology Today* 9, no. 2 (July 1, 1952): 189-196.

———. *The Pastoral Care of Families: Its Theology and Practice.* New York-Nashville: Abingdon Press, 1962.

———. *Counseling and Theology.* Allentown, PA: Muhlenberg, 1956.

Jang, Sung Joon, Byron R. Johnson, Joshua Hays, Michael Hallett, and Grant Duwe. "Prisoners Helping Prisoners Change: A Study of Inmate Field Ministers Within Texas Prisons," *International Journal of Offender Therapy and Comparative Criminology* (2019).

Jackson, Walter C. "Codependence and the Christian Faith: An Introduction to Compassion Addiction." *Review & Expositor* 91, no. 1 (1994): 31–41.
Janzen, J. Gerald. "Metaphor and Reality in Hosea." *Semeia 24*. Chico: Society of Biblical Literature, 1982.
John Aves, "Persons in Relation: John Macmurray." In *Persons, Divine and Human: King's College Essays in Theological Anthropology*, edited by Christoph Schwöbel and Colin E. Gunton. Edinburgh: T&T Clark, 1991.
Johnson, Byron R. *More God, Less Crime*. West Conshohocken, PA: Templeton Press, 2011.
———, and David B. Larson. *The InnerChange Freedom Initiative: A Preliminary Evaluation of a Faith-Based Prison Program*. International Center for the Integration of Health and Spirituality (CRRUCS Report), 2003.
Jonker, H. *Theologische Praxis*. Nijkerk: Callenbach, 1983.
Jones, Alexander, ed. *Jerusalem Bible*. New York: Doubleday; London: Darton, Longman and Todd, 1966. Catholic version by 27 scholars in Great Britain.
Jordan, J. "Lattitude in the Right Place." Accessed April 18, 2011, http://deregnochristi.org/2007/09/30/latitude-in-the-right-place/#comment-2153.
Jüngel, Eberhard. *Justification—The Heart of the Christian Faith*. Edinburgh: T&T Clark, 2001.

Karp, David. *Speaking of Sadness: Depression, Disconnection, and the Meaning of Illness*. Oxford: Oxford University Press, 1996.
Kelly, John Norman Davidson. *A Commentary on the Pastoral Epistles—I Timothy, II Timothy, Titus Black's New Testament Commentaries*. Edited by Henry Chadwick. London: A. & C. Black, 1986.
Kendall, R. T. *Once Saved, Always Saved*. Waynesboro, GA: Authentic Media, 2005.
Kennedy, John W. "Help for the Sexually Desperate: More and More, Christian Men Are Admitting They've Been Caught in a Vicious Cycle." *Christianity Today* 52, no. 3 (2008): 28–35.
Kim, J., and S. Williams. "Linking Childhood Maltreatment to Substance use in College Students: The Mediating Role of Self-Worth Contingencies." *Journal of Aggression, Maltreatment & Trauma* 18 (2009): 88–105.
Kim, Seyoon. *The Origin of Paul's Gospel*. Eugene, OR: Wipf & Stock Pub, 2007.
King, D. E., and B. Dushwick. "Beliefs and Attitudes of Hospital Inpatients about Faith Healing and Prayer." *Journal of Family Practice* 39, no. 4 (October 1994): 349–352. See www.ncbi.nlm.nih.gov/pubmed/7931113.
Kirk, Forrest L. *Chaplains as Doctors of the Soul: Navigating Between the Sacred and Secular while Negotiating a Functional and Ontological Ministry Identity*. Ph.D. diss., New Orleans Baptist Theological Seminary. Proquest, Umi Dissertation Publishing, 2011. Cf., an article abridgement of his diss., http://baptistcenter.net/journals/JBTM_9-1_Spring_2012.pdf.
Kirk, J. R. Daniel. *Unlocking Romans—Resurrection andtThe Justification of God*. Grand Rapids: Eerdmans, 2008.
Kitamori, Kazoh. *Theology of the Pain of God*. Wipf & Stock, 2005 (1st pub. 1946, Japan; John Knox Press, 1965).
———. *Theology of the Pain of God*. Wipf & Stock, 2005 (1st pub. 1946, Japan; John Knox Press, 1965).
———. *Theologie des Schmerzes Gottes*. Gottingen: Vandenhoeck, 1972.
Koberle, A. *Geduld und Hoffnung: Besuch am Krankenbett*. Hamburg: Siebenstern, 1970.
Koenig, Harold G. "MSJAMA: Religion, Spirituality, and Medicine: Application to Clinical Practice." *JAMA* 284, no. 3 (October 4, 2000): 1708. See https://jamanetwork.com/journals/jama/fullarticle/1843381.
———, Dana King, and Verna Benner Carson. *Handbook of Religion and Health*, 2nd ed. NY: Oxford University Press, 2012; 1,192p.
Koenig, Don. "Christian Legalism—the Dark Side of Christianity." Accessed 2005, www.ThePropheticYears.com/comments/The%20dark%20side%20of%20Christianity.htm.
Konrad, George G. "Responsible Christian Counseling." *Direction* 7, no. 2 (April 1978): 23–32, https://directionjournal.org/7/2/responsible-christian-counseling.html.
Kreck, W. *Grundfragen der Dogmatik*. München: Kaiser, 1977.
Kreider, Glenn R. *Jonathan Edwards' Interpretation of Revelation 4:1–8:1*. University Press of America, 2004.

———, ed. *Exploring Christian Theology—The Church, Spiritual Growth, and the End Times* (Bethany House Publishers, 2014).
———. *God with Us—Exploring God's Personal Interactions with His People Throughout the Bible.* P&R Publishing, 2014.
———, ed. *Eschatology—Biblical, Historical, and Practical Approaches* (Kregel Academic, 2016).
Kübler-Ross, Elisabeth. *On Death and Dying.* NY: Macmillan, 1969. Classic on grief.
Kujawa-Holbrook, Sheryl A., and Karen Brown Montagno, eds. *Injustice and the Care of Souls: Taking Oppression Seriously in Pastoral Care.* Minneapolis: Fortress, 2009.
Küng, Hans. *Justification—The Doctrine of Karl Barth and a Catholic Reflection.* 40th Ann. ed. Louisville, KY: Westminster John Knox Press, 2004 (1st 1964).
———. *Gott und das Leid.* Theologische Mediationen 18. Zürich-Benziger, 1974.
———. *Christ Sein.* München: Deutscher Tachenbuch, 1978.
———. *Incarnation of God—An Introduction to Hegel's Theological Thought as Prolegomena to a Future Christology.* Translated by J. R. Stephenson. Hertford, NC: Crossroad, 1987.
———. *My Struggle for Freedom—Memoirs.* NY/London: Continuum, 2003.
Kvanvig, Jonathan, ed. *Oxford Studies in Philosophy of Religion,* 8 vols. Oxford University Press, 2007–17.
Kwee, Alex W., Amy W. Dominguez, and Donald R. Ferrell. "Sexual Addiction and Christian College Men: Conceptual, Assessment, and Treatment Challenges." *Journal of Psychology and Christianity* 26, no. 1 (2007): 3–13.

Laaser, Mark R. *Healing the Wounds of Sexual Addiction.* 2004.
———, and Louis J. Gregoire. "Pastors and Cybersex Addiction." *Sexual and Relationship Therapy* 18, no. 3 (2003): 395–404.
Lartey, Emmanuel Y. *In Living Color. An Intercultural Approach to Pastoral Care and Counseling,* 2nd ed. London: Jessica Kingsley Publishers, 1997.
———. *Pastoral Theology in an Intercultural World.* Eugene, OR: Wipf and Stock Publishers, 2006.
Lea, Henry Charles. "Philosophical Sin." *International Journal of Ethics* 5, no. 3 (April 1895): 325–26.
Lee, Courtland C., ed. *Multicultural Issues in Counseling: New Approaches to Diversity,* 3rd ed. Alexandria, VA: American Counseling Association, 2006; 5th ed., Somerset, NJ: John Wiley, 2018.
Lehmann, Helmut T. "Luther on the Study of Luther." *Word & World* 3, no. 4 (September 1, 1983): 398-404, https://wordandworld.luthersem.edu/content/pdfs/3-4_Luther/3-4_Lehmann.pdf.
Lekkerkerker, Arie Frederik Nelis. *Het evangelie van de versoening.* Baarn: Bosch, 1966.
Lester, Andrew D. *Hope in Pastoral Care and Counseling.* Louisville, KY: Westminister/John Knox Press, 1995.
Leventhal, Barry R. "The Masada Suicides: The Making and Breaking of a Cultural Icon." In *Suicide: A Christian Response,* edited by Timothy J. Demy and Gary P. Stewart. Grand Rapids: Kregel, 1998.
Levine, Stephen B., C. B. Risen, and S. E. Althof, eds. *Handbook of Clinical Sexuality for Mental Health Professionals.* 2nd. ed. Abingdon: Routledge, 2010.
Levine, Stephen B. "What Is Sexual Addiction?" *Journal of Sex & Marital Therapy* 36, no. 3 (2010): 261–275.
Lewis, C. S. (1898–1963). *The Four Loves.* NY: Harcourt, Brace and Company, 1960.
———. *A Grief Observed.* NY: Harper & Row, 1961.
Lewis, Helen Block. *Shame and Guilt in Neurosis.* Madison, CT: International Universities Press, 1971.
Lewis, Michael. *Shame: The Exposed Self.* New York: Simon and Schuster, 1995.
Lillback, Peter, and Jerry Newcombe. *George Washington's Sacred Fire.* Bryn Mawr, PA: Providence Forum Press, 2006; 1,208p.
Lillback, Peter. *George Washington's Sacred Fire.* Bryn Mawr, PA: Providence Forum Press, 2006; 1,208p.
———. *George Washington & Israel.* Bryn Mawr, PA: Providence Forum Press, 2012.
———. *Wall of Misconception: Does the Separation of Church and State Mean the Separation of God and Government?* Bryn Mawr, PA: Providence Forum Press, 2012.
———. "Into the Mystic." *Tabletalk Magazine* (July 1, 2014), www.Ligonier.org/learn/articles/mystic/.
———. *The Binding of God: Calvin's Role in the Development of Covenant Theology.* Grand Rapids: Baker Academic, 2001.

———. "The Reformation and Education." *Tabletalk Magazine* (October 1, 2016), www.Ligonier.org/learn/articles/reformation-education/.
———. "Foreword." *1599 Geneva Bible: Luther Edition*. 500th Anniversary Ed. Dallas, GA: Tolle Lege Press, 2017.
———. *Saint Peter's Principles: Leadership for Those Who Already Know Their Incompetence*. Phillipsburg, NJ: P&R Publishing, 2019; 677p.
———, ed. *Unio cum Christo: An International Journal of Reformed Theology and Life*, www.UNIOCC.com.
———, Charles Colson, Wayne Grudem, and Philip Ryken. *Biblical Perspectives on Business Ethics: How the Christian Worldview has Shaped Our Economic Foundations*. Basking Ridge, NJ: Center for Christian Business Ethics Today, 2012.
———, and Judy Mitchell. *Lessons on Liberty: A Primer for Young Patriots*. Bryn Mawr, PA: Providence Forum Press, 2008.
———, and Richard B. Gaffin. *Thy Word Is Still Truth: Essential Writings on the Doctrine of Scripture from the Reformation of Today*. Phillipsburg, NJ: P&R Publishing, 2013; 1,440p.
———, and David Hall. *A Theological Guide to Calvin's Institutes: Essays and Analysis (Calvin 500)*. Phillipsburg, NJ: P&R Publishing, 2015; 528p.
Linder, R. D. "Antinomianism." *Evangelical Dictionary of Theology*. 2nd ed. Baker, 2001.
Lipton, D., R. Martinson, and J. Wilks. *The Effectiveness of Correctional Treatment: A Survey of Treatment Evaluation Studies*. NY: Praeger, 1975.
Lloyd-Jones, D. M. *Studies in Sermon on the Mount*. Grand Rapids MI: Wm. B. Eerdmans Publishing, 1960.
———. *Great Doctrines of the Bible—God the Father, God the Son; God the Holy Spirit; The Church and the Last Things*. Wheaton, IL: Crossway Books, 2003.
Loewenich, Walter von. *Luther's Theology of the Cross*. Minneapolis: Augsburg Publishing House, 1976.
Longfellow, Henry Wadsworth. *Writings of Henry Wadsworth Longfellow*, vol. 9 of 11, *Divine Comedy of Dante Alighieri, Inferno*. Cambridge: Cambridge University Press, 1886.
Lusk, R. "The Biblical Plan of Salvation." In Brian Schwertley, *The Auburn Avenue Theology*. N.d. Cf. www.reformedonline.com/uploads/1/5/0/3/15030584/chapter_1_auburn_avenue.pdf and https://en.wikipedia.org/wiki/Federal_Vision.
Luther, Martin (1483–1546). *D. Martin Luthers Werke: Kritische Gesamtausgabe* [*works complete critical edition*], vol. 7. Weimer: Hermann Böhlaus, 1897. Commonly known as the Weimar edition of Luther's works, 121 vols., 1883 to 2009, which began in the year of Luther's 400th birthday.
———. *The Liberty of a Christian*. Philadelphia, PA: Lutheran Publication Society, 1903 (variously titled, *On Christian Liberty*, *Concerning Christian Liberty*, or *The Freedom of the Christian*). 1520. See *Christian Liberty* (Philadelphia: Lutheran Publication Society, 1903): https://books.google.com/books?id=jv9EAAAAYAAJ.
———. *Luther's German Bible*. Wittenberg, Germany: Hans Lufft, 1534.
———. *Vermischte Deutsche Schriften (Mixed German Writings)*. Translated by Robert E. Vol. 63. Erlangen: Heyder and Zimmer, 1854.
———. *Luther's Works*. 55 volumes. St. Louis, MO: Concordia Publishing House, 1955–1986. See www.CPH.org/c-2898-luthers-works.aspx. Concordia is working on a complete set, 79 volumes and counting of everything Luther wrote, some never before translated—a massive project.

MacArthur, John. *The Superiority of Christ*. Chicago: Moody Press, 1986.
———. *The Gospel According to Jesus*. Grand Rapids: Zondervan, 1988.
———. "MacArthur's Questions and Answers." Bible Bulletin Board, accessed January 10, 2011, www.biblebb.com/files/macqa/70-9-8.htm.
———. "Genealogy of Grace: Matthew 1:1–17." *Grace to You* (Oct. 14, 2009), www.gty.org/library/articles/A287/the-genealogy-of-grace.
———. "Faith According to the Apostle James." Accessed January 14, 2011, www.biblebb.com/files/MAC/faithaccordjames.htm
———. "Saving Faith." Bible Bulletin Board. Accessed January 15, 2011, www.biblebb.com/files/MAC/80-169.htm
MacDonald, Michael, and Terence R. Murphy. *Sleepless Souls*. Oxford: Oxford University Press, 1990.

MacGregor, Kirk R., and Kevaughn Mattis, eds. *Perspectives on Eternal Security—Biblical, Historical, and Philosophical*, with a foreword by H. Wayne House. Eugene, OR: Wipf and Stock, 2009; compilation of articles from *Testamentum Imperium*, www.PreciousHeart.net/ti.

MacLean, D. Charles, Beth Susi, Nancy Phifer, Linda Schultz, Deborah Bynum, Mark Franco, Andria Klioze, Michael Monroe, Joanne Garrett, and Sam Cykert. "Patient Preference for Physician Discussion and Practice of Spirituality." *Journal of General Internal Medicine* 18, no. 1 (January 2003): 38–43. See www.ncbi.nlm.nih.gov/pmc/articles/PMC1494799/.

MacMurray, John. *Persons in Relation*. London: Faber and Faber, 1970.

———. *The Self as Agent*. New Jersey: Humanities Press International, 1991.

Makidon, Michael. "Justification: God's Plan and Paul's Vision." Book review of N. T. Wright, *Justification—God's Plan & Paul's Vision* (Downers Grove: IVP, 2009). Grace Evangelical Society (n.d.). Reference originally accessed on January 06, 2011 is not longer available, but link is here: https://faithalone.org/journal-articles/book-reviews/justification-gods-plan-and-pauls-vision/.

Mannerma, Tuomo. *Christ Present In Faith: Luther's View of Justification*. Minneapolis: Augsburg Press, 2005.

Maness, Michael G. *How We Saved Texas Prison Chaplaincy 2011—the Immeasurable Value of Religion, Volunteers, and Their Chaplains*. Bloomington: AuthorHouse, 2012; www.PreciousHeart.net.

———. *Ocean Devotions—From the Hold of Charles H. Spurgeon*. Bloomington, IN: AuthorHouse, 2008; www.PreciousHeart.net/ocean.

———. *Queen of Prison Ministry—the Story of Gertha Rogers, First Woman to Minister on Texas Death Row*. Bloomington: AuthorHouse, 2008.

———. *Would You Lie To Save a Life?—A Theology on the Ethics of Love, Love Will Find a Way Home*. Bloomington, IN: AuthorHouse, 2007; www.PreciousHeart.net/love.

———. *Heart of the Living God: Love, Free Will, Foreknowledge, Heaven—A Theology on the Treasure of Love*. Bloomington, IN: AuthorHouse, 2004; www.PreciousHeart.net/foreknowledge.

———. *Heaven—Treasures of Our Everlasting Rest*. Bloomington, IN: AuthorHouse, 2004.

———. *Precious Heart, Broken Heart—Love and the Search for Finality in Divorce*. Bloomington: AuthorHouse, 2003.

———, ed., and Kevaughn Mattis, founder. *Testamentum Imperium—An International Theological Journal*. 2005–present. Mattis founded and directed this from its inception, www.PreciousHeart.net/ti.

Marcus, D. "Men Who Lose Control of Their Sexual Behavior." In *Handbook of Clinical Sexuality for Mental Health Professionals*. 2nd. ed. Edited by S. B. Levine, C. B. Risen, and S. E. Althof. Abingdon: Routledge, 2010.

Marin, D. B., V. Sharma, E. Sosunov, N. Egorova, R. Goldstein, and G. F. Handzo. "Relationship between Chaplain Visits and Patient Satisfaction." *Journal Health Care Chaplaincy* 21, no. 1 (2015): 14–24. Survey of 8,978 patients, with results: "Chaplains' integration into the healthcare team improves patients' satisfaction with their hospital stay." See https://www.ncbi.nlm.nih.gov/pubmed/25569779.

Mattis, Kevaughn, founder, and Michael G. Maness, ed. *Testamentum Imperium—An International Theological Journal*. 2005–present. Mattis founded and directed this from its inception, www.PreciousHeart.net/ti.

Mattis, Jacqueline S. "Religion and Spirituality in the Meaning-making and Coping Experiences of African American Women: A Qualitative Analysis." *Psychology of Women Quarterly* 26, no. 4 (December 1, 2002): 309–321. See https://journals.sagepub.com/doi/10.1111/1471-6402.t01-2-00070.

May, Gerald G. *The Awakened Heart: Living Beyond Addiction*. New York: HarperCollins, 1991.

Mays, James L. *Hosea*. Philadelphia: Westminster Press, 1969.

McCord Adams, Marilyn. *Horrendous Evils and the Goodness of God*. Cornell Studies in the Philosophy of Religion. Ithaca, NY: Cornell University Press, 2000.

McCord, Gary, Valerie J. Gilchrist, Steven D. Grossman, Bridget D. King, Kenelm F. McCormick, Allison M. Oprandi, Susan Labuda Schrop, Brian A. Selius, William D. Smucker, David L. Weldy, Melissa Amorn, Melissa A. Carter, Andrew J. Deak, Hebah Hefzy, and Mohit Srivastava. "Discussing Spirituality with Patients: a Rational and Ethical Approach." *Annals*

of *Family Medicine* 2, no. 4 (July 2004): 356–361. See www.ncbi.nlm.nih.gov/pmc/articles/PMC1466687/.
McDonagh, E. "Mortal Sin." *New Catholic Encyclopedia.* 2nd ed. Washington, D.C.: The Catholic University of America, 2003.
McGinn, Bernard. *The Essential Writings of Christian Mysticism.* New York: The Modern Library, 2006.
McGinnis, Tracy. "Business Has a Prayer." *Forbes* (June 2006).
McGrath, Alister E. "Newman on Justification: An Evangelical Anglican Evaluation." In *Newman and The Word.* Edited by Terrence Merrigan and Ian T. Kerr. Louvain; Paris, Sterling; Virginia: Peeters, 2000.
McGuiness, I. "Venial Sin." *New Catholic Encyclopedia.* 2nd ed. Washington, D.C.: The Catholic University of America, 2003.
McKinnon, Garrett, and Tim Embrey. "2007 Fast Lube Operator of the Year." *National Oil and Lube News* (December 2007).
McMinn, M. R. *Psychology, Theology, and Spirituality in Christian Counseling.* Carol Stream, IL: Tyndale House Publishers, 1996.
McSherry, Wilfred, and Linda Ross, eds. *Spiritual Assessment in Healthcare Practice.* Keswick, UK: M&K Publishing, 2010.
Moffatt, James, (1870–1944). *Love in the New Testament.* NY: R. R. Smith, 1930.
Mohr, Sylvia, Pierre-Yves Brandt, Laurence Borras, Christiane Gillieron, and Philippe Huguelet. "Toward an Integration of Spirituality and Religiousness into the Psychosocial Dimension of Schizophrenia." *American Journal of Psychiatry* 163, no. 11 (November 2006): 1952–1959. See www.ncbi.nlm.nih.gov/pubmed/17074947.
Mercadante, Linda A. "Addiction and Recovery." *Christian Century* 115, no. 9 (1998): 302–303.
Merrigan, Terrence, and Ian T. Kerr. Louvain, eds. *Newman and The Word.* Paris, Sterling; Virginia: Peeters, 2000.
Miller, B. J., J. R. Cardona, and M. Hardin. "The Use of Narrative Therapy and Internal Family Systems with Survivors of Childhood Sexual Abuse: Examining Issues Related to Loss and Oppression." *Journal of Feminist Family Therapy* 18, no. 4 (2006): 1–25.
Miller, James E., Jr. "Hawthorne and Melville: The Unpardonable Sin." *PLMA* 70, no. 1 (March 1955): 91–114.
Minich, Joseph. "Within the Bounds of Orthodoxy." Accessed April 18, 2011, www.Federal-Vision.com/minich_bounds_of_orthodoxy.html; no longer there, see a 2006 version: www.joelgarver.com/docs/Within_the_Bounds_of_Orthodoxy.pdf.
Miskotte, H. H. "Het Lijden is in God: Over Jürgen Moltmann's Trinitarische Kruistheologie." *Rondom het Woord* 4, no. 15 (1973): 35–48.
Moltmann, Jürgen. *Theologie der Hoffnung: Untersuchungen zur Begründung und zu den Konsequenzen einer christlichen Eschatologie.* München: Kaiser, 1966.
———. *Theology of Hope—On the Ground and the Implications of a Christian Eschatology.* London: SCM, 1967.
———. *Der gekreuzigte Gott.* Die Sprache der Befreiung. München: Kaiser, 1972.
———. *The Crucified God—the Cross of Christ As the Foundation and Criticism of Christian Theology.* London: SCM, 1973.
———. *Trinität; und Reich Gottes: Zur Gotteslehre.* München: Kaiser, 1980.
———. *The Trinity and the Kingdom—The Doctrine of God.* New York: Harper and Row, 1981.
———. *Das kommen Gottes: Chrtstliche Eschatologie.* Gütersloh: Chr. Kaiser/Gütersloher Verlagshaus, 1995.
———. *The Coming of God—Christian Eschatology.* Minneapolis: Fortress, 1996.
Morgan, M. "Federal Vision: The Issue for This Generation." *By Faith* 17 (October 2007): 1–14.
Motry, Hubert Louis. *The Concept of Mortal Sin in Early Christianity.* Washington, D.C.: The Catholic University of America, 1920.
Mühlen, Herebert. *Die Veranderlichkeit Gottes als Horizont einer zukünftigen Christologie.* Munster: Aschendorff, 1969.
Murphy, T. *Pastoral Theology.* Dallas, TX: Primedia eLaunch, 2013.
Murray, Alexander. *Suicide in the Middle Ages.* Vol. 2. *The Curse on Self-Murder.* New York: Oxford University Press, 2000/2011.
———. *Suicide in the Middle Ages.* Vol. 1. *The Violent Against Themselves.* New York: Oxford University Press, 2009.

Murray-Swank, N. A., and Kenneth I. Pargament. "God, Where Are You?: Evaluating a Spiritually-integrated Intervention for Sexual Abuse." *Mental Health, Religion and Culture* 8, no. 3 (2005): 191–203.

Nazianzen, Gregory. "Select Orations of Saint Gregory Nazianzen: Oration 40.41." In *A Select Library of Nicene and Post-Nicene Fathers of the Christian Church*, edited by Philip Schaff and Henry Wace. New York: Christian Literature Company, 1894.

Nettles T. "Early Baptists and Easy-Believism." *The Founders Journal Issue* 6 (Fall 1991): www.Founders.org/journal/fj06/article3.html.

Newport, John P. (1917–2000). *Life's Ultimate Questions: A Contemporary Philosophy of Religion*. Dallas: Word, 1989; 644p, a monumental work.

Nicene-Constantinopolitan Creed (AD 381). Accessed November 6, 2010, www.iclnet.org/pub/resources/text/history/nicene381.html.

Nichols, M. P. *Family Therapy Concepts and Methods*. Boston: Allyn & Bacon, 2010.

Noon, Georgia, "On Suicide." *Journal of the History of Ideas* 39, no. 3 (Jul-Sept. 1978): 371–386.

Norton, Herman A. *Struggling for Recognition: The United States Army Chaplaincy 1791–1865*, Vol. 2 of 7 of history of Army Chaplaincy (see U.S. Army ref. for all 7 vols.). U.S. Army, 1977.

Oates, W. E. *Pastoral Counseling*. Philadelphia, PA: Westminster Press, 1974.

———. *The Christian Pastor*, 3rd rev. ed. Philadelphia, PA: Westminster Press, 1982.

O'Conner, Thomas P. "What Works: Religion as a Correctional Intervention: Part II." *Journal of Community Corrections* 14, no. 2 (Winter 2004–05): 4–26.

Oden, Thomas C. *Kerygma and Counseling: Toward a Covenant Ontology for Secular Psychotherapy*. Philadelphia: Westminster Press, 1966.

———. *Transforming Practice: Pastoral Theology in an Age of Uncertainty*. 2nd ed.; Eugene, OR: Wipf and Stock, 2002.

———, and Mark Sheridan, eds. *Ancient Christian Commentary on Scripture, Genesis 12–50*. Downers Grove: IVP, 2002.

Oglesby, William B. *Referral in Pastoral Counseling*. Nashville, TN: Abingdon Press, 1978.

———. *Biblical Themes for Pastoral Care*. Nashville, TN: Abingdon Press, 1980.

Osborne, Grant R., and Clinton E. Arnold. *Matthew. Zondervan Exegetical Commentary on the New Testament*. Grand Rapids: Zondervan Publishing, 2010.

Ott, H. *Die Antwort des Glaubens*. Berlin: Kreuz, 1972.

Otto, E. & O. Schramm. *Fest und Freude*. Stuttgart: Kohlhammer, 1977.

Packer, J. I. *Knowing God*. 20th Anniversary Edition. Downers Grove: IVP, 1993.

———. *Evangelism and the Sovereignty of God*. Downers Grove, IL: IVP, 1991.

———. "Understanding the Lordship Controversy." *Tabletalk* (May 1991). Ligonier Ministries. See www.Monergism.com/understanding-lordship-controversy/, which is a reprint of that article on this massive Reformed site.

Pannenberg, Wolfhart (1928–2014). *Systematic Theology*. Translated by Geoffrey William Bromiley. 3 Vols. Grand Rapids: Eerdmans, 1993 (1991–1998); first published *Systematische Theologie* (Göttingen, Germany: Vandenhoeck & Reupreck, 1988).

———. *Theology and the Kingdom of God*. Westminster Press, 1969.

———. *Theology and the Philosophy of Science*. Westminster Press, 1976.

———. *Anthropology in Theological Perspective*. T&T Clark, 1985.

Park, C. L., C. M. Aldwin, S. Choun, L. George, D. P. Suresh, and D. Bliss. "Spiritual Peace Predicts 5-Year Morality in Congestive Heart Failure Patients." *Health Psychology* 35, no. 3 (March 2015): 2003-201. See conclusion, "Spiritual peace ... were better predictors of mortality risk ... than were physical health indicators." See www.ncbi.nlm.nih.gov/pubmed/26414488.

Pargament, Kenneth I. *The Psychology of Religion and Coping: Theory, Research Practice*. NY: Guilford Press, 1997.

Pascal, Blaise (1623–62). *Pascal's Pensées*. NY: E.P. Dutton, 1958 (1st in French, incomplete at his death, pub. posthumously 1670).

Pastoral Care Council of the ACT. "Spiritual Care." Accessed online in 2016, http://pastoralcareact.org/pastoral.html. Web site set to expire August 2019. ACT: Australian Capital Territory.

Patton, John. *Pastoral Care in Context. An Introduction to Pastoral Care.* Louisville: Westminster/John Knox Press, 1993.

Pausanias (110–180 A.D.). *Pausanias's Description of Greece,* vol. 1. Trans. and commentary by J. G. Frazer. London: MacMillan and Co. Limited, 1898. Pausanias conducted histories of the Athenian topography of the mid-second century.

Payne, Leanne. *Restoring the Christian Soul—Overcoming Barriers to Completion in Christ through Healing Prayer.* Grand Rapids: Baker Books, 1996.

Perry, Greg. "To Know and Be Known: How Christ's Love Moves Us into Intimacy, Humility, and Risk. Sermon on John 13:1–17," in *All for Jesus—A Celebration of the 50th Anniversary of Covenant Theological Seminary,* edited by Robert A. Peterson and Sean Michael Lucas (Ross-shire, Great Britain: Mentor, 2006), 371–76.

Peterson, Robert A., and Sean Michael Lucas. *All for Jesus—A Celebration of the 50th Anniversary of Covenant Theological Seminary.* Ross-shire, Great Britain: Mentor, 2006.

Pink, Arthur W. "Gleanings in Genesis." Accessed September 27, 2010, www.BibleBelievers.com/Pink/Gleanings_Genesis/genesis_21.htm.

Piper, John. *Let the Nations Be Glad!* Grand Rapids, MI: Baker Academics, 1993.

Pitre, Brant. *Jesus, The Tribulation, and The End of The Exile.* Tübingen: Mohr Siebeck; Grand Rapids: Baker Academic, 2005.

Plato (c. 427-347 BC). *Phaedo.* c. 360 BC. See translation with notes by Professor David Gallop of Trent University, Ontario (Oxford: Clarendon Press, 1975), www.faculty.umb.edu/gary_zabel/Phil_100/Plato_files/310585462-Plato-Phaedo.pdf.

Plantinga, Alvin. "A Sermon for Advent: I Believe in Jesus Christ, God's Only Son, Our Lord." In *Exploring and Proclaiming the Apostles' Creed,* edited by Roger E. Van Harn (Grand Rapids: Eerdmans, 2004).

Post, S. G., C. M. Puchalski, and D. B. Larson. "Physicians and Patient Spirituality: Professional Boundaries, Competency, and Ethics." *Annals of Internal Medicine* 132, no. 7 (April 2000): 578–583. See www.ncbi.nlm.nih.gov/pubmed/10744595.

Pratt, John. "Child Sexual Abuse: Purity and Danger in an Age of Anxiety." *Crime, Law and Social Change* 43, no. 4-5 (2005): 263–287.

Preston, Aaron. "Redeeming Moral Formation: The Unity of Spiritual and Moral Formation in Willardian Thought." *Journal of Spiritual Formation & Soul Care* 3, no. 2 (November 2010): 206–229.

PricewaterhouseCoopers. "Driving the Bottom Line: Improving Retention." Saratoga, PricewaterhouseCoopers LLP, 2006. See www.shrm.org/hr-today/news/hr-magazine/Documents/saratoga-improving-retention.pdf.

Puchalski, Christina M., and A. L. Romer. "Taking a Spiritual History Allows Clinicians to Understand Patients More Fully." *Journal of Palliative Medicine* 3, no. 1 (Spring 2000): 129–137. See www.ncbi.nlm.nih.gov/pubmed/15859737.

———, Betty Ferrell, Rose Virani, Shirley Otis-Green, Pamela Baird, Janet Bull, Harvey Chochinov, George Handzo, Holly Nelson-Becker, Maryjo Prince-Paul, Karen Pugliese, and Daniel Sulmasy. "Improving the Quality of Spiritual Care as a Dimension of Palliative Care: the Report of the Consensus Conference," *Journal of Palliative Medicine* 12, no. 10 (October 2009): 885–904. See www.ncbi.nlm.nih.gov/pubmed/19807235, and full article here, https://smhs.gwu.edu/gwish/sites/gwish/files/jpm.2009.pdf.

———, Robert Vitillo, Sharon K. Hull, and Nancy Reller. "Improving the Spiritual Dimension of Whole Person Care: Reaching National and International Consensus." *Journal of Palliative Medicine* 17:6 (2014): 642. See article here, www.ncbi.nlm.nih.gov/pmc/articles/PMC4038982/.

———, and Betty Ferrell. *Making Health Care Whole: Integrating Spirituality into Patient Care.* West Conshocken, PA: Templeton Press, 2010. For Puchalski PowerPoint of essence of book, https://pdfs.semanticscholar.org/1ea2/4c6af3696f2a8ab40881226af2d9ba5e461f.pdf.

Reasoner, Mark. *Romans in Full Circle—A History of Interpretation.* Louisville: Westminster John Knox Press, 2005.

Reed, Sarah J. "Shame and Hope in Sexual Addiction." *Journal of Ministry in Addiction & Recovery* 7, no. 1 (2000): 9–17.

Reisinger, Ernest. "The Lordship Controversy and the Carnal Christian Teaching" (Part 1). *The Founders Journal* 16 (Spring 1994), www.Founders.org/journal/fj16/article2.html.

———. "The Lordship Controversy and the Carnal Christian Teaching" (Part 2). *The Founders Journal* 17 (Spring 1994), https://founders.org/journals/reformation-mindset-issue-16-spring-1994/.

———. "The Lordship Controversy and Repentance." *The Founders Journal* 14 (Fall 1993).

Reynolds, N., S. Mrug, L. Britton, K. Guion, K. Wolfe, and H. Gutierrez. "Spiritual Coping Predicts 5-year Health Outcomes in Adolescents with Cystic Fibrosis." *Journal of Cystic Fibrosis* 13, no. 5 (2014): 593–600. See www.ncbi.nlm.nih.gov/pubmed/24534722.

Ridderbos, H. *Paulus: Ontwerp van zijn theologie*. Kampen: Kok, 1966.

Ritchie, Nelly "Mujer y Cristología," in *El Rostro Femenino de la Teología*, edited by María Pilar Aquino (San José: Departamento Ecuménico de Investigaciones, 1986).

Rogers, Carl (1902–87). *Client-Centered Therapy*, Its Current Practice, Implications, and Theory. Boston: Houghton Mifflin, 1951.

———. *On Becoming a Person*. Boston: Houghton Mifflin, 1961.

———. "Empathic: An Unappreciated Way of Being," *The Counseling Psychologist* 5 (1975): 2–10. A classic definition.

———. *Way of Being*. Boston: Houghton Mifflin, 1980.

Rowland, Christopher, ed. *Cambridge Companion to Liberation Theology* Cambridge: Cambridge University Press, 2007.

Rushdoony, R. J., (1916–2001). *Sovereignty*. New York: Ross House Books, 2008 (published posthumously).

———. *Institutes of Biblical Law: A Chalcedon Study*. Nutley, NJ: Craig Press, 1973.

———. *Philosophy of the Christian Curriculum*. Vallecito, CA: Ross House Books, 1981

Sanders, E. P. *Paul and Palestinian Judaism*. Philadelphia, PA: SCM Press Ltd., 1977.

Sauter, Gerhard, Arthur Sutherland, and Stephen Kläs. "God Creating Faith: The Doctrine of Justification from the Reformation to the Present." *Lutheran Quarterly* 11, no. 1 (March 1, 1997): 17–102. ATLA Religion Database with ATLASerials, EBSCOhost, accessed October 26, 2012.

Schaff, Philip, and Henry Wace, eds. *A Select Library of Nicene and Post-Nicene Fathers of the Christian Church*. VII. New York: The Christian Literature Company, 1894.

Schneider, Sandra M. "Theology and Spirituality: Strangers, Rivals, or Partners?" *Horizons* 13, no. 2 (1986): 253–274.

Schütz, P. *Freiheit—Hoffnung—Prophetie: Von der Gegenwärtigkeit des Zukünftigen*. Hamburg: Furche Verlag, 1963.

Schwertley, Brian. *The Auburn Avenue Theology*. N.d. Cf. www.reformedonline.com/uploads/1/5/0/0/3/15030584/chapter_1_auburn_avenue.pdf and https://en.wikipedia.org/wiki/Federal_Vision.

———. "A Refutation of the Auburn Avenue Theology's Rejection of Justification by Faith Alone." Accessed January 2, 2011, www.reformedonline.com/view/reformedonline/A%20Refutation%20of%20the%20Auburn%20Avenue%20Theology.htm#_ftnref12.

———. *Auburn Avenue Theology: A Biblical Analysis*. Forthcoming, www.ReformedOnline.com/view/reformedonline/A%20Refutation%20of%20the%20Auburn%20Avenue%20Theology.html.

Seegobin, Winston, Mark R. McMinn, Ryan C. Staley, and Kurt C. Webb. "Just What Is Christian Counseling Anyway?" *Professional Psychology, Research and Practice* 41, no. 5 (October 2010): 391–397.

Segundo, Juan Luis. *El Hombre de Hoy ante Jesús e Nazaret*, II/1. Madrid: Cristiandad, 1982.

Senkbeil, Harold L. *Sanctification—Christ in Action*. Milwaukee: Northwestern Publishing House, 2005.

Sethi, Sheena, and Martin E. P. Seligman. "Optimism and Fundamentalism." *Psychological Science* 4, no. 4 (July 1993): 256–259. See www.jstor.org/stable/40062552.

———. "The Hope of Fundamentalists." *Psychological Science* 5, no. 1 (January 1994): 58. See https://psycnet.apa.org/record/1994-29394-001.

Shepherd, V. *Calvin on Justification*. Accessed January 14, 2011, www.VictorShepherd.on.ca/Course/Reformation/justification.htm.

Sherman, A. C., T. V. Merluzzi. J. E. Pustejovsky, C. L. Park, L. George, G. Fitchett, H. S. Jim, A. R. Munoz, S. C. Danhauer, M. A. Snyder, and J. M. Salsman. "A Meta-analytic Review of Religious or Spiritual Involvement and Social Health Among Cancer Patients." *Cancer* 121, no. 21 (2015): 3779–3788. See https://www.ncbi.nlm.nih.gov/pubmed/26258730. "In total, 78

independent samples encompassing 14,277 patients were included in the meta-analysis. Social health was significantly associated with overall R/S [Religion and Spirituality]."
Shults, F. LeRon. *Reforming Theological Anthropology—After the Philosophical Turn to Relationality.* Grand Rapids: Eerdmans, 2003.
Simpson, Michael L. *Permission Evangelism: When to Talk, When to Walk.* Colorado Springs: Cook Communications Ministries, 2003.
Sjöberg, Ekik. "Wiedergeburt und Neuschopfung im palastinischen Judentum (Rebirth and new creation in Palestinian Judaism)." *Studia Theologica – Nordic Journal of Theology* 4, no. 1 (1950): 44-85.
Silva, Moisés. *Philippians.* 2nd ed. Grand Rapids: Baker Academic, 2005 (1st 1992).
Simon, Ulrich E. *A Theology of Auschwitz.* London: Victor Gollancz, 1967. Herein, "Auschwitz" becomes the symbol for the evil that happened there, and he struggles with the Fatherhood of God in that light.
Smedes, Lewis. *Union with Christ—A Biblical View of The New Life in Jesus Christ.* 2nd ed. Grand Rapids: Eerdmans, 1983 [orig. pub. 1970].
Smith, B. *The Grace Escape—Jesus as Savior and Lord.* Nashville: Broadman, 1991.
Smith, Terry Ann. *Think About It, Consider It, Tell Us What to Do—Can Some of the Most Violent Texts of the Old Testament Be Redeemed?* Canada: Essence Publishing, 2002.
———. "Warring Words in the Book of Daniel." In *The Oxford Handbook of Biblical Narrative* (Oxford University Press, 2016; 266–275).
Smith, Terry Ann, and Deborah A. Appler. *Ezra-Nehemiah.* Vol. 14. *Wisdom Commentary Series.* Liturgical Press, forthcoming.
Sobrino, Jon. *Jesucristo Liberador, Lectura Histórico-Teológica de Jesús de Nazaret.* Madrid: Trotta, 1991.
———. *Jesús en América Latina, su significado para la fe y la cristología.* Santander: Salterrae, 1982.
Solberg, Mary. *Compelling Knowledge—A Feminist Proposal for an Epistemology of the Cross.* Albany: State University of New York Press, 1997.
Soothill, K., S. M. Morris, J. C. Harman, C. Thomas, B. Francis, and M. B. McIllmurray. "Cancer and Faith. Having Faith—Does It Make a Difference among Patients and Their Informal Carers?" *Scandinavian Journal of Caring Sciences* 16, no. 3 (September 2002): 256–263. See www.ncbi.nlm.nih.gov/pubmed/12191037. Of 402 questionnaires, "Not surprisingly, both patients and carers with faith identified a greater need for opportunities for personal prayer, support from people of their own faith and support from a spiritual adviser."
Sorajjakool, Siroj. *When Sickness Heals. The Place of Religious Belief in Healthcare.* Philadelphia and London: Templeton Foundation Press, 2006.
Spina, Frank Anthony. *The Faith of the Outsider—Exclusion and Inclusion in the Biblical Story.* Grand Rapids: Eerdmans, 2005.
Steffen, Lloyd H. "Victims and Sinners: Spiritual Roots of Addiction and Recovery," *Christian Century* 115, no. 21 (1998): 728–22.
Stein, Robert H. *Mark. Baker Exegetical Commentary on the New Testament.* Grand Rapids: Baker Books, 2008.
Stewart, Gary P., William R. Cutrer, Timothy J. Demy, Dónal P. O'Mathúna, Paige C. Cunningham, John F. Kilner, and Linda K. Bevington. *Basic Questions on Suicide and Euthanasia.* Grand Rapids, MI: Kregel Publications, 1998.
Stock, Ely. "The Biblical Context of 'Ethan Brand.'" *American Literature* 37, no. 2 (May 1965): 115–34.
Stone, Howard W. *Strategies for Brief Pastoral Counseling.* Minneapolis, MN: Fortress Press, 2001.
Storms, Sam. "The Lordship Salvation Debate." Enjoying God Ministries (2006): www.EnjoyingGodMinistries.com/article/the-lordship-salvation-debate, which deflects to: www.SamStorms.com/all-articles/post/the-lordship-salvation-debate/.
Stott, John R. W. *The Epistles of John.* Tyndale Commentary Series. Grand Rapids, MI: Eerdmans, 1960.
———. *The Message of Acts.* The Bible Speaks Today Series (ed. John R. W. Stott). Downers Grove: InterVarsity Press, 1990.
Stover, Earl F. *Up From Handymen: The United States Army Chaplaincy 1865–1920,* Vol. 3 of 7 of history of Army Chaplaincy (see U.S. Army ref. for all 7 vols.). U.S. Army, 1977.
Strachey, J., ed. and trans. *Standard Edition of the Complete Psychological Works of Sigmund Freud.* London: Hogarth Press, 1962.
Strong, Stanley R. "Christian Counseling: A Synthesis of Psychological and Christian Concepts." *The Personnel and Guidance Journal* 58, no. 9 (1980): 589–592.

Strümpfer, J W. "The Strengths Perspective: Fortigenesis in Adult Life." *Journal for Social Indicators Research* 77, no. 1 (2006): 11–36.
Stuart, Douglas. *Hosea-Jonah*. Vol. 32. *Word Biblical Commentary*. Eedited by Hubbard A. David and Glenn W. Barker. Dallas: Word Books, 1987.
Stuhlmacher, Peter. *Revisiting Paul's Doctrine of Justification: A Challenge to the New Perspective*. Translated by Daniel P. Bailey. Downers Grove: IVP, 2001.
Sweazy, Mary. "The Sexual Addiction." *St. Vladimir's Theological Quarterly* 32, no. 3 (1988): 273–286.

Talbert, Charles H. *Ephesians and Colossians*. Paideia; Grand Rapids: Baker, 2007.
Tamburello, Dennis E. *Union with Christ: John Calvin and the Mysticism of St. Bernard*. Louisville: John Knox Press, 1994.
Tamez, Elsa. "The Power of Nudity." In *Faith Born in the Struggle for Life*, edited by Dow Kirkpatrick. Michigan: Eerdmans Publishing, 1988.
———. "Women Re-reading the Bible." In *With Passion and Compassion—Third World Women Doing Theology*, edited by Virginia Favella and Mercy Amba Oduyoye. Oregon: Wipf & Stock Publishers, 2006.
———. *Las Mujeres en el Movimiento de Jesús, El Cristo*. Quito: Consejo Latinoamericano de Iglesias, 2004.
Taylor, Charles. *Sources of the Self—The Making of the Modern Identity Sources of the Self*. Cambridge, MA: Harvard University Press, 1989.
Taylor, Robert Joseph, Linda M. Chatters and R. Khari Brown. "African American Religious Participation." *Review of Religious Research* 56, no. 4 (December 2014): 513–538.
Temple, C.N. "Lordship Salvation: Is it Biblical? A Study of the Lordship Salvation Controversy Part One." Accessed January 20, 2011, www.DTL.org/salvation/article/guest/lordship-1.htm.
Thompson, Parker C. *From Its European Antecedents to 1791: The United States Army Chaplaincy*. Vol. 1 of 7 of history of Army Chaplaincy (see U.S. Army ref. for all 7 vols.). U.S. Army, 1978.
Thurneysen, E. *Der Mensch von Heute und das Evangelium*. Zurich: Theologiscber Verlag, 1964.
Tipson, Baird. "A Dark Side of Seventeenth-Century English Protestantism: The Sin against the Holy Spirit." *The Harvard Theological Review* 77, no. 3–4 (July-Oct. 1984).
Tillich, Paul. *The Courage to Be*, 2nd ed. New Haven: Yale University, 2000; 1st 1952.
———. *Christianity and the Encounter of the World Religions*. NY: Columbia University Press, 1963.
Tonry, Michael. *Oxford Handbook of Crime and Criminal Justice*. UK: Oxford University Press, 2011.
Torrance, Thomas F., (1913-2007). *Theology in Reconstruction*. Grand Rapids, MI: Eerdmans, 1965; Wipf & Stock, 1996.
———. *Theology in Reconciliation: Essays Towards Evangelical and Catholic Unity in East and West*. Grand Rapids: Eerdmans, 1975; Eugene, OR: Wipf & Stock, 1996.
Torrance, Thomas F. *The Christian Doctrine of God, One Being Three Persons*. Edinburgh: T&T Clark, 1996.
Truman, J. L., and M. R. Rand. *Criminal Victimization, 2009*. Washington, D.C.: U.S. Department of Justice, 2010.
Turner, David L. *Matthew. Baker Exegetical Commentary on the New Testament*. Grand Rapids: Baker Books, 2008.

Utazi, C. M. *The Nature and Subject Matter of Pastoral Theology*. Nairobi, Kenya: Salesian Theological College, 2012.

VandeCreek, Larry, and Laurel Burton, eds. "Professional Chaplaincy: Its Role and Importance in Healthcare." *The Journal of Pastoral Care* 55, no. 1 (Spring 2001): 81–97. See www.ProfessionalChaplains.org/chaplaincy_importance, for this extraordinary joint statement of the five largest chaplaincy bodies representing 10,000-plus members.
Van Dyk, A. *HIV/AIDS Care and Counselling. A Multidisciplinary Approach*. Cape Town: Maskew Miller, 2005.
Van Harn, Roger E., ed. *Exploring and Proclaiming the Apostles' Creed*. Grand Rapids: Eerdmans, 2004.
Van Kooten, Geurt Hendrik. *Cosmic Christology in Paul & the Pauline School: Colossians & Ephesians in the Context of Graeco-Roman Cosmology, with a New Synopsis of the Greek Texts. Wissenschaftliche Untersuchungen Zum Neuen Testament* 2. Tübingen: Mohr Siebeck, 2003.
Van Ruler, A. *Op gezag van een apostel*. Nijkerk: Callenbach, 1971.

Venzke, Rodger R. *Confidence in Battle, Inspiration in Peace: The United States Army Chaplaincy 1945–1975*, Vol. 5of 7 of history of Army Chaplaincy (see U.S. Army ref. for all 7 vols.). U.S. Army, 1977.

Vicuña, Eleodoro Vargas. *Taita Cristo*. Lima: 1963.

Vuola, Elina. *Limits of Liberation. Feminist Theology and the Ethics of Poverty and Reproduction*. London: Sheffield Academic Press, 2002.

Wagner, J., and M. Rehfuss. "Self-injury, Sexual self-concept, and a conservative Christian upbringing: An exploratory study of three young women's perspectives." *Journal of Mental Health Counseling* 30, no. 2 (2008): 173–188.

Wagner, Joyce A. "Sexual Steve: A Schema-Focused, Spiritually Based Approach." *Journal of Psychology and Christianity* 28, no. 3 (2009): 275–279.

Wallace, Daniel B. *Greek Grammar Beyond the Basics—An Exegetical Syntax of the New Testament*. Grand Rapids: Zondervan, 1996.

Wardekker, Willem L., and Siebren Miedema. "Denominational School Identity and the Formation of Personal Identity." *Religious Education* 96, no. 1 (2001): 36–48.

Waters, Guy Prentiss. *The Federal Vision and Covenant Theology: A Comparative Analysis*. Annotated edition. New York: P&R Publishing, 2006.

Watt, Jeffrey R. "Calvin on Suicide." *Church History* 66, no. 3 (Sept. 1997): 463-476.

Weber, Otto. *Foundations of Dogmatics*. 2 Vols. Translated by Darrell L. Guder. Grand Rapids: Eerdmans, 1983.

Webster, D. C., and E. C. Dunn. "Feminist Perspectives on Trauma." *Women and Therapy* 28, no. 3 (2005): 111–142.

Webster, John. *Barth's Ethics of Reconciliation*. Cambridge: Cambridge University, 1995.

———, ed. *The Cambridge Companion to Karl Barth*. NY: Cambridge University, 2000.

Wenham, Gordon J. *Word Biblical Commentary: Genesis 16–50*. Dallas: Word, 1998.

Westminster Confession of Faith. 1646. Accessed January 5, 2011, www.GraceFallBrook.com/westminster_standards/The_Westminster_Confession_of_Faith.pdf.

Westminster Shorter Catechism. 1648. Accessed January 5, 2011, www.PuritanSeminary.org/media/Shorter_Catechism.pdf.

Wheeler, Gordon. "Self and Shame: A Gestalt Approach." *Gestalt Review* 1, no. 3 (1997): 221–244, www.gisc.org/gestaltreview/documents/selfandshameagestaltapproach.pdf.

Whetten, K., J. Leserman, K. Lowe, D. Stangl, N. Thielman, M. Swertz, et al. "Prevalence of childhood sexual abuse and physical trauma in an HIV-Positive sample from the deep south." *American Journal of Public Health*. 96, no. 6 (2006): 1028–1030.

White, Mark A. *Cybersex Temptation and Use among Clergy: Prevalence and Path Analysis of the Role of Sexuality Education, Isolation, and Consequences as Vulnerability Factors*. Ph.D. diss., Texas Tech University, 2009, https://ttu-ir.tdl.org/ttu-ir/bitstream/2346/45370/1/White_Mark_Diss.pdf.

White, Mark A., and Thomas G. Kimball. "Attributes of Christian Couples with a Sexual Addiction to Internet Pornography." *Journal of Psychology and Christianity* 28, no. 4 (2009): 350–359.

Whitehouse, G. "Unimaginable Variations: Christian Responsibility in the Cinema of Broken Identity." *Literature & Theology* 18, no. (2004): 321–350.

Wiles, Maurice. *The Making of Christian Doctrine—A Study in the Principles of Early Doctrinal Development*. Cambridge: Cambridge University Press, 1975.

Wilkin, Robert N. "We believe in Sanctification. Part 2: Past Sanctification." *Journal of the Grace Evangelical Society* 6, no. 10 (Spring 1993): https://faithalone.org/journal/1993i/Wilkin.htm.

———. "We believe in Sanctification. Part 3: Man's Role in Present Sanctification." *Journal of the Grace Evangelical Society*. 7, no. 13 (Autumn 1994).

William J. Hill, *The Three-Personed God: The Trinity as a Mystery of Salvation*. Washington, D.C.: Catholic University of America Press, 1988.

Williams, Jarvis J. *Maccabean Martyr Traditions in Paul's Theology of Atonement—Did Martyr Theology Shape Paul's Conception of Jesus' Death?* Eugene, OR: Wipf & Stock, 2010.

Williams, N. H. *Theology of Sanctification*. Jenkintown, PA: World Harvest Mission, 2002.

Wilson, D. *Reformed Is Not Enough—Recovering the Objectivity of the Covenant*. Moscow, ID. Canon Press, 2002.

Wolff, Hans W. *A Commentary on the Book of Hosea.* Translated by G. Stansell. Edited by P. Hanson. Philadelphia: Fortress Press, 1974.
Woodward, James, and Stephen Pattison, eds. *The Blackwell Reader in Pastoral and Practical Theology.* Malden, MA: Blackwell Publishing, 2000.
Worden, J. W. *Grief Counseling and Grief Therapy: A Handbook for the Mental Health Practitioner*, 4th ed. NY: Springer Publishing, 2009.
Woman's Study Bible. Nashville, TN.: Thomas Nelson Publishers, 1995.
Wright, N. T. *Justification—God's Plan & Paul's Vision.* Downers Grove: IVP, 2009.
———. *New Perspectives on Paul.* Rutherford House, Edinburgh: 10th Edinburgh Dogmatics Conference, August 25–28, 2003, accessed on January 15, 2011, www.NTWrightpage.com/Wright_New_Perspectives.htm.
Wycliffe Bible Dictionary. Peobody, MA: Hendrickson Pub., 1998.

Yong, Amos. *The Spirit Poured Out on All Flesh—Pentecostalism and the Possibility of Global Theology.* Grand Rapids: Baker Academic, 2005.
———. *Theology and Down Syndrome: Reimagining Disability in Late Modernity.* Waco, TX: Baylor University Press, 2007.
———. *The Bible, Disability, and the Church: A New Vision of the People of God.* Grand Rapids and Cambridge, UK: Eerdmans, 2011.
———. *Cambridge Companion to Pentecostalism.* Cambridge: Cambridge University, 2014.

Zastrow, C., and K. Kirst-Ashman. *Understanding Human Behavior and the Social Environment.* 8th ed. Belmont, CA: Brooks/Cole, 2010.
Zizioulas, John D. "On Being a Person. Towards an Ontology of Personhood." In *Persons, Divine, and Human—King's College Essays in Theological Anthropology*, edited by Christoph Schwobel and Colin E. Gunton. Edinburgh: T&T Clark, 1991.
———. *Being as Communion—Studies in Personhood and the Church.* London: Darton, Longman and Todd Ltd., 2004.
———. *Lectures in Christian Dogmatics.* Edited by Douglas H. Knight. London: T&T Clark, 2008.

Indices

Persons 295
Scripture & Semi-sacred References 298
Books, Journals, and Publications 301
General 304

Persons

Abba, 197
Abel, 19
Abelard, Peter, 51
Abraham, 18, 19, 21, 22, 23, 24, 187, 210
Abram, 15, 16, 17, 18, 20, 21, 22
Ackerman, Susan, 35, 36
Ackermann, Henry F., 129
Adam, 19, 176
Adams, Jay E., 148
Aesculapius, 147
Aggebo. A., 254
Aldwin, C. M., 154
Alexander of Hales, 52
Alighieri, Dante, 45, 54, 58, 59
Allen, Guenther R., 34
Allen, Kenneth W., 224, 226
Ambrose, 48, 51
Amnon, 172
Amorn, Melissa, 152
Amundsen, Darrel W., 47, 48, 49, 60
Anderson, Francis I., 36
Appler, Deborah A., 29
Aquinas, Thomas, 51, 52, 53, 54, 55, 56, 58, 191
Aquino, María Pilar, 79
Arends, Carolyn, 166
Aristotle, 46, 55, 89, 91, 92
Arnold, Clinton E., 61
Ascol, Tom, 216, 217
Astrow, Alan B., 153, 154
Athanasius, 103
Augsburger, David, 228
Augustine, 16, 46, 47, 48, 49, 51, 52, 55, 56, 59, 159
Aurelius, Marcus, 46
Austin, J. L., 189
Aves, John, 90

Bailey, Daniel P., 186
Balboni, M. J., 145, 154
Balboni, Tracy A., 145, 153
Barker, Glenn W., 31
Barth, Karl, 242, 249, 259
Bathsheba, 269
Baym, Nina, 59

Belcher, Richard, 213
Bell-Tolliver, LaVerne, xiv, 171, 175
Benner, David G., 144
Bennett, James V., 128
Bentley, J., 164
Berkhof, Hendrikus, 246
Berkouwer, G.C., 97, 99, 248
Bernard of Clairvaux, 52, 196
Beveridge, Henry, 98
Bevington, Linda K., 43, 64
Billings, J. T., 203
Bingham, Jeffrey D., 5
Blake, William, 59
Bliss, D., 154
Bloch, Ernst, 234
Block, S. D., 145
Blokland, Arjan, 129
Blomberg, Craig, 105, 108
Blum, T. C., 155
Boaz, 269
Bock, Darrell L., 61
Boisen, Anton T., 128
Bornkamp, G., 247
Borras, Laurence, 151
Böschemeyer, Uwe, 257
Braaten, Carl E., 192
Brand, Ethan, 59
Brandt, Pierre-Yves, 151
Bridges, W., 164
Brinsfield, John W., 129
Britton, L., 154
Bromiley, Geoffrey William, 100
Brown, Brené, 264
Buddadhumaruk, P., 154
Burton, Laurel, 156
Bynum, Deborah, 152

Cain, 19
Calvin, John/Jean, x, 54, 55, 56, 98, 195, 202, 203, 219
Cardona, J. R., 173, 180
Carlson, Melissa, 145
Carson, Verna Benner, 152
Carter, Melissa A., 152
Castells, M., 233
Chadwick, Henry, 106

Chadwick, Owen, 224
Chatters, L.M., 175
Chavez, Patricia Cuyatti, 67
Chin, M. H., 154
Choun, S., 154
Christiansen, Ellen Juhl, 32
Chrysostom, 46, 48
Ciampa, R. C., 152
Cicero, 55
Clark, P. A., 153
Clement, 48
Clinebell, Howard, 128, 149
Coe, John H., 168
Cohen, Norman J., 158
Collins, C. John, 185
Collins, John J., 187
Collins, Raymond F., 106, 108
Colson, Charles, ix
Crabtree, J. A., 266
Crisp, B. R., 173, 175, 179, 181, 182
Cunningham, Peter C., 43, 64
Cupitt, Don, 84
Curlin, F. A., 154
Cox, Dorian Coover, 5
Cutrer, William R., 43, 64
Cykert, Sam, 152
Cyprian, 48

Danhauer, S. C., 154
Daniel, 186, 187
Dante Alighieri, 45, 54, 58, 59
David, Hubbard A., 31
Dawkins, Richard, xiii
De Jong, J.M., 247
Deak, Andrew J., 152
Dearman, J. Andrew, 31
Deffinbaugh, Bob, 23
Deifelt, Wanda, 79
DelHousaye, John, 185
Demy, Timothy J., xiv, 43, 46, 47, 63, 64
Descartes. René, 88
Didymus the Blind, 17
Dillard, J. M., 229
Dillistone, F. W., 225, 226, 227, 229
Donne, John, 59

Doolittle, B. R., 154
Doré, Gustave, 59
Drain, M., 153
Droge, Arthur J., 47
Dunn, E.C., 173
Dunn, James D. G., 208, 211
Dushwick, B., 152

Ebeling, Gerhard, 247
Edwards, Jonathan, 1
Egorova, N., 153
Ehman, J. W., 152
Eisenberg, Nancy, 128
Eleazar, 188
Emanuel, Linda L., 145
Embrey, Tim, 155
Ephraim, 33, 36, 245
Epicurus, 147
Epimenides of Cnossos, 266
Ernecoff, N. C., 154
Eusebius, 51
Evans, Keith A., 141, 142, 148
Everly, George S., 150
Ezekiel, 186

Faculdade Teologica, 199
Favella, Virginia, 77
Fee, Gordon D., 105
Feller, Bryan, 155
Fesko, J.V., 189, 202, 203, 205
Fiellin, D. A., 154
Finney, C.G., 178
Fitchett, G., 154
Flannelly, Kevin J., 145
Fletcher, S. K., 151
Fontes, L. A., 172, 173, 182
Fouque, L. A., 179
Francis, B., 151
Franco, Franco, 152
Frankl, Viktor, 256, 257
Franklin, Kirk, 272
Frazer, J. G., 147, 279
Freedman, David Noel, 30, 36, 40
Frend, W. H. C., 47
Fretheim, T.E., 243, 244, 245
Freud, Sigmund, 152
Fuchs, Ernst, 247

Galek, Kathleen, 145
Garcia, Frederico Duarte, 162
Gardoski, Kenneth M., 116
Gavielides, Theo, 129
Garrett, Joanne, 152
George, L., 154
Gerkin, Charles, 128
Gerstenberger, G., 253
Gesche, Adolphe., 247
Gifford Lectures, 87
Gilchrist, Sabrina N., 223
Gilchrist, Valerie J., 152
Gillieron, Christiane, 151
Girolami, Remigio de', 54
Glachan, M., 179

Gladding, Samuel, 229
Glanzer, Perry L., 160
Gleuck, Nelson, 35
Golden, Bernard, 264
Goldstein, Arnold P., 128
Goldstein, R., 153
Gollwitzer, H., 255
Goppelt, L., 248
Gorawara-Bhat, R., 154
Greenspun, W.S., 174
Gregoire, Louis J., 162
Gregory of Nazianzus, 95
Grenz, Stanley J., 96, 159, 271
Grossman, Steven D., 152
Grudem, Wayne, ix, 11, 21, 185
Guardini, Roman, 161
Guder, Darrell L., 96
Guillory, William A., 144
Guion, K., 154
Gunton, Colin E., 83, 84, 85, 86, 87, 90, 99, 102
Gushwa, Robert L., 129
Guthrie, D., 248
Gutierrez, H., 154

Hagar, x, 15, 16, 17, 18, 19, 20, 22, 23, 24, 26
Hagner, Donald A., 186
Hall, David, ix
Haller, E., 259
Handzo, George F., 145, 153
Hankin, Harriet, 155
Hannah, John D., 43
Hansen-Flaschen, J., 152
Hanson, P., 34
Hardin, M., 173, 180
Harley, D. A., 229
Harman, J. C., 151
Harris, Sam, xiii
Hawthorne, Gerald F., 4, 5, 6, 7
Hawthorne, Nathaniel, 59, 60
Hays, Richard B., 191
He, M. K., 153
Hefzy, Hebah, 152
Helminiak, Daniel, 158
Hill, William J., 85
Hiltner, Seward, 128
Hodges, Zane C., 214, 219
Homant, Robert J., 129
Home Banc, 155
Hooker, Richard, 57
Horrell, Joseph, 59
Horton, Michael Scott, 96
Hosea, x, 30, 32, 34, 39
Howard, James M., 270, 271
Huddlestun, John R., 30
Huguelet, Philippe, 151
Hull, Sharon K., 143
Hulme, William E., 224, 225, 227, 228, 229

Ignatius, 46
Immanuel, 237

Isaac, 21, 31
Ishmael, 18, 22, 23

Jacob, 31
James L. Mays, James L., 33
Janzen, J. Gerald, 34
Jang, Sung Joon, 129
Jensen, Robert W., 192
Jerome, 47, 48, 51
Jim, H. S., 154
John of Salisbury, 52
John of Wales, 52
Johnson, Byron R., 129, 134
Jonker, H., 248
Jordan, James, 203, 204
Judas, 47, 51
Jüngel, Eberhard, 189
Justice, A. C., 154

Kant, Immanuel, 87, 92
Käsemann, Ernst, 247
Kaufman, Gershen, 264
Kelly, John Norman Davidson, 106
Kendall, R. T., 114
Kerr, Ian T., 193
Kilner, John F., 43, 64
Kim, J., 173, 174, 175, 179, 182
Kim, Seyoon, 267
Kimball, Thomas G., 163, 164
King David, 269
King, Bridget D., 152
King, Dana E., 152
Kirk, Forrest L., 146
Kirk, J. R. Daniel, 189
Kirkpatrick, Dow, 79
Kirst-Ashman, K., 174
Kitamori, Kazoh, 239, 242
Klioze, Andria, 152
Knight, Douglas H., 97
Köberle, A., 254
Koenig, Don, 221
Koenig, Harold G., 151, 152, 153
Konrad, George G., 227, 228, 230
Koop, M., 151
Kreck, W., 243
Kreider, Glenn R., xiii, 1
Krell, Keith, 22
Küng, Hans, 238, 242, 258

Laaser, Mark R., 161, 162
Lactantius, 46, 48, 59
Ladd, G. E., 189
Langston, Michael, 142, 143
Lantos, J. D., 154
Larson, David B., 129, 134, 154
Lathan, C., 145
Lea, Henry Charles, 53, 54
Lehmann, Helmut T., 224
Lekkerkerker, Arie Frederik Nelis, 247
Leventhal, Barry R., 46
Levine, Stephen B., 163
Lewis, Helen Block, 264
Lewis, Michael, 264

Lillback, Peter A., ix, xii
Linder, R. D., 125
Lipton, D., 129
Lloyd-Jones, Martyn, 213
Lombard, Peter, 52
Longfellow, Henry Wadsworth, 58
Louw, Daniël J., 231, 233
Lucas, Sean Michael, 7
Lusk, R., 208, 209
Luther, Martin, x, 54, 56, 69, 107, 192, 219, 223
Lydia, 25

MacArthur, John, 214, 215, 217, 268
MacDonald, Michael, 57
MacLean, D. C., 152
Macmurray, John D., 87, 88, 89, 90, 94
Macrobius, 51
Magdalene, Mary, 178
Makidon, M., 209
Malone, M. P., 153
Maness, Michael G., ix, xi, xiii, xv, 127
Marcus, D., 163
Marin, D. B., 153
Martin, Alan M., xiv, 54, 56, 157, 192, 285
Martinson, R., 129
Martyr, Justin, 48
Mary, 20
Mattis, J. S., 151
Mattis, Kevaughn, xi, xiii, 263
Mays, James L., 34
Mays, James Luther, 39
McCord, Gary, 152
McCormick, Kenelm F., 152
McDonagh, E., 53
McGinn, Bernard, 196
McGinnis, Tracy, 155
McGrath, Alester E., 193
McGuiness, I., 54
McIllmurray, M. B., 151
McKinnon, Garrett, 155
McMinn, Mark R., 230
Melchizedek, 21
Melville, Herman, 59
Merluzzi, T. V., 154
Merrigan, Terrence, 193
Michaels, Gerald Y., 128
Miedema, Siebren, 159, 160
Miller, B.J., 173, 180
Miller, James E., 59
Milton, John, 59
Minich, Joseph, 209
Minos, 58
Miskotte, H.H., 243
Mohr, Sylvia, 151
Moltmann, Jürgen, 232, 236, 237, 238, 240, 241, 242, 243, 250
Monroe, Michael, 152
More, Thomas, 59
Morris, S. M., 151
Moses, 9, 10

Motry, Hubert Louis, 53
Mrug, S., 154
Mühlen, Herebert, 238, 239, 242
Munoz, A. R., 154
Murphy, Terence R., 57
Murray, Alexander, 44, 50
Murray-Swank, N.A., 173, 175, 178, 179, 180

Nahum, 269
Naomi, 29
Navarro, Jacinto, 73
Nazianzen, Gregory, 95
Nero, 46
Nettles, Tom, 216
Newport, John P., 130
Nichols, M.P., 180
Niebuhr, H. Richard, 157
Noon, Georgia, 46, 58, 59
Norton, Herman A., 129
O'Conner, Thomas P., 129, 134
O'Mathúna, Dónal P., 43, 64
Oden, Thomas, 16, 17
Oduyoye, Mercy Amba, 77
Oglesby, William B., 128
Oprandi, Allison M., 152
Origen, 51
Osborne, Grant R., 61
Ott, B. B., 152
Ott, Heinrich, 250
Otto, E., 260, 261

Packer, J. I., 2, 3, 6, 15, 216
Pannenberg, Wolfhart, 100, 101
Pargament, Kenneth I., 144, 173, 175, 178, 179, 180
Park, C. L., 154
Pausanias, 147
Payne, Leanne, 161
Perry, Greg, 7
Peteet, J. R., 145
Peterson, Robert A., 7
Phelps, A. C., 145
Phifer, Nancy, 152
Pilate, 14
Pink, Arthur W., 23
Piper, John, 120
Pitre, Brant, 195
Pitts, Andrew W., 185
Plantinga, Cornelius, 2, 3, 4, 7
Plato, 46, 91, 92
Porter, Stanley E., 185
Post, S. G., 153, 154
Pratt, J., 172
Preston, Aaron, 169
Prigerson, H. G., 145
Puchalski, Christina M., 143, 152, 153
Pustejovsky, J. E., 154
Pythagoras, 55

Radbertus, Paschasius, 51
Rahab, 173, 268
Rahe, R. H., 151

Ramos, Aurelia, 73
Ramos, Enrique, 199
Rand, M.R., 172
Ream, Todd, 160
Reasoner, Mark, 191
Reed, Sarah J., 167
Rehfuss, M., 173
Reisinger, Ernest, 216, 217
Reller, Nancy, 143
Rethelyi, J., 151
Reynolds, N., 154
Ridderbos, H., 252
Ritchie, Nelly, 79
Roach, C. J., 154
Robertson, Archibald T., 103
Rogers, Carl, 128
Roman, P. M., 155
Roosevelt, Theodore, ix
Rozsa, S., 151
Ruth, 29, 269
Ryken, Philip, ix

Sacchi, Andrea, 23
Salsman, J. M., 154
Samson, 49, 55
Sanders, E. P., 207
Sarah, 21
Sarai, 16, 17, 19, 23
Saul, King, 55
Sauter, Gerhard, 226
Schaff, Philip, 103
Schneiders, Sandra M., 158
Schrage, W., 253
Schramm, O., 260, 261
Schreiner, Thomas R., 185
Schrop, Susan Labuda, 152
Schultz, Linda, 152
Schütz, P., 250
Schwertley, B., 207
Schwöbel, Christoph, 90
Seegobin, Winston, 230
Segundo, Juan Luis, 75
Seligman, M. E. P., 151
Selius, Brian A., 152
Senkbeil, Harold L., 74, 80
Sethi, S., 151
Shakespeare, William, 59
Sharma, V., 153
Shepherd, Norman, 203, 207
Sheridan, Mark, 16, 17
Sherman, A. C., 154
Short, T. H., 152
Shults, F. LeRon, 92
Silton, Nava R., 145
Silva, Moisés, 191
Simon, U. E., 249
Simpson, Michael L., 149
Sjöberg, Ekik, 267, 292
Skrabski, A., 151
Smedes, Lewis, 195
Smith, Bailey, 214
Smith, Robert E., 69
Smith, Terry Ann, 29

Smucker, William D., 152
Snyder, M. A., 154
Sobrino, Jon, 75, 76
Solberg, Mary, 76
Solomon, 269
Soothill, K., 151
Sosunov, E., 153
Spike, John T., 23
Spina, Frank Anthony, 12, 25
Spurgeon, Charles H., 127
Srivastava, Mohit, 152
Staley, Ryan C., 230
Stålsett, Sturla J., 79
Stansell, G., 34
Steffen, Lloyd H., 166
Stein, Robert H., 61
Stewart, Gary P., 43, 46, 47, 63, 64
Stock, Ely, 59
Stone, Howard W., 229
Storms, Sam, 215
Stott, John R. W., 147, 148
Stover, Earl F., 129
Strachey, J., 152
Strayer, Janet, 128
Strong, Stanley R., 225, 227
Strümpfer, J. W., 234
Stuart, Douglas, 31, 36
Stuhlmacher, Peter, 188
Sulmasy, D. P., 153
Surber, Christopher D., 111
Suresh, D. P., 154
Susi, Beth, 152

Tabor, James D., 47
Talbert, Charles H., 195
Tamar, 172, 268
Tamburello, Dennis E., 196
Tamez, Elsa, 77, 78
Taylor, Charles, 159

Taylor, R.J., 175
Temple, Christian, 218, 219
Tertullian, 48, 53
Texeira, K., 153
Theon, 188
Thibaut, Florence, 162
Thomas of Strasbourg, 51
Thomas, C., 151
Thompson, Parker C., 129
Thurneysen, E., 259
Tillich, Paul, 226, 235
Tipson, Baird, 57
Tonry, Michael, 129
Torrance, Thomas F., 83, 85, 267, 268
Truman, J. L., 172
Turner, David L., 61

van der Geest, Victor, 129
Van Dyk, A., 234
Van Harn, Roger E., 2
Van Kooten, Geurt Hendrik, 266, 267
Van Ruler, A., 260
VandeCreek, Larry, 156
Vanderweele, T., 145
Venzke, Rodger R., 129
Verani, Guido, 54
Vicuña, Eleodoro Vargas, 72
Virgil, 193
Vitillo, Robert, 143
von Bingen, Hildegard, 52
von Loewenich, Walter, 70

Wace, Henry, 103
Wagner, J., 173
Wagner, Joyce A., 167
Wallace, Daniel B., 7, 188
Walter of St Victor, 51
Walvoord, John F., 20
Wardekker, Willem L., 159, 160

Watt, Jeffrey R., 55
Webb, Kurt C., 230
Weber, Otto, 96, 98
Webster, D.C., 173
Weldy, David L., 152
Weltman, Sheldon J., 29
Wenham, Gordon J., 16, 19
Wexler, A., 153
Wheeler, Gordon, 265
Whetten, K., 173
White, D. B., 154
White, Mark A., 163, 164
Whitehouse, Glen, 157
Wilberforce, William, xii
Wiles, Maurice, 43
Wilkerson, P., 175
Wilks, J., 129
Williams, Jarvis J., 188
Williams, N. H., 222
Williams, S., 173, 174, 175, 179, 182
Wilson, Douglas, 203
Wolfe, K., 154
Wolff, Hans W., 33, 34
Wright, A. A., 145
Wright, N. T., 190, 203, 204, 205, 206, 207, 212
Wycliffe, John, 54

Zastrow, C., 174
Zeboiim, 33, 36
Zeno, 148
Zerah, 268
Zizioulas, John D., 83, 87, 90, 91, 92, 93, 94, 97
Zuck, Roy B., 20

Scripture & Semi-sacred References

*Gen. 1   = Genesis 1:26 on page 115   **Gen. 3, 19, 176, 204   = Gen. 3 on pages 19, 176, 204
    26, 115   ***   16, 194   = and Gen. 3:16 on page 194

*Gen. 1	Gen. 6	5, 20	8, 19	Gen. 22
26, 115	9, 186	6, 187	Gen. 17, 22	14, 22
26-27, 159	Gen. 7	Gen. 16, 15, 20, 22, 23,	1, 18	Gen. 23, 21
Gen. 2	1, 186	26, 27	14, 104	Gen. 25
19-20, 21	Gen. 12	11-12, 20	20, 20	11, 21
Gen. 2-3, 158	10-20, 18	13, 18, 20, 21	5, 18	Gen. 28
**Gen. 3, 19, 176, 204	12-13, 18	14, 21	6, 18	19, 22
***16, 194	15-16, 18	16, 18	Gen. 18	Gen. 32
17, 193	3, 18	2, 15	22-33, 38	30, 22
20, 22	Gen. 12-17, 29	3, 15, 17	24-25, 210	Gen. 34, 181
9, 19	Gen. 14	5, 16	25, 186	Gen. 38
Gen. 4, 19	19-20, 21	6, 17	Gen. 21	26, 186
9, 19	Gen. 15	7, 17	5, 18	

Exod. 4
   24-26, 38
Exod. 12
   15, 104
Exod. 17
   15, 22
Exod. 19-24, 29
Exod. 20
   1, 33
   7, 22
Exod. 23
   7, 186
Exod. 30
   33, 104
Exod. 34
   14, 22
   6, 17
Exod. 13
   2, 69
Exod. 19
   4, 69

Lev. 13
   46, 104
Lev. 23
   40, 267

Num. 5
   1-4, 104
Num. 12
   14, 104
Num. 14
   33, 186
Num. 31
   19, 104

Deut. 4
   8, 186
Deut. 5
   6, 33
Deut. 7
   7-8, 31
Deut. 25
   1, 186
Deut. 27
   26, 193, 211
Deut. 27-30, 211
Deut 28
   1, 186
Deut. 28
   58, 193
Deut. 32
   20, 186
   51, 186

Josh. 2
   1-21, 173, 269
Josh. 6
   22-25, 173, 269

Jud. 2
   14, 251
Jud. 9

   50-55, 61
Jud. 16, 61

Ruth 1
   16-17, 29

1 Sam 12
   9, 251
1 Sam. 20, 29
1 Sam. 31
   1-6, 61
1 Samuel 31, 55

2 Sam. 11
   1-27, 269
2 Sam. 12
   14, 24, 269
2 Sam. 13
   1-20, 172
2 Sam. 17
   23, 61
2 Sam. 7
   4-16, 29
2 Samuel 17, 55

1 Kings 16
   18, 61

2 Kings 1
   2, 61
2 Kings 17
   18-20, 251

1 Chron. 17
   3-15, 29

4 Ezra 4
   42, 194
4 Ezra 7
   75, 193

Job 1
   6-12, 253

Ps. 1
   5-6, 186
Ps. 7
   9, 186
Ps. 11
   5, 186
Ps. 18
   6, 267
Ps. 37
   17, 186
Ps. 40
   1-3, 181
Ps. 77
   10, 36
Ps. 78
   21-22, 251
Ps. 103
   2-4, 37
Ps. 106

   40, 251
Ps. 124
   8, 22
Ps. 139
   14, 225

Prov. 17
   15, 186

Eccles. 3
   1-8, 38

Isa. 1
   2, 17
Isa. 3
   10-11, 186
   24-27, 186
Isa. 13
   8, 194
Isa. 26
   17, 194
Isa. 43, 32
Isa. 45
   12, 17
   7, 252
Isa. 49-54, 36
Isa. 63
   15, 245
Isa. 65
   8-25, 193
Isa. 52
   13-53
   12, 188

Jer. 4
   31, 194
Jer. 18
   11, 252
   8, 252
Jer. 31, 36
   10-13, 36
   20, 245

Ezek. 18
   5-9, 186
Ezek. 37
   5, 107
Ezek. 37, 36

Dan. 7
   9-14, 187
Dan. 12
   2, 186

Hosea 11, 30
   10-11, 40
   1-4, 38
   1-7, 33
   2, 31, 33
   3, 32
   4-7, 33
   5, 33

   6-7, 33
   8, 33, 36, 37
   9, 37, 39
Hos. 13
   13, 194

Joel 3, 186

Jonah 4
   2, 37

Mic. 4
   9, 194

Nahum 3
   19, 270
Nahum 3:1, 269

Hab. 2, 209

Zech. 14, 186

Mal. 4, 186

Mt. 1
   1-17, 268, 269, 286
Mt. 5
   17, 125
Mt. 6
   21, 127
Mt. 6:33, 162
Mt. 7
   21-23, 124
Mt. 8
   5-13, 149
Mt. 9
   27-28, 149
Mt. 10
   38-39, 197
Mt. 11
   19, 197
   28-30, 124
Mt. 12
   31, 61, 63, 65
   31-32, 50, 63
   32, 62
Mt. 13
   3-9, 176
Mt. 18
   17, 108
Mt. 18-20, 149
Mt. 22
   37, 146, 161
   39, 146
Mt. 23
   27, 125
Mt. 27
   3-10, 61

Mark 1

   32-34, 149
Mark 3
   22, 197
   28-30, 61
   29, 61
Mark 5
   22-23, 149
Mark 6
   53-56, 177
Mark 7
   1, 197
   31-37, 149
Mark 8
   22-26, 149
Mark 10
   45, 189
   50-51, 149
Mark 11
   15-17, 181
Mark 13
   44, 194
Mark 16
   9, 178

Luke 1
   31, 20
Luke 2
   40, 3, 10, 11, 52
Luke 5
   12-16, 149
Luke 10
   30-37, 146
Luke 12
   10, 61
Luke 15
   20, 242
   21, 163
   22, 164
   24, 164
Luke 17
   11-19, 149
Luke 23
   46, 192
Luke 24
   27, 187
   36-37, 24

John 1
   10-11, 2
   12, 177
John 3
   16, 242
   19, 62
   7, 12
John 4, 12, 22, 23, 25,
   26, 27
   16, 13
   20, 12
   26, 14, 23
   27, 13, 14
   29, 14
   34-38, 14
   39, 23

4, 15	17–21, 147	1 Cor. 10	1, 114	8, 11
42, 14, 25	18, 147	13, 179	14-16, 117	Heb. 6
46–54, 149	22, 147	1 Cor. 12, 179	5-6, 267	4-6, 63
5, 12	28, 266	1 Cor. 13	8-9, 124, 219	5, 193
6, 12		2, 196	Eph. 3	Heb. 7
9, 12, 13, 14	Rom. 1	1 Cor. 15, 246	14-18, 176	7, 21
John 5, 4, 12	17, 192	35-44, 189	Eph. 4	9-19, 21
10, 8	Rom. 2	4, 189	20-24, 202	Heb. 12
15, 8	13, 205		25, 29, 149	7, 121
16, 8	Rom. 3	2 Cor 5	26, 181	Heb. 13
17, 8	21-26, 192	21, 6	31-32, 181	5-6, 177
18, 8, 11, 14, 26	22, 191	2 Cor. 1	Eph. 5	
19, 10, 26	23, 176	5, 197	31-32, 195	James 1
2, 12	26, 191	2 Cor. 10	Eph. 6	14-15, 178
25-29, 187	3, 191	3-5, 178, 183	10-18, 183	James 2
31-36, 9	Rom. 4	2 Cor. 3	12, 168, 179	1-4, 7
37-40, 9	12, 191	18, 116, 121		14-26, 7
39, 9, 11	25, 189	2 Cor. 4	Phil. 2	17-18, 118
40, 9	3, 187	18, 268	3, 4	James 4
45, 10	Rom. 5	4, 116	4, 4	10, 6
45-47, 9	1, 190	2 Cor. 5, 267	5, 5, 27	
46, 10	14-21, 205	17, 177, 194	6, 5, 7	1 Pet. 3
46-47, 9	19, 195	21, 195, 268	6-11, 5	14, 195
John 6	8, 6		7, 5	16, 195
35, 13	8-9, 115	Gal. 1	8, 192	1 Pet. 5
John 7	Rom. 6	13-14, 196	Phil. 3	10, 195
1, 14	1-2, 122	3-4, 193	8-11, 190	1 Pet. 5
John 10	12-14, 176	4, 192	9, 191	15, 149
16, 12	23, 176	8-9, 195		
25, 26	Rom. 7	Gal. 2	Col. 1	2 Pet. 3
27-29, 165	15, 158	16, 191	13, 193	17-18, 166
37-38, 26	24, 225	17, 190	15, 86	2 Pet. 3
John 12	24-25, 121	19-20, 195	15-17, 266	18, xii
34, 12	Rom. 8	21, 192, 196	15-23, 160	
John 13	15, 197	Gal. 3	24, 259	1 John 2
1-17, 7	18-23, 194	1, 192	Col. 2	27-28, 195
31-32, 119	19-22, ix	10, 193, 211	12, 191	1 John 4
John 14, 24	28-29, 118	2, 192		1, 195
10-11, 26	29, 86, 116, 160	22, 191, 192	1 Thess. 2	1 John 1
15-31, 193	30, 190	26, 192	2, 235	8, 121
6, 62	32, 242	Gal. 4	1 Thess. 5	9, 123, 167
9, 115	3-4, 205	12-20, 197	3, 194	1 John 3
John 15	Rom. 10	6, 193, 197		1-3, 268
18-25, 48	3-4, 119	Gal. 5	2 Thess. 3	16, 6
4, 195	9-10, 177	16, 196	14-15, 109	1 John 4
John 16	Rom. 12	16-26, 202		16, 6
18, 24	1-2, 177	19-21, 176	1 Tim 3	19, 6
8-11, 62	Rom. 15	22, 196	15, 10	20-21, 162
John 18	13, 259	5, 190		8, 6
37, 14	17, 117	6, 196	2 Tim. 4	9, 6
John 20	5, 258	Gal. 6	2, 149	1 John 5
11-18, 178	Rom. 16	14-15, 193		16-17, 53, 63, 65
9, 12	17, 106	17, 197	Titus 3	20, 195
		2, 196	10, 106	
Acts 1	1 Cor. 1	5, 190		2 John 10, 106
18-19, 61	23, 192	8, 190	Heb. 1	
8, 149	30, 195, 268		2, 80	Rev. 12
Acts 2	9, 123	Eph. 1	Heb. 2	2, 194
39, 96	1 Cor. 5	3-5, 98	1-4, 214	
Acts 16, 25	2-7, 105	3-6, 126	18, 123	Zech. 3
Acts 17	5, 108	6, 267	Heb. 4	1-5, 267
16, 147	1 Cor. 7	7-8, 167	16, 270	
16–34, 146	4, 16	Eph. 2	Heb. 5	--------------------

1QS 4	44, 188	15-17, 193	2 Esd. 7	Jub. 23
25, 193	1 Macc. 9	2 Apocalypse of Baruch	50, 193	23-31, 193
1 Macc. 13	10, 188	56	2 Macc. 8	Jub. 4
4, 188	1 En. 62	6, 194	21, 188	26, 193
1 Macc. 17	4, 194	2 Bar. 32	4 Macc. 16	Targum Psalms 18
21-22, 188	1 En. 72	6, 193	27-29, 188	14, 194
1 Macc. 6	1, 193	2 Bar. 44	Jub. 1	
	1 En. 91	12, 193	29, 193	

Books, Journals, and Publications

101 Most Puzzling Bible Verses, 43, 63
A Select Library of the Nicene and Post-Nicene Fathers of the Christian Church, 103
A Way of Being, 128
Actuality of Atonement—A Study of Metaphor, Rationality, and the Christian Tradition, 85
AIDS Behavior, 154
All for Jesus—A Celebration of the 50th Anniversary of Covenant Theological Seminary, 7
American Journal of Medicine, 153
American Journal of Psychiatry, 151
American Literature, 59
Ancient Christian Commentary on Scripture, 16, 17
Annals of Family Medicine, 152
Annals of Internal Medicine, 153
Apocalyptic Imagination—an Introduction to Jewish Apocalyptic Literature, 187
Archives of Internal Medicine, 152
Articles of the Synod of Dort, 201

Baker Exegetical Commentary on the New Testament, 61
Basic Questions on Suicide and Euthanasia, 64
Basic Types of Pastoral Care and Counseling, 149
Basic Types of Pastoral Care and Counseling Resources, 128
Being as Communion—Studies in Personhood and the Church, 90, 93
Belgic Confession, 201
Believers Church Bible Commentary, 34
Bible Knowledge Commentary: An Exposition of the Scriptures, 20
Biblical Themes for Pastoral Care, 128
Bibliotheca Sacra, 1, 224
Black's New Testament Commentaries, 106
BMC Palliative Care, 145
Book of Concord, The Confession of the Lutheran Church, 68
Book of Hosea, 31

Cancer, 145, 153, 154
Care of Souls, 144
Chaplaincy Today: Journal of the Association of Professional Chaplains, 136
Chaplains as Doctors of the Soul, 146
Christ Present In Faith—Luther's View of Justification, 192
Christian Counselor's Commentary, 148

Christian Doctrine of God, One Being Three Persons, 85
Christian Faith—A Systematic Theology for Pilgrims on the Way, 96
Christian Faith—An Introduction to Christian Doctrine, 87
Christian Origins and the Establishment of the Early Jesus Movement, 185
Christian Theology, 51
Church History, 55
City of God, 16, 49
Client Centered Therapy, 128
Commedia, 58
Commentary ad Matthew, 47
Commentary on the Book of Hosea, 34
Commentary on the Pastoral Epistles, 106
Communiloquium, 52
Compelling Knowledge—A Feminist Proposal for an Epistemology of the Cross, 76
Concept of Mortal Sin in Early Christianity, 53
Confidence in Battle, Inspiration in Peace: The United States Army Chaplaincy 1945–1975, 129
Contemporary Mental Health Issues Among African Americans, 229
Cosmic Christology in Paul & the Pauline School: Colossians & Ephesians in the Context of Graeco-Roman Cosmology, 267
Cost-effectiveness and Preventive Implications of Employee Assistance Programs, 155
Counseling Psychologist, 128
Counseling—A Comprehensive Profession, 229
Covenant in Judaism and Paul—A Study of Ritual Boundaries as Identity Markers, 32
Criswell Theological Review, 1
Curse on Self-Murder, 44

Dallas Theological Seminary Catalog, 11
Dasein für, 238
Discovering Jesus in Our Places—Contextual Christologies in a Globalized World, 79
Divine Comedy, 45, 58, 59
Divine Commitment and Human Obligations: Selected Writings of David Noel Freedman, 30

Effectiveness of Correctional Treatment, 129
El Hombre de Hoy ante Jesús e Nazaret, 75
Empathy and Its Development, 128
Empathy: Development, Training, and Consequences, 128

Encouraging Faith, Supporting Soldiers: A History of the U.S. Chaplain Corps 1975–1995, 129
Engaging Ephesians—An Intermediate Reader and Exegetical Guide, 185
Ephesians and Colossians, 195
Epistle of Diognetus, 48
Eschatology: Biblical, Historical, and Practical Approaches, 1
Essential Chaplain Skill Sets, 141, 142
Essential Writings of Christian Mysticism, 196
Evangelical Dictionary of Theology, 125
Exploration of the Inner World, 128
Exploring and Proclaiming the Apostles' Creed, 2
Exploring Christian Theology: The Church, Spiritual Growth, and the End Times, 1

Faith Born in the Struggle for Life, 79
Faith of Jesus Christ—An Investigation of the Narrative Substructure of Galatians 3:1-4:11, 191
Faith of the Outsider, 25
Faith of the Outsider—Exclusion and Inclusion in the Biblical Story, 12
First Corinthians, Sacra Pagina Series, 106, 108
Forbes, 155
Foundations of Dogmatics, 96
Four Books of Sentences, 52
Fourth Eclogue, 193
Free Gift, 219
From Its European Antecedents to 1791: The United States Army Chaplaincy, 129

Galatians, 189
Genesis 12-50, 16, 17
George Washington's Sacred Fire, ix, 284
Gleanings in Genesis, 23
God with Us: Exploring God's Personal Interactions with His People Throughout the Bible, 1
Gospel According to Jesus, 214
Greek Grammar Beyond the Basics, 7, 188

Handbook of Religion and Health, 152
Harvard Theological Review, 57
He Was Always There, The U.S. Army Chaplain Ministry in the Vietnam Conflict, 129
Health Psychology, 154
Heart of the Living God—Love, Free Will, Foreknowledge, Heaven, 127
Heaven—Treasures of Our Everlasting Rest, 127
Heidelberg Catechism, 201
Hesed in the Bible, 35
History of the U.S. Chaplain Corps 1975–1995, 129
Homilies, 48
Hosea—A New Translation with Introduction and Commentary, 36
How We Saved Texas Prison Chaplaincy 2011, 127

Inner-Change Freedom Initiative, 129
Institutes of the Christian Religion, 98, 195
International Journal of Behavioral Medicine, 151
International Journal of Ethics, 54
International Journal of Offenter Therapy and Comparative Criminology, 129

JAMA Internal Medicine, 153, 154
Jerusalem Bible, 266
Jesucristo Liberador, Lectura Histórico-Teológica de Jesús de Nazaret, 75
Jesús en América Latina, su significado para la fe y la cristología, 76
Jesus, The Tribulation, and The End of The Exile, 195
Joint Commission Journal on Quality and Patient Safety, 153
Joint Federal Vision Profession, 204
Jonathan Edwards' Interpretation of Revelation, 1
Journal for Biblical Manhood and Womanhood, 185
Journal Health Care Chaplaincy, 153
Journal of Aging Studies, 151
Journal of Clinical Oncology, 153
Journal of Community Corrections, 134
Journal of Cystic Fibrosis, 154
Journal of Family Practice, 152
Journal of General Internal Medicine, 153
Journal of Ministry and Theology, 116
Journal of Offender Counseling, 129
Journal of Palliative Medicine, 143, 152
Journal of Pastoral Care, 156
Journal of Pastoral Care Publications, 136
Journal of the Evangelical Theological Society, 5
Journal of the History of Ideas, 46
Justification—God's Plan & Paul's Vision, 190
Justification—The Heart of the Christian Faith, 189
Justification—Understanding the Classic Reformed Doctrine, 189
Kindred Spirit, 64
Knowing God, 3, 6, 15

Las Mujeres en el Movimiento de Jesús, El Cristo, 78
Law of Moses, 104
Lectures in Christian Dogmatics, 97
Let the Nations Be Glad!, 120
Liberty of a Christian, 192
Libri Quattuor Sententiarum, 52
Life's Ultimate Questions, 130
Living Human Document, 128
Luke, 61
Luther's German Bible of 1622, 69
Luther's Theology of the Cross, 70
Luther's Works, 56
Lutheran Quarterly, 226
LXX, 17, 188, 193, 194

Maccabean Martyr Traditions in Paul's Theology of Atonement, 188
Maccabees, 188
Making of Christian Doctrine—A Study in the Principles of Early Doctrinal Development, 43
Mark, 61
Martyrdom and Persecution in the Early Church, 47
Matthew, 61
Matthew, The New American Commentary, 105
Medicine, Society, and Faith in the Ancient and Medieval Worlds, 47
Meditations, 46
Message of Acts, 147
More God, Less Crime, 129, 134

Most Real Being—A Biblical and Philosophical Defense of Divine Determinism, 266
New Catholic Encyclopedia, 53, 54
New England Quarterly, 59
New Dimension Faith, 223
New Perspective on Paul, 203
Newman and The Word, 193
Nicene-Constantinopolitan Creed, 1
Nicomachean Ethics, 46
Noble Death—Suicide and Martyrdom among Christians and Jews in Antiquity, 47

Ocean Devotions, 127
On Becoming a Person, 128
On Genesis, 17
On the Incarnation of the Word, 103
Once Saved, Always Saved, 114
Our Legacy—The History of Christian Doctrine, 43
Oxford Dictionary, 264
Oxford Handbook of Biblical Narrative, 29
Oxford Handbook of Crime and Criminal Justice, 129

Paradise Lost, 59
Pastoral Counseling, 128
Pastoral Crisis Intervention, 150
Paul, the Community, and Progressive Sanctification, 270, 271
Penguin History of the Church, 224
Pausanias's Description of Greece, 147
Personality and Social Psychology Bulletin, 264
Personnel and Guidance Journal, 225, 227
Persons in Relation, 89
Persons, Divine and Human, 90
Perspectives on Eternal Security, xiii
Permission Evangelism, 149
Philippians, 6, 7, 191
PlainViews, 136
PLMA, 59
Policraticus, 52
Precious Heart, Broken Heart—Love and the Search for Finality in Divorce, 127
Professional Psychology, Research and Practice, 230
Promise of Trinitarian Theology, 84
Psychological Science, 151
Psychology of Religion and Coping, 144
Psychology of Women Quarterly, 151
Psychology Today, 264

Reforming Theological Anthropology—Ater the Philosophical Turn to Relationality, 92
Religion in Crisis and Custom, 128
Review of English Studies, 59
Revisiting Paul's Doctrine of Justification, 186, 188
Responsible Selfhood, 157
Right Moves For Youth, 223
Romans, 46
Romans in Full Circle—A History of Interpretation, 191
Routledge International Handbook of Life-Course Criminology, 129
Routledge International Handbook of Restorative Justic, 129

Sage Journals, 136

Sancti Bernardi Sermones in Cantica, 196
Sanctification—Christ in Action, 74, 80
Scandinavian Journal of Caring Sciences, 151
Scripture and the People of God—Essays in Honor of Wayne Grudem, 185
Scivias, 52
Select Library of Nicene and Post-Nicene Fathers of the Christian Church, 95
Self as Agent, 88
Semeia 24, 34
Shame and Guilt in Neurosis, 264
Shame—The Exposed Self, 264
Skilled Helper, 128
Sleepless Souls, 57
Solace for the Soul, 180, 183
Song of Songs, 196
Sources of the Self—The Making of Modern Identity, 159
Southern Medical Journal, 154
Splendour of the Three, 95
Spirituality in the Workplace, 144
Struggling for Recognition: The United States Army Chaplaincy 1791–1865, 129
Suicide in the Middle Ages, 44
Suicide in the Middle Ages. Vol. II, The Curse on Self-Murder, 50
Suicide in the Middle Ages: Volume I: The Violent against Themselves, 50
Suicide—A Christian Response, 43, 46, 47, 64
Sumerian myth of Dilmun, 193
Summa Alexandri, 52
Summa Theologica, 53
Systematic Theology, 21, 100
Systematic Theology—An Introduction to Biblical Doctrine, 11

Table Talks, 56
Taita Cristo, 72
Taking Leave of God, 84
Ten Commandments, 56
Testamentum Imperium, ix, x, xiii, xiv, xv, 127, 263
The Church, 97
The Courage to Be, 235
The First Epistle to the Corinthians, The New International Commentary on the New Testament, 105
The Journal of Pastoral Care & Counseling, 136
The New Workforce, 155
The Snow-Image, and Other Twice-told Tales, 60, 281
Theological Guide to Calvin's Institutes, ix
Theology for the Community of God, 96
Theology in Reconstruction, 267, 268
Theology of Auschwitz, 249
Theology through the Theologians—Selected Essays, 1972-1995, 99, 102
Theology Today, 225
Think About It, Consider It, Tell Us What to Do: Can Some of the Most Violent Texts of the Old Testament Be Redeemed?, 29 Three Forms of Unity, 201
Three-Personed God—The Trinity as a Mystery of Salvation, 85
Today's New International Version, 178
Torah, 187, 188, 192

U.S. Army Chaplain Ministry in the Vietnam Conflict, 129

Understanding the Big Picture of the Bible, 185
Unio cum Christo—An International Journal of Reformed Theology and Life, ix
Union With Christ—A Biblical View of The New Life in Jesus Christ, 195
Union with Christ—John Calvin and the Mysticism of St. Bernard, 196
Union with Christ—the New Finnish Interpretation of Luther, 192
United States Army Chaplaincy, 129
United States Army Chaplaincy 1791–1865, 129
United States Army Chaplaincy 1865–1920, 129
United States Army Chaplaincy 1920–1945, 129
United States Army Chaplaincy 1945–1975, 129
Unlocking Romans—Resurrection and The Justification of God, 189
Up From Handymen: The United States Army Chaplaincy 1865–1920, 129
Using Chaplains as Key Leadership in Evaluating and Enhancing Workplace Spirituality, 148

Vermischte Deutsche Schriften, 69
Vetus Testamentum, 35

War, Peace, and Christianity—Questions and Answers from the Just-War Perspective, 43
Westminster Confession of Faith, 201, 206
Westminster Larger Catechism, 56, 210
Westminster Shorter Catechism, 56, 210
What St. Paul Really Said, 206
Wherefore God?, 250, 254
Who am I?, 174
Wissenschaftliche Untersuchungen Zum Neuen Testament, 267
With Passion and Compassion—Third World Women Doing Theology, 77
Woman's Study Bible, 177
Wood of the Self-Murderers—The Harpies and the Suicides, 59
Word & World, 224
Word Biblical Commentary, 36
Word Biblical Commentary, Hosea-Jonah, 31
Would You Lie To Save a Life?, 127
Wycliff Bible Dictionary, 218

Zondervan Exegetical Commentary on the New Testament, 61

General

125 Chaplains facilitated, 131
19,602 Critical Illness/Death Notices, 131
20,000 Volunteers, 131
4,000,000 prisoners in attendance, 131
400,000 visits, 131
500,000 hours, 131
99.8%, 131

Abrahamic Covenant, 29
ACA, 273
Adam's sin, 193
Admah, 33, 36
adventus, 232, 234, 242
adventus, future as, 231
African Christian College, 157
Agnosto Theos, 147
AIDS, HIV, 234
Allied Holdings, 155
American Correctional Association, 135
American Correctional Chaplains Association, 135
American LubeFast, 155
Ancient of Days, 187
apatheia, 236
Apollo, 147
Areopagus, 146

Articles of the Synod of Dort, 201
Associated Chaplains in California State Service, 135
Association for Clinical Pastoral Education, 136
Association of Professional Chaplains, 136
Assyria, 33
Assyrians, 104, 269, 270
Athenian soldiers, 188

Baal, 30
Babylonians, 104
Bacchus, 147
Banner Thunderbird Medical Center, ix, 141
Baptist, 130
Barna Group, 141
Beer Lahai Roi, 21
Being of God, 245
Belgic Confession, 201
Bered, 21
b^{e}rith, 35
Biola University, 83
Body of Christ, 101
BPP Law School, Manchester, ix, 263
Bride of Christ, 101
Bridegroom, 196
Bureau of Justice Statistics, 172

California Department of Corrections and Rehabilitation, 135
caminata, 79
Canaanite worship, 30
Canadian Association for Pastoral Practice and Education, 136
Carnal Christian theory, 217
Catch-22, 218
Catholic, 135
Catholic University of America, 53, 54
Celebrate Recovery, 165
Chalcedon, 1
Chaplains I–IIIs, 135
cheap grace, 216
Christian hope, 233
Christology, x, 5
Cnossos, 266
Coast Guard, 43
Cogito ergo sum, 88, 89
communication idiomatum, 93
communio sanctorum, 263
communion sanctorum, 270
Community of God, 83
Constantinople, 107
Cornell University, 154
corporate dimension, 233
Cosmic Christology, 267
co-suffering, God's dynamic, 240

cotidiano, 77
Council of Braga, 47, 56
Council of Carthage, 47
Council of Gaudix, 47
Council of Nicaea, 5
courage to be, 235
crimen, 50
cross, theology of, 236
crucified God, 236

Dahingabe, 239
Dallas, 130
Dallas Theological Seminary, ix, 1, 11, 43
Davidic Covenant, 29
Day of Atonement, 267
Day of Judgment, 213
De civitate Dei, 49
dei, 12
Department of Developmental Services, 135
Department of Health and Human Services, 155
Department of State Hospitals, 135
Department of Veteran's Affairs, 135
derelictio, 237, 240, 262
derilictio of God, 232
Deus crucifixus, 241
Devil, 51
diabolo instigante, 51
diakonia, 232
dialectic event, 241
dialectics, 256
Diana, 147
Dilmun, Sumerian myth of, 193
dimension, corporate, 233
dimension, environmental, 233
dimension, existential, 233
dimension, ontic, 234
dimension, psychic, 233, 234
dimension, social, 233
dimension, spiritual, 233, 234
dimension, structural, 233
dimension, transcendent, 233
Division of Juvenile Justice, 135
divorce, 127
Drew University, 29
Duke University's Center for Spirituality, Theology and Health, 151
duplex gratiae, x
dynamic view, 270

easy-believism, 216
Egypt, 17, 31, 33
ekkesia peccatorum, 69
ekklesia, 69
El Rostro Femenino de la Teología, 79
elpida dikaiosunē, 190
en Christō, 195
enfleshment, 238
ens realissimum, 266
ens realissimus, 266

ensarkosis, 238
ensouled embodiment, 235
environmental dimension, 233
Epicureans, 147
epikataratos, 193
eschatologia crucis, 231, 235, 237, 250, 261
eschatologis crucis, 259
eschatology, 235, 236, 240, 250, 256
eschatology of the cross, 235
eschaton, 246
Eucharist, 261
euthanasia, 47
existential angst of shame, 263
existential dimension, 233

Federal Bureau of Prisons, 128
Federal Vision, xi, 200, 202, 203, 204, 206, 207, 208, 210, 213, 221, 279, 294
Federal Vision Controversy, 200
Federal Vision theology, xi
Feminist hermeneutics, xi
fertility rites, 30
foreknowledge, 127
Formgeschichte, 247
fortigenesis, 234, 235
fortigenetics, 232, 233, 234, 261
fortis, 234
fortology, 234, 235
Free Grace view, 220
free will, 127
future as *adventus*, 231
future hope, 234
futurum, 231, 234, 242

Galilee, 12
George Washington Institute of Spirituality and Heath, 143
God all in all, 240
God in our suffering, 245
God, crucified, 236
God, static v. pathetic, 238
God's Divine Being, 241
God's dynamic co-suffering, 240
God-forsakenness, 240, 241
God-Logos, 238
Golden Hour, 138
Good Friday, 72
Good Samaritan, 146
Good Shepherd, 166
Grand Canyon University College of Theology, 141
gravissumum, 50
Graylock, 59
grief of God, 240
guilt for being raped, 176

hamartiology, 44, 45
harlot, 173
Harpies, 58
harpy, 58
heaven, 127

Hebrew Prophets, 186
Hegelian, 243
Heidelberg Catechism, 201
Hellenistic, 188
Hellenistic anthropology, 108
hermanas, 78
hermeneutics, 233
hesed, 35, 39
Hingabe, 241
hingebende Vater, 241
hingebendes Verlassen, 241
HIV & AIDS, 234
Holy Communion, 261
Holy One, 37, 38, 39
homo apatheticus, 237
homo faber, 257
homo festivus, 261
homo patiens, 257
homo sympatheticus, 237
huper, 187
Hyperides, 188
hypostasis, 94

IFI, 134
Imagine Me, 272
Imago Dei, 115, 116, 123, 125, 160, 163, 270, 271
immanent Trinity, 240
in ipsa fide Christus adest, 192
Inferno, 45, 58
inhabitation theology, 235
InnerChange, 134
Inter-American University, 199
International Academy for Practical Theology, 231
International Center for the Integration of Health and Spirituality, 134
International Network for the Study of War and Religion in the Modern World, 43
International Society for Pastoral Care and Counselling, 231
intertrinitarially, 241
inter-Trinitarian, 240, 241
Islam, 180

Jahwê, 231, 232
Jerusalem, 12, 196, 269
Judaism, 180
Judea, 12
Jupiter, 147

Kadesh, 21
kiwwah, 259
kurios, 218

Law of Moses, 104
liberation theology, xi
Liberation Theology, 75
Liberty Baptist Theological Seminary, 141
Lordship Controversy, 200

Lordship Salvation, xi, 200, 213, 215, 219
Lutheran School of Theology, ix
Lutheran World Federation, 67
lutron anti pollōn, 189
LXX, 17, 188, 193, 194

Marine Corp, 43
Mars Hill, 146
martyrdom, 48
Masada, 46
mazzot feast, 260
meaninglessness, 250
Mercury, 147
Messianic suffering, 236
Middle Ages, 50
miggēn, 33
Moabitess, 269
monophysitic, 243
Montrouis, Haiti, 111
mortality, 38
mortificatio, 258
Mosaic Covenant, 29
Mosaic Sabbath, 9

Narrative Therapy, 180
National Association of Catholic Chaplains, 136
National Association of Jewish Chaplains, 136
National Oil & Lube News, 155
Navy, 43
Nazareth, 3, 10
nec plus ultra, 50
Neptune, 147
New Brunswick Theological Seminary, ix, 29
New Orleans Baptist Theological Seminary, 127
Nicaea, 107
Nicene-Constantinopolitan Creed, 1
Niveheh, 269
non compos mentis, 57
noödynamics, 258
North-West University, ix, 199
novum, 234

Oklahoma Christian University, ix, 157
ontic, 234
ontic dimension, 234
ontology, x, 234
Ordo Salutis, 206
ousia, 92

pan-entheism, 246
Paralysis of Toxic Shame, 264
Parker College of Chiropractic, 141
parousia, 232, 246, 249, 258
parrhesia, 233, 235
pascha, 260
pascha feast, 260
passio Dei, 232, 235

passio hominem, 236
pathetic v. static God, 238
patricompassionism, 241, 243
peccatum, 50
Pentateuch, 3
perfectum, 246
perichoretic, 267, 271
Persians, 104
phil, 146
Philippi, 25
philosophy of hope, 234
philoxenos, 146
philoxenosology, 146
Phoenix Seminary, ix, 185
physician-assisted suicide, 47
pistis, 191
pistis Christou, 191
pneuma, 108
pneumatology, 235
polygamy, 16
promissio, 246, 262
promissio-character of hope, 232
promissio-instigated action, 259
promissiological, 256
promissiology, 231
promissiotherapy, 257
propositional transformation, 117
Prosgymnata, 188
Protestant Reformation, 263
prototokos, 266
Providence Forum, ix
psychic dimension, 233, 234
psychofortology, 235

rape, 171
red flag (sexual addiction), 164
Referral in Pastoral Counseling, 128
Reforma Dos Escuela de Ministerios, 199
Reforma Dos Ministry at Center Church, 199
religious hysteria, 46
Rome, 49
Roper Center for Public Opinion, 154

Salve Regina University, 43
Samaria, 12
Samaritan, 12
Samaritan woman, 23
sapientia, 235
sarx, 108
schemas of self, 264
sed non fides quae est sola, 215
Selbstentäusserung, 238
self-absorption, 158
self-transcendence, 158
Seminario Campbell Morgan, 199
Seminario Mayor Escuela de Teologia y Ciencia de la Religion, 199
Seminario Reformado, 199
sexual abuse, 171
sexual addiction in men, 157
sexual assault, 174

Sheep Gate, 12
Shepherd Controversy, 200
Shur, 17
Sic et non, 51
Sikhism, 180
simul justus et peccator, 67
social dimension, 233
Socrates, 46
Sodom and Gomorrah, 210
sola fide, 270
sola fides iustificat, 215
sola gratia, 270
soteriology, 45
Southwestern Baptist Theological Seminary, 127, 130
spiritual dimension, 233, 234
spiritual fortigenetics, 261
spiritual noetics, 235
spiritual transformation, 117
static v. pathetic God, 238
staurological Trinity, 240
staurology, 240
Stellenbosch University, ix
Stoics, 46, 48, 148
Strategies for Brief Pastoral Counseling, 229
structural dimension, 233
suffering God, 232, 237, 238, 239, 240, 243, 244, 254
Suffering Servant, 188
Suffering Servant-Son, 189
suffering, Messianic, 236
suicide, 47
suicidium, 51, 60
Sumerian myth of Dilmun, 193
Supply and Multiply, 111
Sychar, 12
sým, 33
Synod of Dort, 107

Taco Bell, 155
Talbot School of Theology, 83
Talbot Seminary, ix
teleion, 255
teleologically, 256
telic, 255
Temple Baptist Seminary, ix, 141, 148
Ten Commandments, 56
Texas Department of Criminal Justice, 127
theodilitic crises, 150
theologia crucis, 231, 232, 245
theologia gloriae, 261
theologia resurrectionis, 231, 249, 262
theology of hope, 233
theology of the cross, 236
theopachitic theology, 232
theopaschitic, 241, 242
theosis, 94
transcendent dimension, 233
Trinity, x, 3, 61, 240, 271
Trinity Theological Seminary, 141

Trinity, immanent, 240
Trinity, staurological, 240
tsadīk, 186

U.S. Navy War College, 43
überhaupt, 249
unio mystica, 195
University of Arkansas, ix, 171
University of London, 263
UNKNOWN GOD, 146
Upper Mesopotamia, 269
Urereignis, 250
US Naval Chaplaincy, ix

Venus, 147
verherrlichende, 242
verlassende Hingeben, 241
verlassenen Sohn, 241
victims of sexual assault, 174
Vital Issue > Coping with Life & Prison, 130
Vital Issue > Cycles & Stages of Life, 130
Vital Issue > Derivation & Purpose of Law, 130
Vital Issue > Destiny of Humankind, 130

Vital Issue > Essence of Good—Evil, 130
Vital Issue > Essence of Humankind & Principles, 130
Vital Issue > Eternity & Annihilation, 130
Vital Issue > Existence—Being—Non-Being, 130
Vital Issue > Family—Marriage—Separation, 130
Vital Issue > God, Supreme Being &/or Spirit, 130
Vital Issue > Identity & Sexuality, 130
Vital Issue > Life Crises & Goals, 130
Vital Issue > Moral & Social Accountability, 130
Vital Issue > Nature of Growth & Death, 130
Vital Issue > Origin—Beginning—Ending, 130
Vital Issue > Purpose of God & Humankind, 130
Vital Issue > Purpose Pain & Pleasure, 130
Vital Issue > Purpose—Meaning in life, 130
Vital Issue > Scripture Interpretation, 130

Vital Issue > Sources of Authority, 130
Vital Issue > Transcendence, 130
Vital Issue > Truth—Dignity—Honor—Love, 130
Vital Issue > Universal Forces, 130
Vital Issue > Wisdom & Life Skills, 130
Vital Issues, 140
vivificatio, 258
vulnerable God, 232

Wake Forest University, ix, 223
Weggabe, 239
Westminster Theological Seminary, ix, xii
Worms, 107
WWJD, 11
WWYD, 11

xenos, 146

zētountes dikaiōthēnai, 190
zig zag realism, 253
Zoroastrianism, 180

www.PreciousHeart.net/ti

www.ingramcontent.com/pod-product-compliance
Lightning Source LLC
Chambersburg PA
CBHW050621300426
44112CB00012B/1598